PENGUIN CANADA

THE LAST SEASON

Roy MacGregor is the author of many bestselling books, including *The Home Team, A Life in the Bush, Road Games, Home Game* (with Ken Dryden) and *The Seven A.M. Practice.* He has won more than a dozen national and international awards for his writing, including most recently the 2000 Rutstrum Award for *A Life In the Bush,* judged to be the best North American book on the environment or wilderness 1995–2000. *A Life in the Bush* also won the 2000 Canadian Authors' "Birks Family Foundation" Award for biography and the 2000 Ottawa-Carleton Book Award. His most recent book is *Escape: In Search of the Natural Soul of Canada.* In fiction, in addition to *The Last Season,* he has also written *Canoe Lake,* a novel on the death of Canadian painter Tom Thomson, which has recently become a multi-week bestseller on *The Globe and Mail* list. His children's mystery series, *The Screech Owls,* is an international success, with more than 1 million copies in print in Canada alone, as well as publication in Sweden, China and the Czech Republic.

D1004385

THE LAST SEASON

ROY MACGREGOR

PENGUIN
CANADA

PENGUIN CANADA
Published by the Penguin Group
Penguin Books, a division of Pearson Canada, 10 Alcorn Avenue, Toronto, Ontario, Canada M4V 3B2
Penguin Books Ltd, 80 Strand, London WC2R 0RL, England
Penguin Putnam Inc., 375 Hudson Street, New York, New York 10014, U.S.A.
Penguin Books Australia Ltd, 250 Camberwell Road, Camberwell, Victoria 3124, Australia
Penguin Books India (P) Ltd, 11, Community Centre, Panchsheel Park, New Delhi – 110 017, India
Penguin Books (NZ) Ltd, cnr Rosedale and Airborne Roads, Albany, Auckland 1310, New Zealand
Penguin Books (South Africa) (Pty) Ltd, 24 Sturdee Avenue, Rosebank 2196, South Africa

Penguin Books Ltd, Registered Offices: 80 Strand, London WC2R 0RL, England

First published by Macmillan of Canada (A Division of Gage Publishing Limited)
First published in Penguin Books, 1985
Published in this edition, 2002
10 9 8 7 6 5 4 3 2 1

"Grey is the Forelock Now of the Irishman" from *It Was Warm and Sunny When We Set Out* by
John Finnigan (The Ryerson Press, Toronto, 1970). All rights reserved. Reprinted by permission.

The author is indebted to the Canada Council and the Ontario Arts Council for financial support.

He is also grateful to the Parliamentary Library and the Canadian Centre for Folk Culture Studies.

Warm appreciation is due to David Halpin-Byrne, Professor David Staines, Eero Rautio, Doug
Gibson, and Linda Press Fisher, and especially to two sensitive editors, Jack Hodgins and Rick
Archbold.

*Publisher's note: This book is a work of fiction. Names, characters, places and incidents either are the
product of the author's imagination or are used fictitiously, and any resemblance to actual persons living
or dead, events, or locales is entirely coincidental.*

Manufactured in Canada.

NATIONAL LIBRARY OF CANADA CATALOGUING IN PUBLICATION DATA

MacGregor, Roy, 1948-
    The last season / Roy MacGregor.

ISBN 0-14-301329-7

I. Title.

PS8575.G84L37 2002   C813'.54   C2002-903431-0
PR9199.3.M3174L3 2002

Visit Penguin Books' website at **www.penguin.ca**

Contents

For the Toronto Maple Leaves (*sic*),
who added me to the roster for
their tour of Finland, April 1981,
and for Ottawa's Canterbury Rusty Blades,
who let me dress the rest of the time.

". . . Talking with Batterinski in Finland this past spring, there was absolutely no hint of what was coming. We sat, measuring out his curious career in coffee spoons and flat beer, in a small restaurant in Lahti, a small city a hundred or so kilometers north of Helsinki. That evening Batterinski's Tapiola Hauki would meet Lahti in the first round of the SM Liiga Hockey Championships. He seemed completely content with himself, a great tickle of a grin spreading over the face that 'seems to have been shaped by a furious Greek sculptor with his fists,' as Philadelphia sportswriter Jim Kennedy once wrote.

He was going out a winner, he said. He was wrong, of course, but it was as hard to see then where he was going as it was to understand from where Felix Batterinski came. His own past he shied away from the way others avoided the arena corners he would patrol that night. They have a saying for this in hockey, and that is that the player 'hears footsteps.' And whenever it came down to Batterinski's early life and what had shaped him, he would suddenly turn on edge, wary, almost as if something might be sneaking up on him from behind.

And so he lied. His father, he said, was 'an entrepreneur.' Much later I would discover that Walter Batterinski, a tall, silent man with the flattened face of inherited oppression, was nothing other than the owner of a dilapidated live bait business up a long dirt road that seemed to dead-end twice, once at his doorstep, and again in the small Ontario backwoods village of Pomerania.

It was here where a couple of hundred beaten Poles came following their failed revolution of 1863. And here they remained beaten. The local economy is simple and double-edged, lumbering or welfare, each compensating the other. Opportunity is equally simple: it lies elsewhere. And no one would ever understand that better than Felix Batterinski.

Incredible as it may sound for those of us whose first memory is of television, he grew up in a tar-papered shack, without electricity, with no running water, hot or cold, no toilet, no privacy, confused by one language at home, another at school, and yet another at the Latin Mass celebrated at the massive St. Martin's Roman Catholic Church that sits at the top of the village's largest hill, ever watchful.

The Batterinskis were people without a past. Felix would say he was a Polish Canadian, but nothing else. I asked Walter once about the family background and he just bit his lip and shook his head, almost as if to say he was ashamed not to know where they had come from. A simple family that could not even keep track of itself. . . ."

Excerpted by permission from "Batterinski's Burden," by Matt Keening, *Canada Magazine*, June 1982.

I CAN SEE POPPA PLAIN AS DAY AND IT HAS GOT TO BE — what? — twenty-two years if it's been a day. The silly bugger sitting in the Rileys' very own kitchen and waving his damned Polack newspaper around like a fly swatter. You'd think he felt he had to pound the lies into me. All I can say is I'm glad I was there to catch his knock. Thank the Christ none of the neighbors saw him snooping about. They'd have called the cops, sure as sin.

Poppa looked like a degenerate. He would have shaved before flagging down the bus as it flew through Pomerania, but by mid-afternoon he always managed to look like other men do at the end of a hunt, no matter what. He had on his church clothes: the black pants that rode too high on the belly and shone like polished pews under the ass, the white shirt buttoned tight, no tie, and the heavy gray sweater with Batcha's pink darning in the left elbow. Pink on gray — the old bitch must have been going color blind.

But the hat. My good God, the *hat*! That he must have picked up downtown at the year-end clearance at Vacationland Sports. It was straw woven in a fedora style, with a hollow plastic golf ball sliced in half and stapled onto some slime-green plastic grass that rode up top. And sticking up out of the band was a red plastic flag with the number "4" on it.

He had to be nuts. Imagine the silly bugger coming all the way over here from Pomerania, six bucks on the Ottawa-to-Vernon milk run, just to tell me this. And him swallowing it in the first place. But there it was, written up like it had really happened, in the *Polonia*, his damned Polish newspaper, practically the only mail we ever got apart from the baby bonus.

The *Polonia* was full of the appearance of the Virgin Mary on a church steeple in downtown Warsaw. Poppa claimed she'd been there four weeks, surrounded by some goofy glow and smiling down with big sad eyes on the crowds that were gathering each night to see her. The paper said the police could barely keep order. They had to marshal the crowds into six-deep ranks and then march them around the church so everyone could get a fair look. Some said they saw only the aura. Some said they saw her completely. But no one, naturally, had the guts to admit that they saw sweet screw-all.

"Krasinski was right!" Poppa shouted. "Poland *is* God's daughter!"

Krasinski? Christ, but there it was smack in the middle of page two of the *Polonia*, Poppa's long spruce cone of a finger tapping on the damn poem like he was trying to make a frog jump. Poor dumb Poppa, expecting me to remember Krasinski like he lived back home in Pomerania, maybe just down the road from our shack in a hollowed-out maple somewhere between Dombrowski's and Shannon's. But I could barely remember. The name of Krasinski's damn poem, yes —"Przedswit" — and perhaps one or two lines . . . "Be thou then the Truth, as Jesus is" —no, no, no — "as *He* is, everywhere. Thee I make my daughter." Only a dumb Polack could swallow that kind of crap.

Far more than the words, I remember Jaja's bony knees, me sitting on my grandfather's lap before the old man died, the smell of split cedar on his clothes and pipe tobacco on his breath as he tried night after night to teach his only grandson that silly poem. And all that garbage about this Krasinski being a distant relative of the Batterinskis and how I should be so proud.

Hell, Krasinski should be so proud to be related to me. Hadn't they just named me to the Muskoka midget all-star team? Hadn't Felix Batterinski been voted first-string defense? I made the front page of the Vernon *Muskokan*. Krasinski only made the second page of the *Polonia*. And no picture, either.

But here was Poppa, acting like I should model my game on someone who'd been dead for a hundred years.

He didn't even seem interested in my hockey. Once we'd disposed of the Virgin Mary, he had to go over all the latest news from home. Uncle Jan had just bought another new car, a Chevrolet Impala with power steering and automatic transmission, which caused Poppa to half spit and say it was the same as having a chauffeur. Uncle Ig was still the same, which was to be expected for someone who was so retarded. But at least I could smile about Jan's car and good old Ig, who next to Danny Shannon was probably my closest friend. Poppa expected me to do the same for Batcha, but I couldn't. So what if she was now making more money on her phoney cures than Poppa had all summer on worms and minnows? I hadn't given a sweet damn about her since Jaja had keeled over in the chicken coop and left her a widow in permanent mourning. I still carried the scars on my neck from that memory of the bitch. So no thanks, Poppa, all I wanted to know was when he was going. Before he was seen.

"Why have you come, Poppa?"

"I want to see my son play hockey."

"We don't play tonight. It's juveniles tonight. Midgets don't play till tomorrow."

"Fine then. I'll stay till tomorrow."

Den. Den. Fine den. What did the old bugger say down at Vacationland Sports when he pointed out the hat? "I tink I'll take one a dem tings?" Christ, until I heard him I hadn't realized how much I'd lost. It was amazing what laughing behind your back could do for your front; I fell asleep thinking "th" and woke up saying it.

"Never mind," Poppa said quickly, though I had said nothing. "I'll get a room at the hotel."

I couldn't be sure whether he expected me to argue with him or not. But how could he have possibly stayed at the Rileys'? If he went to the bathroom he wouldn't even know to flush.

"This is a dandy place, son."

Dis. Dis. What was next? *Prit near?* He sat drinking in the place, gawking around like he'd suddenly realized he was in out of the rain. I knew what he'd be noticing: paint on the walls, and wallpaper, and no big spikes anywhere to hang up coats and hats and rusted cables he'd never use; real fancy dinnerware that's all the same color; four different sizes of Canada geese on the wall rather than four calendars — all from the same year; a four-piece toaster and sharp red plastic on the breakfast nook table rather than oilcloth you can't make the pattern out on anywhere except where he'd hammered the overlap back up under.

"What does this Mr. Riley do?" Poppa asked.

"He owns his own business."

Poppa laughed. "So do I!"

"You saw the hardware store on the corner where the bus came in?"

"No."

"Well, that's his."

I would have told him about the size of it, about all the gear and delivery vans and everything else, if he'd asked, but I knew from the way he picked at his knees he wasn't interested.

Then he smiled. "Where's Danny Boy?"

"Just up the street a bit."

"Nice place like this?" *Dis.*

"Yah, sure."

"Free, too?"

"Yah, sure."

"Just for playing hockey?"

"Just for playing hockey."

"By God, you hang on to that, son."

"I will. Don't worry."

"You been going to mass?"

"Father Schula's uncle is the priest here, Poppa. You remember that."

"I didn't ask about him. I asked about you."

"We play Sundays. Usually."

"We pray Sundays. Usually." Poppa thought this very funny, slapping the table so hard the knife-and-fork drawer rattled.

"What's that?"

"Just the drawer. Utensils."

"Utensils?"

"Yah. Knives and forks and spoons."

Poppa bent down and examined it, whistling. "Say, that's a hell of an idea." *Dat's.*

I had to get him out of there before the Rileys returned. My nerves must have shown, for Poppa shook his head and wagged a finger at me.

"You haven't been going to church, have you?"

"We're going to start serving after Christmas. Danny, too. Mr. Riley's arranging it."

"Riley. Irish Catholic, eh? Watch them, Felix, they'll steal the wine right off your tongue, eh?"

"Mr. Riley doesn't drink."

"Then he can't be Irish. How's about school, how's it?"

"Fine. Fine."

"Grades good?"

"Got none yet."

"You working hard?"

"Danny says he's quittin' the day he turns of age."

"That's a Shannon. You're a Batterinski. You think your Matka and Jaja would like to hear that?"

How typically Poppa to call on the dead to do his work for him.

Did he really believe I had anything to do with my mother's death any more than I could have caused my grandfather's heart attack?

"How can they hear that? They're dead."

The tongue cluck. Always the tongue cluck. "You get your schooling, son. Something to fall back on after hockey."

After hockey. Always the same phrase: *after hockey*. Like I was going for a crap or something.

Poppa was talking too much. Maybe he was as nervous about the Rileys coming home as I was. He had his big hands on the table, fingers drumming, and I could make out every line in his skin by the black. He'd scrubbed, I knew that; I could practically feel the pumice stone rising from the can he'd hammered in above the basin. But it did little good. Ever. Poppa's hands always looked like they'd just left a transmission.

"Well," he said, rising and reaching for his idiotic hat. "I'd better get going if I'm going to get a room. You'll have supper with your father, eh? I'm buying."

"Mrs. Riley's got a roast on special tonight. Can't you smell it?"

Poppa sniffed the air like a deer. Probably nothing had got through that mat of nasal hair in years.

"She'll expect me to be here," I added quickly.

"Sure. Sure. But you'll come after supper, eh? And bring Danny Boy. Maybe show me the town, what do you say?"

"Yes, Poppa. I'll come down as soon as I eat."

"Here," he said, grabbing up the copy of *Polonia* again. "You keep this. I can get another from the church."

He set it down so the paper faced me properly and I realized that the big story had pictures of the crowds but none of the main attraction. "If she was there, Poppa," I said, "why didn't they get a picture of her for the paper?"

Poppa scowled. "The Holy Mother would not come down to pose for newspaper photographers, Felix. Don't be sacrilegious."

"But they could have taken one anyway. She didn't come down for them maybe, but they were there. They got pictures of the crowd."

"That's not important," Poppa said, snatching back his copy. "What's important is that she chose Poland to appear in. You think about that, son. Why Poland?"

"What if it had been China, Poppa?"

"Don't be smart with me, son."

He said it so matter-of-factly, so soft and free of anger, that I felt immediate guilt and stood up, smiling, to see him to the door. Another awkward handshake and then he was gone, the straw hat with the plastic golf course bobbing down the walk, past the cedar hedge and down the road toward Main Street and the hotel. He was whistling. I couldn't hear, but could see the fine stream of his happy breath in the cold air — Poppa, drawing attention to himself. I watched for a moment and then ran. I had too much to do.

Downstairs, where my bedroom was just off the family room, what Poppa's doorbell had interrupted lay all over my bed, accusing me. Four *National Geographic* magazines were laid out like little tents, their straight pins lined up at rest along my homework table. I had to work fast to get everything back together and clean again. Every month when the magazine arrived, Mr. Riley ceremoniously handed it over to Mrs. Riley so she could head upstairs and do her censoring. On a good month she'd return it with at least five pages pinned together. A pin for each corner and one along each side so it was impossible even to peek inside.

But this afternoon, with them out driving in their brand-new Pontiac Fire Chief, I was downstairs with the pins out and the pages open. Africans, but at least you could see their boobs. Not great, mind you, kind of flat and triangular like a splitting wedge, but when you're fifteen years old even a hot water bottle looks good.

I didn't mention Poppa at all during supper — not that he was in Vernon, not that he'd be at the game. Nobody ever said much at all when the Rileys ate; there was never the time for it. They were on their second bowl of neapolitan ice cream when I excused myself and went to the washroom to work on my hair and zits. The hair only took a second; there was only so much you could do with a brushcut.

Some of the guys had been saying I looked like Tim Horton and that was just fine with me. I thought I played like him, too. Horton looked then like the Maple Leafs cut his hair on the skate sharpener, grinding it down, but I made do with Herb Broadbent's scissors and not a damned thing else. The style was a natural for me and Herb was even talking about hanging my picture, complete with hockey uniform, in his shop window to advertise.

But I knew he wouldn't. A picture of Batterinski wouldn't look like an advertisement for hair, but like one against zits. I was convinced I had zits because I was Polish. No one in my family had good skin; no one in Pomerania, as far as I had seen, ever had either, except for a few Irish like Danny Shannon. Maybe it was all the sugar in the *mazureks*, because Poppa, Jaja, and Ig all had swollen noses, moles, blackheads and broken vessels. Maybe it came from not pronouncing "th" properly, I don't know.

At least I had hair. Hair like Poppa's, too, not poor Ig with his damned Scotch tape and floor sweepings from Hatkoski's barber shop. How could they have been brothers, Ig with a quarter of Poppa's brain and not a speck of his hair? And goddamn that Danny, too — him going on after practice yesterday to Powers and Bucky, telling them all about my Uncle Ig taping on somebody's white hair over some of Danny's own cuttings. Danny Shannon should have known better. Sometimes I wondered, who's the more retarded, Danny or Ig? The real difference was Ig couldn't help himself and smartass Danny could, but didn't bother. The prick.

If he wasn't my best friend, I'd have killed him. And he knew that, which is why he was even friendlier than usual when I called on him.

"Your old man's *here*?" he asked when I said I was heading down to the hotel to see him. "Jaisus — I'd give anything for my gang to show up for a game."

I very nearly said I'd gladly trade him, but let it go, knowing full well Danny's enthusiasms weren't necessarily tied to what he really felt. Danny Shannon put popularity before all other considerations and Vernon seemed ready-made for him. He'd only been in town a day when he had his first telephone call. A girl, naturally, and since then hardly a day went by without a call, a single female screech "You're cute!" and then a banged receiver. Cute, yes, I couldn't deny that, Danny with his curly hair black as a puck and those big sleepy brown eyes and what Poppa always calls "that damn sneaky Irish charm." But I never begrudged him that. It was all he had, really. He wasn't a first-stringer on the team, not like me, and he sure as hell wasn't going to make any go of school. His personality was as crucial to him as my hips were to me. What people knew you by.

Vernon had a great Main Street, snaking up from the river past the hotel and the theater and on up into the hill where the water reservoir sat. The river ran between two lakes, the one back of the arena called "Fairy," and Danny found it impossible to walk by the sign over top of Riley's Hardware without splitting a gut. All it said was "Oddfellows Club, Fairy Branch," which was good for one laugh but hardly what Danny had turned it into. I knew I'd have to make sure we kept to the other side of the street if we took Poppa anywhere, God forbidding.

The only similarity between Pomerania and Vernon was the amount of walking you had to do. Vernon had a covered arena with artificial ice; Pomerania had an outdoor rink, ice pebbles and spring muck. Vernon had four thousand people; Pomerania had maybe two hundred—and most of them hidden in the pines. Once we had eleven hundred spectators out for a game in Vernon; in Pomerania once, maybe, we had eleven.

But the walking—that was entirely the same. You either climbed leaning into your direction or fell away backwards to compensate for the long steps down. The coach, Teddy Bowles—a hell of a nice guy nicknamed "Sugar" by the town, "Toilet" by a couple of players, Danny Shannon included — he said it was our great fortune to live in a place like Vernon. "You'll build legs here that'll last you the rest of your life." Danny said he'd rather have a car that would last him the rest of his life, but he didn't have a car, so we walked. We walked up and down Main Street, the two of us always in our Pomeranian bantam jackets, yellow with black arms, me with "Asst. Captain" stitched in below my number, 7, the same number Tim Horton wore for the Leafs.

But I'd have given up the number just to walk like Danny. With his fists jabbed into his jacket pockets he seemed to leisurely tip forward and kind of flow into his walk, casually breaking a sure fall with the toes of his feet. Me, I was gangly, and where Danny's cords draped perfectly over top of his desert boots, my jeans were too short and showed a big gap of white sock between cuff and sneakers. I gawked around when I walked like I'd never been there before, whereas Danny would glide along with his head held straight on as if he was watching television and the town was simply slipping off the screen and folding around him as he passed. He became the center, no matter where he was. And me, I always felt at the edge, circling like a seagull until my own chance came along.

I stood a moment at the hotel desk, waiting, but the man in charge sat reading a war comic, ignoring my stare. I had to clear my throat to get him to look up, revealing a nose even larger than Poppa's. Beneath it he was smiling.

"Hi there, son. Your dad's in room 404."

I stared, blinking.

"You wonder how I know, is that it? I know you. And I know your buddy there. How ya doing, Danny?"

Danny smiled back. "Good, Arch. How's she going?"

"Good. Room 404, boys." The nose tipped down, the eyes settling back on the comic book.

Danny was up ahead, already on the stairs. "How do you know that guy?" I asked.

"Shit. Don't you notice nothing? He's always at the rink, hanging around. Powers bets he's a fruit, so you got to watch him, eh?"

I nodded, marveling at Danny's knowledge of the town after two months. We ran to the fourth floor of the Muskoka, where the toilet sign on one of the doors announced that this was where the cheap rooms were.

"Hey, Danny!" Poppa shouted when he yanked open the door. "How's the boy?"

"Good, good, Mr. Batterinski," Danny said, reaching for Poppa's hand. "Great to see you."

They seemed more pleased with being together than Poppa and I had earlier. "I bought some chocolate bars for you boys," Poppa said, grabbing them off his bed. "Here."

Danny took his eagerly. I shook my head, no.

"Hey, that's not my son."

Dats. Jesus.

"He's afraid of getting zits," Danny said, and laughed.

"Zits?" Poppa asked.

"Pimples," Danny explained and they both laughed. I could feel it rising inside of me, the urge to burst and the relief that would follow.

I could taste Poppa in the room. It was like he'd brought all the smells of home with him. One whiff was all anybody needed to know right off how poor we were, and that Poppa worked with a chainsaw. I looked at Poppa and realized how lucky I'd been he had his shirt buttoned up tight when he showed up at Riley's;

open now, I could see his longjohns, the pink ones, the ones he says are flesh-colored but which look more like a dirty bandage than anything made of human skin. But then Poppa didn't look like he had human skin, either. If you saw him naked you'd swear he'd been hand-painted, with a big "V" of dark red from the wind and sun spreading down his neck, up his throat and over his face as high as his cap mark, and then again on his forearms from the elbow down. Everywhere else the skin he never exposed was pure white, the line as clear as the difference between skin and pulp when you bite into a ripe apple.

"You have anything to eat?" Danny asked Poppa.

Any-ting. Christ, Danny was talking like he was home for the holidays.

"Had a sandwich," Poppa said. "What do you boys want to do? Treat's on me."

Fearing Danny might mention the hockey game, bright lights and Vernon people, I acted. "What about the movie?"

"What's on?" Poppa asked, excited.

"*Judgment at Nuremberg,*" Danny said with evident disinterest. "Supposed to be a drag."

"Naw," I said. "It's about the war."

"The war?" Poppa said. "Geez, I'd like that."

Finally, we flipped a coin. The Virgin Mary must have been standing on top of the Muskoka Hotel because I was blessed with victory. But I won only time. The movie was, as Danny said, a drag; all the right people — Lancaster, Tracy, Widmark — but too much talk and not enough action. Poppa was sitting between Danny and me and kept excusing himself to go to the snack bar and the can. At first I thought he was sneaking off with a mickey, vodka maybe, and I simply couldn't smell it on him. He kept coughing, too, and once when I looked I realized the cough was being faked. When he took his red hanky up to his face it went to his eyes, not his mouth. And he was wiping away tears. Poor Poppa, he saw so few movies — perhaps two before this one — that he hadn't yet learned that this was all acting and not real at all. Not at all.

Even in the forty below weather of Pomerania, I always had to be the first one to the rink. And I kept it up in Vernon. Coach Bowles — to me he deserved being nicknamed Sugar — he got so tired of seeing me standing around the side entrance when he arrived to set up that he slipped me my own key so I could come and go as I pleased. The day Poppa came to watch I left Riley's about noon, even though we weren't playing until seven. I'd told Poppa I'd see him after the game, that I needed the time before to unwind and get ready, and he seemed to understand. And I took the same crazy route to the arena I've followed since we won our opening game of the season against Orillia, shortcutting across the curling rink parking lot, hopping the chainlink fence around the war memorial—wreaths just now starting to wilt after a week in the cold and rain—then over across the field back of the Legion Hall, through the lane between the houses, down the slope by the river and up again to the rink. Someone down toward the docks was burning wet leaves and the smoke was rolling along the river, sharp and delicious. For some reason it made my stomach growl.

Sugar was already there, sharpening in the skate room. I could hear the stone and smell the dry grind, and though I loved to watch him work, I passed and went directly to the dressing room. The lights were on over the ice and I could hear Bull Tate tripping the tank levers as he began his first flood. Usually I loved to watch that too, the water spreading wet and glimmering behind him, the steam rising from the spread rag and the taps, but this I passed on too.

It was not a matter of trying to be first. I *had* to be first. And far worse in Vernon than back home. At our very first skate in Vernon we all dressed together, and Tom Powers, who had already been made team captain by Sugar, stopped right in front of me, pointed straight at my drawers and shouted: "Christ, if you're going out there in *that*, forget the equipment—no one's going to come near *you*!"

No one had ever said anything like that in Pomerania. I'd been expecting to be called "Polack," had even specially remembered the great line Jaja's hero, Wally Stanowski, had when he played for the Leafs, so I could use it, too: "I train on Polish sausage, the breakfast of champions." But they weren't laughing at my heritage—it was my underwear! I couldn't just jump up and paste Powers, so I leaned over and pretended I'd lost something in my duffle bag, scrounging around till I felt some of the burn leave my face. So I didn't have nice, new, bright white insulated underwear—big goddamned deal! I was angry and I couldn't shake it.

I carefully checked out Powers during the warm-up, the way he'd skate in over the blueline and then let the puck drop back from the blade to his skate, kick off over onto the other skate and then kick the puck back up to the blade, the illusion being that he had lost it. I skated around memorizing his move and gathering myself, enjoying the season's first waft of arena air on my face, giving my little extra kick as I rounded the net so I came out of the turn with pants hissing and the ice behind me making a sound like I'd just been withdrawn from a scabbard. And then, when scrimmage began, I simply waited for Powers to try that little suck move on my side, aiming for his head rather than the puck, and I put him up so high he did a complete somersault in the air and came down so hard on his brand-new Tackaberry skates that the left blade bent and Sugar, smiling rather than angry, had to go off with him into the skate room and pound it straight with a mallet.

After that I never had a moment's trouble from Tom Powers. After that, though, I never failed to be the first one dressed either. Not that I had to any more. At the very next practice I arrived to find a brand-new cellophane-wrapped set of Stanfield longjohns resting on my seat. The only other person in the rink was Sugar Bowles, sharpening, but he never said a word about the underwear, and I never mentioned it either. But it had to be him.

I could hear Sugar coming along dragging a new bundle of sticks and I got up and caught the door for him. I'd been imagining I was Tim Horton sitting there yakking up a storm with Stanley and Bower before we took to the ice. But it was hard to think of Sugar as Punch Imlach. Sugar had more hair sticking out one ear than Punch had on his entire head. Sugar's face was all squashed up like a bulldog and his hair began, I swear, about an inch above his eyebrows, hair like Poppa's, black and thick and dry-looking like he'd just washed it, though I doubt Poppa and he had had a half-dozen washes between them over their lifetimes. Punch looked like a bank teller; Sugar like the holdup man. Sugar had this huge scar on his face running from the corner of his right eye down across the cheek and sliding off his jawbone. The right eye seemed to look at you but was cloudy, the left one nearly as black as his hair. Tom Powers put it about that Sugar had lost his eye in a hockey fight, kicked by a skate when he was down, but Sugar hadn't verified this story. Powers also said Sugar was once a prospect himself, but when Danny pressed him on the way back from a North Bay game, Sugar denied he'd even played the game and told us all to shut up and try and get some sleep.

"Batterinski."

"Yah," I said, looking up. The cloudy eye seemed to have me fixed. Sugar was still taping, but not thinking about it.

"What do you think of Fontinato?"

"He's okay."

"You ever hear of Sprague Cleghorn?"

It sounded like a disease to me. "No. Why?"

"Cleghorn'd eat Fontinato for breakfast."

"He played?"

Sugar nodded and spit. "Five times they arrested him for hurting players. Five times."

I shook my head. I didn't know what else to do.

"Newsy Lalonde," he said, letting it hang.

I looked at Sugar, unsure.

"Sent more'n fifty guys off the ice on stretchers."

Sugar finished taping the first stick, bit off the tape and picked up another, his head turning so the left eye could catch me directly. "Who do you like in the NHL, Batterinski?"

"Horton," I said.

"You take a look at Fontinato," he said. "And maybe even this new guy Eddie Shack. You understand?"

I didn't. Sometimes no one could figure out Sugar or his crazy riddles. Talking with him was always like breaking an oar halfway across the lake. But I did like some of his sayings. He really pissed Powers off one practice when he said: "You don't have enough talent to win on talent alone," and when Powers came up after practice and asked Sugar if it was meant for him in particular, Sugar just said: "If you have to ask, you must have a question." Beee-utiful.

One of the sayings was meant for me in particular, and I knew that for certain because he gave it only to me, all folded over and placed in an envelope with my number on it. "The unforgiveable crime is soft hitting," it read. "Do not hit at all if it can be avoided, but *never* hit softly." Underneath was this name, Teddy Roosevelt, which sounded vaguely familiar to me, but I didn't have the nerve to ask.

The other guys straggled in, Terry LeMay, the goaltender, Powers and his sidekick, Bucky Cryderman, then Danny.

"Hey, Bats," Cryderman said, laughing, "you want I should call your old man in here to tighten your skates?"

"Screw off," I said, closing the issue. Danny was a loudmouth.

Ten minutes before warm-up Sugar was ready for his talk and slammed a stick into the equipment box for our attention. "All right, then," he began. "We should be ready. You all remember Parry Sound from the exhibitions, so you forwards know if you get a chance you shoot. Goalie's weak on long ones to the stick side; but don't try to suck him because he's good in tight and flops well. So keep it simple and make your first shots count. I'll be juggling lines to keep Powers' line away from their checkers, so if I touch your shoulder that means *you* are on, not necessarily your line, so just keep track of yourselves, okay?

"These guys like to carry the puck and they like to make the pretty play, but they don't seem as keen when the going gets rough. Batterinski?"

"Yah?"

"You set the pace, you understand?"

"Uh huh."

"Sprague Cleghorn, remember. Now the rest of you are going to be seeing a very small player out there and though he's a defenseman they'll probably play him up front 'cause he's only pee-wee age."

"A *peewee*?" Powers said, falling into giggles.

"Laugh once and get it out of your system," Sugar said, eyeing Powers with the black left ball. "His name is Orr and I've seen him and he's already a better player at twelve than any of you are at fifteen. Understand that? Don't let his size fool you and watch him. Defense, I want you to stick to him like snot to an oven door, understand?"

All around the room we grunted that we did.

"Cryderman," Sugar called, kicking at Bucky's skates stuck out in front of him like he was about to take a nap. "What's the toughest fish in the ocean?"

"Huh?"

"Come on. You guys think you're all big fish in a little pond. What is it?"

"I dunno," Bucky said. "A shark, I guess."

"That's very good, Cryderman. Now there's something special

about sharks that I want you all to consider. There's one thing that makes sharks different from all other fish . . . anyone care to guess what it is?"

"The fin," said Powers.

"Nah."

"The teeth," Danny shouted, showing his.

"No."

Sugar waited, scanning the room, then he smiled. "A barracuda's teeth are just as nasty, maybe worse. What makes a shark truly unusual is what he *doesn't* have. And that's a swim bladder."

Someone laughed. Powers, probably. Or Bucky.

"Go ahead," Sugar said. "Laugh. But let me tell you first what it means. A shark has to keep moving constantly. A shark does not float, like other fish. A shark can't float. He has no swim bladder, see. He can't let up for a minute and that's what makes him top dog. You think about that awhile, okay?"

Sugar walked out the door and closed it silently and no one said a word. No laugh, no burp, no fart. No one would dare destroy Sugar's pregame silences because they worked. We were leading the league.

Danny and I could hardly believe it when we first got here. We were used to Father Schula's prayers that no one got hurt, but so far this year we had had Sugar read aloud from *Tom Sawyer*, quote John Kennedy and Winston Churchill and some Chinese guy I'd never heard of and give lectures on everything from why water droplets scoot on a hot pan ("Keep the puck away from the traffic") to how vultures in Egypt break open ostrich eggs by dropping small stones on them ("You can't do it all yourself").

By tradition, I went onto the ice first. Number seven was the first sound in the arena always, first scrape on the ice, first slice of the corner, first stick on a puck, first crash of puck against the boards. In a way I created the game, just as I so often finished the game. With my hands.

I didn't see Poppa until "God Save the Queen." The record always skipped slightly and Al Willoughby, the arena manager, had piled so many pennies on the arm the record had slowed to a near growl. But no one sang along anyway, so it didn't matter. I quickly scanned the seats, skinny Wilemena Bowles, Sugar's wife, in her usual seat, clutching the gong of her cow bell so it wouldn't sound, and behind her a plastic golf hat held over a heart. *Poppa*.

And he was singing along, or trying to. The only one in the arena fool enough to even try.

Powers won the first face-off and got it straight back to me. I circled slowly, shifted, then doubled back and cut across ice when the winger charged me. At their blueline I hit Powers with a perfect pass and he stopped, a give-and-go play. I followed through, slipping up the far wing and into the clear, and Powers put on the shift I figured he would, a shoulder dip, but when he tried to thread the pass through the defenseman's skates the puck was suddenly stopped and Powers was standing there looking like a fool.

It was the *kid*! They'd *started* him for Christ's sake, and on defense too. He looked like a mascot out there, but suddenly the puck was sailing off his stick high through the air and perfectly into the glove of the winger who'd originally rushed me. I was caught up ice. Parry Sound came in two on one, a deke, a flick pass and a stab and poor old Terry didn't have a prayer. Parry Sound 1, Vernon 0.

Sugar let into us on the bench. What had he said in the dressing room about floating? Why did Powers stop? What made me so sure I could just walk away from my position? We took it all, heads down, not saying a word. Sugar waited through ten minutes of stopped time before he tapped my shoulder again.

At the start of the second period Danny got the puck back to me at the point and I slammed a low, hard one, and Danny, just like we used to practise back home, skated in front and let his stick dangle so it just ticked the shot straight down onto the ice and suddenly it was 1–1. I slapped Danny's pads and went straight back toward the face-off circle, skating bent over, stick riding both knees, looking up from the ice just once to see how much time was left. I wanted to look at Poppa, but couldn't. But I could imagine what he must have felt hearing his family name crackling out over the P.A. system. Had a Batterinski ever before known such glory?

A minute left in the second period and I was last man back with the blond kid breaking over center, intercepting a bad Bucky pass over to Powers. He looked like an optical illusion coming in on me, too small, too compact, rushing in a near sitting position, but still accelerating too fast for me to simply ride off into the corner. I forced him slightly to my left, then stepped right, where he came, and stopped and thrust out my hip with a little bit of knee I hoped the referee wouldn't catch. I had him clean. But then I didn't. All I felt was the wind from his sweater on my face as he somehow stepped yet another way and was gone. I turned and lunged, sweeping his feet out from under him, but even that was too late. The red light came on even as he flew through the air past Terry, and before he landed I could see him smile and raise his hands in victory, as if he'd somehow had control even as he sailed through the air.

MacLennan began the third period in my place, the ultimate humiliation, the first opening face-off I'd missed since arriving in Vernon, penalties excepted. I tried to convince myself it was because Sugar wanted to talk to me about stopping the blond kid. But of course it wasn't. I knew Poppa would be looking for me at every player change, but Sugar's hand never landed on my shoulder.

And MacLennan was botching things. Danny was playing his heart out, twice carrying right through the team only to hit the goal post once and fan on his backhand the other time. He was playing his heart out for my Poppa. I sat, stick handle pressed between my eyes, staring over the boards. I could feel the heat rising. I could sense every one of the eight hundred or so spectators knew that I'd been benched because of some goddamned twelve-year-old kid. I'd been made a fool of; once I thought I heard laughter from behind the bench, and since there was nothing funny about the game I knew the one thing they could be laughing at was me.

I was sweating harder on the bench than I would have on the ice. There was a noise, a steady, rhythmic rap that seemed to fill the arena, until I realized it was me doing it, ramming my skate toes into the boards in front of me.

Poor Poppa. He'd come all this way for nothing. Nothing. Up at three to catch the bus; money he didn't have; and now nothing to show for it. I could see him skulking out of the Vernon arena and not even waiting to see me, back by bus to Pomerania with a good word for Danny Shannon's family, and then not able to lie about me to Father Schula or the Jazdas or Dombrowskis or Hatkoskis or even the old bitch herself, Batcha. I could see her smiling, knowing all along. I could hear her tongue cluck with the disgust that seemed to fill her mouth as easily as spit.

I wanted to hit something. Bad.

Sugar barely touched me and I was over the boards as dumb-ass MacLennan stepped off. The little blond kid was no fool, obviously; figuring to catch us on the line change he sent a long pass up my side to this skinny creep whipping along with his head down. I skated backwards just to the blueline, then cut sharply, forcing skinny toward the boards. I jumped from going backwards into an instant charge and caught him flush, stick rising just as he hit the boards, rising in just under his chin and ear, and lifted with all my strength. I could hear him groan. I could feel him cave and smell him sweat, frightened. The whistle was screaming even as I lifted, stick and knee, and thrust him on over the boards, sprawling and shouting into the front row of terrified spectators.

Now I felt fine.

Just as the linesmen arrived, Parry Sound's big defenseman charged up and threw his stick down. I kept mine, which flustered him immediately. I could feel the linesman's arms around my shoulder and neck in a half nelson: it was a feeling I enjoyed, the gentleman's agreement that we would struggle, but within limits, that it would look like more than it was. I pulled angrily toward the defenseman and my linesman pulled back in agreement. The big defenseman, already toothless at sixteen, spit at me and I spit back, but the other linesman had moved in to pull on the defenseman and so neither of us landed our shots. I pulled; he pulled; they pulled; we shook; we circled. It was as if the players were heavy life-sized dolls and the linesmen were struggling to work them, unsuccessfully. I laughed at the defenseman, which made him puff up and charge like a goose. But he got nowhere.

I could hear their coach screaming. He was up on the boards, balancing and calling for a major. Good—that meant blood. Their trainer was slipping across the ice on the arms of one of the Parry Sound players and he was carrying a white towel, deliberately chosen to show the blood.

"How about somebody your own size, asshole!" the defenseman shouted. Without his teeth he lisped, so it came out "athole."

I spit, landing on his shoulder. "Faggot!" I shouted. And spit again.

"Cool it, boys, or you're both out of here," the bigger linesman warned.

I was willing to let things die, but not the defenseman. My spitting seemed to have him worked into a rage and he caught his linesman off guard by ducking down and twisting out of his hold. He came at me swinging and my linesman wouldn't let go, so I ducked and could hear the crack of the defenseman's fist on my linesman's head. I take things like that personally. My linesman released me, perhaps deliberately, but I had time only to follow through my duck with a bear hug around his middle. I lifted him but he pummeled my head. Not that it hurt, but it looked bad; so I lifted more and pushed forward, cracking his head on the ice like a .22 short, but it didn't bother him much. He swung at my face with one hand and tried to claw at my eyes with the other. I could feel the sting of a scratch. Pulling up his sweater over his head so it tied his arms, I drilled him right through the Parry Sound Shamrocks' crest, a direct hit on the mouth. Twice more and I could see the sweater staining red through the crest and, mercifully, both linesmen fell on me and pulled me away. My defenseman merely rolled over onto his side, moaning. Finished.

Naturally the referee threw us both out of the game. As I stepped off the ice a stretcher came through—the ultimate proof that I'd won. The leeches stood six deep along the corridor, but this time they were silent and did not touch. Silent with admiration. Not touching out of respect.

The linesman escorted me to the home dressing room, waited till I sat down, then closed the door carefully, leaving me entirely alone with the sucking of the urinals and the flutter of the rubber vents over the hot air duct. I slouched back and let the sweat run freely down over my forehead, over my nose, down onto my lips, and here I drew it back inside, getting back what I'd given out. I tasted like a man.

I knew it wasn't right, but it felt great. I could feel my defenseman on my knuckles and when I touched them they stung with his jaw, just as I knew when he moved this week he would feel me and I would be with him, his better, for weeks to follow. He had my mark on him. I too had swelling and redness, but on the knuckles it shone with pride. Where his swelling made him less, mine made me more. I tried to feel his fear of me, and in trying this, my respect for myself grew. I went to the half-shattered mirror but saw no pimples. Just *Batterinski*, hulking in his pads, solid from blade to brushcut, a man oddly at ease while others about him panic.

Danny always talked about how quickly things take place. "He never even saw the puck," he'd say. But it was never so with me. I was like Willoughby's recording of "The Queen." When attention was on me, time slowed down. In a fight, I relaxed. I could sit in the dressing room in the hours before a game and twitch so bad sometimes a foot would jump right off the floor. But when my defenseman charged I was aware even of my own breathing. He came in flailing, but to me it was like watching someone swim toward me doing the crawl. I could sense his intention and I could feel his blind fury. When I had him about the waist it almost felt as if I was comforting him. That I didn't just keep squeezing until his own insides poured out his mouth was an act of charity. I put him down and I ended his humiliation quickly for him, even hiding his face under his sweater when it happened. He should have thanked me.

The horn went to signal the end of the game and Danny was first in to confirm what I already knew.

"Ugga-bugga!" Danny shouted. His victory call. "Five–four for us, Bats."

I smiled. The rest poured in, shouting, slapping, tossing sticks and gloves. As they passed by they looked with the respect of the leeches but had no fear in touching, which I was glad for. I felt their hands and their sticks praising me.

"You fucking near killed that twit, Bats!"

"I heard the ambulance."

"Best check of the season."

"You turned it around, Bats old fart."

I said nothing in return. I sat there, completely dressed but for my gloves at my feet and felt no different than if I was lying in bed on a Saturday morning. The trainer, Biff, came in with a tray of Pepsi and made sure I got mine first. Then came Sugar, making like he was scribbling the final score down on his clipboard in case he'd somehow forget. He stopped, looked with the good black eye and winked it.

"Teddy Roosevelt," he said.

I said nothing, just smiled and looked down and began undressing slowly. Not undressing, more like dismantling: sweater, elbow pads, shoulder pads, lift off the braces, take off the skates, pants, undo garter, socks, shin pads, jock. Each piece dropped off with reluctance. If only the people who saw me on the street could see me in full uniform, the big "A" over the heart, the number "7," the tuck of my sweater into the back of my pants. I knew the uniform spoke better for me than I did myself.

Coming out of the shower Sugar reached out and caught my arm, turning me toward him. He whispered:

"That your dad waiting out there?"

Danny! The son-of-a-bitch.

"Yes."

"You want me to call him in?"

I shook my head. Sugar hung his thick lower lip out and nodded his understanding.

When I was dressed though, Sugar insisted on leaving the dressing room with me. Poppa was outside, leaning on the nearest edge of the snack counter, chewing on a Coffee Crisp like a little kid. There were chocolate and wafer crumbs all over his chin and front.

"Mr. Batterinski?" Sugar said before I could say a word.

Poppa looked like he was about to get into trouble with the law. "Yes?"

"I'm Ted Bowles, sir. Felix's coach. Delighted to meet you."

Poppa took Sugar's hand like it was some sort of trick. I began praying he would say nothing with "th" in it.

"How'd you like the game?" Sugar asked.

"Yes." Poppa said, brushing the crumbs off his chin like he hadn't properly heard the question. "Some of it."

"Your boy here," Sugar said, smiling, "he turned it around for us."

Poppa looked startled. "He did?"

"Sure he did. We were flat as pancakes before he shook things up." Sugar smacked me on the back of the head, reaching up to rub his knuckles into my brushcut. I knew I was turning red. "You got any more like this back home, Mr. Batterinski?" Sugar asked.

"No. Sorry." Poppa said it as if he was actually at fault. He shifted restlessly, anxious for dismissal. I kicked a Pepsi cup, then looked up to see Mr. Riley's shock of red hair just off to the side behind Poppa, he and his nervous wife both standing there, grinning widely and waiting to meet the bumpkin.

"Way to go there, Felix," Mr. Riley shouted, but not looking at me, at Poppa. Poppa turned, startled.

"Des Riley, Mr. Batterinski," Mr. Riley said, introducing himself.

"This here's the wife."

Poppa nodded at Mrs. Riley and tentatively shook hands with Mr. Riley. The Rileys looked as if they were dressed for church, his suit and tie indicative of his rising position on the local hockey executive. She had on her black wool coat with the beaver collar and her knitted hat. She was offering one of her tight smiles and nodding, but as I knew from past experience, not listening. Her only true interest lay in the church and Mary Maxim patterns.

"You should be very proud of Felix," said Mr. Riley. "He's a fine young man."

"Felix should not fight."

"Ah," Mr. Riley snorted, as if it were a point of utter insignificance. "He never started it. But he sure as heck finished it, eh?" Mr. Riley laughed loudly and looked around for approval.

"He's a good boy," Poppa said, and that seemed to satisfy everyone. But he meant it, I thought, in argument.

Sugar gave me another whack, reached over and shook Poppa's hand again and moved on into the leeches who were waiting to go over the game with him, as if the game could not be fact until they all agreed they'd seen the same thing. Well, at least this time I knew they'd have a good fight to talk about. I began to move away myself, but Poppa surprised me by starting up again.

"He goes to mass?" he asked Mrs. Riley directly. She tried to speak but her mouth wouldn't work. No one in the arena had ever spoken to her in preference to her husband before. He spoke for her anyway.

"Sure he does. You've no worries there, Mr. Batterinski."

"His first coach," Poppa said, "Father Schula, he wants Felix and Danny Shannon to serve Christmas Mass."

"Wonderful," Mr. Riley said, looking at me with pride. "They're both fine boys."

"I know."

"No trouble with them two."

School was to let out December 21, a day so bitterly cold the smoke rose above the boiler room like toothpaste from the tube. The windows in geography class were thick with frost so that at first we could only hear the ambulance siren as it bounced around the skinny pass between the shop entrance and the main building. The sound was so loud that Mrs. Hay couldn't continue, and eventually even she went to the windows and began rubbing with her hand to see what all the fuss was about.

It was a bit like looking underwater when the frost melted, but I was able to see the ambulance pull up just beyond the shop by the teachers' parking lot and cut the siren. And I could see both Old Man Morgan and the vice principal, Biggins, holding what seemed to be a pail of steaming water. They were standing near the rear of Morgan's three-tone Ford Fairlane, and they were bending over looking at something.

It was Danny Shannon.

He was right up to the side of the car like he was leaning into it. And he was screeching. I could hear him all that distance, his own siren wailing away. I thought at first Morgan must have driven over his foot and stopped on top of it, but that didn't make sense. He would have moved the car by now.

"Away from the windows, class," Mrs. Hay called, her voice rising shrilly. "Immmmeeeed-iately!"

"I still got the bastard," Danny said later when I went to visit him in the hospital. It seemed like a foolish boast, considering the two months of detentions he'd picked up and the great bandage that lay between his legs.

"It was pretty dumb," I said.

"I didn't figure on the cold," he said. "All I meant to do was piss in his gas tank and get out of there. How'd I know I'd stick to his goddamn gas tank. It was colder'n I thought, eh?"

"I still say it was pretty stupid."

"It'll ruin his engine," Danny said, forcing a smile.

"It almost ruined yours," I said.

"To hell with it," he said. "I'm quittin' anyway."

I stared at him, not following.

"School!" Danny shouted. "I'm quittin' *school*, asshole."

"You can't."

"Fucking right I can. You just watch me, lad."

"When?"

"Soon's I'm sixteen."

"You tell your family?"

"I'll tell 'em over the holidays."

I stared between his legs. "They going to let you out of here?"

Danny just smiled. "I already got my bus ticket — and a half-dozen safes to boot."

I giggled, couldn't help myself. "What the hell for?"

"Lucy Dombrowski, arsehole."

Danny looked at me as if he couldn't believe I'd question it. I looked at him like I couldn't believe he'd imagine it.

"Look," he decided to explain. "Sugar told you he thought you could play injured, didn't he?"

He was dead serious.

Danny made the bus home for Christmas, as promised, and he never stopped talking about what he was planning to do to poor Lucy until the bus passed into the high hills east of Algonquin Park. Here Danny fell asleep, leaving me to sit staring into the bush and seeing nothing but Lucy Dombrowski's marvelous ass wiggling back at me. Danny couldn't possibly be thinking he'd get her, could he? He'd be damned lucky to get a hand on her tit in the condition he was in.

Still, a tit was a tit, and more than Batterinski had touched at fifteen years of age. I was beginning to worry about the chances of going through an entire life pretending you'd done it all when in truth the closest you'd come was *National Geographic*. What if everyone flew around nude in heaven and you didn't know what to do? Would they send you down?

All I wanted was a tit to hold. All I'd wanted for as long as I could remember was to grab one, and I'd never even *seen* a real one. Lots of pictures, but I didn't even know what one would feel like. A cow's udder? Soft and cool like when I stabbed my hand into the bitch's flour bin? Or firm and hot like the Rileys' hot water bottle?

Hard to believe, but the first set of bare tits I ever saw were at Jaja's funeral. Well, not precisely at the funeral, but outside, in Uncle Jan's latest car, a Meteor, I think, and they weren't real tits that you could touch or anything, but you could sure see them when you put your eye up to the plastic steering knob Jan had bought and fitted onto his steering wheel.

Will I ever forget that day? We were supposed to have a squirt practice that morning—it had to be squirt, I was nine—and Jaja said he'd gather up my eggs for me so I could get in, but when I got there the ice was nothing but scab and muck, so Father Schula cancelled and sent us home. Danny and I goofed a lot on the way back trying to open up Sabine Creek early by dropping boulders off the bridge, and by the time I got back for dinner, they had

Jaja completely wrapped up tight in a camp blanket on the couch, and Doc Rafferty was sitting at the dining room table filling out papers as calmly as if he was doing a grocery list. And thank Christ he was there too. The bitch lunged at me out of her room screaming, *"Vjeszczi! Vjeszczi!"*—which means something idiotic like "monster"—at me and by the time Poppa and old Doc pulled her away she'd already ripped my neck half off. He had to clean me up with iodine and four stitches, which hurt worse than the original. And there was blood all over my sweater, which I wanted left on so Danny could see.

Uncle Jan was good to me that night. I was upstairs crying about Jaja and moaning about my neck when he came up and scooped me up and took me out to where he already had the Meteor warming up. On the front seat were a couple of Cokes for me and some beer for himself, and while Jozefa, Ig's and Poppa's only sister, and the other women were inside getting ready for *pusta noc*, the empty night, we sat out and listened to the Detroit-Leaf play-off game fading in and out from Toronto, Foster Hewitt in the gondola, which was to me even holier than the heaven I knew Jaja was off to. Uncle Jan grinned through his big moustache, gunned the car, showed me the steering knob and my first set of tits with the interior light, and cursed Lindsay and Howe like we were both grown men and the words were every bit as much mine as his, though of course I never used them. Ever since, when I think of Jan I think of that night, the heat puffing out from under the dash, the sour smell of beer—and tits. I must have forgotten about my neck because I fell asleep before Detroit wrapped up the series. Jan must have carried me up and put me to bed.

Poppa made the bitch apologize in the morning. He took me to her in the death room. She was already in Jaja's rocker, and her not even his real wife, Poppa's and the others' mother. She wasn't even one of us, just a replacement Jaja had brought out from the old country, and now she was acting like she was in charge. She had her black hair back in that tight bun covered with the net, and her lips were shaking like she was about to spit. But she did apologize, even if the words meant nothing compared to the stare of those wolf eyes. I knew she blamed me. And Poppa knew too. He even had Doc Rafferty take me aside and explain how the heart attack could have come at any time, picking eggs or even asleep, that it was no one's fault, and that, as far as he was concerned, it was the best way to go, because he'd seen them all. It didn't help though. Batcha hated my guts, plain and simple.

Christ, but I wish Danny had seen Ig that day of the funeral. He wouldn't have made all those cracks at practice if he had, because Ig looked and acted magnificently. But Danny wasn't there to see. Ig had taped-on hair that was a perfect match for his own gray-red horseshoe — you'd almost think Hatkoski the barber had been saving up his sweepings for a special occasion — and Aunt Jozefa had taken the time to fold the tape over neatly for him so for once it wasn't shining through. God, he looked great.

I could still feel him poking me on the march in to the cemetery. *Feelie, Feelie, Feelie, will ya ask, eh? Will ya ask?* Until finally I hurried up to Father Kulas and Father Schula and the pallbearers and asked Poppa if Ig could have a turn carrying. Ambrose Dombrowski, Lucy's father, dropped out, I remember, and Poppa took one side of the head and put Ig on the other, even though he could barely reach the box. Down the dirt road toward the village they went, five men solemnly carrying, Ig hopping along beside them like he was hanging from his fingertips, giggling, shaking his head, his mouth wrapped in a smile that would have you think he was bringing a bowl of fresh-picked raspberries back to the house, not carrying his own father to his grave. But Ig's mind was on the carrying, not the contents. One thing at a time for Ig.

And Batcha earlier walking up to the open casket with Jaja's eyeglasses and standing there cleaning them with her hankie before she put them on him. Worried about smudges in heaven. Acting like St. Peter's come down with the flu and left her in charge. The bitch.

And her again, pushing me up and half in with him. *Do it, Felix. Kiss your grandfather. Remember, you'll never fear the dead once you've touched them.* I'd rather have touched him than her, any day.

But it is Ig who deserves remembering, not the bitch. Ig running up to the barn when he found out how it had happened, and Ig trying to hurt the hens with their own eggs. Yolk splattered on the beams and straw and all over the dirt floor. And Ig screaming at them until Poppa came in and did what he always did at these times, held his brother's arms down and tight and used his own chin to squeeze Ig's head in tight to his chest, the two of them standing like that until it was over. Ig and his muffled screams. Poppa as expressionless as if he were waiting for an engine to cool before he took it apart.

And Ig at the cemetery, not knowing what to do when Poppa took Batcha's arm and led her back toward the church. Which left me to bring along Ig. Poppa had a snapshot Uncle Jan had once taken of me when I must have been about three, and I have this harness on that Poppa put on me when the creek was high with spring runoff, and the picture is of Ig walking me like I'm his dog, and Ig is laughing. But Jaja was dead, I was nine and it was Ig who needed leading. Him crying for Jaja and bawling because Poppa has pointed out my own Matka's grave, dead giving birth, which I sometimes think is why Batcha really hates me. I have him by the hand and we are moving back toward the church when Ig suddenly stopped and asked me to kiss him and pat his back, which I did. And from that moment on, we had changed positions. My uncle asking for a harness, for the nephew to care for him the way you might a dog. Now me the master, him the pet. But so what, Danny Shannon — big fucking joke. Brainless or not, there is no one on earth I love more than my Uncle Ig. So stick it with your big laughs with Powers and the rest of this half-assed team.

If I thought leaving Pomerania was a shock, it was nothing compared to the return. The bus dropped us at the White Rose two days before Christmas, and Danny and I walked up the highway together and turned off onto our road, which hadn't been plowed. We had to highstep past the rink — Danny groaning with every lift — over the tracks, past the bluff and the gravel pit and the cedars. The snow had stopped falling but it was still higher than our knees. We passed Dombrowski's, where Danny, holding a mitten to his crotch like he'd just blocked a shot, had the nerve to suggest we sneak up and see if we could catch Lucy undressing, an idea I talked him out of when I pointed out we'd leave tracks, and on past the other poor shacks with their single, weak lights in the kitchen, and on until we got to Shannon's, where the windows burned almost as brightly as those in a Vernon home.

There was a huge cedar wreath on the door and his sisters had sprayed the windows with canned snow in the shapes of snowmen, Santas and reindeer. Danny asked me in but I said no. He fairly ran to the door, jumping through the snow so he left funnel-shaped holes behind him, and when the door opened the lure of the Shannon home poured out: the collie barking, Beatrice, Colleen and Terry shouting at him, the sound of Christmas carols on the old wind-up Victrola. I saw Danny drop his duffle bag as the family pounced and the door slammed shut, suddenly silent, leaving me alone.

I half wished Danny's pants would mysteriously fall down so they'd see the hickie Old Man Morgan's Fairlane had left. That'd shut them all up.

It was like I'd gone deaf once the door closed. No one to make jokes about the team, no one bragging how he was going to get Lucy Dombrowski over the holidays. Just me with myself, alone. I walked down across the flats and over Sabine Creek, where a rifle crack made me wonder if it was the bridge, the ice or just a maple sounding the cold. Not like Vernon. Here it was dark and lonely and threatening, like a wolf might burst out of the bush at any corner. In Vernon, coming home from a late practice, it was like moving in perpetual daylight, the snow so white and clean, the street lights, the porch lights, the glow in every window, the blue flutter of a television from the living room. And the cars, always the cars, their chains growling, their headlights sweeping between the banks and around the corners. But here, here there was nothing. No cars had been on the road for days and it probably didn't matter to anyone. Where was there to go?

Up ahead through the spruce I could make out a single light as it winked through the weighted branches. At least Poppa had thought to hang the lantern. I could make out the shadows of the shed and the barn. I knew if it were daylight and I were a stranger I would have to look twice to tell which building was the house. Unless there were smoke from the woodstove I wouldn't even be sure anyone lived there. No aluminum siding here. No window trim. No reds, yellows, browns or blues — all black, black or nothing. Tar-paper along the north, west and east sides. Gray, sun-baked slabs along the south, cracks filled with straw, horse manure and river clay.

Puck started barking as I neared the door. Some name, Puck, but Poppa said when I left he needed someone besides Ig to do things with. So I had been replaced by a black mongrel from the mill cookery, supposed to be part Labrador, but more accurately, partly there. Like Ig.

The door gave a bit, caught and then opened with a stubborn grind. Poppa stood beyond, scowling and holding Puck by a rope until he settled down, and behind them stood Ig, complete with a new head of Hatkoski's hair, Irish red, and the old mouth-open smile. He was cheering and punching the air with his fist —"Hip, hip, horray! Hip, hip, horray!"—like I'd just scored a goal. Puck, once he'd realized it was me, began wetting himself all over the floor. Poppa booted him in the side, which made him pee all the more, and the dumb dog yelped and skulked quickly to his mat beside the wood box.

"Welcome home, son," Poppa said, smiling and putting his hand out like he was about to jimmy a jammed ax. His hand was scrubbed and shining, the week's work scraped and ignored on every finger.

Ig slapped my back, squealing. "Feelie! Feelie! Feelie! Did we ever miss ya! Holy old smokes, Feelie!"

I made as if to hug Ig but he stuck out his own hand in the same manner as Poppa. I took it and we shook violently, continuing the shake until Ig started giggling and I screamed "Uncle!" and he let go. I wondered if I was still four or five or eight years old in his eyes, or whether he was capable of such memory. I remembered once wondering if Ig had any understanding of time and then being pretty sure he hadn't. But he'd missed me, obviously; this wasn't a greeting for an eight-year-old coming in from a late practice.

Poppa had coffee on and some crisp apple *placek* sitting in a bowl on the table. Ig had one in my hand as soon as I shook free of my coat and boots. "Batcha made 'em special for ya, Feelie!"

"Where is she?" I asked Poppa.

"Asleep."

Ig pressed his palms together and held them to his cheek, closing his eyes and snoring through a wide grin.

"She doesn't have a lot of strength these days," Poppa explained. *Deez*—I could see myself falling instantly back into Pomeranian talk. "She wanted to stay up to see you home, Felix."

I just bet. She was probably lying at this very moment in her room counting off her rosary and praying I'd be gone by morning.

"Where's your hockey stick, Feelie?" Ig asked.

"Won't need it here," I said.

"How's it going?" Poppa asked, pouring out the coffee. An eggshell fell into my cup and he plucked it out with a black finger and dropped it back into the pot. Mrs. Riley would have fainted.

"We're in first place."

"Your Mr. Bowles is a good coach," Poppa said, as if he were expert enough to judge. Sugar had called him "Sir," so obviously Sugar could do no wrong.

"Sugar's all right," I said.

"*Sugar?*" Poppa said, his eyebrows caving.

"Yah, like in sugar bowl, eh?"

Poppa snarled, displeased. "You shouldn't be smart, son."

"Danny calls him 'Toilet,' " I said in defense.

Ig shrieked. "Toilet! Toilet Bowl! Toi-let Bowl!"

Poppa lightly tapped Ig's shoulder and Ig shut up instantly.

"Danny Shannon is an Irish," Poppa said sternly. "They talk toilet all the time."

Ig giggled, but a simple signal from Poppa — almost a soft crokinole shot in the air between them — put an immediate end to the joy.

"Danny's been dropped back to the third line," I said.

Poppa looked surprised. "Why? What's his problem?"

"How would I know? Sugar — Mr. Bowles — he thinks Danny's homesick."

"What do you think?"

"I guess he is, maybe. He talks about his family all the time."

"And you don't." Poppa looked at me, eyes steady, while I shrugged and looked at the table. He was starting to speak like old Jaja, even the same regrets. Surrounded by Polish and Irish families that bred like rabbits, the Batterinskis were slipping down some unfair funnel into oblivion. Jan childless, so far; Jozefa unmarried and not expected to ever be so; Ig impossible; Poppa with one dead wife and only one child. And me handed the name without asking or caring enough. For Poppa's sake, anyway.

"I made district all-stars," I said.

Poppa's eyebrows went up again. "Is that good?"

"Yah, sure. In February we're going to be playing an exhibition against the midgets from St. Mike's."

"*The* St. Mike's? In Toronto?"

"Uh huh."

"Hip, hip, horray!" shouted Ig, pounding the table.

Poppa was impressed. "Some of those boys turn pro with the Leafs, you know."

"Of course I know. There's going to be scouts at our game."

"Scouts?"

"Bob Davidson's going to be there. He's chief scout for the Leafs."

"He'll be watching *you* play?" Poppa asked.

"Yes."

Poppa blinked. This was almost as remarkable as the Virgin Mary herself coming down for a look. But at least you could photograph Bob Davidson.

"We'll pray you do good, Felix," Poppa said.

Ig folded his hands and bowed his head, ready to pray, but Poppa did his finger snap again. This was new since I'd left. I half expected Ig to crawl away to his mat or wet the floor like Puck, but he just reached for another *placek* and mushed it into his mouth.

"I got something to show you, Feelie," Ig said with the crumbs pouring out his mouth.

Ig started getting up from the table. I looked at Poppa but he was in such a shock over Bob Davidson that he was spooning brown sugar absent-mindedly into his coffee and shaking his head. The Virgin Mary he could understand; this he could not. She'd at least picked Warsaw. What in God's good name made Bob Davidson pick Vernon and his son?

I followed Ig to the door, where he signaled me to swipe the second coal oil lamp so we could see. I picked it up, turned the wick up slightly and we started up the stairs to his room. The creaks were all the same, and the third board from the top was still so loose you double-stepped over it. And the smells. How could I have forgotten? The house smelled of grease and coal oil and must and wood smoke and old clothes and urine from Batcha's and Ig's potties. And probably Puck now too. Back in the kitchen you could sometimes smell the lime Poppa poured down the outhouse hole, once in a while the pumice soap Poppa liked and sometimes the turpentine he used to get the grease off his hands; but these were the only *clean* smells. Mrs. Riley's kitchen always smelled of Success floor shine, the basement of Lestoil, and the cellar floor of Dustbane. She had Fleecy in her washer, pine scent in the family room and Dutch Cleanser in the bathroom. There was even a crazy thing the size of a small hockey puck hanging down the inside of the toilet bowl, white and smelling like moth balls. There, I never knew who'd been to the bathroom before me; here, I knew who, when and precisely what they'd done.

Ig was giggling madly and rubbing his hands together. The lamp was dancing with the drafts and the light played oddly on his face, but it struck me Ig looked exactly as he had always looked. I had never known him with hair; had I been given his brain I might have believed he'd grown the Scotch tape naturally.

"Looky," Ig said, spreading both his arms.

I put the lamp down on the table and adjusted the wick so the fog lifted from the chimney. Ig's table had been laid out like a forest, clumps of moss holding Princess pine, a small saucer of water, some stones, and all through this terrain little plastic animals, red and brown and blue and black bears, deer, squirrels, beaver, wolves, foxes, rabbits. The fox beside the rabbit; the wolf beside the deer.

"Poppa bought 'em for me at the Barry's Bay Stedman's."

"They're great, Ig. What do you play with them?"

Ig looked at me, not understanding but too smart to say anything for fear he'd been caught dumb. I realized he played nothing with them, as if once put in place they were forever in place, the wolf courteously beside the deer, the rabbit content with its fox. Ig lived in a world with no winners or losers. But then, he was a loser and didn't want reminding. I was a winner. I needed losers to remind me.

Batcha's reputation as a *carovnica*—something I never even realized she was until after Jaja's death—had grown in the few months I'd been gone. The white witch of Pomerania was a damned industry now. She was even taking business away from Old Frank, the *jiza* from down by Black Donald Lake. A wicker basket sat beside her old rocker completely filled with poplar branches to be knit together in the form of crosses and sold. She could hardly keep up with demand, Poppa said. A quarter to Batcha for a cross and you were in the clear: *smentek* the devil bat wouldn't suck out your blood while you slept.

With Ig's help and Poppa's vise and hacksaw, she was splitting and selling nickels to other old women who were frightened of the *mora* nightmare, the girls cursed at baptism who unwittingly suck others' blood at night. For a dime they could buy here consecrated maple keys to bury under the front door and make sure *smolôk* the devil didn't sneak into their house when they were away. A dollar and she'd lance a boil with the old otter claw she kept in a special chest in her room.

Growing up with her always around, it had never seemed all that unusual to me. But now, coming from Vernon where Mrs. Riley had her sparkling medicine chest filled with every cure the television promised, Batcha seemed outrageously impossible. How, in 1960, could people still believe that every stroke of lightning in a storm strikes a devil or that the small whirlwinds that circled in the snow were caused by the souls of children who had died without being baptized? Yet Batcha and her customers believed precisely that, and I suppose at one time I believed it myself, at least until I got to California where every day the papers were full of the kind of insanity such thinking leads to.

I had myself seen her cure swollen cows' udders over at the Jazdas' by scratching the teats with a mole's foreclaw. And I remembered how when Jaja died she had forced Poppa to walk around the yard telling everything, chickens, bushes, trees, even a chipmunk, that the old man was dead, while she came along behind making the sign of the cross over everything Poppa spoke to. I remember he seemed embarrassed. But I also remember he did it. So not much had changed in Pomerania — they were still buying the old bitch's tricks.

The first morning back and I was awakened by Puck's barking and a pounding on the front door. Going downstairs, I could see my breath in the dawn light. The linoleum was frosted around the camp blanket Poppa had kicked against the door when we finally went to bed, and the storm door would barely open up, it had become so tightly stitched with frost; beyond, beating their arms against their sides, woolen scarfs tied completely over their faces, an old man and woman asked for Batcha. I invited them in and made the fire, me putting my big coat on out of necessity while they took theirs off out of habit.

When they had unwrapped, I could see they were old Sikorski, from down by Black Donald Lake, and his wife, a woman so thin she seemed merely the skeleton for the body she had just removed and hung over an empty spike. But Sikorski seemed not to recognize me. He asked if I'd mind checking to see whether Batcha would see them and then he sat down silently and uninvited on a kitchen chair.

I made a fire while Poppa and Ig got up, and soon Poppa had

coffee and *Makowiec* cake out for them, which Sikorski gobbled up while his wife refused. She didn't look real, less like a person than something that had been drawn with a protractor, all angles, bends and lines. The only thing about her that was round was her face—she had one of those flat, expressionless looks so common in Pomerania, as if all the women were sisters and all their feelings a family secret.

Batcha came out in her black housecoat and slippers, slouched slightly and stepping stiffly, her brown leggings riding low and wrinkled around her ankles. She had her hair tied back in a tight black bun—not a single gray hair to show for more than seventy years, the gray all reserved for eyes that moved like a cop's flashlight over the couple. Sikorski fidgeted with his cake and spoon and ran his other hand over and over a great dent of a scar in his forehead while pretending to comb his hair with his fingers. His wife was crying.

Batcha smiled while the wolf eyes maintained their own scowl, and she indicated with a toss of her head that they were to follow her to her room. Sikorski looked nervously at Poppa and Poppa nodded and Sikorski got up and took his wife's bony hand and led her off behind Batcha. Watching, I saw his hand slip behind him as he entered Batcha's room. I saw the palm extend and then the ring and small finger fold back. The *mano pantea*, protection from the evil eye.

We ate our own breakfast while they stayed with Batcha, cries and prayers occasionally filtering out.

"Why have they come here?" I asked Poppa.

Poppa looked as if I should have known. "His wife has the cancer."

"Shouldn't she see a doctor?"

Poppa shrugged. Ig giggled over his hot chocolate.

"She has and nothing has helped."

"But what can Batcha do?"

"I don't know," Poppa said. "Offer hope, maybe."

"But is that fair?" I asked.

"Fair?" Poppa shrugged again. Ig was ignoring us, wolfing great spoonfuls of chocolate direct from the Nestle's Quik can into his mouth. "Nothing else has been fair to her."

I shook my head. "Why do you let her do it?"

Poppa poured himself another cup of coffee. I could see the

heavy grains floating in it. Mr. Riley always had instant coffee, but I doubted Poppa had even heard of such a miracle.

"Your Batcha is very well thought of around here, Felix," he said.

"She spooks me," I said.

Poppa laughed. Ig joined in, too loud and not even aware of what might be the joke, just wishing to be involved.

"You're fifteen years old, son. Has she hurt you yet?"

"When's your birthday, Feelie?" Ig asked. He started singing "Happy Birthday," high and tuneless.

"No, she hasn't hurt me. But she's hardly been nice to me, either."

Poppa shook his head. "Batcha loves you in her own way, you know that."

"Is today your birthday, Feelie?" Ig shouted.

Batcha's door opened and the Sikorskis emerged. The wife's eyes were red but her body seemed to have puffed out with them, as if somehow Batcha had packed her bones with new flesh while they sat praying in Batcha's room. I saw in Sikorski's hand at least a dozen poplar crosses; it was the hand of the sign, but the sign against the evil eye was no longer there.

"Today is Feelie's birthday!" Ig shouted at them.

Both Sikorskis smiled at me. I shook my head. "No, it's not."

Ig whined. "But you said it was," he said to Poppa.

Poppa ignored him. He was setting the Sikorskis' cups back out. Old Sikorski held out his free hand and indicated that he would be having none. They went straight for their coats. Poppa went and stood by them as they bundled up again in silence. Batcha, without so much as a farewell or a nod, returned to her room. Sikorski looked up when he heard her door click shut.

"You tell her we'll be back, Walter."

"I will," Poppa said.

Sikorski nodded to his wife as if she were a chainsaw Poppa and he were trying to figure out. "The doctor in Renfrew," he said, "he said three weeks."

Mrs. Sikorski looked down, avoiding Poppa's mechanic's stare. Poppa shook his head, as if it was no use, hopeless.

Sikorski went on. "They want her in the hospital. People die in hospitals."

Poppa nodded.

Mrs. Sikorski looked up to get her scarf from the spike and I could see her eyes had been watering again. She looked quickly at Poppa, nodded a silent thank you and tied her scarf tight as her husband pulled at the door. It stuck fast.

"You have to lift it and then pull," Poppa said. Sikorski did and the door popped open, a gush of cold air that made the hemlock roar in the box stove. The Sikorskis jumped out without a word and the door slammed shut.

Poppa stood for a while staring straight at the door, then turned and walked slowly back to the table. Puck, dumb enough that he probably figured Poppa was just coming in, wiggled out of his bed and across the floor, tail whipping against the chair legs, and tried to jump up on Poppa. Poppa cuffed him across the nose and Puck cowered down, peeing on the linoleum. Ig giggled and dug his spoon deep into the Quik. Poppa reached over as he passed by and grabbed up the chocolate, capped it and slammed it down on the shelf as he went through into the wood shed, closing the door behind him.

Puck whimpered in his corner. Ig whimpered at the table. The pee began flowing toward the far window, forming a long, thin, yellow trail. The old house had heaved. Jaja, who mitered even a birdfeeder and who carried a small clip-on level like a pen in his shirt pocket, would have been annoyed to see this. The home he had so carefully built had fallen out of balance.

True to their word, the Sikorskis came back in the late afternoon, two bundled wretches walking up the blue snow of the lane and carrying a burlap sack between them. Puck was squirting all over the floor even before they knocked, sniffing at the door crack and squealing, and when they came in, leaping at the sack and barking until Poppa booted the dog back to his blanket. The Sikorskis went into Batcha's room with the sack, and a bit later the old bitch herself came out to the kitchen and gathered up a large bowl, the butcher knife and some towels.

"What's going on?" I whispered to Poppa, but he only shook his head and refused to answer.

I went up to my room, wishing I was back in Vernon and able to lose myself in some *National Geographic*. I thought I could nap, but the house seemed filled with murmured prayers and Mrs. Sikorski's crying so I got up, came down, bundled up and went out to split some of the hardwood Poppa had stacked back of the shed.

After a while I forgot about what was going on in the house. And might have forgotten completely had I not gone to get one of Poppa's splitting wedges. Where we threw the ashes back of the shed someone had kicked a hole in the snow and then covered the work over again. But the frayed edges of the top of Sikorski's burlap sack were sticking free, hardened with the cold, black with frozen blood.

I began to kick at it, imagining that inside might be Mrs. Sikorski's cancer. Had Batcha gone completely insane and begun to think of herself as a surgeon? But when I moved the sack around with my foot and forced the opening with the ax tip, I saw that whatever was inside had fur. It couldn't possibly be anything to do with the sick woman. Picking up the sack by the bottom, I shook hard. The blood cracked around the opening, split, and reluctantly the sack released its contents.

It was a cat. A black cat, with white paws. And there was a great black and matted slice in the chest where the heart had been.

Batcha was obviously sicker than even I had imagined. I threw the sack over the corpse and kicked snow back on top. The ground was too hard to bury it; the stink would be too much to burn it; I left it, knowing the foxes would soon enough find it and dispose of the thing properly. But whether to laugh or feel sad? What was worse, the Sikorskis' gullibility or their desperation? Or the fact that the bitch was profiting on others' fear?

I found the wedge and returned to the woodpile, quitting only when blisters broke on each hand. But by then the bitch and her lunacy had been worth a cord and a half of rock-hard maple.

I had a feeling this might be my last Christmas holiday at home. It was not just my disgust with Batcha and her ways. No matter what I did, nothing seemed to have the old feel to it. Ig and I set snares up along the cedar lines and caught six fat rabbits, but we would have had a dozen or more if Puck hadn't peed over every wire we set. We went ice fishing on Black Donald but caught only pike, no pickerel. And Father Schula made sure Danny and I came out to a bantam practice, obviously to show us off, and even that felt funny. The ice was all cobbly and some of the boards had given away in the corners. And while we had our own skates with us, Danny had to wear his brother Terry's equipment and I got stuck with Father Schula's.

I had no reason to feel astounded that a priest would have a jock, yet I was: I was conscious of the feel of it all the time, a kind of unholy sensation like getting an erection during mass, and it made me skate bowlegged as if I was protecting my privates with the chalice.

Father Schula also arranged for Danny and I to serve the midnight mass after the Christmas eve *Oplatck*. Poppa and Ig's maiden sister Jozefa had come from Pembroke, and their brother Jan arrived with his new girlfriend Sophia, a horse-faced woman from Renfrew with perfumed Kleenex stuffed up each sleeve and down the bubbling front of her fancy dress. Good old Uncle Jan had another new car, a big green Chevrolet Impala with rear fenders like blue heron wings and a trunk full of four cases of India Pale Ale. We spent *Oplatck* gathered around the kitchen table, Batcha leading Ig in prayers, Poppa leading Jan in beers, and all of us trying to swallow this thin, dry thing Batcha made which was supposed to cleanse us of all our sins of the past year. Naturally my *National Geographic* thoughts quickly led to Lucy Dombrowski's ass and from there to Danny Shannon's hands, and so by the time Uncle Jan's big Chevy pulled in to the St. Martin's parking lot I was desperate for news of Danny's Christmas resolution.

He was already down in the basement, picking through the cassocks for one that would show off his new snake boots to best effect.

"Well?" I asked.

Danny smiled his coolest. "Got my hand on a boob last night."

"Whose?"

"Whose do you think!"

"Lucy's?"

Danny just smiled wider.

"You shoulda felt it," he said.

I could feel my heart skipping. "Inside or out?" I asked.

Danny snorted. "Shit, I was *outside* last summer."

Danny said this as if he was talking about a twelve-pounder that had been taken out of Black Donald Lake, almost as if his accomplishment should have been in the Renfrew paper, Danny standing there with a big smile and one hand on the outside of

Lucy Dombrowski's fabulous boob, and the reeve, Hatkoski, in his chain of office standing there shaking Danny's other hand in recognition.

Father Schula assigned me to candles and the Gospel side, meaning I had little to do during the actual communion mass but think about Danny getting inside on Lucy. I tried taking my mind off it —staring up first at the sad, black-faced Our Lady of Czestochowa and then off to the plaster heaven-and-hell sculpture to the right, with the worried skull separating the peaceful angel above from the poor tortured bugger burning below, even thinking of Jaja's funeral—but it was no use. A slight cough from the congregation and I'd be staring out over Pomerania, each family in their named pew, the clothes deteriorating visibly the further away from the altar they sat, the round and flat faces, the dark and poorly shaven faces, the awed look of the young, the desperation of the old. They were all there, even old Sikorski and his wife with the runny eyes. She did not look at all well. I thought of the poor cat and its missing heart and wondered who would pray for it. A few dollars for the witch, a few more for the collection plate. Covering their bets.

Ah, who could say? Perhaps they'd been right in going to Batcha. I looked back down the pews and saw Ig's hair sticking up. Jozefa had done it this time and it looked almost natural, from a good distance. Ig was blowing his nose, loudly. Poppa was praying beside him, and Jozefa and Jan, Sophia. . . .

Batcha was staring right at me!

She was kneeling but not praying. Her face was the only one turned up in the entire congregation. Father Kulas was mumbling in Latin and Father Schula and Danny were busy with the wine. Only Batcha and I were aware of anything at the moment but prayer. I could feel her wolf eyes rake. I looked away, off toward the confessional, but could not prevent myself from looking back. And she was still staring, scowling. I looked away again and shortly, a sneak peek back. Still she stared.

I coughed. I coughed again and this time my throat caught and I choked. I coughed and choked and my eyes started to water and Father Schula had to leave the wine and come over and slap me on the back and have me sit in the bishop's chair along the side, where the choir girls stared and giggled and where finally I gathered myself enough to stand back up and move back into position. But still I had to look. I glanced as quickly as I could back toward the Batterinski pew, but this time she was not staring back. Her head was down and covered with her black shawl. Praying, of course. I kept fighting the thought that she was laughing. At me.

The choir and sidesmen went to work. The Dombrowski pew spilled out its contents and suddenly I was caught up in Lucy's floating twist to the communion altar. She had on a new dress, cotton, floral pink, a sheer purple scarf around her neck, a skull-fitting red hat and big winter boots. Not dressed as well as some of the Vernon girls, but as Danny had already said, you throw out the wrapping and keep the present. She looked delicious. I saw her eyes calculate as she stepped up the three stairs to the rail, a quick glance at me — nothing in it — and then a long drink of Danny, followed by a sweetly holy curtsey to the black Madonna. When she knelt and came forward, hands cupping to receive Father Schula's bread, I could see past the buttons to the white lace of her brassiere. I could almost see Danny's palm print.

At collection time Danny and I were sent to receive the take from the four sidesmen. Both of us held a huge black-felt-lined golden tray for the men to place their wooden plates on to be returned to the altar for the blessing, while Father Kulas stared to the heavens in silent thanksgiving. When we bowed I detected Danny's left hand move ever so slightly, almost imperceptibly, but not so little that I did not see the ten-dollar bill being crumpled into his fist. When Father Kulas took the trays and we returned to our positions, Danny reached inside his cassock for a hanky and safely deposited the money, replacing the hanky, after a flamboyant but definitely dry blow, into the other pocket.

"How could you?" I asked later in the basement.

"How could I resist?" he said, laughing.

"It's stealing from the church," I said, furious with him.

"Ah, bullshit it is. How's the Pope going to miss a tenner?"

"You won't say that if you end up in hell," I said very righteously.

"I'll tell you where Danny Shannon's going. Straight to heaven." He kissed the bill. "This here'll take me to the Renfrew show with sweet little Lucy."

The bill kissed for luck, he then stuffed it into his jacket pocket and kept it rammed there as we pushed through the choir stragglers, up the stairs and through the priests' line. Danny went first, and both Father Kulas and Father Schula seemed to awaken visibly when they saw who was next in line. The procession stalled completely, leaving the sidesmen, linen women and entire choir to wait and simply gawk as Danny yakked on about hockey in Vernon and lied about school and built up his chances in the big time. You'd have thought he was the Bethlehem Star himself, not a third-stringer; yet when it came to me I was welcomed, patted, shaken and yanked quickly through and out into the cold punch of the parking lot and the careful-not-to-swear shouts of men looking for booster cables. Uncle Jan had the Chevrolet waiting, purring with heat. Poppa was razzing him for letting it idle for two hours, saying it had cost him a quarter of a tank of gas, but Ig was cheering for the radio and Sophia, Jozefa and Batcha all seemed asleep.

I got stuffed in back with the women, with no one to talk to all the way back. It was a half moon and too cold for cloud. I remember how the birch stand on this side of the creek ran over the window so it made me imagine a zebra, and almost instantly I thought of bear, the shadows making me damned glad I wasn't taking this road on my feet, alone, as I had previous Christmases.

How, I wondered, could Danny have shaken hands with the priests using the very hand that had stolen from the church? Part of me felt they should have known, that they should have at least treated me with a little more of the respect I had always been careful to return. But for whatever reason they never seemed to feel comfortable around me, or me too much around them. Unlike Danny. His right hand had moved from Lucy Dombrowski's boob to the communion chalice to a dip in the collection plate to the priests' congratulations — and he probably hadn't washed it once in all that time. Me, I believed. I prayed. I was a good Catholic even if I sometimes slept in to give me strength for a Sunday game. And I always meant to do right, to respect the church and to get to heaven, where the only flaw in the paradise I envisioned was that it couldn't possibly have room for a Danny Shannon.

But there was always this thing between me and the church. Almost as if I might have something that threatened them, hiding in the same pocket Danny had stuffed his tenner into. But what, I didn't know.

My fist? Why would that bother anyone unless I made it do so.

Batcha?

"Well?" I said when Danny and I met to catch the Pembroke bus for the run back to Vernon the following Thursday.

"Well what?"

"How did it go with Lucy?"

"Okay, I guess."

"You *guess?*" I said, bewildered. "Did you or didn't you?"

"I did," Danny said slowly, then smiling. "But she didn't."

"Oh, come on. How is *that* possible?"

Danny kicked the snow and continued to laugh. "Anything is possible in the back seat of a '59 Dodge."

I could see the bus cresting the hill at St. Mark's and panicked. "Come on. What do you mean?"

Danny turned sheepish, blushing. "She saw my bandage before I could get if off, eh?" he said very low, kicking violently at the snow. "She wouldn't believe it was just an injury. She figured I had V.D."

The driver eventually came back and said we couldn't sit together any longer unless I stopped laughing.

Six weeks back in Vernon and Danny proved good as his word on another matter. He quit school immediately on his sixteenth birthday, just as he'd promised, and his hockey began to go downhill as quickly as Main Street. At first I blamed it on his pool playing, but soon enough I realized the one thing he was truly practising was stealing.

Danny's favorite hit spot was the tiny smoke shop, Denton's, and some days it seemed he carried most of the store's stock in the inside of his hockey jacket. Denton's was run by a woman in a wheelchair and her half-blind mother. It never occurred to Danny that he was taking unfair advantage or that it might be something to be ashamed of. He'd march up to the tobacco sign guarding the glass door and knee the Macdonald's lassie right in the face, entering without even taking his hands from his pockets.

His specialty was the magazine rack, pretending to be deciding between *Hockey Pictorial* and *Mad* while really stuffing the inside of his coat with *Sir* and *Gent* and *Men Only* and *Sun Worshipper.* I was, admittedly, caught both ways, bothered by his gall and stealing but desperate to get my own fluttering paws on one of those magazines. He gave me a *Sun Worshipper* and I took it—receiving stolen goods, I know—and it was absolutely the last time I ever bothered with the pins in the damned *National Geographic*. Not that *Sun Worshipper* was the greatest magazine; it had too many old people, too many fat people, too many young kids and —worst of all —not a single person with nipples or pubic hair, thanks to some fuzzy, erased area you had to fill in with your imagination. But at least they weren't wearing bones through the nose.

I came out of school one cold Monday toward the end of the month and Sugar was waiting at the corner, the exhaust from his old yellow Studebaker practically making him invisible. He had to call out before I realized who it was.

"You want a ride home, Batterinski?" he asked.

"No sweat, Sugar. It's just up the hill."

"Get in," he growled.

I did. But first he had to get out. The passenger door wouldn't stay shut and so he'd fastened it by an inner tube running from the door handle to the steering column. I had to slide across and hoist my legs over the rubber tube and sit more like I was in a bathtub than a car. Sugar slammed his door twice and then proceeded to drive off in the opposite direction from Riley's. I said nothing. We went out the snow-covered road toward the river locks, towards where I knew Sugar lived, the shockless car waving over the road like a speedboat.

"What the hell is wrong with your buddy, Batterinski?" Sugar said, finally.

I figured Danny had been caught shoplifting and was in custody somewhere.

"Danny?"

"Yes, of course Danny. Who else? You know him best —what's wrong?"

"In what way?" I asked, unsure what Sugar was getting at.

"In all ways! Damn it! He's got as much God-given talent as Powers, you know. But Powers is first-line center and I'm one game away from benching Shannon. I swear."

"Benching him?"

Sugar nodded. Air sucked defiantly up his nose.

"He's had some trouble in school," I offered.

Sugar wasn't biting. "Shit, he already quit school."

"Well, he wasn't very happy with it."

Sugar pulled the car out of a drift, spinning the wheel like a ship captain as the Studebaker floated down along the river run.

"Is he homesick?" Sugar asked.

"I don't know."

"What's his family like?" he asked, tilting his head to focus me with the black eye.

"Great."

"His dad, does he booze?"

"Mr. Shannon? Yah, he drinks a bit."

"Heavy?"

"Well, I wouldn't like to say, but sometimes, yes."

Sugar dipped in and circled in the locks parking lot, rising back onto the road and into the blindness of his own exhaust.

"How's Shannon thought of back there?"

"He's popular," I said. "Just like here."

"He was star of the team, though, back there."

"Yah. When we played bantam he was."

"In your opinion, Batterinski," Sugar said, "did he play better back there than here?"

"Yes."

"I'm thinking of sending him back there," Sugar said.

For a while we drove in silence, but I had to know. "When?"

"At the end of the season," Sugar said. I breathed with relief. "No use humiliating him. You don't mention this, I won't. Understood?"

"Understood," I said.

Beyond the cemetery he pulled off and down the road leading toward the Rock Hill and the summer lookout. Then he turned down across the swamp road and up toward the arena, still not going anywhere near the direction of my ride home.

"How about you, Batterinski, you like it here?"

"Sure," I said.

"Homesick?"

I shook my head. "Not a bit."

Sugar smiled at this. "Good. Good. Tell me, how do you think you're doing?"

"Not as good as I'd like to."

Sugar nodded in approval. "Good. Good. How do you see yourself as a player?"

I shifted, uncomfortable with the question and miserable with the rubber tubing across my legs. They were asleep, singing with blood.

I cleared my throat and sneaked a look at Sugar. I knew he was waiting. So was I.

"I don't know." I said. "Good puck sense, I guess. Never caught out of position."

Sugar grinned. "Never?"

"Well, not since Parry Sound much, anyway."

Sugar stopped the Studebaker outside the arena and leaned his shoulder heavily into his door; it opened with a loud crack. "I'd like to show you something personal, son," he said.

I crawled out after him, my legs collapsing and now stinging. *Son?* Sugar never called anyone *anything* but their last name. He led me around to the side entrance and pulled his key from the sliding holder clipped to his belt. It hissed out and easily into the lock, turned and then snapped back with a metallic ring. The door opened on my favorite smell: the arena, empty and waiting. Only the night lights were on, making the lobby shadowy and cold and the ice beyond dark and rippling red where the distant exit lights bounced along the surface. Sugar reached without looking, tripped a switch and the lobby lights went on. I could see the dried swirls where the mop had gone over the cement floor, could smell the Dustbane. For me, coming into the arena was like crawling back in under the bed covers.

Sugar walked through the lobby up toward the turnstiles at the entrance, stopping under a long row of old pictures. He tapped the third one from the end.

"You see this here?"

I walked over. I saw the usual two rows of players, coach seated between the goaltenders, trophy complemented by crossed sticks out front, a few leeches in business suits and hockey jackets diving in from the sidelines. An old picture, by the haircuts.

"This here," Sugar said, continuing to tap the glass with a thick knuckle. "That's me. Same age as you. See."

I looked but could not see Sugar. The man he was tapping was smiling and sharp-eyed, the face thin and full of cockiness, the hair split dead center and slicked down tight to the skull. He wore the team captain's "C" and sat to the right of the goalie.

"The year after this was taken," Sugar said, "I played at St. Mike's. Straight into junior 'A', you understand. No midget, no junior 'B', nothing, straight into the second-best hockey league in the world. You understand?"

I nodded.

"Sixteen years old I made second-team all-star. That's up against Fern Flaman, Doug Harvey, Alan Stanley, a half-dozen others who went on, right?"

"Yah."

"I lost my eye in the all-star game."

Sugar turned to face me, almost as if he thought I might not have noticed before. I glanced quickly through him and then back at the picture. It was impossible. They couldn't even have been distant cousins. I read some of the names underneath. Carrington, C., Wilson, R., Cox, W., LaCroix, J., Bowles, E. (capt.).

"You think that's a sad story, I guess," Sugar said.

I was getting afraid he was going to start crying.

"Well . . ."

"Bullshit it is!" Sugar shouted. He rapped the picture again, this time the knuckle slamming into the face of a good-looking guy on the back row, left side, "This here's the real tragedy."

I had no idea what to say. I said nothing and soon sensed that Sugar was staring at me, waiting.

"You know who this is?" he asked.

"No."

"Archie Cargill, that's who."

I had no idea who he meant. It must have shown.

"You know him," Sugar said impatiently. "If this was a side view you'd recognize his nose."

I looked again. Archie Cargill . . . Archie — *Archie!* From the hotel desk. The leech. *No way. Impossible.*

"Archie Cargill was the finest prospect ever came out of this one- horse town. Could shoot both ways, just like Howe. Could make the puck dance like he had a string on it. Beautiful skater. Archie went off with me to St. Mike's and three weeks later I put him on a bus home crying his eyes out."

"Why?"

"Homesick. Scared. Gutless. Same as your pal, Danny. No heart. Archie Cargill had no heart. I'm going to tell you one thing, Batterinski, and I want you to remember it: talent is what begins hockey games, heart is what wins them."

I looked at him, not sure whether to cheer or be hurt.

Sugar smiled. "Don't worry, son. You've got talent. You've got to have that to start with or there's no use even talking about it. But Powers has probably got as much talent as you, and maybe even your buddy Shannon has too. But they won't make it. You will because you want it, you understand."

"I guess."

Sugar laughed this time, once and loud. "Maybe you won't ever have the kids dreaming about you, Batterinski, but you sure as shit'll have the general managers."

I had no idea what he meant.

Not then.

"Ugga-bugga!"

Danny could hardly contain himself. "You only got five minutes to get ready!" he shouted over the phone. I pulled it tight to my ear, worried the Rileys might hear all the way down in the television room. "Powers got the bottle, just like he said he would. Bucky Cryderman's got his old man's car. And I'm supposed to pick Maureen the Queen up later at the Mug Shop."

"You're sure," I said, uncertain.

"Ugga-bugga!" Danny shouted and hung up on me.

They came by for me at seven. Bucky's old man drove an Edsel, the only one in Vernon, a massive chrome-plated brown and white two-tone that infuriated Bucky when people joked about it. But we did it because Bucky and the car were opposites. Bucky was fat and ugly, with teeth like one of Jaja's old stone fences. The car was exquisite: huge, plush seats of real leather, electric everything, more dials than a jewelry store. They had the bottles tucked into the glove compartment, a cherry whiskey and a lemon gin, and Powers made us each hand over two bucks before he'd even show them. Once we'd paid, Bucky drove cautious as a priest's housekeeper out past the golf course to the gravel pit, where he tucked in behind a fresh- bulldozed bank and sat with the heater blasting full. Danny pulled free the cherry whiskey, giggled, skidded the cap off right through the seal by rasping it across the full palm of his hand, pushed down the window button and tossed the cap outside into the snow as if he'd spent his entire Pomeranian youth drinking expensive booze in fancy cars.

"Hey!" shouted Bucky. "What did you do that for?"

Danny laughed. "You weren't planning to save any, were you, Bucky?"

Bucky looked hurt, worried. "Just don't spill any on the upholstery, eh?"

Much to my surprise, after Danny took the first swig he handed the bottle back to me. Not Bucky, who owned the car. Not Powers, who'd bought the stuff and was team captain. But me, Felix Batterinski. I took it and smelled first. Smelled all right. I tasted: sweet, warm, thick. But the true effect wasn't until I swallowed. It hit my stomach like flaming gasoline. I gagged, choked—choked just like at Christmas Mass, when Batcha was staring at me—and started coughing madly while the others, especially Danny, laughed like it was the greatest show they'd ever seen.

The next time the bottle came around I drank slower and neither choked nor coughed. And the next and the next. I began to feel warm, content, a bit proud when Bucky went on about how I'd sucker-punched the big goon from Collingwood on Saturday. It was nice to hear my name mentioned by friends. And me, I was talking more, not just more but better; I even told a joke about why a woman is like a stove—"With both of them ya got a lifter, the leg and poker"—and all of them laughed and Danny never even squealed that I'd picked it up from his old man. It felt good. The car was warm and glowing magically with the dash lights. The bottle came around again and I drained it. I pushed the window button, listened as it hummed down and then hurtled the bottle by the neck straight into the bulldozer blade, where it shattered magnificently in the stillness. It was my sound. My night.

"Ugga-bugga!" Danny shouted.

"Let's crack the other one," I said.

"Just hold your horses," Powers said. "That's the one for Maureen, eh?"

"Oh yah," I said. Had I really forgotten?

"Ooooooooooeeeeeeee!" screamed Danny. "Let's get at her. I'm hornier than a three-peckered owl."

Bucky started the Edsel, snapping on the radio at the same time and twisting the volume up — "*Pleeeeeez, Mistah Custah . . . Ah don't wanna die*"—as he spun wildly out of the gravel pit, bouncing off the far banks and fishtailing down the golf-course road like a tangled spinner.

"You better all have safes," Danny warned. "Maureen's not exactly the Virgin Mary."

Father Kulas's face rose out in the headlights, then vanished. Blindness. Spines dissolving. Rotting forever in hell.

"I haven't," I said.

"Huh?" Danny said, his mind racing on to Maureen.

"I haven't got a safe."

"Aw shit, Bats. Yous guys got an extra?"

"Not me."

"Nope."

Danny slammed the dashboard, causing Bucky to look over in a panic. "Well," Danny said. "We'll just have to get you one."

"Where?" I said. At the hospital? Emergency?

"Bucky," Danny said, taking control. "Drop us first at the Shanghai, eh?"

"Sure."

Powers whooped and slapped his knee and I looked over at him. He was looking down into his lap as if he'd just broken his neck. It seemed to be dangling side to side, in time with the music but not natural. I'd expected him to hold his booze better, but since I doubt he'd had any more practice than I had myself, I couldn't waste time worrying about him. I had other problems. How did you get a safe at a Chinese restaurant? I knew there was no machine in the washroom. Could you order it? "A Number Three to go, please?"

Bucky moved the Edsel up through town. The street lights, dancing hypnotically as they slid across the hood, were cut off by the roof and flashed again in the rear window. I realized I wasn't quite right. Woozy, kind of. Further up Main Street the show was just getting out and I stiffened at the thought of running into the Rileys coming home from *North to Alaska*. Danny, however, was going to give me no chance to worry.

"Here," he ordered, leaning back over the seat. "Give me your finger."

"Huh?"

"Your pointer, arsehole. Straight out like this." Danny held his out like a gun. I followed suit.

"Now keep it still."

Danny had a dollar bill in his other hand, all crushed and beaten with the air of a collection plate grab, and he first smoothed it out before wrapping the bill carefully around my finger until it fit tight as a Chinese finger trap.

"There," Danny said, satisfied. "Now put it in your pocket."

What was this, one of Batcha's tricks? Got a toothache? Simple, just suck all day on a nail and then hammer it into a maple on the night of the full moon and the ache will disappear. Need a safe? Nothing to it — just wrap a dollar bill around your finger, stick it in your pocket and your pecker'll suddenly turn to rubber.

"What the fuck am I supposed to do with this?" I asked, afraid Danny might be making a fool of me. Powers and Bucky were already giggling.

"Just you go in there and show it to Kim on the cash," Danny said.

"Kim?"

"He's the Chink with the glasses."

Danny turned toward the restaurant, leaned forward and rubbed the steam off the window. "There. He's on now. Get going."

"Just show it to him?"

"Just show it to him."

"Hurry up," Bucky shouted. "Maureen won't keep."

I got out of the car and realized when I put my feet down that I had lost half of my weight. I had to concentrate completely on my walk, but I couldn't remember precisely how it was I *did* walk. I stepped too carefully, like I was walking down the tracks back home; then I tried imitating Danny. It didn't feel quite right, but it worked.

I pushed quickly through the Shanghai door into the blasting heat from the overhead fan, then through the inner doors, and suddenly found myself face-to-face with an older man who looked up from his newspaper and smiled. His teeth were as yellow as a Pomeranian bantam crest.

"Yes sir," he said. "Can I help you with anything?"

He caught me off guard. I stared at him, not sure what to say. I had my wrapped dollar finger, still stiff, rammed into my jacket pocket and I made as if to remove it.

Kim jumped up and back a bit, his jaw trembling. He thought I had a *gun*! I had the finger halfway out and suddenly realized this might be one of Danny's sick jokes.

"Don't worry," I said, as if to say it wasn't loaded. Unlike me.

I couldn't stop the finger and it was out, lying pointing at him along the rubber-tipped change mat. Kim saw it and relaxed. He smiled at me, winked, quickly checked for observers and then peeled the bill in one motion from my finger. He leaned down and picked up a cigar box from well under the till, set it down,

opened it, patted in the dollar and closed it. I was absolutely convinced the dollar had come from the collection plate. Perhaps
Mrs. Riley's, destined, she thought, for the "poor orphans" she
was always fretting about when her daughters turned their noses
up at turnip. How could a well-intentioned dollar become so
misguided? Nothing to it when Danny Shannon's the middle
man.

From another cigar box, this one beneath the cigarette display
case, Kim took a small package that I first thought were penny
matches. But it was an Indian picture, in full headdress, and when
he handed it over I realized this was the key to Maureen the Queen.
I rammed the safe into my pocket and fled.

"*Ugga–bugga!*"

That was me, stealing Danny's cry.

Danny came back with a loon call. Bucky gunned the Edsel and
we were off, up past the theater and the holy rollers, down along
past the bay and the train station and the lumber yard, out Main
Street until it trickled into darkness and the occasional light of a
gas station. Maureen was waiting, as she promised, at the south-
end truckers' stop.

We watched from the parking lot as Danny picked her up. They
stopped on the way out while Danny paid her bill and also bought
three packs of Sweet Caps and a handful of what might have been
Double Bubble gum, it was difficult to see through the frosted
glass. This, I presumed, was her price.

It was always my belief that Maureen played for the juveniles,
not the midgets. She looked older than Danny, coming out on his
arm, but it was difficult to say just how old she was through her
make-up. She wore her usual clothes: the shiny black slacks tight
from the moment they rose from her white rubber boots till they
rounded an ample butt tucked in under a pink ski jacket with
false rabbit's fur around the hood and wrists. Her jacket puffed
out in front with the hint of a marvelous bust, but there was
nothing at all subtle about Maureen's face: she'd done it and it
showed. It was a small, possibly quite pretty face cupped by
spongy, teased brown hair, the eyes made up as if she'd been
punched, the mouth as if she had bled.

Danny opened the door and Maureen bounced in with a flood
of lilac, checking around past me instantly to Tom, who'd steadied his head somehow and slapped a lecherous grin onto it.

"Hi, there, Maureen," he said. His voice seemed to be coming from back in his throat.

"How's Tommy," she said, her high voice rolling back like satin sheets. I had trouble catching my breath.

"Nice car," Maureen said to the driver. Bucky beamed and goosed the engine so the Edsel bucked like a horse. When it settled he moved the shift into drive and pulled away slowly, with extreme caution.

So Bucky, too, was worth recognition. But not me. He had his old man's fancy car. I had a face full of pimples, mercifully hidden in the dark, and a Chinese safe which for all I knew was just a book of matches. I hated her for ignoring me and part of me wanted to punch right through the seat into the back of her spine; another part, however, would like to have snaked right through Bucky's treasured leather, right through the pink ski jacket, the blouse, the brassiere, right until I had her cupped in my hands and screaming for more.

Christ, I wished we were sitting here in our uniforms. Surely she'd notice my "A". Big Number "7". Shit, if Willoughby was introducing the starting line-up here in the car Bucky and Danny wouldn't even have been mentioned, but now here they were, Danny with his arm around Maureen and Bucky driving with his leg pressed right up against those incredible slacks. She snuggled in tight to Danny and when he squeezed, Maureen went off like a puffball, filling the car around her with perfume and making me choke slightly as I accidentally got ahead of my breath.

Maureen stretched, purred. "What've you boys got to drink?"

"Gin," we all said at once.

"Fab — where'll we go?"

"We already went through one at the gravel pit," Bucky said. "May as well try her again?"

"Uh uh," Maureen said, her voice full of experience. "Cops check there this time of night."

"My parents are home," Bucky said, needlessly.

"I haven't got a home," Danny said. Maureen laughed and snuggled in tighter to him.

"Not my place," Powers said, reviving his head lolls just long enough to beg out.

"How about you?" Maureen asked, turning her face so she could see me.

I cleared my throat like I was about to give an oratorical. "No," I said.

"Just lovely," she said with disgust. "We may as well go right back then. I'm not going to no fucking gravel pit."

Fucking? A girl had said *fucking?* I couldn't believe it. I could feel myself rising, my heart skipping.

"No wait," Danny said, chewing his lip as he thought. He turned and faced me, smiling, the Irish charm already at work. For what, I hadn't a clue. Not Riley's, surely!

"Bats?"

"What?" I said quickly, the tone unwelcome.

"You've got that key to the arena still, eh?"

"Hey, yah!" shouted Bucky, and he leaned on the horn for emphasis.

"Oh, no," I said.

"Why not?" Danny said, smiling over the top of the seat. "It's going on midnight. Won't be a soul around. C'mon, eh?"

I shook my head. "No."

"Bats," Powers said, rallying, pleading. "How can we hurt anything?"

"We'll get caught."

"Bullshit," Danny said. "Who's to catch us?"

"Come on, Bats. It's perfect."

"Sugar gave me the key on condition I use it just for getting in early," I said.

"But he'll never have to *know*," Danny groaned.

Maureen turned, fluttered her punched-out eyes and smiled. "Felix," she pleaded. *How'd she know my name?* She reached over and poked my Adam's apple gently, running her nail up along my jaw and off my chin. I nearly went berserk. "For me, okay, Felix?"

For me! I could feel my heart stampeding. I had to straighten my left leg my crotch hurt so badly.

"Well," I said, reconsidering. "Sure, why not?"

Danny went into his loon call. Bucky hit the accelerator and the horn at the same time. Powers leaned over and slapped at my shoulder but missed, the hand slamming into my pecker like a hammer. I recoiled forward, holding in. Powers never even noticed; he went back to his head-lolling, giggling.

My hands shook so badly at the side door that Danny had to take the keys away from me and do it himself. The door gave immediately and we were inside, safe. No one would notice the car. Bucky had insisted on leaving it up by the high school rather than anywhere even remotely close to the empty arena lot. And as long as we didn't spring the big lights it was impossible for anyone to know we were inside. But we could still blow it. Danny had the lemon gin in his hand and was dancing with it, whipping himself around the lobby pillars and booting the garbage pails as he passed. Bucky was jumping up and punching at the ceiling, but missing. Even Powers had come alive, bopping along snapping his fingers and humming some incomprehensible song. Maureen followed him, pretending it was stripper music, wiggling out of her ski jacket as she laughed and danced along.

Danny went straight for the "home" dressing room. I would have preferred "visitors" in case we busted something, but Danny was going to have nothing but the best. He even insisted on sitting in his own spot, setting the bottle ceremoniously on the equipment box and dramatically opening it and tossing the cap the length of the room basketball-fashion, dropping it perfectly into the far trash bin. Bucky rounded up some Dixie cups somewhere and set five of them out on the box. Danny poured.

"To the team," Danny announced, picking up the last glass when it was filled. We all grabbed and drank. The lemon gin wasn't nearly as sweet and nice as the cherry whiskey, but it didn't bother Maureen; she drained her glass and plunked it back down for seconds, which Danny was eager to oblige. I sipped at mine, convinced it somehow tasted like pine needles, even though I was sure I'd never tasted a pine needle. Thinking of pine needles made me think of the wood shed, Poppa's wood shed, and suddenly I felt like I might be sick. Whatever it was swept over me it left me slightly shaken, like I was being watched or about to be found out. I looked out the door, thinking Sugar might be there writing notes to himself on his clipboard: Powers . . . Cryderman . . . Shannon . . . Batterinski . . . all cut. Ha! — cut. Cut both ways, eh? Cut from the team and . . .   I shook it off. Maureen finished her second and Danny poured a third. She tossed that back and poured a fourth. Score: Maureen 4– Vernon 1.

"To Toilet Bowles!" Danny announced, picking up his second drink and screeching like a loon. "The one-eyed prick."

"Piss off, Danny," I said.

Maureen's eyes snapped at me. They were green behind the black. A nice green. She was measuring, expecting a fight. Not frightened but eager, anxious. But she didn't know Danny Shannon and Batterinski.

"Just kidding, Bats."

"Keep it that way."

Danny turned to Maureen. "Come on, Maureen. Let's dance."

There was no music, nothing, but Danny swung Maureen up onto her feet, both of them giggling and hanging onto their cups, and they waltzed perfectly around the equipment box. Danny started humming "Mr. Lonely" and picked up the pace. I could see Maureen pressing it as tight as she could to Danny's pants, rubbing up and down as he pushed back and forth. My heart very nearly stopped. Danny started kissing her and I saw her tongue go straight into Danny's mouth and then they weren't dancing at all, just standing in front of the chalkboard grinding away and French kissing. I looked down into my cup and swirled it. I didn't know what to do: watch? leave the room? go up behind her and rub from the other side? I looked at Bucky and he was blushing but giggling. Powers was leering, his head rock-steady now.

I looked again at the chalkboard, trying to settle myself. The plays from last game were still visible through a half-hearted wipe and I could see that I was the circled "X" in the upper corner. Danny Shannon wasn't even on the board.

Danny started pawing her, pushing against her breasts through her sweater. Maureen giggled, the air passing from her mouth into his, making his pop open like a weak bubble; she pushed his hand away but the other one went immediately to the other breast. She backed off and shot him a look of fire, but not anger. She leaned and whispered something in Danny's ear and Danny nodded. Hand in hand they left the room, turning toward the ice. We sat, not knowing what to do, and then heard the pass key turning in the referee's room. Maureen shrieked with delight and the door slammed shut.

The three of us were left with the bottle but no one made a move to refill their glass. "That goddamned Danny," Powers said, shaking his head in amazement. "I'd give my right arm to be in his pants right now."

"Go ahead—they'll be on the floor by now," Bucky said, laughing.

"You know what I mean," Powers said. "Goddamn it—the lucky bastard."

Bucky got up and poured fresheners. Powers refused his. His

neck had gone back to being boneless. I tried to drink more but it didn't want to go down. The room was as if it had gone underwater, with currents moving through it. I didn't feel good but I knew I, too, desperately wanted to trade places with Danny. I knew if it was going to happen, it was going to happen right here, in my element. If I couldn't get laid at the arena I might never get laid anywhere.

The referee's door rattled again, but this time closed quietly, and then came the sound of Danny's bare feet slapping along the rubber mat. He came into the dressing room with his shirt off and his pants only belted up, the fly wide open. His chest looked like he'd just played a game, all red and welted with slashes and butt ends.

"Powers," Danny said, tossing my key back. "Maureen wants to see you right away."

Powers' neck suddenly went hard. He took a quick drink of the cup he'd been avoiding, cleared his throat and stood up. Danny let loose with a loon's call followed by a hyena laugh. He punched Powers on the shoulder and pushed him out the door, where Powers slipped slightly and then stumbled down the hall toward the ref's room.

Danny sat down and poured a tall drink. He picked it up, eyeing it as if the cup were somehow glass. He closed his eyes. "*Fan*-tastic!"

"She good?" Bucky asked. He seemed nervous as if, stalled on the tracks, he had looked out and seen the train coming.

"Great," Danny said. "And she's just getting warmed up, lads."

Danny winked at both of us. I swallowed and looked at Bucky, who seemed extremely nervous now. He was rubbing his hands and his right foot was jumping like a jackhammer.

"Was this your first?" Bucky asked. Danny looked at him as if he'd just asked if this was Maple Leaf Gardens. We sat in silence awhile, Danny sighing and Bucky's heel typing like mad on the cement. Then came the sound we were waiting for: the ref's door opening and closing, this time very quietly. Bucky coughed and rubbed his hands. I closed my eyes, wanting to pray but worried that God might not appreciate being called on in a situation like this.

"Okay, Bucky," Powers said when he came back in. "Your turn."

Bucky seemed relieved. He bolted out the door on a breakaway.

Powers hit at his bum as he scooted, but missed, and Powers let his arm sweep back in a lazy loop that ended in a handshake with Danny. He fell down into the seat beside Danny and shook his head. "Wow!"

"I know," said Danny.

I didn't.

The fear was rising and I took another drink, not wanting the gin but not knowing what else to do. It seemed like I had no right talking with Danny and Powers, both sighing on the far bench. A barrier had come down between us: men and virgin. I knew they were looking down at me. One was first, the other second, I'd be fourth.

I wished I had my uniform on. I fingered the package in my pocket carefully to make sure what was inside was rubber, not wood and sulfur; and just as I determined it was the real thing, the sound of a door opening came in from the corridor. Christ, Bucky had only been gone two or three minutes! I could feel the sweat breaking out on my forehead and running down my back. I hoped my shirt wouldn't stick to me when I took it off. I prayed —yes, this time prayed, God would have to know—that I wouldn't smell like a skunk.

Bucky's big feet came shuffling along slower than the other two. And he didn't come in. I couldn't see out the door but I could tell from Danny's quizzical expression that he was being signaled. He got up and went out. I took another drink, a stiff one, and felt again for the safe. I leaned over and folded my arms, sitting as I would during an ice flood. I tried to think hockey.

Danny came back in with Bucky trailing behind. Danny had on his best Irish, his eyes coming down on me like Doc Rafferty's the time I had the mumps.

"Bats," he said with great gentleness. "Maureen says she's through, okay? No more."

"Yah," added Bucky, hitching up his pants. "She's exhausted, eh?"

I knew he was lying.

"Tough luck," Danny said, putting his hand on my shoulder. "We should've let you go earlier, I guess."

I batted his hand away with all my might. "Fuck off!" I shouted at him. I took out the key, shook it and threw it at him so it bounced off his chest and he caught it.

"Lock the fucking place up," I said. "I'm going home."

I waited outside the arena, on the crest of the parking lot leading down toward the river, and I bawled. Right out loud I bawled. That bitch! I wanted to kill her. I waited and I waited. But they never came out. Tired, my ass. She hadn't fallen asleep. They were all back for seconds.

Pimples! I slugged myself in my face. Once, twice, three times.

Talk! Why couldn't I talk like Danny or even like dumb-ass Bucky? I spit and spit and spit and spit. The tears rolled down, stinging until they froze on the edge of my chin.

When the fury rose I didn't even bother to try and contain it. Let it come. I ran out across the ball diamond, jumping through the snow, leaped and pulled the scoreboard clean off the posts, snapping it in half so it cracked like a .303. The sound was so incredibly loud in the cold that it scared me off and I ran out across the field, plowing through the higher drifts, up beyond the high school. I thought about phoning the police as I ran. Telling on them. That'd fix them. But it was my key they had. Besides, it was her, really. She'd done it to me. Not Danny, not Powers, not Bucky. But I hated them for knowing. The *bastards!*

Out beyond the high school on the river road a single car was parked, probably frozen up. A 1958 Dodge, black, I thought in the bad light, with an aerial. No houses around, nothing. Not even a street light. I grabbed the aerial as I walked past and twisted and it gave almost instantly. I took the broken end and ran it along the side of the car, digging it as deep as I could into the paint. Then again. I whipped the aerial off into the trees, watching as it spun, listening for it to land, but it hit the powder without a sound.

I should have walked away. I should have gone home and cried or beat my pillow or whatever, but I didn't. I went around behind the car and stepped up onto the trunk, then walked up the rear windshield onto the roof. I could feel it giving slightly, bouncy like the swamp back home. I jumped twice and a side window popped, spilling like gravel down the side of the car. I jumped again and another window gave. I jumped again and another window gave. I jumped harder, slamming my heels down onto the roof as I landed each time and each time the roof gave a little. It was like driving fence stakes. Then the rear window gave, turning first like honeycomb and then falling slowly into the back window ledge over a box of Kleenex.

When the windshield gave it burst, exploding out and in and ringing, skidding, scraping out along the hood and silently out into the snow. I jumped and jumped and jumped and the roof fell until it rested perfectly along the backrest of the front seat.

I stepped down, quiet and calm, and walked away slowly, turning up the first side street that would bring me back into town and Riley's and my bed.

Maureen the Queen stayed behind, in the car.

" 'We're going to have to do something about all this violence,' the late Conn Smythe once said, 'or people are going to keep on buying tickets.'

Nothing proved Smythe's point better than hockey's early expansion years, when a baby boom of diluted talent combined with easy investment money to produce, in six short years, *thirty* major professional hockey teams in North America, where in 1967 there had been only six.

The vast majority of expansion took place in the United States (in the 1974–75 season fifteen of the NHL's eighteen teams were American-based) where the customers were too often hockey unsophisticates. ('How do they pump the air into that li'l black thang?' a Houston fan asked Gordie Howe.) Hockey had to be sold, and any ticket outlet knew wrestling outdrew the symphony: the stage was set for a Schultz, a Kelly and, of course, a Batterinski.

In 1972–73, the Philadelphia Flyers set a new all-time penalty record with 1,756 minutes, a full thirty games' worth of playing at a man disadvantage, nearly ten hours more than the next most surly team, the Boston Bruins. The following year, in 1974, the Philadelphia Flyers won the Stanley Cup. Evil was triumphant.

The years in Philadelphia were Batterinski's glory; the years in Los Angeles his demise. 'Hockey wasn't the first priority out there,' remembers Batterinski's then close friend, Torchy Bender. 'Not the second, either, nor third, fourth or fifth. He wasn't used to meeting people who didn't already know him through his statistics.'

In Finland, however, they knew him well by reputation. His hiring was controversial, a subject of debate in both the sports and editorial pages. 'No true Finnish hockey fan,' wrote Arto Pakola, the country's most respected columnist, 'can condone violence, but neither can he deny convincingly that Finnish hockey might gain much by a little infusion of aggression. Batterinski does not deserve to be written off as a plague, at least not yet. Who knows but one day we may honor him as the turning point in the ill fortunes of Finnish hockey.' "

Excerpted by permission from "Batterinski's Burden," by Matt Keening, *Canada Magazine*, June 1982.

THEY ARE PAYING ME TO COACH AS WELL AS PLAY, BUT it is not like hiring an electrician or a plumber. I have no training. There are no instructional manuals. The parts don't come with numbers on them. They simply name you coach and if the team wins they slap your back and if the team loses they stab it.

It's always said that journeymen make the best coaches. These are the guys who have spent so much time warming the bench they have no choice but to try and sound knowledgeable about the game. It's kind of like being one of those phoney artists whose paintings so obviously stink that their true art becomes their tongue. The tongue gets them press and the press gets them sales and eventually the sales turn around and give them respect. A hockey coach, then, is simply a player who handles his mouth better than a stick.

My problem is maybe I was too good an NHLer to make a great coach. I know I've still got to work on my tongue. I don't seem to be able to talk them into a victory, so I've been searching for an appropriate charm to help us. Don't get me wrong, I'm no Phil Esposito. I don't have to do everything according to ritual—which leg you stick first through your long underwear, things like that—but I'm not beyond wearing the same clothes when we're on a winning streak.

Lately, I've taken to walking to the Ishallen hockey stadium by different paths each game, hoping one of them will work.

I'm still hanging in at the Inter-Continental, room 622. No one got too upset when I said I wanted to stay right here in Helsinki. Sudbury with a harbor, I called it at first, but at least it's a city and there's a bit of action. The team executive seemed to expect I'd be reluctant to move out to Tapiola. Besides, it's only about ten miles away and all we have is the odd practice out there, and that's about it. Our major practice every second week is a day-long affair up at the sports complex at Vierumaki, maybe 80 miles or so straight north. And until Tapiola gets a proper arena we'll continue playing out of Helsinki, so there's every reason for me to stay right here.

They insisted I at least go on a tour of Tapiola and sign some autographs at the big shopping center. No problem. I agreed. But I had a hell of a time keeping from throwing up. A miracle city, they kept bragging, everything planned perfectly by one man, houses like you'd see surrounding a model train track in a Christmas window, bicycle paths through the pines. At the town center I took a good look at the people, and they weren't at all like Helsinki Finns. I've seen that type before, in places like Ottawa and Washington, cities where skinny, bird-muscled men in suckhole beards jog but won't compete, and where their wives speak calmly to screaming brats in supermarkets. No thanks, not for me.

The Inter-Continental suits me quite well. There's a pool, sauna, and Broom Hilda waiting at her rubber-sheeted table for you to drop your shorts and climb on so she can sand you down with hot, soapy water and a sponge like a Brillo pad. There's a disco and bar on the top floor, another bar down below; I can run around the lagoon or walk to the Jaahalli Ishallen, where we play. Tram 3B takes me downtown, 3T brings me back. The use of a rented Saab 99 whenever I want.

The Inter-Continental is also on the same street as the Viisi Pennia, which Pekka — he's our best forward and already my best friend here — says means "The Five Pennies" and refers to some jazz trumpeter I never heard of named Red Nichols or something. Everyone goes there after practices and games. I like it because I haven't had to introduce myself once.

Batterinski's table is always center table at the Viisi Pennia. They can't get enough of what I can tell them or make up. They want to know all about cocaine and Mr. Snow with the New York Rangers; they want to know who are the perverts (better they ask who aren't) and who besides Murdoch has gotten fouled up by drugs. I tell them what former L.A. player had the league's smallest penis and what former import from Sweden was found out to be a faggot. It's the type of information you can't find in the NHL Guide or The Hockey News but, I swear, these are the records the true hockey nuts discuss most. They all know the same published material. Statistics are just a courteous step toward the true obsession of hockey fans: individual dirt.

I'm better with dirt than praise anyway. But too often they want to talk about The Kid, Gretzky. His picture seems to be in the Urheilu section of the paper twice as often as my own, for Christ's sake, and he's not even in the Finn league.

He looks like he's got a perm now, kisscurls. Just like all the other asshole Goody Two Shoes. Him. Gary Carter. All of them. But only I see through this crap. Every night it's the same question: "Do you know him?"

I don't, no. He came up when I was falling down. We might have met several times around the blueline if I hadn't lost a step or two, as they say. But every night it's also the same answer: "Wayne? Shit, you kidding?"

"He's very good looking," every sweet young thing at the table will say.

And always someone will ask: "Is he as good as they say?"

"He's lucky," I usually say, leaving it at that.

It's funny the way things go in cycles. Right now hockey is all Gretzky and those damn Czechs, the Stastny brothers in Quebec, and the Swedes, and guys like Perrault and Dionne again. Five years ago it was all me and Hound Dog and Battleship and Bird and Schultzy and the Bullies. Cycles, round and round and round, like a whirlpool sucking deadheads like me and Hound Dog down.

Gretzky. What is he, twenty? If we met and he was twenty and I was twenty those kisscurls would end up in casts, I tell you.

Still, talk like that serves its purpose. It draws the talent. It's a simple system: throw a few big names in the air like you expect them to walk in through the door any minute, and before you know it you're walking out the same door with the trophies that fell for the lure.

Fleeting victories, perhaps, but at least I was winning at something — unlike this team. Sometimes I wish a few of these guys had pimples like I once had, anything that might give them some spunk, even if only to bust up a few opposition faces that had never been struck with anything, least of all fists. As they say back home, we *own* the basement. And we deserve it.

That's not to say we are exactly nobodies. We are Tapiola Hauki, *hauki* meaning "pike" in English — the ugliest, meanest, most taste-less fish we know back in Pomerania. It refers to the giant Finnish firm that takes little pieces of balsam wood, whittles them down so that they vaguely resemble creek chub, paints them fluores-cent orange and green and blue and silver, glues on a couple of treble hooks and a plastic lip to make them dive and then sells them at five bucks a shot to North Americans who snag them on deadheads before the first week is out and buy another. Hauki obviously makes so much money that management can't figure out how to spend it, which is the only rational reason for Tapiola becoming the eleventh entry in SM-Liiga, Finland's poor-man's version of the NHL. As of last night, the standings were as follows:

	GP	W	L	T	GF	GA	PTS
Karpat Oulu	8	8	0	0	41	17	16
IFK Helsinki	7	7	0	0	31	13	14
Tappara Tampere	8	7	1	0	35	23	14
TPS Turku	8	6	1	1	34	22	13
SaiPa Lappeenranta	7	4	1	2	28	26	10
Assat Pori	6	4	1	1	27	22	9
Jokerit Helsinki	8	3	3	2	43	31	8
Ilves Tampere	8	3	4	1	29	36	7
Kiekkoreipas Lahti	7	2	5	0	21	39	4
Lukko Rauma	8	2	6	0	19	41	4
Tapiola Hauki	7	0	7	0	13	52	0

I make no excuses for our showing. The goddamned press set me up as some kind of savior when I arrived in September, but I'm too old to fall for that crap again. Sportswriting serves the same purpose in any language — the spreading of lies.

You learn two things immediately when you make the NHL: one, you keep your head up; two, you don't trust the press. You take your average sports reporter in North America and you've got a fat slob who can't keep his shirt tucked in or his pimples popped. If he hasn't got a speech impediment he bites his nails. If he's not an old washed-up drunk he's an up-tight kid who'd look more

comfortable carrying a purse than a Sherwood P.M.P. Never listens
— if he's not talking he's eating, for free, of course — and even
those who pretend to listen screw it all up in the end anyway, out
of sheer stupidity. I cut out the *Sports Illustrated* quote from Norm
Van Brocklin when he was recovering from a big operation last
year. "It was a brain transplant," the old quarterback said. "I got
a sportswriter's brain so I could be sure I had one that hadn't
been used."

I'd hoped they'd be different over here. But no, everybody has
to keep pointing out how Carl Brewer came over here and suddenly IFK Helsinki were league champions, but they neglect to
point out that IFK Helsinki was an established team before Brewer
ever arrived in town. Apart from me, Tapiola is a joke. Well,
Pekka's not bad: he was first draft choice from the slush pile the
other teams made available last spring. He has that long, extended
look of the better European skaters, and he's a beautiful stick-
handler, almost in the class of Marcel Dionne. But back in L.A.
when a puck spilled out from a crush of players in the boards,
Dionne was there waiting to rifle it into an upper corner of the
net; here, when a puck spills out, Pekka is usually just another
Finn scrambling in the other direction to avoid having to carry it
through the heavy going.

They can talk all they want about the differences between the
two styles of hockey and I say it's all bullshit. It's not rink size,
not skating, shooting, passing or even all the malarkey about them
playing in five-man units. The difference is that Canadians have
a need to possess the puck — control meaning power for them;
and I don't give a damn how many times Gretzky says the first
thing he thought about when he scored his fiftieth goal was that
it helped the *team*, the simple absolutely honest truth about Canadian hockey players is that the individual comes first, the team
second. Europeans play like they'd rather have someone else do
it; all they want to ensure is they don't get blamed for the screw-
ups. There's something all too precious about European hockey.
Pretty to look at but hollow within, like an Easter egg.

That's why they need a bit of Batterinski. *Hardboiled.*

Tapiola's boss is Erkki Sundstrom. I call him "Jerkki." He's got
one of those round Finn faces with thin hair plastered close to
the scalp, a perfectly round face and perfectly round wire-rimmed
glasses, so it looks like somebody drew him up with a compass

during a study break. He's gone on record saying I'll turn this team around in the second half of the season, and I somehow kept shut about it. *This* team? We've got a left winger named Jorma Aura who insisted on wearing a silk scarf when he played, like he was Douglas Bader in *Reach for the Sky*. First intermission of the first game, I ripped the scarf off his neck in front of the whole team, blew my nose in it and threw the damn thing into the garbage can at the entrance to the dressing room, and that was the end of that, not that it improved his play much.

Tapiola *should* be a great team. The first time we had a sauna together up at Vierumaki I couldn't believe my eyes. There can't be five pounds of flab among the twenty players out. All thick-necked and big-armed with wide shoulders. Naked, they looked like they could eat hockey pucks. I had to think of all the dressing rooms I'd been in and could only shake my head. Phil Esposito's big tire of flub, Butch Goring's grade-six build, Guy Lafleur coughing for a weed and looking like he's sixty years old, Bobby Clarke looking like you'd have to search for the card tied to his toe to figure out who he was.

But they, at least, are hockey players. These guys here are engineers and students and mechanics and civil servants first, hockey players second. Hockey is more like a hobby to them. Only three of them — Pekka, big Timo, my defense partner, and, for some unknown reason, our weak-ankled goalie with the glasses — make more than fifty thousand Finmarks and that's only about eighteen thousand dollars. I'm getting twice that and feel I'm being gypped. Some of them are getting only six or seven grand for the year.

But that's not the only thing that separates us. They all have their teeth. All of them, all of their teeth. And that says all anyone ever needs to know about European hockey, as far as this boy's concerned.

Pekka's on the phone. He wants to know what I'm up to with this free weekend, last one till January.

"I was thinking maybe I'd drive over to Turku."

"*Turku?*" Pekka roars. "Finns go to Turku to die, man."

I cannot tell him there's an eight-hundred-year-old castle there that the tourist guide says was once ruled by a Polish princess, Katarina Jagelonica. I thought maybe a postcard of that and a

few souvenirs and Poppa would lay off about me going to Poland.
What am I supposed to do? Race over so I, too, can riot over horse
flesh? What does he expect of me? Join Walesa? Does Solidarity
even have a team?

"I don't know. Maybe I won't."

"Pia and I, we are off to Stockholm," he says in his precise,
singing manner, the voice too high, the words always coming out
like he is reading, not thinking. The way they all sound, at least
the few who speak English. In Finnish they sound like Poppa's
diesel-fired washing machine.

"Great."

"Come with us."

"Nah, you two go off and enjoy yourselves."

"There is to be three of us."

"Who else?"

"Come and see for yourself, man."

No doubt, they are truly different over here. A blind date for
the weekend? I couldn't believe it. But Pekka told me to be at
the Siljaline boarding platform on the south harbor at five and
to look for the *Newbuildings* — a ship, not a construction pro-
ject. When I found it they were already there, Pekka in that
powder-blue three-piece suit that makes him look more like an
insurance salesman than a hockey player, Pia in a thin green coat
that with her red hair makes her look like an iris in full bloom,
and Kristiina. . . .

. . . Kristiina . . .

I see her as I am coming up the gangplank. She stands just to
the side of Pekka and Pia, the two of them waving frantically and
Kristiina just smiling patiently, perhaps not even smiling at all
but braced against the harbor wind. Her hair blows, soft maple-
colored bangs lifting as if they were electrically charged, light
blue eyes, high cheekbones, a full mouth. The kind of talent about
which Torchy would have said you'd expect to find staple marks
in her belly. I race up the rest of the gangplank glad my leather
jacket is open, proud of the loud jangle of metal around my neck,
pleased that the winter sun is glinting, with luck, on the hair that
spills over the highest button in my Lou Myles pink silk shirt. I
run and smile like an Old Spice commercial.

"Hey, man," Pekka shouts. "We thought you were not coming."

"Traffic," I explain.

"The weekend," he explains back.

Pia kisses me on the cheek, filling my nose with that bewitchingly lewd smell she wears as if it's perfectly natural for people to walk around snorting in each other's neck.

"Bats," Pekka says. "This is Kristiina. Kristiina, I would like for you to meet Felix Batterinski."

"Hi," I say.

"Hello."

I reach for her hand and feel foolish, as if we are business acquaintances or something. She takes it, her hand long and slender and without nailpolish, no jewelry, and when I shake and let go the hand drops back quickly, unsure.

"I'm pleased to meet you," I say stupidly.

"And I am most pleased to meet you," she says, smiling as if I am a child she is dealing with. "Much has been said about you."

I feel the old burn moving toward my ears.

A long time ago I decided that hockey was *the* masculine game. Sports go roughly like this, from masculine to feminine: hockey, football, baseball, soccer, tennis. Hockey requires both strength and thought. Football requires strength, the thought they send in from the sidelines. Baseball would qualify higher if they allowed body contact, but they don't. Soccer requires a weak mind that won't get bored while running up and down a lawn never scoring. And tennis, of course, rewards those with limited skill with the illusion that they are actually playing properly. Only hockey has it all: the basic skill level required, strength, quick thought, imagination, body contact, conquest. Back in the early seventies — I think when I'd just gone to the Flyers — some academic in Montreal published a book claiming hockey was a metaphor for sex (man with big stick fires projectile past goalie's legs into net to score and triumph), and all the hockey writers were doing snide columns on this guy and calling him a goof. Not me. He was onto something, I say.

What I'm coming to is groupies. Doesn't matter what city or what hotel you're in, they find you. They're easy to spot because they have a common-denominator look: skinny in tight pants, larger than average boobs, braless and showing it, heavy eye shadow, and so much orange blush on their cheeks that some look like you have to peel them like a tangerine, nervous hands,

giggles, frightened eyes. They ask for nothing and they refuse
nothing, which is what delights guys like my buddy Torchy Bender
and spooks guys like me, who are always convinced they're either
lying about their age, or their health, or both. Torchy, though, he
never backed away from any of them, which is why part of him
has never left Chicago, where he played before we joined forces
once again in Philadelphia. He fell in with the Plaster Casters when
he played with the Black Hawks; they'd come to the Stadium looking for Joe Cocker and ended up, somehow, with Torchy; and
before the night was out there was a full-scale plaster-of-Paris
replica of Torchy Bender at his mightiest, the skin down one side
included. They had to graft from his shoulder to fix him up, and
five years later in Los Angeles he was still dining out on the old
joke that ever since he's had bursitis down there and is under
doctor's orders never to lift anything heavy. He usually said that
to rookies at the urinal. Then he'd add that it's always stiff no
matter how much he rubs it.

It would be a lie to say I am myself pure. There are names and
faces and rear ends I no longer recall in all twenty-one National
Hockey League cities. I have gotten down on my knees (not always
willingly) and thanked God for penicillin. And since I got to
Helsinki, room 622 has seen Lise, Hilder, another Pia and, I think,
an Annie, all overseas equivalents of the National Hockey League
groupie, these discovered eager-eyed and willing at the Viisi Pennia rather than the elevator of the Mariott or the lobby of the
Westbury. I offer no excuses. Ten beers into one a.m. and a hockey
player's in love with himself anyway, so letting a mutual admirer
come back to the room for the night is simply an act of kindness.
But eight-thirty a.m. and the sun comes white and cruel across
Toloviken pond and I find myself lying there listening to the trams
squeak to a stop outside the window and I can't even remember
her name.

It never works out for me. Never. I've been close; I've been
disappointed; I've been grateful. Poppa always goes on about me
being thirty-six years old and never married, the last of the
Batterinski line, childless, and I always give him the same bull
about never having met the right girl. A convenient stopper, corny,
but true.

And now Kristiina.

The *Newbuildings* lowers the vehicle ramp, closes the chute
and pulls away from her slip. We stare out silently, all four of us,

and I concentrate deliberately on the day, fixing the white sky against the green dome of the cathedral, its gold cross glinting in the pale light. The market is busy, red canopies snapping in the air, gulls thieving, balloons, the crowd shimmering in a rainbow of ski jackets. And I realize I have been unfair. This is not Sudbury with a harbor. This is Helsinki. Kristiina could not have come from Sudbury. Bertha came from Sudbury.

"To the bar, man?" says Pekka, raising himself stiff-armed from the railing as if the harbor is a movie that has bored him.

"Yes," says Pia.

I look at Kristiina and she shrugs and smiles and I smile back, but it is not a meeting of equals. My smile is forced, I know; it's been that way since I lost my teeth. My upper lip hangs down like it's still afraid a puck's coming. Kristiina's teeth seem anxious to get out and show off. Next time I smile, I will have my moustache go it alone.

We head off to the main lounge but it is full and Pekka leads us up a narrow stairway to a smaller, darker bar on the port side where there is a table near the back under the fish net and traps. There are only two waiters, however, and service is slow. Pia seems determined to sell me to her friend. I am not just Canadian, she tells Kristiina, I am also a Pole.

"I cry every time I think of the Poles," Kristiina says. "It seems to me so sad and unnecessary, I think." Her voice is like water rolling over stone. She should be talking about puppies, not Poles. I half expect Pekka's idiotic joke: *What's a Polish Rubik's cube? All one color.* But he resists.

"How does it affect you, Felix?" Pia asks. She leans forward onto her folded hands, grim. What am I supposed to say—it makes me itch?

I shrug. I wish I had a drink to look down into, a nearly empty glass to pick up and swirl. What do they want me to do? Stand up and sing that idiotic anthem the way Poppa would? (*"Poland is not yet lost as long as we are alive . . ."*)

"They are saying in the broadcasts that there are fourteen thousand Solidarity members in prison," Kristiina offers, "perhaps even more."

The conversation rolls around me and I shake my head in amazement, nod in agreement. The illusion is that all that goes about the head is also held within. But I know none of this stuff.

No meat. No chicken feed, no chicken, no milk, fruit or toilet paper, no heat at home and none at work, line-ups to join line-ups, twelve bucks a month for a six-day-a-week job . . .

"It breaks your fucking heart," Pekka says to the table, his awkward use of the dressing-room word nearly making me laugh. "But how could they go on in such a system that requires you to sacrifice everything for your children and then twenty years later you look at those children and they are worse off than you?"

We all nod. I eye the room, hoping to catch the attention of a waiter.

"You are a Pole," Kristiina says to me. I melt. "What do you think of Lech Walesa?"

How do I answer that? *Walesa?*

"Oh," I say finally. "I think he's great, great."

"He will win the Nobel prize," Pekka says, as if it's fixed.

"If he is alive," Pia says.

Thank God the waiter comes, finally. Pekka orders first, two *koskenkorva*, a schnapps-like drink he and Pia always mix with 7-Up and which I always say tastes like coal oil. I shake my head when the waiter tips his pencil my way and concede to Kristiina.

"*Lakka*," she says.

"What's that?" I say, grateful to be leaving Poland.

"Try one," she dares.

"Sure. Why not?"

The drinks come and Pekka orders another round before the first sip is taken. I eye this *lakka*. It seems thick, syrupy, a light orange with a wine smell to it. A girl's drink.

"Lovely," I lie to her after the first sip. "What is this stuff?"

"Cloudberry," she says. "It is a liqueur. Very popular in Finland."

"What's a cloudberry?" I ask.

"It grows up north, man. Wild," Pekka says with enthusiasm. "In the wet areas — what do you call them?"

"Lakes?"

Pekka snorts. "No. Bad water. Muddy."

"Swamps."

"That's it. Swamps."

I lift the drink and spin it professionally in the light. "We have wild berries where I come from. Blueberries and raspberries. Blueberries grow around swamps. Are they like that?"

"Lakka aren't blue. Red."

"What is a raspberry?" Pia asks, leaning toward me, curious.

I give her one, loud and spitting, my upper lip burbling over my tongue like an outboard motor. I expect laughter, but the table offers only confused stares. The Finns at the next table are turning as if something is out of order at our table. Something is. Me.

"It's a joke," I explain badly. "We do this thing in Canada and call it a 'raspberry,' see. When we hear something we don't like. It's just a joke." I can feel my ears burning.

"I see," Pia says and smiles into her drink. When she looks up I can sense that Kristiina is signaling, and the two women stand up together and leave for the washroom.

"She's fantastic!" I whisper to Pekka.

"Yes, my man, she is."

"Who is she?"

"Pia's friend. She's an architect."

I swallow. "I don't think I made a very good impression."

"Not to worry you," Pekka says, slapping my shoulder and laughing. "Different cultures and all that. We're used to it. It is nothing."

The waiter and the women return together. I have calmed a little, warmed by the second drink. My leather jacket is off, but I feel steamy inside. I can sense the ship rolling, creaking; it seems to walk up, hang, then dip quickly, groaning with each drop, then a repeat, rise, run, hang, drop . . . rise, run, hang, drop . . . rise, run, hang, drop . . . rise . . .

"Felix?"

It is Pekka, concerned. I open my eyes.

"You all right, man?"

I nod. "Maybe I'll just get some air," I say. "Too hot in here."

Outside is instant relief, but cold. I am not alone. All along the railing are others, all staring blankly at the water. But out here the rolling makes sense. The draw of the hull rises and then lowers as the ship cuts through each new wave; and when the hull sinks the sea foams away in hissing swells. I can see progress here and feel better for it.

There is nothing in the distance. Already dark, there is neither light nor line to be seen. This, I suppose, is the Baltic Sea. I had envisioned it for years, all because of the small bronzed plaque on the back wall of St. Martin's with the names of the four Pomeranian boys who died in World War II. *Boys.* I imagine that is the first time I have thought of them like that. When I was a boy their pictures turned them into men, their glory made them heroes. When I was their ages —nineteen, twenty-one, two were twenty-two —they seemed removed, lost, like old newsreels, their hair wrong, their faint moustaches goofy; they seemed somehow still older. Now, though, I am thirty-six. Old enough to be a big brother, an uncle, perhaps even a father to the youngest of them. I think I remember the quotation: ". . . lost in action somewhere over the Baltic Sea, August 26, 1942." *Somewhere.* Here maybe? I look out into the black nothing and wonder if Pomerania has come to this spot twice. Why else would I think of it? He was a Dombrowski. Perhaps Lucy's uncle. Dead at nineteen. When I was nineteen years old I showed up at my first NHL training camp, the world by the ass. And now look: we both end up here. *Felix Batterinski, lost in action somewhere over the Baltic Sea,* December the what? 1981 . . .

. . . I feel better holding the railing. Repeat. Repeat. Repeat. All the sounds are wet here, all the sensations moving. Repeat. Repeat. Repeat.

I am praying. *Me?* Praying? But the words rise with ease, followed by my stomach. . . .

There is a soft touch on my hand. Warm. Skin. I glance at it, forcing my eyes open, and it is what I fear: long fingers, pale, ringless, unpolished, pure.

"Okay?" Kristiina asks.

"Yes," I lie. "I just needed some air."

She says nothing. I stare out at the sea, stunningly aware there is nothing there to be looking at. She stands beside me, hand still gracing my own. She is fortunate I am not holding hers; this ship is fortunate the railings are steel.

"Did you receive any medicine?"

"No."

"I will see that you get some."

Like cousin Jazda's old pony, Joe, I allow myself to be led away and back inside, but not toward the bar again. We take another turn, go down a stairway and come into a narrow, poorly lit corridor with cabin numbers on the doors. She stops at one, checks her key, inserts it and opens the door. I follow, expecting to find Pekka and Pia waiting, presuming this to be the women's place for the night.

"Where's Pekka?" I ask.

"Your friend Pekka is next door," she says. Her voice is cool.

"Pia?" I say unnecessarily.

She jerks the key toward the wall. "Pia is there, too. It is Pekka's little joke, I think."

"I'm sorry," I say.

"That is not necessary," she says. The cool is gone from her voice. Yet I take no joy from it. I do not wish Kristiina to be here, nor Pekka. All I wish is that I could be somewhere else, steady.

I lie down, thinking it may have all passed outside, and Kristiina gets two pills down my throat. I sleep, I think, but only for a moment. When I come to it is as if the bed has been turned to elastic, sinking deeper with every dive, soaring higher with each rise. Standing up, convinced the floor will be sturdier, I am suddenly thrown to my knees as if Eddie Shack has pole-axed me from behind; I am almost unconscious, creeping on hands and knees to the toilet, where I am ill again. Yet when it is over Kristiina is still there, waiting, a cool washcloth ready for a hot forehead. She helps me back into the bed and through the night it is the same cycle, each time astonishing only in that it has come again. But always Kristiina is there waiting. That son of a bitch, Pekka. Some little joke. Some impression I'm making.

It is over again, I think. I'm sure I have been sick again. The washcloth is cool, fresh, so I must have been. There are voices at the door. Not Pekka. Not Pia. Official voices. I feel hands on my clothes, unbuttoning, unzipping. I feel my underwear being rolled down and quick, cool hands spreading my cheeks. *Suppositories!* I feel them rise, two of them, up into my rectum like a shiver, tickling and spooking at the same time. I bury my face in the pillow, cursing Pekka.

"Hi."

It is Kristiina's voice, fresh as first meeting. I roll over in the bed, focusing. "Hi," I say back. "Sorry."

"There is nothing for you to be sorry for, Felix. Do you feel better?"

"Much, thank you."

I stare at her and she looks down smiling. There is nothing of the night on her: eyes still clear and bright, hair as light as Queen Anne's lace. I run my hand up through my own hair. It is greasy, matted.

"You should shower," she says, reading my mind. "Then we will go up for some breakfast."

The shower is weak but welcome, the hot water peeling off the sick shell and letting the old skin breathe again. The spray is so hot it almost burns, but I cannot adjust things. Either hot or cold, no in-between. The steam fills the stall and I close my eyes and hold my arms around my chest like I'm holding a baby. I suppose in some ways I am.

"We have come," Pekka announces once we have checked into our hotel, "to study the Swedish perverts close up."

"How close?"

"As close as you want, old man. What's your choice: basic screwing? S and M? dogs? sheep? donkey? gays? lesbians covered in mud? rubber costumes? There's even a man here who does an act with a vacuum cleaner, if you wish."

I blush, not for me but for Kristiina.

"Look!" shouts Pia. "He's embarrassed. Isn't that sweet?"

I look at Kristiina, feeling for her, having to put up with this. But she, too, is laughing.

"I suggest the Chat Noir," she says.

"*Bor*-ing," Pekka says, drawing out the word as he has heard me do so many times previously.

"Fantasia," Pia says.

"Ohhh, yes," agrees Kristiina.

I look at her, confused — but I dare not ask what it is.

Nor do I have a chance to ask Pekka before we get there. Fantasia is a hole in the wall, a simple red neon sign and a sandwich board set up on the sidewalk to tell you who is on whom tonight. A staircase leads down to a vast cavern of darkness and strobe lights and music that pounds like the ship's hull. But no one dances. There is no room. We check our coats and I see, faintly, that Kristiina has changed to a shiny black, slightly slinky, dress. The contrast on her skin is startling, almost lewd, forcing me to focus on the rising line heading down between those marvelous breasts. She should have covered up more.

Up on stage are two men and a woman, but I can only tell this because spotlights are shining on their genitals. Over their heads they wear white sacks with eye slits. The woman is well built, like she has just stepped out of a *Playboy* cartoon, and the one man is tall and skinny while the other is short and fat, Mutt-and-

Jeff style. The short man has a tuba tied to his back and he carries it as if he is a hunchback. The woman lies down on a raised mattress, spreads her legs, and the short man with the tuba crawls onto his stomach until he fits into the "V" her legs make. The mouth piece of the tuba disappears into her pubic hair. The tall man, now visibly excited, comes up and begins thrusting his penis into the bell of the tuba. Over the speakers comes a flatulent burp, which I shortly realize is a tuba solo. I recognize the tune but cannot name it, and I stand there holding Kristiina's perfect hand while three people and a tuba go at it on stage, and then suddenly it comes to me that I don't recognize the song because of its location, not its melody. The last time I'd heard it was in St. Martin's Roman Catholic Church in Pomerania.

O Come All Ye Faithful.

I am out leaning against the railing of the *SiljaStar*. But I feel fine. A different ship, a different voyage; this time the seas are calm, wall-to-wall blackness under a sky unlike any I have ever seen before. It's depth, that's what: the sky has depth here, the constellations at different distances, three-dimensional. I am too used to city skies with outer shells. Or, in L.A., no sky at all.

Kristiina stands beside me, sucking in the air as if she had a straw running the forty feet or so down to the water line. When she releases the air it is with a shiver of resignation.

"Pekka cannot understand why you are so angry with him," she says.

"Pekka pissed me off, I guess."

"Why — what did he do?"

"Ah, everything had to be sex. He was grossing me out, a bit anyway."

"*You?*" she laughs. "The big National Hockey League star?"

"Well, there were women there," I say defensively.

She laughs. A shriek. I can sense the other stargazers turning from their constellation to me. The Big Dipper.

"You were upset because Pia and I saw?" she asks incredulously.

I shrug, hoping to shake it off. I know when I'm entering a no-win situation. Talking is one game I do not play well.

"We are grown girls."

"That's not the point," I say, not having a clue what the point is by now. I just want to finish, wrap up, get out. "Stuff like that should be banned, that's all."

"Banned?"

"Yes. Should be a law against it."

She is still smiling. I *love* the smile. But I want it for me, not against me.

"A law to protect whom?"

"You. Other women. Kids."

"But it's all right for you, is that it?"

I detect a chill entering her voice.

"No. I wouldn't be able to go either."

"But you're not worried about yourself?"

"No. I'm not."

"Tell me, big hockey star, by what right do you decide what's proper for someone like me to see or do?"

"Oh come on, Kristiina — "

"No. *You* come on. What about the film we saw. It was mostly women."

"Yah, but . . ."

"But it's different for them, is that it?"

"They're different kind of women."

"What about the men that pay to watch?"

"They're men. They . . ."

"Men! It's all right for them to pay money and watch women performing with each other."

I sense I have her. I speak gently, wrapping up perfectly. As a gentleman.

"They're adults. They can decide for themselves."

It doesn't work. She doesn't smile. Doesn't laugh. She snorts.

"And *we* cannot decide for ourselves, is that it?"

I say nothing. I am retracing my steps, reviewing the argument. It works. Can't she see it?

"Batterinski," she says gently. I turn toward her, ready for peace, eager for victory. "I think I like you better sick."

She turns and is gone. And I do not know how to follow.

We part at the docks, Kristiina heading east with Pia and Pekka, me choosing to walk up first to Stockmann's, the big department store, to pick up a warmer coat and then to the 3B tram back to the Inter- Continental. All I take from her is a light kiss on the cheek. Sixty hours together, naked bodies and genitalia around us all weekend, one night complete in the same bedroom, and all I have to show for it is an aunt's buss on the cheek.

Batterinski and another chance blown — nothing new there. I head up, head down, toward the market stalls and past the gathering drunks. Bad *sisu*, Pekka calls it, as if to say the drunks are an unavoidable blight, the disease we require to understand what health is. The first time I saw them here, sitting on the benches with their paper bags and taped-on rubbers and torn coats, staring at me with their rheumy eyes and scabbed noses and swollen lips and tongues, I had a momentary thought that I'd seen them before. I had to work backwards: Griffith Park (no, not quite, too much clothes on here); Philadelphia, by the shipyards (no, wrong color); Edmonton, down along the river (no, no Indians here). And then it came to me. Pomerania. And not bad *sisu* or out-of-work blacks or drunken Indians. But Poppa. And Martin Shannon. And Dombrowski. And Jazda. It could have been Easter back home. The women in the living room with their colored-bread sandwiches and tea and shortbread, the men in the woodshed with their bottles and curses and busted lips and bruised fists. Home Sweet Home.

"Batterinski!"

I turn, unsure. A surly-looking, black-faced devil stumbles forward, holding his coat wrapped around him by the force of his hands in his pockets. It has no buttons.

"Batterinski!" he says, challenging.

"Yes."

He smiles, broken black teeth over swollen gums, the tongue thick and wet, searching for something. Finally he finds it. "Polish," he says. "Polish."

I nod.

He thumps his chest. "Me Polish."

He sticks out his hand, letting the coat flop open to reveal nothing beneath but gray, filthy long underwear. I have to take his hand. His fingers are dirty, knobby, like carrots that haven't been thinned properly and have grown together in clumps. He won't let go.

"Poland," he says, grinning proudly.

"Poland," I say.

"*Solidarnosc*," he says with great sadness. I detect tears welling in his eyes, I think, but it is hard to tell.

I nod again, and smile. How strange. He thinks we are brothers simply because he has seen my picture in the papers — proba-

bly woke up on a bench one morning to find me staring him
straight in the face — and deduced from that that we are both
Polish. I am tall; he is short. I have styled hair; he has none. I have
just left Kristiina; he has just left his bottle, his love. I have money;
he wants it. I set down my bag and rummage in my pocket for
some change, pulling out a mittful of Finnmarks.

"Here," I say.

He looks at the money and then back at me. I think for a moment
he is going to bat my hand away. He looks angry, as if I have
insulted him. How do you insult a bum? But then, quickly, he
scoops up the coins and pockets them.

"Poland," he says, as if it were a salute.

"Poland," I say.

He turns and walks away, not even a thank you or a further
word. He doesn't look back. He is probably thinking I gave him
the money because we are both Polish, brothers.

How appropriate: I am still thinking Poland when I get back to
the hotel and there is a thick letter —no, a thick envelope —waiting at the front desk from Poppa. I take a shower and while I'm
drying my hair order up three Koff beers from room service;
then I'm ready to read:

R.R. #2,
Pomerania, Ont.,
Canada

Dec. 11, 1981

My dear son,

First the news here, okay? This winter's a corker. Snow
and freezing rain and snow and thaw and freezing rain
again and more snow have made the lakes impossible. Can't
go out on the skidoos. Can't ice-fish and probably won't be
able to even later. Ice'll be too thin with all that crust up
top, if you know what I mean.

Poor deer this year. Dombrowski got his and Hatkoski
got his but none of us out here got any at all. I say it's the
crust. It's thick enough for the wolves to ride but the deer
break through and get caught. You can hear the wolves
any night, mostly down in the swamp but once, anyway,

close enough I blasted with the 12-gauge just to button them up.

Batcha's not too good. It's her blood. A kind of cancer I don't know anything at all about. Doc Jarry says she's too old — she's ninety-four, you know, son — to bother with putting her through tests and stuff like that down in the city. He says it's up to you and me whether we tell her or not and since you're not here my vote wins cause I say no. I can't say what she doesn't know won't hurt her but what she could know wouldn't do her any good either. So that's it, decided.

Now, about this letter. You know as well as anyone that I'm not your average "retired" gentleman. I'm 76 years old, I worked hard all my life — *and could still work hard if I had a job, I'm telling you*, I'm strong, I feel real good, I still got all my faculties (or at least those I had to begin with). I'm less like Danny Shannon's father, spending his government pension down at the beer parlor, and I'm more like Jaja was when he was this age. Not interested in slowing down. But the problem is, son, I haven't got much to do with my time. Until now, that is, and if you're agreeable.

You'll remember those crates of Jaja's, the wooden boxes piled in the cellar just by the kindling box? You maybe didn't pay too much attention to Jaja all those nights he sat at the desk scribbling away under the coal oil lamps [Does Poppa really think I, who had to memorize Krasinski, would not remember?], but what he was doing was writing a kind of family history. [Still trying to convince himself Krasinski was a relative, like the Jazdas no doubt.] It's all in Polish — he was a very smart man in that language, your Jaja — and I must admit I'm not up to translating it. The heavens, however, have chosen to smile on us and I'm being helped by the goodness of your cousin Marie Jazda (*Hi, Felix, hope it's going well — Marie*) and she's helping me and putting everything into good English and typing up everything nice and neat, like this here letter. (*I need the practice. I'm hoping to get on with the Polish-Canadian Congress translating the tapes they do of immigrants, so this helps me as much as it does your father — Marie*)

How we work is I read the original, then mark lightly in pencil sections I think you would be interested in, and then Marie and I go to work translating, though she does most of the work and takes what she calls "liberties" with the wording. (*Not too many — Marie*) I'm lucky if I mark up one page in every twenty or thirty. You mind Jaja was a man of detail.

Anyway, I guess you're wondering why. Well, I already explained I want to do something, but I also want you to have this, Felix. It's a record of who we are, see. It's all there should you or your *children* ever want it. I hope you will. I need not remind you that the Batterinski name is now yours alone. Your beloved Matka, may that saintly woman, my dear wife, rest in eternal peace, she would have wanted you to have this, I am sure.

Jaja must have known what would happen to him. At the top of the first box I found a note dated January 1, 1955. That's the first day of the year he passed away, of course. I personally would have liked to have examined all this stuff years ago, but Batcha would never hear of it. I suppose it brought up too many memories of her dear husband for her. She still doesn't like it (*She'll hardly speak to me! — Marie*) but I've told her she's just acting silly. After all, it's been nearly 27 years. Anyway, here's what he said.

January 1, 1955

My dear children,

I began writing this history in September of the year 1951. It was the evening after young Felix went to his first day of school and I realized then and there that he was to be instructed entirely in English. The Separate School Board of Education in Renfrew (made up, I remind you, of Irishmen) had decided Polish could exist only as what they call an "extra-curricular" subject, which I translate to mean they consider Polish second-rate.

A people's language is not a hobby. I decided that I would encourage my grandson to learn Polish and our own Cassubian in the hopes that it would not be lost for ever. Other families decided likewise. And I also decided to write down what I knew of the Batterinski name and what it means to be a Batterinski, for it is a proud name in our people's history.

I had at one time the idea that these papers might be published, but Canada does not care about the Poles. The first volume I sent off to the publishers in Toronto and it was returned unread. They don't publish in Polish; they could care less to translate.

No, the Canadians aren't interested in Polish history. No Pole should ever forget the words of the Reverend George Eaton Lloyd, Anglican Bishop of Saskatchewan, who called us "dirty, stupid, reeking of garlic, undesirable Continental Europeans" and who, after we had been falsely blamed for the General Strike in Winnipeg in 1919, began a movement to send us back. We stayed, of course, but they called us "Bohunks" in the Depression and much of the hatred continues to this day: I myself have been called "D.P." (*"Displaced Person"* — *Marie*) by those I know for a fact arrived in this country after us. And this is why I decided to keep up the records after all hope of ever publishing was done with. It is for you, my children, and for your children, and their children. To be a Batterinski is something. I pray to the Black Madonna of Czestochawa that no Batterinski ever forgets what it means to be one of us.

Yours in faith,

Karol Batterinski

So there you go, son. Right now I'm working Marie's fingers to the bone (*See the blood — just kidding — Marie*) and we'll be sending along parts as we finish. Marie is typing carbons so we got a copy for me and one for you. Here's what we got so far, son. Enjoy yourself!

Has Poppa flipped? Enjoy myself? I've already heard and *forgotten* most of this shit at the knee of the old man himself. I wasn't interested then, either. Hell, I could save Marie enough carbon paper to finish off her old man's shack with, if she was interested in the present rather than this crap.

You want to know about the Batterinskis, Marie? Try page 366 of the *National Hockey League Guide*, right in-between a nobody named Rudy Bastion — a total of *one* NHL career goal in five seasons — and a mean bugger called Baxter who took an ill-timed run at me once when he was with the Nordiques.

Just look, Marie, and tell me who's got three-quarters of a whole page all to himself, eh? Seven teams in four leagues, fifteen full- or part-seasons in the pros, 926 games played, 64 goals, 286 assists, a nice round 350 points and a stunning, remarkable, atrocious, magnificent 2,038 minutes in penalties.

That's just a single slash short of thirty-four hours. Hell, in the shaky lumber market, Danny Shannon's lucky if he gets that much work in a week. And for what? Two hundred ugly bucks? Maybe. You know what those same hours paid Batterinski? I'd guess a million. Hadn't been for that weasel Wheeler I'd know for certain, but I'll still say a million. At least on paper. That's *one million dollars*.

This Batterinski is a goddamned millionaire, Poppa. Or at least should be. Not a worm picker. Not a painter of roadhouse shit- houses. Not a fucking poet. And certainly not *dead*!

And not a "D.P." either. But precisely where he belongs — smack dab in the record books. You could look it up, Marie.

God, just look at the trouble they've gone to, the poor, pathetic fools. Them sitting over there thinking this is what I've spent my whole life waiting to read. Poor, poor Poppa! Lord knows I love him, but Jesus H. . . . I will glance at it, okay . . . and thank him for it in a letter . . . if I can stay awake. . . .

The Batterinski History
by Karol Batterinski

I, Karol Tadeusz Batterinski, am the first and only son of Tadeusz Kosciusko Batterinski who was born in the year 1816 or thereabouts, the records are not accurate. He was born on a farm in Pomerania, some fifty *wiorsta* from Gdansk. (*Felix, this is a measurement I cannot track down. I'm sorry — Marie*) The family was Kashube. His father was Dominic and his mother, I believe, Jozefa. Again, the records are sketchy but I know, when his life is told, the reader will understand why so little is known of the father by the son.

It would have been a small farm, for I know my father was very poor and had three older brothers who would stand to inherit before him. My father told my mother,

Danuta, that he believed his father to be a romantic, for he named him, obviously, after Tadeusz Kosciusko, leader of the tragic 1794 Insurgents. The Poles were even then fighting Russian oppression. They fought under Kosciusko with scythes. Farmers, all of them, and all they wanted was to own their own small plots of land and not have to kill themselves working as poor serfs with no hope at all. For a while under Kosciusko they had hope. But they were only farmers, remember. They had no training, no weapons, no strategy except their own anger. What organization they had came from Kosciusko alone, and he must have been a remarkable man. He'd fought with Washington in the American War of Independence and had been one of the main officers involved in the successful fortification of West Point. The United States Congress later rewarded him for his act of bravery by granting him huge tracts of land in, I think, Maryland. He could have been a wealthy man, waited on by servants, his work done by slaves if he'd so wished. But what did Kosciusko do? He was completely unselfish and a true Pole. He came home and he fought. And when he was wounded and had lost, he went into exile in Switzerland. He sent instructions to the the United States of America that his many lands be sold. The money, he stipulated, was to be used for one purpose alone: the buying up and setting free of American negro slaves.

Some would call that naive, foolish. Undoubtedly, the money from the land sales ended up in somebody else's pocket, and what negroes were set free probably were again slaves within the day. But that is not the point. The point is that it is a Pole's nature to think of others first. And in that way the Pole is too easily taken advantage of, on earth. In heaven, however, it is another matter. The Pole is a pauper on earth, a king in heaven.

Our destiny, it seems, is to fight. The Kashubes have fought throughout their history and there has been little time for anything else. A few poets, a composer, I'm sure (but can find none, certainly not on the level of our revered Chopin or Paderewski, my personal favorite, as you well know), some painters, but above all fighters, warriors. The Israelites say they are the lost tribe, the chosen people. The Kashubes are also chosen, chosen to suffer. Poles know what it is to be outcasts. No one needs to describe abuse or oppression to the Poles.

History teaches a Pole that in the end he stands alone. I quote Napoleon Bonaparte in Verona, Italy, speaking in September of 1796, when revolution and new promise was riding the winds of Europe and America. "I like the Poles," Napoleon said. "When I have finished the war in Italy I will lead the French myself and force the Russians to re-establish Poland."

We know now what Napoleon was doing. He was firing up the Polish volunteers, many of them the very best fighting men he had. Toss an empty promise into the air and a Pole is sure to charge head down and full-throttle out of the trenches. It works every time. It will work again.

Churchill did it in World War II—just look at the glorious accomplishments of the Polish pilots in the Battle of Britain, and for what? To fall under Russia's boot heel again! Woodrow Wilson did it in the Great War. We were even included in his famous Fourteen Points, you know. We were point thirteen. Any Kashube could have told Wilson what that meant.

In all my reading (and here I must thank the good Fathers for opening up their libraries to me) I have come across but one non-Pole's opinion that was totally accurate, and that, incredibly, comes from the founder of Communism, Karl Marx. Nevertheless, he was right. Writing in the September 6, 1848, issue of *Neue Rheinische Zeitung*, Marx said to the Prussians: "You have devoured the Poles, but you will not succeed in digesting them."

You have devoured the Poles, but you will not succeed in digesting them. Think about that! It was true more than a century ago; it is true today; I fear it will also be true tomorrow. The Poles continue to be devoured. All that ever changes is those who bite into us.

The Prussians came and tried to abolish our language. At a time when the Romantic poets were celebrating the dignity of man, the Prussians established throughout Polish territory Gestapo-style organizations called Gustav-Adolf Societies, which were charged with making us over in their own image. They had the right to walk

into a death home and tear the Polish books off the
shelves and shove them in with the dead. Then they
would cart the coffin off to make sure the old Poles and
their old ways were buried forever. Some Poles,
determined to hang on to what they were, *were forced to
rob their own parents' graves in the dead of night.* Just
think about it. . . .

My father was fifteen or sixteen years old in 1831 when
the Poles decided to fight back. I know nothing of the
circumstances but he ended up in the so-called army of
General Sowinska. This army numbered perhaps sixty
thousand, mostly farmers, and had only anger to fight
with. Yet somehow they swept across Poland, thanks, I
believe, to Nicholas II's obsession with sending his
Russian troops into France to rectify the July Revolution
and return Louis to power. The Russians and Prussians
simply ignored Sowinska's rebels until they were
ensconced in Warsaw. And when they did finally get
around to routing them, the rebels won even though they
seemed to lose. Many fled with Sowinska to Paris where,
because their ragtag revolt forced Nicholas to abandon
his assault on the French, they were the toast of France.
Amis des Pol societies sprang up all over the country.
They took the threadbare refugees in, clothed them, fed
them and gave them shelter for free and sustenance
money each month with no strings attached.

They were known as The Emigration. I know from my
mother that my father was in Paris with General
Sowinska and that he, the poor farmer's boy, was trained
as a typesetter by Paris sympathizers. He was involved in
the publishing of tracts and poetry that were smuggled
back into Poland to keep the resistance going. Here he
apparently met Frederic Chopin, who was then all of
twenty-one years of age and a composer of international
reputation. My father also knew Adam Mickiewicz, the
immortal poet, whose *Books of Polish Pilgrimage* were,
with Chopin's music and the writings of Zygmunt
Krasinski, the most powerful weapons Poles back home
had to fight with. Words are in the mind and music in the
heart, and neither can be imprisoned in coffins, buried
and forgotten.

*(Felix, your grandfather goes into long, long quotations
from Mickiewicz at this point and your father has marked*

*them for you. I feel uncomfortable translating them. I
consulted Father Schula and he had some parts already
translated in a book. I send you, then, a portion of*
Pilgrimage *that he suggested:*

> "I shall beat one wing against the past,
> The other against the future,
> And steering by the dictates of the heart,
> Strive toward the feet of God."

*I can send more if you want, Felix. Just say the word. —
Marie)*

So Father Schula suggests this passage, does he? And he wants
me to beat my wings, is that it? Has the old coach gone soft, too?
Him and Poppa? If Father Schula thinks Batterinski is "The Bird,"
then he's got me mixed up with my old Flyer pal Saleski, only for
Don the poem would have been written a little different, I'd say.

"I shall beat one wing against the Bruins,
The other against the Canadiens,
And charging by the dictates of Shero,
Strive toward the cup of Stanley."

What in Christ's name does Poppa expect me to do with this stuff?
Clutch it to the bosom and weep? Sing the Polish National Anthem?
Hijack the *Newbuildings* and invade Gdansk harbor with a bri-
gade of Volvos?

I find it hard to even picture Father Schula today. Where is the
priest who was more coach than knee-banger? Where have the
days gone when I would sit opposite him in the St. Martin's confessional running my left hand up and down the velvet curtains
because it made me feel horny? *Bless me, Father, for I have sinned
and I confess to almighty God and to you, Father.* Schula's voice
lowered, sadder, the yelp from the rink missing, but the questions, *How long since your last confession?*, more filled with concern for my shoulder than soul, the Hail Marys aimed more at
Renfrew and the upcoming game than at heaven and the upcoming judgment.

Confiteor Deo, omni potenti . . . Christ, I'm surprised I can still
remember it. I suppose it's like a reverse breakout pattern. See it
once in chalk and you never have to see it again. . . .

My father had the sense to give up on phony French
promises and return to where the real fighting needed to

be done. In 1843 he arrived in Gdansk. That same year Krasinski's *Przedswit* was smuggled into Poland and I choose to believe [Aha, so now he's not so sure! I can almost feel Jaja rocking me.] that it was my father who was the carrier of this powerful message, which I am proud to say I have passed on to my sons—alas, not to Ignace, for whom I have memorized it twice as perfectly —and to my, so far, only grandson, Felix:

> "... and I heard
> A voice that called in the eternal sky:
> As to the world I gave a Son,
> So to it, Poland, thee I give.
> My only Son He was —and shall be,
> But in thee my purpose for Him lives.
> Be thou then the Truth, as He is, everywhere.
> Thee I make my daughter!
> When thou didst descend into the grave
> Thou wert, like Him, a part of humankind."

(Felix, Father Schula again — by the way, he sends his best — Marie)

Krasinski died a bitter drunk at the age of forty-seven. [Christ, if he'd told me this back then, maybe I'd have listened better.] Still, it is the poem not the man that matters. He may have been, as some have claimed, simply a carrier of a larger meaning, as the Holy Mother herself was. *Przedswit* became the basis for what the skeptics have referred to as Poland's messianism. Not even Chopin, with his Revolutionary Etude no. 12, op. 10, was to have such an effect. The idea spread that Poland had been called on by the Holy Father to suffer crucifixion, just as Jesus had. Why? Well, the true Poles argued that this was because Poland, again like Christ, stood for a universal truth, the cause of human freedom. Poland thereafter was seen as a Christ metaphor, rising from the dead.

We are still waiting. I apologize for my cynicism but I am an old man and I have been waiting all my life. Perhaps you, my children, will see Poland return to her proper glory. I am convinced I will not.

My father vanished between 1843 and 1856. Where, I

do not know. My mother believes he was in Gdansk, working in the shipyards. I do not know. Whatever, in the autumn of 1859 "A Circle of Brotherly Help" surfaced in Warsaw. Obviously father was there, for he courted and married my mother—a sister of Krasinski who, sadly, never knew her older brother as he had gone to Paris when she was a child and was dead when she was a woman—there that year. [Jaja's giving away his old age here. I just did a quick check and his father had to be forty-three or forty-four when he married. It's a wonder he did marry. Thank the Christ he did, though. Or there'd be no proof of the Batterinskis in the NHL *Guide*, let alone this.] Several others from The Emigration were also there; the group was now some twenty-eight years in existence. The Circle of Brotherly Help was filled with young men caught up in Rousseau's *Liberté*. They wanted agricultural reform and better working conditions, but more than anything else, control of their own affairs and ownership of Polish land by Poles. In other words, they wanted Russia out.

Tsar Nicholas had died and Alexander had succeeded him, and Alexander had even gone so far as to legalize the Agriculture Society three years earlier, making them, the Circle charged, "the authorized revolutionaries." The Agriculture Society was led by Andrew Zamoyski, a dull, highly conservative man who naively believed Poland's difficulties as a country lay in the ground. Zamoyski's call was for "organic work," thinking that by working hard and together the unsullied peasants could somehow triumph over the greed and cruelty of the regime. No wonder Alexander eagerly endorsed the Agriculture Society. In reality, it was working for him, getting the peasants to produce more.

Just imagine the confusion. Krasinski, Poland's most famous poet, was speaking to the country's highly religious, downtrodden people to look above for a solution—God, surely, would never abandon His daughter—and Zamoyski was telling them to look at the ground itself for the answers. The men of the Circle knew that the only answer lay somewhere between heaven and earth. It lay in the space of men and action. They were entranced by the Franco-Austrian war and, later, by the

unification of Italy; they felt all they needed was their
own Cavour or Garibaldi — men who could change
history — and Poland would be saved.

The Russians were holding up the carrot of Tsarist
ukase, the abolishment of serfdom, and were convinced
Zamoyski's Agriculture Society would unwittingly play
into their hands. The Poles would be appeased but hardly
independent. The Russians failed to realize that the Circle
saw through this lie. The Agriculture Society set its
convention up for the end of February. On February 27,
1861, my father and other members of the Circle marked
their arms and hats with the sign of the Circle and set off
carrying banners to demonstrate in full view in the
Krakowskie Przedmescle. They marched in an orderly
fashion, no rock throwing, and they gathered, four
hundred strong, and began a chorus of shouts they knew
would be carried into the meeting hall of the Society.
More Russian Hussars arrived on horseback, carrying
lances straight up, but the protesters held their positions
and the Russians contented themselves with a show of
force, riding up and down along the face of the crowd in
formation, turning and quietly retracing their steps.

What happened next no one knows. I suppose someone
threw a rock. Perhaps it even missed. Whatever, shortly
after noon the Russians spurred their horses into the
crowd and leveled their lances. The crowd panicked and
broke. The Russians moved in methodically, riding two
abreast, lances out, leveling the Circle brethren in great
wide swaths, turning and running again. For the most
part it was simple cruelty, harassment; but toward the
end of the panic a Russian rifle brigade kneeled and fired
a single volley. Five clearly identified brethren of the
Circle died immediately, their bodies left to bleed into the
gutters.

My father was one of them. The revolution had just
begun and he was already dead, never to realize it was all
for nothing. I do not even know what he looked like. . . .

Bor-ring! There is more, far more, but I am too tired of it to go on.
I'm sorry, Poppa, but that's just the simple truth.

A nap, I guess, and then something to eat, maybe give the soggy pizzas from Davys' a last chance. . . . But I will not dream about what he looked like, Jaja, neither bleeding to death in that gutter or jumping across the border with a dumb poem hidden in a false heel, or whatever. I know what Torchy would say — *Shit, is that all they had to smoke in those days?*

No, I will dream instead about Kristiina and how it might have been if I wasn't such a goddamn big jerk.

Two days later Kristiina phones. I've been thinking about her constantly, trying to figure out how I might call her and not have it sound awkward. All the way up on the team bus to Lahti I thought of ways I could get to her. Erkki Sundstrom was sitting beside me, the boss and the coach traveling side by side while the team slept and joked and played whist behind us. Erkki was biting his nails, as usual, undoubtedly sweating over our remarkable record of victories: none. He kept glancing over at me, trying to gather the nerve to interrupt. He must have figured I was deep in thought, perhaps engineering a solution to our dismal forechecking or coming up with a scheme to break up the long lead pass that's been killing us lately. I kept shifting my position in the seat, looping one leg over, then back, then trying to stretch. As far as Erkki could tell, the team problems were eating me up, and he left me alone. My real problem was that I had an erection.

"Hello, Felix?"

"Yes. Who is this?"

"Kristiina . . ." she says hesitantly, as if I might not remember.

"Kristiina!" I shout. "Hi! How are you? I didn't recognize your voice."

"You were expecting another call," she says, still unsure.

"No. No. Of course not. I sometimes get crank calls though, and the odd switchboard screw-up."

She laughs and I remember the sound. A laugh you could drink.

"Why do you stay there?" she asks.

"Here? Well, it's awfully convenient. Why?"

"A hotel is not an idea of a home."

"It suits me. They wanted me to move out to Tapiola."

The laugh again, delightful. "The assembly line."

"Ticky-tack," I say.

"Pardon?"

"It's a song."

"Ahhh," she says, not following, not bothering to pursue. "Pekka tells me that you play ice hockey on Saturday night."

"Yah. Home against Tampere. They're in second place."

"And on Sunday? Do you have an ice hockey practice?"

She wants to come to a practice? "No. Nothing Sunday. We practice Monday."

"Good," she says. "If I come to the game, how would you like on Sunday to come up to my cottage?"

I'm shocked. *"You* are asking *me* out?"

"Yes. Is that all right?"

"Well, of course it's all right. Where is this cottage?"

"It is my parents' cottage, actually. It is north of Lahti, just beyond a small village called Kalkkinen. They are on the lake."

"Sounds great," I say. "But it's hardly cottage weather."

The laugh. "It is if you are a Finn."

"I'm Canadian."

"Then you should feel right at home."

Already it is Saturday, game today. Not even for the Stanley Cup have I ever been so tight before a match — and I am not talking here of hockey. It's Kristiina. And I'm as rattled as if my assignment was Lafleur. But it's not that easy: Lafleur's weak spots would be in the scouting reports; here, I'm on my own. And the weak spots, I fear, are all mine.

Deliberately, the route I take to the Ishallen is leisurely, so I will have time to gather my thoughts. Up Mannerheimvagen, turn right on Helsinginkatu, then onto the footpaths through the rock park. They're not shoveled, but enough Finns are fool enough to walk here that there's a crude path through the snow; it reminds me of the back trail over to Jazda's. Then off the rock path and onto Paavo Nurmentie, a park named after the Flying Finn of some long-forgotten Olympic glory — there's even a statue of him in the middle, and on up past the Olympiastadion to the rink.

It is so cold today I seem to be the only one bothering with the park. Even the hippie assholes Pekka calls *diinarit* must be indoors jerking off with barbed wire, or whatever it is those perverts do. Pekka says they take their name from James Dean, but, shit, Dean had class. He was an original. These Finn kids are all carbon copies: the kind of jeans they used to call dungarees in the old comics, black scuffed Wellingtons, filthy torn jean jackets with goofball buttons and confederate flags, another jacket or sweater tied

around their waist — a lot of good that does you at ten below
zero. Their hair is a roar: double parts, sides straight back over
the ears, hair pushed up and rolled forward over the parts until
they meet and hang down over the forehead like a tangled horse-
mane. Sometimes Jazda's big horses used to look like that in the
summer if they'd been out all night in the wind. Batcha blamed it
on the forest dwarves, naturally. She'd love these kids, the old
bitch. *Zgrzidlok*, she'd call them. Evil. The devil's helpers.

Those goofy jerks have me thinking of home again, and it's got
to be because so many of them have Mohawk cuts, three-inch
shags down the center of the skull with the rest shaved clean.
Pekka says they're the punk rockers of Helsinki, that they even
have this one hero they pay to see who plays electronic music on
a chainsaw. Arrogant little fops. Christ, if I spoke Finnish I'd tell
them Danny Shannon had a Mohawk cut twenty years ago in
Vernon. And what he did with a chainsaw one night to poor Maurice Duschene's outhouse was a performance none of them are
likely ever to see, no matter how much they pay.

Danny, Danny, Danny . . . You just peaked at the wrong time. If
you'd been thirty instead of thirteen when the best moments rolled
along you might have cashed in. You just peaked too soon. All
that curly hair, nice clear skin, all that charm, the big smile, the
great walk—what happened to it? One season in Vernon and the
rest of your life in the minors in Pomerania, putting on so much
weight they call you "Moose," and then so much more weight
that "Moose" gets embarrassing and you're back to Danny. If
you still had the Mohawk cut it would look like a couple of passing lines. You'll be what, soon—thirty-six? And what do you have
to show for it? A closet full of hockey jackets that no longer fit?

My God but I think of that silly bugger a lot. I must be getting
homesick. But I shouldn't be. I never did in L.A., or Philly, or
even goddamn Wichita. But here I keep thinking of home, and
Danny and Poppa. It's got to be because of Jaja's history, not
because of some damn mixed-up punks.

What was it Jaja said? A Pole walks alone? He does if he's in
this park, anyway. I'm completely alone. There's only the wind
shipping the large flakes of snow more up than down. Damn
things, they catch in my eyelashes and blur the vision. I walk,
wiping, and know that from a distance it must appear I am crying. I
walk by the statue of Paavo Nurmi, and he looks unreal, all black
and dark green contrasting against the snow, his shoulders and

nose and one raised calf solidified in frozen pigeon droppings. Nurmi is in full stride, his empty eyes staring straight ahead beyond the stadium, and he is completely naked. His pecker looks too small in summer, too large in winter. In this weather it should be sucked right up inside.

. Pekka tells me that when Nurmi died they did an autopsy and discovered he had a very bad heart. Weak medically, perhaps, but he won nine gold medals for God's sake. That is the kind of heart Sugar Bowles would have loved. Nurmi must have been a great, great man. A story like that and they erect a hollow naked statue to him. At least I *think* it's hollow. There is no one around so I may as well find out. I step quickly up to the pedestal, pull off a glove, and ping him on the ass with my fingernail crokinole style, the way Poppa always settled Ig down. It rings. Hollow, as I thought.

I pat Nurmi's bum and move on, laughing at the sudden thought that someone might have seen me.

I am standing in the center of the dressing room, feeling all eyes on Batterinski the legendary coach, and while my tongue is tripping my brain is actually down on its knees, praying I had Sugar's ability to fire up players. But I haven't got it and I know it. I slam a stick against the equipment box, make them all shout *"Saa vuttaa!"* — something Timo offered up as a rough translation of the "Go for it!" we used to scream in Los Angeles — and then they get up and walk out as calmly as if class has just been dismissed at Vernon District High. Christ, if this was the old Flyers' dressing room they'd see something. Clarkie, snarling with his teeth out, screaming in their faces and slamming every player in the shins as they stepped out the door, Bill Barber with his sick-looking black eyes, Schultz like he should be wearing one of the chrome-plated Nazi helmets his fans have on in the crowd, Moose Dupont looking like he came to eat, not to play, the Watsons with their hired-killer stares. You wouldn't smell cologne in the dressing room of the Broad Street Bullies. But now, kissing the inside of my sweater as I pull it down, that is what I do smell: perfume. It makes me want to puke.

I noticed one thing right off about the Finn players. The way they smelled. Like room fresheners. It sure as hell wasn't like hockey players. Danny Shannon and I, back when we played together in Vernon, we used to say there were two absolutely distinctive smells in this world. Torchy Bender argued there was a third the day he showed up at practice with his right middle finger wrapped in gauze after a night with Juice Larocque, but our two were a brand-new car and a hockey dressing room. Danny claimed one day he'd make a million bucks by bottling that arena odor and flogging it to older guys who were messing around behind their wives' backs on the nights they were supposed to be out playing shinny with the boys. Screw all night, splash on a dash of Danny Shannon's special sweat- and-stale-underwear smell, and head on home to a wife who'll actually be pleased to hear you scored.

You know something, Danny? I miss you.

I put on my helmet — ultimate suck symbol, law here — snap the chin tight, look slowly around the empty dressing room and head out—hard to believe I once had to be first on the ice and am now last—to discover half the crowd would fit comfortably into the penalty box. What can we do to draw? Helsinki IFK has been on fire since they dumped New York Rangers in exhibition play, and Jokerit are hanging onto their old fans and drawing new ones with the young kid, Petäjäaho. Why would anyone but wives and girlfriends bother with Tapiola Hauki? Erkki Sundstrom is already pacing and chewing his nails back of the north boards, undoubtedly praying enough lures are snagged and replaced next summer that the board of directors won't notice all the red numbers in the promotions budget.

I don't give a shit, quite frankly. All I know as I skate around is that there is nothing sweeter than the music of my own skates. I know that for the next two hours or so I am locked in, set. The lines have been set out and all I will have to do is shout out one of five numbers to get what I want, power play to penalty-killing unit. The puck will drop and I will know precisely what to do and when. I will be wearing exactly what I feel best in. I will not have to talk. I will hit once and feel the marvelous state of alertness that seems to wash from first contact. All the hits to follow will only increase that feeling until, as the game's intensity grows, I become calmer and calmer. When Erkki is at his worst, I will be at my best. Knowing what to do and doing it.

Kristiina *is* here! There, beside Pia, to the right of the home bench. I take my eyes off her instantly and will not look back again. I see Pekka doing his silly signal, removing his helmet and pulling his ear for Pia. Who does he think he is, Carol Burnett? Batterinski has never waved. Batterinski has never acknowledged any crowd, ever.

Erkki, in his growing terror, has arranged for a scouting report on Tampere. Kamppuri, the goaltender, has trouble clearing pucks. Lehtonen, at center, likes to hold onto the puck. Sevon has a good slap shot. Susi checks well. I threw the report away. I could have written my own descriptions: chicken, hog, loafer, screw-up. Shorter, simpler and more to the point, but in the end useless. It applies to all Finn teams. What do I tell my players? They play like you, so imagine you're up against a mirror. All Finns play like they're made out of glass anyway.

We line up for the anthem, Timo to my left, Pekka to the right, and I stare up at the rafters listening to this strange song soaring and fluttering about. It sounds more like an opera than a hockey game. But I do not laugh. They have suffered enough for Tapiola Hauki.

I love the moment of the opening face-off, when the arena is full of held breath. There is silence as the puck slaps the ice and then, with luck, a stick will slap it quickly back to me and suddenly I am in command of time. If I hurry, they panic. If I look up and lazily stickhandle back and forth, waiting, they circle nervously, waiting, too. No one wants to be the first to test Batterinski.

Sometimes along the boards I can hear my name, but not from Kristiina's mouth. I do not expect that. She is above that. She will notice me, and acknowledge me when I hit. Lehtonen has the puck at his own blueline now and Pekka misses with a fool's play, a poke check. Lehtonen has too much reach to fall for that. He sweeps wide and center ice opens up for him.

Timo moves to head off Susi but he is wasting his time. I can see Lehtonen's eyes and I know that his thoughts are there for anyone to read. Lehtonen checks the puck and then Timo. He looks at Timo, not Susi, meaning he has no intention whatsoever of passing. He does not look at me but that is because there is no need. He knows precisely where I am. He is trying to dupe me with his eyes, getting me to bisect between him and Susi. But I do not. The ice cuts soft under my skates as I grind backwards, angling toward him.

Lehtonen looks up, surprised. He now must deal with me

immediately. He crosses the blueline, dips his shoulder left and fakes a stick shift to the right. As I knew he would. He then double-shifts and does move to the right, and my shoulder is there to welcome him. I forget the puck, leaving it and Susi to Timo. I forget all but the pressure of my shoulder along his chest. I can hear his breath, popping. We hit the boards and I dig in with my skates and thrust upwards, sending Lehtonen so hard against the glass that it warps back and jumps out whole from its side channels and into the first-row crowd.

How perfect for Kristiina. The Tampere bench is shouting but the referee doesn't have the guts to call anything. It is a per-fectly clean check but, for Finland, an unnatural act. I look at the clock and it is 1:39 into the first period. I have my hit. I feel the calm in my blood. There remains a wonderful, growling mur-mur in the stadium, indecipherable but absolutely clear: the sound of amazement.

I would give anything to see Kristiina's face but I cannot look. To look would be to admit that it happened. A great hockey player is oblivious to his effect on the game. This I learned from Orr, the true master of distancing himself from what is going on on the ice.

The glass reinserted, the game continues, but it is not the same game. I have established myself and my territory. Now when Tampere comes up across center they look for me, not daring to chance deceiving me with their eyes. And once I have their eyes, I have them. It's as simple as that.

But I cannot do everything. The larger ice surface makes con-trol more difficult, especially in our own end when it seems to me there is a second rink grafted behind our net. We survive, barely, a power play by them when Timo goes off for tripping, though they keep us bottled up in our own end for virtually the entire two minutes. But we make it through, thanks to me block-ing a half-dozen shots from the point. Then they draw a penalty trying to stop Pekka breaking up center. I get five straight shots from the point but no one has the sense to tip them in. Christ, I wish Torchy was here—or even Danny Shannon, fat and bald, he could still show them a few tricks. I get an unbelievable sixth chance and just slap it blindly at the net. It goes off Kamppuri's stick handle into an upper corner. 1–0 for Tapiola. We have the lead!

In the second period they tie up the game. We go up 2–1 on a sweet shot by Pekka on his backhand, but immediately they get one back. The scorer is a big defenseman named Esa Välioja and after his goal — a floater from the point that goes in only because of Timo's screen — he skates backwards to center ice, drops to his knees and begins somersaulting toward his own goaltender, who skates out to congratulate him.

This I despise. I hated Tiger Williams when he rode his stick like a damn horse. I hated Shack when he stuck his stick back down his glove like he was sheathing a damned sword. I hate all hot dogs, except, of course, Torchy. When Batterinski scores, it is like he's not even there. Same with Orr or Lafleur or Bossy.

When Välioja comes over my blueline in the third period I am ready. He somersaults again, but no goal is scored. I hit him like a mule, blindsiding him with his head down, and he hits the boards like a car accident. I don't even turn to see. I watch their box, and when the trainer comes onto the ice I know I have hurt him.

"Kanadalainen vittu!"

The tone translates for me. *Fucking Canadian.* I look up and Välioja's fat-faced defense partner is standing with his stick out, thrusting the blade at me. I straighten up and stare at him, the calm in my blood so thick now that I see everything in slow motion. Even the stick, rising and then falling, and then suddenly time changes gears on me and it is racing. Time is running from me! I know I am on the ice and I know there is a towel against my eye but I do not know how I or it got there. It feels like I'm back on the ship, floating, nauseous. I open my eye and stare up at Pekka, leaning over. He swims on me. I feel hands under me, lifting. My eye feels warm, except the warmth is not comforting: it burns with fear.

I want desperately to look now for Kristiina. Only now I cannot see.

Kristiina is not concentrating on her driving. The gears grind as she speaks. "I'm not so sure you should be going ahead with this."

I grind, listening, slowly finding my own gear: a lie.

"I'm sure. The doctors said it looks far worse than it is."

"Okay then. Let's go."

I am glad to be in the passenger's seat. This way, if I stare straight ahead she will not see the fat man's work. My right eye is swollen shut. Under the small bandage on the side of it are twenty-seven stitches, nineteen inside which will dissolve, eight on the outside which will be removed in a couple of weeks. I was damned lucky. So was the team — we managed to hold onto the tie.

Twenty-seven more puts me over the two hundred mark. That's respectable. I remember Derek Sanderson saying his father used to cut out the stitches and store them in a jar, and when he'd collected a hundred of Derek's stitches he threw them away, saying Derek had proved himself. Not like Poppa. Every time I got a stitch he'd tell me it didn't pay to fight. Bullshit it didn't. Every stitch I took brought me one step closer to the National Hockey League.

"Are you in any pain?" she asks.

"No."

"You're awfully quiet."

"I was just thinking."

"About your game?"

"Feels good. Our first point."

"You can sit there like that and say it *feels* good?" she says, smiling.

I half turn toward her with a smile. She is smiling back, but the difference between our two acts is so immense they should not even have the same word. I must look like a geek. Kristiina looks stunning, the sun playing through the window on her hair, the Lapland sweater all blue and red and purple and white and dazzling in the morning light, mesmerizing in what it holds.

How odd all this is. Her date, her car, her cottage, her plans. I feel weakened by it all.

"I imagine you've been up this road a lot," she says.

"Yes. But I like the drive." It is not the same, though. No loud bus this time, no laughter around you, no music — "Queen" in the rear fighting with "ABBA" in the front — and no Erkki gobbling up his fingers. This time I see the drive. I see the young boys ice-fishing as we go over a bridge. I see the skiers. I see an old man burning brush from a road clearing. He stands like Poppa, leaning over the fire as if he is chewing it out.

We pass several parked cars, people removing their equipment from the trunk and their skis stabbed into the bank on the side. "Think you're ready for that?" she asks.

"Sure. Why not?"

"The doctors didn't say you couldn't?"

"No. I'll be playing Wednesday's game, too. So don't worry about me. I'm fine."

"Great."

"What is it, rope tow or chairlift?"

She laughs. My laugh. "Cross-country, silly. Nordic. Not downhill."

Oh my God — winter tennis!

Kristiina's father, thank heaven, is not here. He's pretty well my size but he must be a fairy. I am in his fishnet underwear, his yellow- and-green-checkered plus fours, his purple-braided knee-socks, his yellow corduroy waistcoast and his green fluorescent toque. Kristiina says I look smashing. I say smashed.

It is hard for me to appreciate whatever pleasure it is she takes from this sport. Kristiina's only advice is that I pretend I'm walking like Groucho Marx, but I still slide backwards on the slightest knoll. She is far ahead of me, a flash of pure white corduroy, pink stockings and toque, a high backward kick that looks from here as if she is falling on her face, but which ends up producing a long smooth glide until her next kick. She has waxed the skis and abandoned me, which I am in a way grateful for — a true athlete hates nothing so much as instruction.

Her bottom drives me on. To get her kick she must shift it quickly and the result is a fascinating shimmer that pulls me along like a magnet. I kick and scramble and hammer my poles into the snow and her bottom stays gloriously in sight. But I am tired. For a sissy sport I feel exhausted already. I must have lost more blood than I realize. She heads up a long, twisting, pine-covered hill, climbing first sideways, then herringbone, then slamming her skis onto the trail for grip and moving straight ahead. I feel like I'd be better off carrying my skis but cannot let her see me, so I struggle on and eventually the trail flattens and comes out onto a magnificent view of the lake and surrounding hills. The snow glints harshly on the eyes. Or in my case, eye.

"Come over here!" Kristiina calls. She is just beyond the larch, on a better outcropping. I try my best to ski over gracefully and do, but am forced to stop by stabbing my poles ahead and leaning into them, and this causes me to stumble and almost fall. Kristiina laughs. Her cheeks have lost their whiteness; they seem cooked now, pink-orange like the flesh of lake trout. There is a light, delicate frost on her upper lip and chin. I would kill to thaw it with my tongue.

"It's beautiful," I say. I cannot say more. I have no breath.

"You, can see a good part of the lake from here," she says proudly.

"What's it called?"

"Paijanne."

She raises a pole and points down toward the near shore with it. "See. There's the cabin." I look and, from here, it looks much improved, more like an illustration in a children's book. There is smoke rising from the fire she set and more smoke coming out of the sauna by the edge of the lake. Closer up, it is just a primitive cottage. No floor insulation, no ceiling tiles, cheap pine panelling, a musty smell. Back home it would be a magnificent hunting cabin, or a poor man's cottage.

"Our sauna awaits us," she says.

"I need a drink."

"A sauna first. Come on. I'll race you back."

She is gone, the skis whispering away from me, teasing down the rise and in through a pocket to the coverage of the pine trees. I have no choice but to chase. I push off and my skis fall into her grooves, sighing. I feel the air moving fast into my bandage, stinging.

When I get to the cabin Kristiina is nowhere in sight. Her skis stand in the snow to the side of the sauna, poles beside them with gloves hanging empty in the straps. There is now more smoke coming out of the sauna than the cottage, so I can only presume she has stoked up the fire even more. I sweat just thinking about it.

"Kristiina!"

No answer.

I put her father's skis beside hers and take only one step, my foot breaking through the snow in those funny, long-toed boots and pitching me forward onto my elbows in the deep snow. I am glad she has not answered. I am glad she has not seen.

The sauna is divided into two sections, a small dressing room and the actual sauna, the two areas separated by a thick, unpainted birch door. The building smells of birch, hot and sweating. I check first in the dressing room and her ski clothes are *all* there, hanging from a large wooden peg.

"Kristiina!"

Nothing.

I am trapped. She must be able to hear me in there, but chooses not to. What I want to know is not where she is, but what she is wearing. I have brought my bathing trunks with me, expecting the sauna, but they are in my suitcase up in the cabin. Can I break in on the daughter wearing the father's fishnet underwear?

"Kristiina!"

Nothing.

I think I hear her little laugh, but can't be certain. I have no choice but to step out of her father's clothes, keeping on his kinky shorts, and hope she rescues me somehow. But there is nothing. I step out and jump across the cool hallway between the two rooms and knock. No answer.

"Come on, Kristiina — are you in there?"

Laughter is my answer.

"Now I'm coming in. All right?"

Nothing.

I push open the birch door, leaning in, but the sauna is filled with steam and my one good eye winces in the heat. I enter and the heat boots me solidly in the chest. My lungs fill and turn to fire. I expel, but the replacement air is even worse. I blink, rub my eye and look again.

Kristiina is inside, sitting on the upper ledge, her legs crossed, *naked.* In the air she seems partly vaporized, but it is no dream. She is dimpled with sweat, the beads running high and thick and round along her shoulders, sliding thin and long and runny down and off her breasts. I feel like something more powerful than steam has hit my lungs. She is smiling at me, welcoming me. No, she is laughing at me, and she points to my drawers, to her father's drawers. I turn, step out of them awkwardly, open the door and toss them across the hallway into the door of the dressing room.

"I didn't expect you to be so bashful," she says.

"I didn't expect you to be so naked."

"Come on. Up, beside me." She pats the plank beside her and I step up into a mightier blast of hot air and settle down. The air seems cooler as I sit. She shifts over, her bare skin against mine. I cannot speak. I watch instead as she picks up the wooden dipper from the bucket and splashes more water on to the rocks. It strikes like gunpowder, the steam exploding off the rocks into the air, bouncing off the roof and punching me again in the lungs.

"Enough! Enough!"

Her laugh. "You'll get used to it."

"I doubt that," I say.

"It's good for you. It's *löyly*."

"It's what?"

"*Löyly*. The vapor. It's very good for you, they say."

"Who are they?"

"Finns. Everybody."

"I don't believe it."

"You will."

For ten minutes she continues to throw on the water. Then she tosses some liquid from a small bottle and the smell of birch intensifies. I lean back and relax, watching the sweat rolling unevenly through the hair of my chest, dashing down my belly onto my thighs and then dropping onto the planking. It feels good. My eye is giving me no trouble, and each time I breathe it is as if I am sloughing off waste, being cleansed. I feel fine.

"Had enough?" she asks.

"Just getting used to it," I say.

"You must not stay in too long."

"Why?"

The laugh. "You'll die."

"I believe it," I say, laughing with her. "Where's the shower?"

Again the laugh. "No shower here."

"Well, what do we use, then? That bucket?"

She says nothing. She stands, stoops and steps down, taking my hand as she goes. The motion makes her skin shimmer, a calm lake at sunset. It is hypnotic.

She goes out into the hall, pulling me behind her, then surprises me by turning not into the dressing room but to the outside door and opening it. She steps out into sunlight sharp as a knife blade and cold that lunges as the steam did inside.

If only Danny could see me now. I'm standing starkers beside a naked goddess in the middle of a Finland forest in the middle of winter. I blink and focus in on Kristiina. She is standing less than six inches from me, smiling up happily, her big teeth white as the snow, the steam rising in clouds from the top of her perfect head. She has her eyes closed, her mouth open. No one is so dumb that they'd mistake that.

I lean into her, and even Kristiina tastes like birch. I am bewildered, but not fool enough to stop and ask why. I can taste salt and birch and feel her tongue moving, surprising me as it darts high and tickles along the ribs of my roof and then slipping quickly back inside her own mouth. I feel her pressing tightly against me, her breasts flattening soft and luxurious against my lower ribs, the flat part of her stomach firm and promising against my groin.

But it is her arms that puzzle me. She seems to be pulling, forcing me down as if we are in a hockey fight and she is trying to knock me off my skates. I place my feet wider and hold fast, my mouth suddenly bubbling over with her wonderful giggle. She breaks away.

"You wanted to cool off," she says.

She pulls and I follow, falling, pressing together as we hit the snow and the snow gives to form around us. We roll and the snow flattens and she wraps her legs suddenly completely around me and just as quickly I am wearing her and we are pounding together to form a cast of her wonderful bottom in the snow.

I open my eye to see if it is really happening and I see the snow steaming all around us, our lovemaking rising into the winter air and then vanishing.

Our own personal *löyly*.

"It was not just a triumph for the Montreal Canadiens when they defeated the Philadelphia Flyers in four straight games to win the Stanley Cup in 1976, it was a victory for the purists. 'To sweep them,' Montreal captain Serge Savard said at the time, 'maybe we put an end to all the crap they stand for.'

No names were required. Schultz was soon gone from the Flyers, and McIlhargey, and Batterinski: new fists for old. The fall would be in the same manner that had led to the rise: the classic Greek interpretation of *hubris*. The fists no longer worked.

Yet Felix Batterinski was not the first tragic figure in this passion play. The first was the strange, bitter man who, in a manner of speaking, constructed Batterinski. His name was Ted Bowles, known as 'Toilet' to Danny Shannon and other players who despised the man. It was necessary, however, to disguise their feelings, for Ted Bowles was the Vernon midget-level coach. He was a short, ugly man who never recovered from the junior hockey accident that destroyed both his right eye and his career. He returned to Vernon, worked in maintenance at the arena and inherited the thankless job of coaching the local midgets. He coached winning teams, but his tactics were so controversial that eventually he had to be fired.

'It was a nasty business,' says Desmond Riley, the president of the local hockey association and, ironically, the man who boarded Felix Batterinski when he first arrived in Vernon. 'Teddy Bowles had old-fashioned ideas and refused to change. He wouldn't work on his Level II or Level III or, for that matter, Level I qualifications. He said pencil pushers had nothing to teach him, and he even turned down our offer to pay for the coaching courses. You can understand our situation — we had to act.'

Since Bowles's dismissal, and subsequent death, Vernon has failed repeatedly to win another midget championship. Riley dismisses this by saying that they were too soft on Bowles's case from the start, that he won not because of what he knew but because of who he had — read Batterinski — and that the Bowles system was so diseased by the time Batterinski left that it has yet to recover.

'Felix came into my house a shy, good boy,' says Riley. 'Then Bowles got hold of him and before the year was out this . . . child . . . was leading the league in penalties, slipping in his schoolwork and getting caught drinking beer.'

'I remember our very first practice,' says Tom Powers, the

captain of that year's midget team and today the owner of a small local trucking company. 'We couldn't keep from laughing at this hick and the way he talked — "duh" for "the," you know — and his underwear — Jesus! his *underwear*! It looked like someone had used it to plug up a radiator.'

Batterinski bought new underwear, changed his pronunciation and determined that no one would ever laugh at him again and get away with it. Once Batterinski had moved up to junior with Sudbury, a North Bay player named Simon Billings would make that mistake and pay for it with his hockey future. That fight, Batterinski would say to me nearly twenty years later, had 'served its purpose.' No explanation needed.

His nickname in Sudbury during those years was 'Frankenstein.' Again, no explanation needed."

Excerpted by permission from "Batterinski's Burden," by Matt Keening, *Canada Magazine*, June 1982.

DANNY TOLD ME I'D BE BEATING THE AMERICANS TO THE moon and he was right. I smelled Sudbury twenty miles before I ever saw a building. At first I thought the old lady with the two shopping bags in front of me had let go a squirter; but no, it was the stacks. When I looked out to the left I could see the smoke; the sky, which all the way had been as clear as Ig's eyes, now looked like some kid had thrown a rotten squash up against it, yellow streaks heading off farther than the eye could see. Along the roadside the bush disappeared, not gradually but instantly, the spruce and rolling hills suddenly giving way to a landscape that could only be described as rusted out. Like Danny said, the moon. The Americans were spending millions to get there; I'd found it for seven dollars and thirty-five cents.

The bus pulled into the Sudbury depot in ninety-degree heat, the air rippling above the downtown rocks. Sudbury looked like a junkyard for other towns, the dump where they unloaded everything that didn't fit or had broken down or was too old to be of any use anymore. I figured my hockey career was over before it had even begun. The only scouts this hole had ever seen would have been looking for Indians, or the way out.

"You Batterinski?"

I turned, shocked anyone would come to meet me. Surely not a player — how could they dare let one near the bus terminal without losing him to a one-way ticket home? But this was obviously an athlete: young enough, big enough, cocky enough. He had on a Sudbury Hardrocks T-shirt, jeans, and a pair of laceless sneakers that looked like they'd just been burped out of the smelter. He had Danny Shannon's practised smile, a bent nose and hair like a devil's paintbrush. He was to become — forever, I once thought — my best friend on earth.

"Yah," I said.

He stuck out his hand. I took it, slowly.

"I'm Al Bender," he said. "'Torchy.' Coach sent me down to welcome you."

"Yah."

I couldn't dampen him. He swooped up my duffle bag, then took my suitcase and started off, leaving me nothing to carry but the *Cracked* magazine I'd picked up in North Bay. I had to hurry to catch up.

He talked over his shoulder like I was in a cart he was pulling. "You'll love it here. Never mind how it looks. You ever been here before?"

"No."

"Most people hate it at first. It's like they died and went to hell. But then they love it."

"Where you from?" I asked.

"Kirkland Lake."

"Is that right?"

"Yah. I know Dick Duff a bit."

"Christ," I said, impressed.

"Shit, everybody knows old Duffy. Where're you from?"

"Vernon."

"Oh yeah. Lotsa cottages, eh?"

"You got it."

"What's your old man do?" Torchy asked.

"My father owns a hardware store. A chain, actually."

"Geez, great."

"What does your father do?"

"My old man?" Torchy shouted back at me, still hauling ahead. "He's a fucking drunk."

Torchy Bender. Torchy. Funny, but when I think of him now I always see him as he was then, not as he became in L.A. Torchy played center for the Hardrocks, nifty with a head fake that made him look like his body had somehow separated at the waist, like a child's Slinky toy. Torchy could come over the blueline, deliver the head fake, tuck the puck between the defenseman's legs, leap four feet straight up and over the hip check and land in full flight, completely clear. In regular-season play over 1963–1964, he had fifty-seven goals and sixty-one assists for a hundred and eighteen points and precisely two minutes in penalties. I had seven goals, forty assists, for forty-seven points and a hundred and thirty-seven minutes in penalties. We both made second-team all-star. The perfect pair: him the dream, me the nightmare.

The second year we even lived together, free of charge, in the basement apartment of the team owner, Gus Demers. It was a magnificent setup, a large red-brick home out Ramsay Lake Road, dynamited straight into the rock so our bedrooms were suspended out over the water. We had our own entrance and our own refrigerator, always fully stocked. Gus gave us full access to the inboard- outboard cruiser, the sailboat and the white Valiant convertible; Torchy assumed access to the owner's daughter, Lucille.

I'm not even sure Gus minded. As long as it helped the team, anything was all right by him. Torchy would be pumping her down in the boathouse long after swimming weather and fifty feet away Gus would sit in the family room with the television blasting and his big, beefy hand wrapped around a fourth double rye and Coke and he'd turn to me — me always drinking milk straight from the carton because I was convinced Coke would turn my face into its own Sudbury — and he'd squish up his fat eyes and say something like, "Dirty fucking Jesus Christ, Bats — aren't them two ever coming in?"

Maybe Gus liked the idea. Maybe Torchy pumping Lucille, like Gus's exaggerated swearing, somehow made him feel more like one of the boys. Torchy was always saying how Gus didn't want to be the owner, he wanted to be stickboy. He didn't look down on us; he looked up, like we were something he'd never been able to be. I'm sure he'd always been too fat to play the game. Even at supper the sweat would be rolling down through his greasy hair just from the scramble for the third porkchop. He competed with his mouth, always cursing, promising, praising, backstabbing, lying. Harmless, though. And kind. And simple. Lucille's virginity probably had as much value to him as an empty refrigerator. Gus Demers's theory was the same for screwing, eating and hockey: if you see an opening, fill it up.

Lucille. She was seventeen years old, a brilliant student who applied her ample brains to far more than isosceles triangles. She beat Ed Sullivan to the Beatles and San Francisco to free love. A genius who never guessed wrong. Torchy used to say she was fine as long as you kept a paper bag over her body, which was a bit nasty because Lucille did have a marvellous face, and fine, long brown hair sheltering fawn eyes. Her flaw was no tits, that's all, and maybe a few extra pounds on her hips. Torchy was convinced he'd failed somehow, having gotten into her pants almost immediately, but under her brassiere never. "It's like a goddamned Band-aid," he'd say. "I bet if she took it off her little titties would flake off."

I never found out. She kept her brassiere on for me too.

For months it had been my impression that Lucille was Torchy's girl, though Torchy clearly felt no commitment beyond the boat-house, the back seat of the Valiant, the television room, the ping-pong table, and, once, he claimed, the breakfast nook, where the cornflakes stuck to Lucille's ass. Lucille was like a magazine Torchy kept hidden under the mattress. He reached for her when he needed it, dropped her the second he was finished. And, again like a copy of *Gent*, she took it all, lying low and never changing expression from one session to the next. I wondered what it was she got out of it all. It never occurred to me that perhaps she just liked it.

One Sunday night shortly after nine I was lying on the couch eating a sardine sandwich and half-watching *Bonanza*. I'm con-vinced it was that episode where Hoss meets the leprechauns, or maybe I'm just remembering magic and nothing else; whatever, that night it finally happened to me. Lucille's parents were out to dinner at the in-laws and Torchy was on the milk run back from Kirkland Lake, where he'd gone for his mother's birthday. No one home but the two of us.

Lucille came downstairs, wearing her housecoat and carrying a huge ice cream float.

"Any good?" she asked.

"Oh, not bad. Hoss has fallen in with these little Irish lepre-chauns."

"Sounds great," she said, with her marvelous snottiness. She fell into the chair opposite, flat on her back, her head barely tilted up by a pillow so she could get at her straw. She made a loud, sucking sound, not even at the bottom of the glass yet.

"I'm bored," she said. "Aren't you?"

I turned to answer her, but couldn't. *She'd forgotten to put her panties on!* She sat, legs wide apart, housecoat riding like a can-opy over the entrance. I couldn't possibly tell her. I turned back to *Bonanza*, aware of the blood rising within, in two places.

She slurped again, louder.

"You like that show better than this one?" she asked.

I couldn't turn. I couldn't answer. I turned the other direction and slapped the pillow straight and shifted.

A slurp. "I thought," she said, laughter teasing in her voice, "that you were the league bad boy, eh?"

"I get my share," I said. I meant penalties, but I know she didn't take it that way. Lucille howled with laughter.

I heard her set her drink down. "Maybe you'd like to show me just how bad you are?" she said.

I swallowed and said nothing. Suddenly Hoss vanished and the picture whistled away in shrinking light. Lucille had kicked off Gus's remote control that he'd rigged up to deal with Lestoil commercials.

"Well?" she said. She had her left leg cocked over the side of the chair, dangling.

"Well," I said. I didn't know what else to say.

"Well?"

She stood, letting the housecoat drop over her shoulders onto the floor. No panties, but a bra. I stared, remembering Torchy's line that he'd heard of "A" cups but Lucille had the saucers, but I hardly felt like laughing. I coughed and covered my mouth, but she took my hand and pulled it away and fell into my lap and mouth at the same time.

Her tongue tasted of Pepsodent; mine, shocked by hers, must have tasted of sardines — half the sandwich was still sitting on the coffee table, with half a dill—but she hardly seemed to mind. I'd French-kissed before — I wasn't *that* innocent — but up until Lucille I'd been the instigator and I'd believed tongue-touching was simply a wetter, warmer way of holding hands. Lucille tongue-kissed like Hinky Harris stickhandled, fast and with so many deceptive dekes that my own tongue flattened itself to one side in terror.

My only thought was that I didn't know what to do. Fortunately, it didn't matter; Lucille took complete charge, even to unbuckling my pants. She kept on her brassiere; I kept on my socks. In thirty seconds there I was, fitted to her like a plug to a socket while she supplied the current. She pumped; she bucked; she groaned, moaned, grunted, shunted; and never once did her tongue leave my mouth, though God knows I could have done with a deep breath. This was harder than starts and stops in practice.

I'd never even thought to put on protection and suddenly I wondered what I should be doing. I wished I'd taken my socks off and then I'd have something to cap it with if I yanked out. But it never came to pass. Lucille's big hips bounced us over to the remote control and onto it and suddenly Pa Cartwright was shouting at us over the dinner table. If he thought Little Joe should hop to it, he never saw us. Before I realized it was Pa shouting and not Gus, I had my pants back on and was reaching, instinctively, for the sardine sandwich. Lucille had also been spooked and was holding her housecoat to her already covered chest — what else to you call it when breasts aren't involved? — and from upstairs came the sound of a door dinging open.

Five minutes later I was working on the pickle, nodding while Gus argued that Chrysler's slant-six engine was going to run General Motors out of business and then we wouldn't have to suffer all this commercial shit at the end of *Bonanza.*

Thank God he didn't ask about the show itself.

I find Torchy Bender difficult to explain. One example seems to cancel the next. On a trip back from the Soo after an exhibition match I saw Torchy's hand sneak off with Dennis Bannerman's leather briefcase — D.S.B. stamped in phoney lettering along the handle. Bannerman was my first defense partner, a jerk in Perry Como sweaters who refused to swear and who wrote up biology experiments on the bus while the rest of us were playing hearts. He fell asleep on the late haul down Highway 17, his homework done, his prayers said, and when he opened up his briefcase next morning in Grade 13 physics, he discovered Torchy had convinced the entire first line to take a dump in it.

I saw Torchy cry the day they shot President Kennedy. I saw Torchy pick up a garter snake and snap it like a whip, the guts turning out of its mouth as he tossed the reptile in a high, twisting circle toward a group of terrified public school girls.

I saw Torchy pick up a small girl who'd lost her mother at what passed for the Sudbury Plaza. He settled her down, dried her tears and then walked around carrying the child and shouting the mother's name like a bullhorn until he found her leafing through romance magazines in Steinberg's.

I saw Torchy steal Gus Demers's .22-caliber semi-automatic Cooey and sneak over to the Ramsay Lake Golf and Country Club, hide in the cedars just off the 250-yard mark on the eleventh hole and use a mushroom long rifle to blow up a Titleist another twenty yards to the left. When the foursome that was playing the eleventh hit the fairway in terror, Torchy coolly sprayed six shots over their heads, running for it only when the clip ran out.

I saw Torchy impersonate poor Alvin Dorsett's stutter until Dorsett broke down and quit the team and then I saw Torchy turn around and talk him into coming back out and threaten to drop the first person that made a joke about his friend Alvin.

I saw Torchy phone his mother in Kirkland Lake every Sunday night at ten, the voice rising from his throat so childish and removed from the brute who held the receiver that it looked, at first sight, like a telephone joke, Torchy phoning up some poor old woman and pretending he was something he was not. In a way he was; in another way, not.

I saw Torchy Bender quietly pick up first Snap and then Clearasil at a time when it was beginning to look as if my pimples were growing me rather than me them. It had gotten to the point where I was afraid to shake hands for fear pus would explode out of my nose. Torchy bullied me to wash carefully each night — not, however, with Dr. Jarry's pumice stone, which he threw out when I wasn't looking — and then go to sleep with a brown mask of Clearasil, which I would scrub off in the morning. For a week I looked like a trampled strawberry patch, but then, mysteriously, the season of Batterinski's pimples ended.

It was the least the bastard could have done for me, considering my teeth. I lost them in a four-pointer against North Bay Trappers. Whoever won would head into the second part of the season in first place, so it was a game we were all up for—but no one quite so much as Torchy, who was also chasing the Soo's Reinholdt for the first-half lead in league scoring.

Torchy was in magnificent form, moving in on the Trappers' net like a hummingbird at Batcha's honeysuckle and leaving the North Bay defense slamming the boards in frustration. Even with the crowd on him and the Bay's thug, Simon Billings, chopping away at his ankles, Torchy still managed to score twice and set up a third—a carom pass to me at the point and a low, hard one that Alvin Dorsett somehow tipped in as Billings flattened him with a cross-check — and we went into the first intermission up 3–0. All thanks to Torchy.   Up 6–2 halfway through the third I went down Bill Gadsby-style — knees flat out, hands to the side the way Al Jolson finished "Mammy" — and was just turning my face away from Billings's exaggerated slapper when I felt a painless, almost soft, certainly silent push against my mouth that sent me over in a perfect backwards somersault and left me spitting blood and my remaining front teeth onto the left face-off circle. There was no pain whatsoever.

I looked up and Torchy was bent down looking worried. "That

fucking Billings," he said in a low hiss. "He did it on purpose."

I leapt up in a rage, still spitting blood and teeth, and spun like a cornered raccoon. Billings was standing off to the side, leaning on his stick and talking to a teammate, with a big, laughing smile on his puss. I wrestled Torchy's stick away and ran at Billings, holding the blade out at him like it was a stropped razor. His eyes nearly popped. The linesman caught me for a moment, and before I could shake free Billings had turned and was skating toward his bench. I reached out and tripped him and he dove headfirst, turning and wrapping his arms and gloves around his head as he crashed back first into the boards. I could see his eyes: afraid to look; afraid not to look. He squirmed like a netted trout.

The blood was warm and thick on my chin. It felt good. There was still no pain. I felt warm all over. Around me was total panic: referees' whistles, the crowd howling, the Trappers' bench screaming. I felt none of this. No panic, fear or even anger. I felt sensible, knowing the purpose of the coming act. Time had slowed respectfully, as if this was somehow more important than the game. Revenge was due and I was delivering it. Billings's arms flailed and I picked an opening carefully, without hurry. Torchy's stick came down once between an elbow and a face; the stick snapped at the blade; Billings opened his mouth to scream, but all that came out were bubbles, red.

As far as I was concerned it was over. Hockey, unfortunately, is without proper balance. If it worked sensibly, Billings and I would have gone off to get our stitches, the game would have resumed and, with luck, maybe I would have made it back for the last shift. But no one else was willing to admit it was over. Both linesmen were hanging off my shoulders when this short little bald-headed man in a Trappers' booster jacket hit the ice after climbing over the screen and he grabs up Billings's stick and comes slipping across the ice at me, his face all twisted up and the stick cutting madly out in front of him like a scythe.

What could I do? With the linesmen on me I was a dead duck. But Torchy, God bless him, was free and charged the old geezer like he was coming one-on-one with me and I was the goaltender. Torchy blindsided him with a hip and the booster spun twice completely in his rubber boots before he buckled straight over backwards, his head striking the ice with a sound that made me think of the hollow wild cucumber we used to fire against trucks on

Highway 60 so drivers would think they'd struck something big.

But this was no joke. He was hurt — I could tell by the way he stayed down, not even hoisting back on reflex alone, but staying on the ice like he'd gone halfway through and was stuck. The other linesman and the referee both jumped Torchy, and a good thing too.

The crowd went berserk. They threw rubber boots, programs, cups, even a set of car keys at us. Three North Bay cops had to come out onto the ice and escort the two of us, first to the dressing room and then out to the bus, where a crowd of punks screamed insults, knowing the presence of the cops meant their fists wouldn't have to follow through on their tongues. They had a heyday. By the time I got out to the bus with an ice pack my mouth had swollen shut. I couldn't even yell back at them.

It didn't stop Torchy, though. As soon as he was sure the door was locked tight, he mooned them.

It took eighteen stitches for me and four sessions for plate fitting at Gus Demers's dentist. Billings, I heard, needed thirty stitches, so there's no doubt who won that exchange. Torchy also lost when Demers refused to let him dress next time we went back to North Bay, a decision which Torchy has always claimed cost him the league scoring title. Stupid bastard, Gus probably saved his life.

I found out later the little bald man was Billings's father.

I found out much later that Torchy Bender had tipped the shot, so Billings had been completely innocent.

"But you told me he'd done it on purpose," I said.

"He was pissing me off. I wanted him off my back, okay?"

Maybe I should have hated him, but I loved Torchy forever — at least I thought it would be forever — after that. I guess I was one of Jaja's true Poles even then, always walking alone. No one had ever fought my fights for me; no one had ever been expected to; damn sure no one had ever been asked to. But Torchy had done it on his own, and given a shit less for the consequences. He did it for *me*, and as long as I could remember no one had ever done anything for me before.

He made it rough, but I stuck by him. I awoke to a pillow in my face, usually, and more than once to a bare butt impersonating an elephant charge about six inches from my nose. I had to lie for

him and Lucille. I had to let him crib from my history notes —
funny, it just struck me that history was my best subject, so I
must have more Jaja in me than I realize — and then, when he
failed and I passed, I somehow let him talk me into quitting Grade
11 with him.

But what can I say? The one time I needed him, he was there.
And if Torchy Bender was willing to walk with the guy he loved
to call "the big, dumb Polack," I was willing to let him walk and
get away with it. But only Torchy.

In hockey it is called a "rep," short, of course, for "reputation."
Mine grew out of North Bay: one game, one moment, the clock
stopped, the game in suspension — and yet it was this, nothing to
do with what took place while clocks ran in sixty-eight other
games, that put me on the all-star team with more votes than
Torchy. Half as many, however, as Bobby Orr. But still, it was Orr
and Batterinski, the two defensemen, whom they talked most
about in Ontario junior.

Bobby Orr would get the cover of *Maclean's*. I almost got the
cover of *Police Gazette* after the Billings incident. My rep was made.
The *North Bay Nugget's* nickname for me, Frankenstein, spread
throughout the league. I had my own posters in Kitchener; there
were threats in Kingston and spray-paint messages on our bus in
Sault Ste. Marie; late, frantic calls at the Demers house from
squeaky young things wanting to speak to the "monster."

They didn't know me. I didn't know myself. But I loved being
talked about in the same conversations as the white brushcut
from Parry Sound. Orr they spoke of as if he was the Second
Coming — they sounded like Poppa praising the Madonna on the
church in Warsaw; for me it was the same feeling for both Orr
and the Madonna — I couldn't personally see it.

Orr had grown since I'd seen him first in Vernon, but he was
still only sixteen in 1964 and seemed much too short to be compared to Harvey and Howe, as everyone was doing. He'd gone
straight from bantam to junior, but Gus Demers still said he was
just another in a long list of junior hockey's flashes-in-the-pan.
Another Nesterenko, another Cullen.

We met Oshawa Generals in that year's playoffs, and the papers
in Oshawa and Sudbury played up the Batterinski-Orr side of
it. "Beauty and the Beast," the Oshawa *Times* had it. The *Star*

countered with "Batterinski's Blockade," pointing out that the Hardrocks' strategy was to have Batterinski make sure Orr never got near the net, though no one ever spoke to me about it. I presume it was understood.

On March 28 we met on their home ice, the advantage going to them by virtue of a better record throughout the season. I said not a single word on the bus ride down, refusing to join Torchy in his dumb-ass Beatle songs, refusing even to get up and wade back to the can, though I'd had to go since Orillia. My purpose was to exhibit strength and I could not afford the slightest opening. I had to appear superhuman to the rest of the team: not needing words, nor food, nor bodily functions.

If I could have ridden down in the equipment box I would have, letting the trainer unfold me and tighten my skates just before the warm-up, sitting silent as a puck, resilient as my shin pads, dangerous as the blades. The ultimate equipment: me.

I maintained silence through the "Queen" and allowed myself but one chop at Frog Larocque's goal pads, then set up. Orr and I were like reflections, he standing solid and staring up at the clock from one corner, me doing the same at the other, both looking at time, both thinking of each other. We were the only ones in the arena, the crowd's noise simply the casing in which we would move, the other players simply the setting to force the crowd's focus to us. Gus Demers had advised me to level Orr early, to establish myself. Coach Therrian wanted me to wait for Orr, keep him guessing. I ignored them all. They weren't involved. Just Orr and me.

His style had changed little since bantam. Where all the other players seemed bent over, concentrating on something taking place below them, Orr still seemed to be sitting at a table as he played, eyes as alert as a poker player, not interested in his own hands or feet or where the object of the game was. I was fascinated by him and studied him intently during the five minutes I sat in the penalty box for spearing some four-eyed whiner in the first period. What made Orr effective was that he had somehow shifted the main matter of the game from the puck to him. By anticipating, he had our centers looking for him, not their wingers, and passes were directed *away* from him, not *to* someone on our team. By doing this, and by knowing this himself, he had assumed control of the Hardrocks as well as the Generals.

I stood at the penalty box door yanking while the timekeeper held for the final seconds. I had seen how to deal with Orr. If the object of the game had become him, not the puck, I would simply put Orr through his own net.

We got a penalty advantage toward the end of the period and coach sent me out to set up the power play. I was to play center point, ready to drop quickly in toward the net rather than remaining in the usual point position along the boards and waiting for a long shot and tip-in. Therrian had devised this play, I knew, from watching Orr, though he maintained it was his own invention. I never argued. I never even spoke. I was equipment, not player, and in that way I was dependable, predictable, certain.

Torchy's play, at center, was to shoulder the Oshawa center out of the face-off circle while Chancey, playing drop-back left wing, fed the puck back to me, breaking in. A basketball play, really, with me fast-breaking and Torchy pic-ing. The crowd was screaming but I couldn't hear. I was listening for Orr, hoping he might say something that would show me his flaw, hoping he might show involvement rather than disdain. But he said nothing. He stared up at the clock for escape, the numbers meaningless, the score irrelevant. He stood, stick over pads, parallel to the ice, back also parallel, eyes now staring through the scars of the ice for what might have been his own reflection. Just like me, once removed from the crowd's game, lost in his own contest.

The puck dropped and Torchy drove his shoulder so hard into the Generals' center I heard the grunt from the blueline. Chancey was tripped as he went for the puck, but swept it as he fell. I took it on my left skate blade, kicking it forward to my stick, slowing it, timing it, raising back for a low, hard slapper from just between the circles. I could sense Orr. Not see him. I was concentrating on the puck. But I could sense him the way you know when someone is staring at you from behind. I raised the stick higher, determined to put the shot right through the bastard if necessary. I heard him go down, saw the blond brushcut spinning just outside the puck as he slid toward me, turning his pads to catch the shot. His eyes were wide open as his head passed the puck; he stared straight at it, though it could, if I shot now, rip his face right off the skull. He did not flinch; he did not even blink. He stared the way a poker player might while saying he'll hold. Orr knew precisely what my timing was before I myself knew. I saw

him spin past, knew what he was doing, but could not stop; my
shot crunched into his pads and away, harmlessly.

The center Torchy had hit dove toward the puck and it bounced
back at me, off my toe and up along the ankle, rolling like a ball in
a magician's trick. I kicked but could not stop it. The puck trickled and suddenly was gone. I turned, practically falling. *It was
Orr!* Somehow he'd regained his footing even faster than I and
was racing off in that odd sitting motion toward our net.

I gave chase, now suddenly aware of the crowd. Their noise
seemed to break through an outer, protective eardrum. There
were no words, but I was suddenly filled with insult as the screams
tore through me, ridiculing. It seemed instant, this change from
silently raising the stick for the certain goal, the sense that I was
gliding on air, suspended, controlling even the breath of this ignorant crowd. Now there was no sense of gliding or silence or
control. I was flailing, chopping at a short sixteen-year-old who
seemed completely oblivious to the fact that Batterinski was coming for him.

I felt my left blade slip and my legs stutter. I saw him slipping
farther and farther out of reach, my strides choppy and ineffec-
tive, his brief, effortless and amazingly successful. I swung with
my stick at his back, causing the noise to rise. I dug in but he was
gone, a silent, blond brushcut out for a skate in an empty arena.

I dove, but it was no use. My swinging stick rattled off his ankle
guards and I turned in my spill in time to see the referee's hand
raise for a delayed penalty. I was already caught so I figured I
might as well make it worthwhile. I regained my feet and rose
just as Orr came in on Larocque, did something with his stick
and shoulder that turned Frog into a lifesize cardboard poster of
a goaltender, and neatly tucked the puck into the corner of the
net.

The crowd roared, four thousand jack-in-the-boxes suddenly
sprung, all of them laughing at me. Orr raised his hands in salute
and turned, just as I hit him.

It was quiet again, quiet as quickly as the noise had first burst
through. I felt him against me, shorter but probably as solid. I
smelled him, not skunky the way I got myself, but the smell of
Juicy Fruit chewing gum. I gathered him in my arms, both of us
motionless but for the soar of our skates, and I aimed him carefully and deliberately straight through the boards at the goal judge.

Orr did not even bother to look at me. It was like the theory
you read about car accidents, that the best thing you can do is
relax. Orr rode in my arms contentedly, acceptingly, neither angry,
nor afraid, nor surprised. We moved slowly, deliberately, together.
I could see the goal judge leaping, open-mouthed, back from the
boards, bouncing off his cage like a gorilla being attacked by
another with a chain. I saw his coffee burst through the air as we
hit, the gray-brown circles slowly rising up and away and straight
into his khaki coat. The boards gave; they seemed to give forever,
folding back toward the goal judge, then groaning, then snapping us out and down in a heap as the referee's whistle shrieked
in praise.

I landed happy, my knee rising into his leg as hard as I could
manage, the soft grunt of expelled air telling me I had finally made
contact with the only person in the building who would truly
understand.

If it would stop there, the game would be perfect. But I knew,
having taken my best shot, I would have to deal with the rebound.
My hope was to clear it quickly. I pushed Orr and began to stand,
only to be wrapped by the linesman trying to work a full nelson
around my shoulders. I went to him gratefully, shifting with false
anger, yanking hard but not too hard, according to the unwrit-
ten fighter-linesman agreement. He was talking in my ear the
way one does to calm down a dog who has just smelled porcupine.

"Easy now, fella. Just take it easy now, okay?"

I said nothing. I pulled hard; he pulled back hard. He twisted
me away; I went with him, scowling, delighted.

"Get the trainer!" I heard the referee shout to one of the
Generals.

I twisted back. Orr was still down on the ice. The other linesman stood above, waiting to embrace him, but Orr just lay there,
eyes shut, face expressionless.

"Chickenshit!" one of their larger players yelled at me and then
looked away quickly, afraid to own up to his words. I lunged
toward him, but gratefully let the linesman reel me in.

"Just easy now! Easy, easy, easy," he said in my ear. I felt like
barking, just to throw him off.

The referee signalled to the linesman to get me to the box, and
I let him wrestle me over with only a few stops and twists. Some
of the crowd was hanging up over the glass and screens, throw-

ing things, spitting, screaming. They looked like the muskrat Danny had once taken on a tip trap and failed to drown; we'd put it in a box and stabbed cattail stems through the cardboard at the little fucker until it ran at the screen we'd placed over top, screeching and spitting at us as if it would have torn us to pieces if it hadn't been blocked from us. These rats seemed voluntarily caged. Unlike the muskrat, they welcomed their confinement. If they broke through and got to me they'd have trouble finding the courage to ask for my autograph.

Orr did not return to the game. We won 4–1 on Torchy's hattrick. I scored the fourth on a desperate empty-net attempt by Oshawa, and the slow slider from center was booed all the way into the net, making it as sweet as if I had skated through the entire team and scooped it high into a tight corner as the last man back slashed my feet out from under me. I even asked the linesman for the puck, just to rub it in.

But such sweetness never seems to last. The X-rays went against us, Orr returned for game three and after six we were out of it, retired for the season. Orr scored or set up seventeen of the Generals' twenty-two goals over this stretch. I scored twice, set up three and spent sixty-two minutes in the penalty box, twelve of them for boarding him. But Orr and I did not make contact again until May 19, 1974, when Eddie Van Impe, Moose, the Watsons and I set up the defensive minefield that even the Great Orr with perfect knees couldn't have penetrated. Philadelphia 1, Boston 0. The Flyers take their first Stanley Cup in six games.

Thinking back on it now, I don't know why I went home that summer. I think I told Torchy and some others it was so I could get in shape, work out, add some upper-body strength, but it was a lie. I think really I had some vision of Batterinski returning as the conquering hero. But how to do it? Could I walk up and down Black Donald Hill carrying my scrapbook, wearing the three team jackets, pointing out the new teeth, carrying the team trophy for top defenseman? I had no idea. I was just going home for the first summer back since my first year in Vernon. No more wrestling with the front-end loaders at the mine. No swelter in the smelter. Just Poppa, Ig and me.

And Danny.

Shit, and Batcha.

At twelve noon on June 4 the Pembroke bus pulled in to the White Rose at Pomerania. I checked on my new Timex with the date and "The Hardrocks" where there should have been numbers. A gift from Gus to the team. I wondered who would notice first.

Outside the air-conditioned Gray Coach the air was thick and humid, a haze turning Black Donald Hill into a ghost where the church began and the steeple vanished. I felt foolish not having a car. Torchy and I had become so used to the white Valiant that we had come to regard it as personal property, much like Lucille. I had a suitcase, a duffle bag and that cursed two-mile walk ahead of me.

No thoughts of a glorious parade through town now, only that of trying to slink home without being seen. The big jesus hockey hero, carrying his own luggage, walking. Oshawa had given Bobby Orr his own car so he could race back home to Mommy and Daddy in Parry Sound. Gus had given me a watch, so I'd know how long it would take to walk.

"You make your old Poppa very happy, Felix. You know that, don't you?"

Dat. Yes, Poppa, I said to myself, I know dat only too well.

Poppa chewed on a pig's knuckle while I nodded in agreement. I had forgotten. He'd written and asked me to consider coming home for the summer, for him and for Ig and for Batcha. Perhaps the decision hadn't been mine to make at all. No wonder I'd been confused as to why I'd ever come back.

Poppa looked happy, if older. Every second seedling on his face was now white and the effect was a deathly look, much like the bums in Sudbury's Borgia district back of the Nickel Inn. But Poppa had probably shaved in the morning. I'd forgotten how black and tight his skin was, and how the beard always looked like he'd be better hammering it back rather than shaving.

Ig sat beside me. Same table. Same dishes. Same scraps, for all I could tell. The only improvement I could make out was that Poppa's damn whining Puck was now housetrained and no longer pissed all over the floor. Ig had a tin of Nestle's Quik open and was spooning the crystals directly into his dry mouth. He suddenly seemed aged himself, like he'd gone to sleep last night a happy little boy and had awakened in the morning slow and senile.

Ig had Jaja's liver spots now, and neck wattles. His hand shook as he worked the spoon up and down, in and out. He no longer bothered with the Scotch-tape hair; he wore a red-and-white-striped Ivy League cap now, a bit too large, pulled down nearly to his eyebrows with the front snap open, and it was filthy.

But it was Ig, with the same milk-clear eyes and, as always, totally delighted to see me. Batcha had said hello crisply and then gone immediately to her room to lie down. To hell with her — I hadn't come for her anyway.

"There might be some work with the highways," Poppa said, still chewing. He meant painting craphouses for the tourists, but this made it sound more respectable.

"I've got nearly four hundred dollars," I said. Pretty impressive, considering Gus Demers was only forking out thirty a week.

"Four hundred dollars," Ig repeated, still spooning chocolate. "Holy Moley, that's a lot, Feelie."

Poppa took another knuckle out of the pickle jar. "I'll be drawing later. You can help me cut if you like."

"Sure," I said. "Be good for the forearms."

"Pulp's down this year."

Dis. I nodded. I didn't care.

Ig pinched my arms and shook his head, giggling. Did he want to see if *I* was awake?

"I might not be able to pay you," Poppa said.

"I don't want anything."

Poppa nodded, picked with a fork at his teeth. Until now, the fork hadn't been used. He held the fork out to look for success, then stared at me through the prongs.

"When do you find out?"

"I'll get a letter."

"And?"

"And if I get invited to camp I'll be gone."

Poppa picked without thinking. "What are the chances of that?" *Dat.*

"Good."

"How good?"

"Very good. Excellent."

Poppa wasn't satisfied. In his book no one dealt with strangers without getting screwed.

"And how does this 'contract' work?" he asked.

"They pay me while I'm at camp, and then if I make the team I get more. It depends on what level I make or whether I make it at all, I guess."

"And if you do make it?"

"All the way?"

"American league, say."

"Maybe $10,000. Maybe $15,000 if I stay with the top team."

Ig whistled and hit my shoulder with delight. It could have been fifteen thousand chocolate crystals, for all he cared. He just liked long-sounding numbers. He had no comprehension of how they got there.

Poppa wiped the grease off his mouth onto the back of his hand, the back of his hand onto his pants.

"Who is taking care of all this?"

"Mr. Wheeler."

The name meant nothing to Poppa. Hadn't he read my letters?

"You know, the guy who wants to represent me."

"Uhhh."

"Vincent Wheeler, the agent," I added impatiently.

"Can you trust him?"

"Of course."

"Where's he from?"

"New York City."

I loved the way it came off my tongue. Like an answer to a quiz, like a secret, like a prayer. Once I said New York City Poppa was convinced. Wheeler must be the best. Poppa couldn't comprehend another human getting by in Sudbury, let alone surviving in New York City. Obviously, Wheeler knew what he was doing.

"He's the buy who signed Terry Bartholomew with Chicago last year," I added.

Ig giggled. Poppa closed the pickle jar.

"How much will he take?"

"I don't know. Ten percent, I guess. The more he gets for me, the more he gets for himself. That's how it works, Poppa."

"Only there, son." *Der.*

Poppa was finished with agent talk. He stood, the smell of gasoline and sawdust rising with him.

"Let's go, then. Time's wasting."

So much for the vision of my homecoming. My scrapbook still sat in the suitcase, seventy-three filled pages of clippings from the Sudbury *Star*, North Bay *Nugget*, Kitchener-Waterloo *Record*, Oshawa *Times*, Peterborough *Examiner*, Toronto *Telegram* and the *The Globe and Mail*. Pictures for Ig, words for Poppa, and they hadn't even seen it yet. I couldn't just go and get it. That would ruin the effect. They should beg it out of me.

But Poppa said *Time's wasting*. Almost as if it had wasted so quickly no one had noticed I was gone most of the time over all those years. I may as well have walked in to Hatkoski's for a haircut and just come back, for all it seemed to matter. No glory, no party, nothing. It was just like I'd never left.

Even Danny Shannon was much the same. Forty pounds heavier, maybe, his walk even looser, if possible, hair thick and dandied, same smile, but everything else the same: loon calls, *ugga-buggas*, booze plans, sex jokes. He had no interest in hearing about Sudbury or about Billings or about Orr or about the new league penalty record or the all-star selection or even about my chances of making it. He wanted to stuff his green '62 Chevy with his new chums from down at O'Malley mill — Tiny Fetterly, who couldn't have made our old Pomeranian team as stickboy, Dominic Toposki, Stan Lacha, any mix of a half-dozen others — and then he wanted to do nothing but drive around making up lies about his year in Vernon and having me verify them for him. Talking about Maureen the Queen like she was Ann-Margaret or something.

He was using me, the bastard, and I was helpless. I knew if I balked he could always tell the true side of what happened between Maureen and me, and I would rather have Bobby Orr make a goat of me in front of four thousand hometown fans than have that get out. As far as I was concerned, he could use me all he wanted as long as I got equal time. But though I waited it never came.

I had told Torchy that Pomerania was like stepping into a time machine, but I hadn't realized how right I was. The sole concession to modern times was cars. The guys Danny worked with worshipped Detroit the way the older Poles thought of Czestochowa. The new confessional was Household Finance over in Renfrew, undoubtedly with the same proportion of lies. Danny claimed his Chevy had clocked 117 down on the flats. He had chrome moons, Lake pipes, a modified Thrush shift and a hydraulically suspended record player that could take 45-rpm records. All this, parked each night in front of a house that only last summer got running cold water, that still used an outhouse, that burned slabs from the mill in a welded oil drum with duct-work hammered out of truck fenders, that didn't get a single newspaper or magazine in the mail, that didn't, in truth, ever get mail.

If I'd been a car they might have been impressed. After all, I had shut down Bobby Orr.

But they could care less. Anything beyond Pomerania lay like snakes below the bed. Danny and his friends were perfectly will-ing to accept anything about me that was still Pomerania but the other stuff I could keep. They weren't interested in taking the blinders from their eyes to see what it was I had become.

Piss on them. I looked around Pomerania and saw water to haul and wood to chop, freezing all winter, slapping flies all summer, rotting turnips and soft carrots and wizened-up pota-toes from February on, disaster when you missed your moose, people willing to take a quick deer at the expense of a front fender, people sweating about what the priest knew, hating Hatkoski of the barber for his two-year-old Buick, cursing the endless stream of American tourists and camper trailers and Airstreams and the songs of rich, blond-haired kids as their chartered buses hurtled through town on their way to the summer camps in Algonquin Park, where roughing it meant having to share a horse. Piss on them all.

It finally came to me that I had been wrong. The outside world wasn't the place to escape to; Pomerania was the escape, was still the escape just as it had been a hundred years ago when all the frightened, petrified Jazdas and Dombrowskis and Hatkoskis and Batterinskis were told to head up the Bonneclare River until they came to a big damn hill that wouldn't grow anything and would kill most of them before they reached forty, but where at least the Russians and the Prussians and the damn Germans wouldn't find them. Pomerania was still their fortress. All that had changed was they no longer felt a need to defend it.

Who would want in?

At least Poppa now had a telephone. One long, two short. It quickly got so I couldn't bear to be in the house: every ring would leave me wrapped in cold, clammy slime. At least the mail didn't come to me. I went for it, and in that way felt protected when away from box 14 in the rusted green row by Dombrowski's turnaround. But when I did go I felt weak, then weaker yet when the box revealed nothing but its usual black, empty space.

The work was a welcome distraction. Poppa landed a contract hauling for O'Malley Brothers back of the abandoned grist mill on the creek. Seven in the morning and we'd be stepping lightly across the broken trestle and off into the bush, forcing wet, cold pants through yet more spruce undergrowth. I carried the two chainsaws, Poppa the gasoline, oil mix, six-quart basket of screwdrivers, wrenches, chain tightener, sharpener, lunch and extra spark plugs. Two miles straight back to avoid the bog along the creek, up over the hardwood hill following a blaze he'd set with orange fluorescent paint he'd snitched from the highway's depot, down the bluff, across a slope of birch and poplar, over a smaller creek and then into the spruce and jack pine and tamarack bog where the creek led in to Kaszuby Lake.

Poppa went rain or shine. June was mostly shine, and by midmonth the mosquitoes were like a second shirt by the time we'd arrived at the cut. Citronella didn't work, nor 6–12, finally only tump pots of old oil, rags and our own pee, pots that worked but which we couldn't light until we got to the clearing, meaning the two-mile hike in was a free buffet for the little bastards. It made the work more of a distraction, less of a welcome. I bought a couple of green hats with cheesecloth netting for our heads, took to long-sleeved shirts, tucking my pants into gray work socks and even gloves, but all to no avail. Poppa said nothing, blinking through his shell of flies like they were nothing more than the confusion of first wakening.

I remember we cut all that month. Poppa felled and I trimmed; then, the last week, cousin Jazda came in with his horses and we hauled what would move easily out to the bush trail coming in at the south side of the lake and moved the rest with a rope system Poppa devised for hauling pulp from the swamps. Two men on block and tackle, the other, me, trussed up like a work horse in hip waders, slugging the trees out to where the horses could move without breaking through the bog. When we were finished we had better than two hundred cord and I felt strong enough to put both of Bobby Orr's knees permanently in the goal judge's cage.

School let out on the twenty-eighth, and the first tourists passed through town that evening. The pulp would have to wait until fall and early winter now. Summer meant live bait and four out of every five dollars Poppa would earn this year. It could have been much more, but Poppa had no imagination. A mile up from the White Rose he had nailed a single plywood board to a tree with one large word, "Bait," written on it, and below that two more, "Batterinski's Road."

"It's useless," I said.

"People find me," he said.

"You'd get two, three, maybe five times as many if they knew exactly where," I argued. They can't tell from that whether you're a hundred yards or a hundred miles away or in what direction. You could be in Vernon for all they know."

"They find me."

Dey could have him. Poppa didn't understand the first thing about selling. Riley, despite his faults, knew he'd starve waiting for people to find his hardware store. You had to suck them in.

I tore down the sign. Danny drove me to Renfrew and I bought a proper stencil and a small brush and two cans of paint, one black, one white. I got a large plywood board from town and spent the weekend turning it into two signs, one for each direction on the main highway. I nailed them back-to-back at the end of the road where it bleeds into the main highway, each with a huge arrow at the bottom pointing up our road.

BATTERINSKI'S LIVE BAIT
NEXT TURN
TWO MILES IN
ALWAYS OPEN, 24 HRS.
Worms
Leeches
Frogs
Minnows
Crayfish
FREE FISHING HINTS

"I have no leeches," Poppa said.

"You say you're out of them."

"What does it mean, 'free fishing hints'?"

"It means you tell them to go over to Black Donald for pike or up Sabine creek for speckles."

Poppa thought the whole thing absurd and said he wouldn't lie to people, not even tourists. But once the car horns started honking he seemed to find the lies easier to hold on to than the leeches or crayfish, which we never seemed to have in stock. Ig took to sitting down at the end of the drive on a big rock, cap pulled down almost over his eyes, and at the first sound of an engine he'd come running up screaming for Poppa or me that we had customers.

Customers. I wondered what they thought. First thing I'd check would be their license plates. Michigan, Pennsylvania, New York — and if Ontario I'd check where they bought their big cars, Ottawa, Toronto, Hamilton. Stationwagons bottoming on the ruts, Cadillacs humming as the power steering ground around the final lane turn, tiny Morris Minors and Volkswagens with two bars where they would be tagged on behind silver Airstream trailers. What did they think in their pork-pie hats and Bermuda shorts and once-a-year sissy beards? They'd pull in with their soft bodies and obvious wealth and fine teeth and be met by an aging retard with a goofy cap pulled halfway over his head, giggling and walking around the cars trying to see himself in the mirror or tapping on the windows and smiling toothlessly at the little boys and girls who'd shrink back and shriek while their father held onto his brand-new sparkling white Styrofoam minnow pail and pretended everything was just fine — all the while watching poor Ig like he's a strange dog about to lift his leg. Then along would come Poppa, all gruffness and pitch-black hands and broken nails and egg yellow caked along his chin and the smell of small engines, worms, coal oil, chickens and gutted fish wafting up from him like a shed pail that's just been opened after a year.

"Yah?" Poppa would say.

"You got any worms?"

"Yah."

"Great. Great day, huh? Great day for fishing."

"How many?"

Nervous, shaking, desperate for small talk that wouldn't come out of Poppa unless he was related to you, the tourists would follow him into the shed, passing by the outdoor toilet, sniffing the lime confusedly, stepping over every stain and spill like it might be a nest for tsetse flies. I tried to handle every customer I saw. I tried to talk to Poppa about the importance of "return customers," and Poppa said they'd come back when they ran out of bait and he wasn't about to go suckholing to a bunch of slickers for a lousy sixty cents a box.

I quadrupled his business. I filled pickle jars with leeches just by leaving the jars overnight in Dougald Pond with an uncooked pork hock in the bottom. I built a net out of cheesecloth and filled burlap sacks with frogs from the creek. I got extra minnow traps at the Renfrew Canadian Tire and could get more than we'd need in a week just with bread crumbs and an overnight sit in Sabine Creek. But they wouldn't keep in the heat, so with Ig's help I diverted the trickle in the small creek that used to run under Jaja's milk house, cut out the aspen that had grown up there and dammed off a small reservoir with stones, hammering fine mesh behind so they couldn't escape downstream and another mesh about ten feet upstream, hammered onto posts and then down deep into the muck. It worked. The perfect holding tank.

The first week the signs were up we made $220, more than Poppa would usually make all July. On Wednesday of the second week, with Ig and I prepared to go down and turn over rocks in Black Donald Lake until we had enough crayfish to fill a washtub, Poppa came up with a longer than usual face.

"I took down the signs this morning."

I looked up. "You *what?*"

"Batcha don't like all the honking. It upsets her."

I couldn't believe it. Ig began to giggle.

"It *upsets* her!" I said, very near shouting. "Does $220 also upset her? You want we should throw that away too?"

"You wouldn't do that," Ig said, covering his mouth not to laugh.

"She's not well, Felix," Poppa said. "You've got to understand."

I didn't.

"What if I put up a sign at the end of the lane telling them not to honk?"

Poppa shook his head. "Just let thems come who know us."

Dems. And even with a "th" it was wrong.

"They don't have to honk," I said. "We'd have a sign and Ig's always there anyway. You could stop them, couldn't you, Ig?"

"You betcha, Feelie. I'd stop 'em." Ig made a loud honking sound and then throttled himself, giggling.

I looked up at Poppa, pleading. I didn't want to lose the business. It wasn't the money but the distraction. I hadn't thought of Wheeler or the NHL in days.

"Let's go for a walk," Poppa said.

I got up and looked at him. *Go for a walk? Here?* Batterinskis have lived here for a hundred years and no one *ever* went for a walk.

"A walk!" Ig shouted. "Let's go for a walk!"

Poppa fixed him with his hard look. "You can dump the dishwater."

Ig whooped and jumped up. For him, that was even better. He'd get to throw the water over the ashes back of the workshed and perhaps there'd be mice lying there from last night's traps. Ig believed dishwater on their coats made them seem alive again. If they were stiff already and the flies hadn't gotten to them he could set them up in the soft ashes like they were real again and throw stones at them. Squealing, Ig ran off in anticipation.

Poppa stood waiting. I let him lead back across the garden and past the coop to the old milk house with its buckled roof and the new minnow corral. There Poppa stopped.

"It's this," he said.

"It's what?"

"When you put this in you cut out the trembling aspen."

"It was in the way."

"I know, but she thinks it's sacred, you know that."

I was so angry I could spit. "No," I said, blood rising. "I did not know that."

"Some of the older ones say aspen was the tree that sheltered the Holy Family when they ran from Herod."

I couldn't believe it. I felt like laughing, the way Ig handled difficult moments, but knew I'd better not.

"Well, that may be," I said, trying to sound reasonable. "But I doubt they passed through here."

"Don't be smart, son. She thinks it and that's it. She's very upset."

"So let her be upset. Why should she always get her way."

"She's not well."

"Bullshit," I said.

Poppa's hand moved slowly across my face, snapping my neck half off as it hit. The force seemed all out of proportion with the speed. I'd seen it coming enough to duck but couldn't because it was Poppa. My eyes filled with tears, helplessly. I wanted to ask him why he and everyone else always caved in to her, why they let the bitch ruin their lives, why he let her stay on when she wasn't even a proper member of the family. She only came along after my true grandmother, Poppa's real mother, was dead. The bitch wasn't one of us, not really.

"Break your dam," Poppa ordered.

"But why? How will that bring back her damn trees?"

"Just break the dam. And no more questions, please."

Sacred. How distant the meaning of the sermons at St. Martin's from Batcha's bizarre interpretations. Father Schula would call the painting of Our Lady sacred; Batcha would say the barn swallows are sacred. Father Kulas would talk about the baptismal waters, the host, the communal wine, the cross—all sacred; Batcha would say blindness was caused by the parents of the blind person harming a swallow or a lark. She would place three crosses on the door to the chicken coop, maple twigs under the doors, maple keys buried under the threshold. Every person has a star, his value decided by its size, his life ended by its fall. Every stroke of lightning kills a devil. Sacred, all of it.

Bullshit, all of it.

My relationship with Batcha was even cooler now than before, if that was possible. Our warmest moment was her greeting, the flicker of a smile and then to her room. She sat each day in her rocker with the window view of the yard, the rungs of the chair grinding on the floor as she shifted slightly down the floor slant from the Bible table to the potbellied stove. If she remembered, she took the Polish bible with her, not reading but holding it gently on the afghan covering her lap, eyes closed, lips moving silently. If the door opened the wolf eyes also opened. A body moved, me, and the eyes moved with it.

I like to think I tried. I bought lemons for the old bitch when I picked up the minnow traps in Renfrew. She believed a wedge rubbed over the face would tighten wrinkles. I brought her a sheaf of supple poplar from our pulp cut for her stupid cross-making, but she burned them and insisted on cutting her own down by the creek. After that we rarely spoke.

I might have gone mad but for two people: Uncle Ig and Danny

Shannon. Ig went everywhere with me during the day, while I took charge of Poppa's scaled-down bait business. Together, we checked the minnow traps and looked for crayfish. We even took that stupid dog Puck with us, but stopped when he kept spooking everything we wanted. Ig was good daytime company. Agreed with everything, laughed at everything, and took his pay in Mars bars. For nighttime company, there was Danny. He'd come out with his trunk full of beer and haul me off to the bridge over Sabine Creek where we'd let bobbers and worms drift down toward the hold under the bent hemlock in the hopes a speckle might be holding in the fast water.

"I don't give a fuck, you know. Giving it up."

"What?"

"Hockey," Danny said. "I don't care. I like it here, eh? All the lads is still here, except you, of course. O'Malley's is steady."

"Yah." I said half-heartedly.

"I move to $1.60 an hour after the first."

"Good."

"That's $76.80 a week. Take-home works out to $57.20."

I laughed. "You sound like you've spent it already."

"How much they pay you?" Danny sounded almost resentful.

"Thirty a week."

He said nothing. Was I supposed to think $57.20 take-home for ten hours a day of hustling rack sticks around the yard was somehow better than thirty a week under the table for three practices and two games a week, money you never had to spend, either, with everything paid for, local celebrity, clippings, giggling phone calls and a chance, maybe, to become everything you ever dared dream of — was Danny really implying that?

I said nothing. I opened two fresh beer and handed Danny one while he dropped his empty in the creek and watched it drift down past the quiet bobbers. I found I had little to say to Danny.

If only Torchy was here. We could have talked about training camp, what an agent could and could not do for you, who I'd pick for my first fight, who he thought he'd score his first NHL goal on, what we'd say in our first "Hockey Night in Canada" between-period interview. Danny, though, he wanted to go backwards. He was nineteen years old and it was like he'd retired.

To listen to him tell his buddies, his whole life had taken place from September to April during one long winter in Vernon. He treated our 1960–61 season together like we'd been overseas, to war, and when he talked about that time he seemed to expect everything should stop out of respect. As if to say here was all one needed to know about life and living, and Danny Shannon had seen it all.

Night after night that summer we sat there cleaning up and polishing his past. He'd ask if I thought he was National Hockey League caliber, and naturally I would say he was and that would seem to satisfy him — for the evening. Next time we'd go over it all again. But I knew one evening we would have to talk about me. And I dreaded it.

It came on a day when the trout were surfacing down under the hemlock, but not biting. It was an evening so calm you could hear them break surface, a soft kissing sound followed by a swallow as the river took them back in. I remember it perfectly, the clouds high pink to low purple over Black Donald Hill, the night air rushing cool out of the cedars onto the water, a bullfrog on the piling over the center pier. I had a letter in my pocket and it was burning.

"Shit," I said. "I almost forgot."

"What?" Danny said. He turned, worried.

I pulled out the letter like I had suddenly remembered it had been there for days. Danny grabbed it and read, quickly, quietly. Then:

"*Ugga-bugga!*"

The bullfrog went silent and the shout bounced off the high rocks on the bluff opposite the cedars. Danny read the last part aloud: "You will report to rookie camp in Peterborough, Ontario, on August 23rd. A room will be held under your name in the Shamrock Motor Inn until six o'clock in the evening of the 23rd, after which, if you have not appeared, this offer will appear null and void. We look forward to seeing you then. Have a good summer! Yours, in hockey, Chuck Holloway."

I said nothing.

"Holy old shit!" Danny said. "You get this today?"

I nodded.

"You show your old man?"

I nodded.

"And?"

I couldn't contain my smile. "He's pleased."

"I guess so, eh? You hear from your man? What's his name — Wheeler?"

"He phoned around supper. He'd already heard."

"And?"

"Says nineteen, four . . . conditional."

"Meaning?"

"I have to make the team."

"You will," Danny said. "*You fucking will!*"

Danny spoke with such conviction that I realized I wasn't destined for the NHL for my sake, but for his. I had to make it to justify the myth that he had created for himself. If I failed, then he had failed worse, in Vernon. If I made the team, then he would have as well, if he'd wanted to. The Gospel according to O'Malley's Millyard.

A prayer was the least I could do. On Sunday, Uncle Jan and Sophia and their new baby girl came up in his Rideau 500 from Renfrew. Sophia had gone to fat, her thighs whispering nylon when she heaved about the room trying to show off the bald kid like it was too bright to let eczema hold it back. Jan at least was much the same, more interested in showing off the new Ford than the child.

Jan's hair was thinning like Ig's now, but he was still a kid when it came to cars. Poppa, Ig and I had to stand for half an hour before the yawning hood while Jan took off the air filter and explained what a four-barreled carburetor meant. The baby he left entirely to Sophia, as if it was her machine to demonstrate. But now, in church, I imagined them switching roles, Jan pulling open the brat's mouth to show where the built-in enamel would rise automatically once she hit teething gear, wrapping a fist around a calf to call attention to the rocker panels, yanking down the diaper to demonstrate the dual exhaust.

I began to snort. Poppa poked me in the ribs. Ig began to snicker and Poppa kneed him from the prayer position. I looked over, guilty for getting Ig going, and saw not him but the wolf eyes scolding back at me from beyond a dozing Jan and pious Sophia. Batcha stared until I settled back.

I tried sobering church thoughts. Jaja's funeral. The war plaque at the rear of the church. I thanked God and Jesus and the Holy Ghost and Our Lady of Czestochowa. I prayed with all my might that Felix Batterinski would never become like the four dead soldiers, missing in action. Never. I felt invincible. Blessed, almost. I prayed so hard my sinuses ached, and when I looked up toward the altar my eyes burst alive with tiny stars that spun around inside my skull, formed, faded and finally vanished.

Could it have been a sign?

Father Schula moved to the pulpit. Father Kulas was dead and Father Schula had begun to look like him, thinning out, balding, the nose rising higher than I had ever remembered. He began speaking and even his voice had become Kulas's reedy accusation. He would speak, he told us, of the church of the Laodiceans, from the third chapter of the book of Revelations.

I would like to have dozed off, but Poppa wouldn't let me. Schula read from the scriptures.

"And to the angel of the church of Laodicea, write: These things saith the Amen, the faithful and true witness, who is the beginning of the creation of God:/ I know thy works, that thou art neither cold, nor hot. I would thou wert cold, or hot./ But because thou art lukewarm, and neither cold, nor hot, I will begin to spue thee out of my mouth."

I heard Ig giggle and saw Poppa's knee slam into Ig's shorter leg. Ig stopped, let a squeak go and then slumped down. I guess Ig had never made the connection between Nestle's Quik and the Lord before.

One long, two short.

"Batterinski's Bait."

A laugh. "Tackle your own worm."

"Danny! Watcha doing?"

"Good. You?"

"Good. What's up?"

"Me 'n' Dominic 'n' some-a the lads from down at the mill want to have a little party for you. Supposed to be a surprise but we're going to go all night, so maybe you should know, eh?"

"For me?"

"Sure. National Hockey League, eh?"

"Not yet," I said, laughing hollow.

"You okay for tonight, then?"

"*Tonight?* That's kind of short notice, isn't it?"

"What's the matter, you going to the opera, or something?" Danny's sarcasm was hardly subtle. The Shannons always remembered Jaja's love of Paderewski, as if listening to Chopin meant Jaja was putting on the dog or something. No one in our family ever got snotty about Danny's wet-eyed old man sniffling about

those God- awful Irish ballads, like he was pretending to be an
outlaw leader hiding out in Black Donald Hill.

"Where?"

"I'll pick you up."

I thought Torchy and Larocque could drink, but somewhere along
the way I'd lost contact with what beer drinking means in
Pomerania. In Sudbury you drank until you passed out and that
was it. Maybe you threw up, but preferably not. In Pomerania
you drank beer and more beer and rye and rum and gin and
vodka and moonshine and, if necessary, aftershave, Scope, vanilla
extract, antifreeze sucked through potatoes, and — in Danny's
case at least once — shoe polish strained through a white silk
church shirt. You drank until you were sick, and once you were
sick you were considered empty, not ill, and started all over again.

Danny rolled in with the horn of his souped-up open Chevy
blasting, causing a moan from Batcha's room.

"You crazy fart!" I shouted as I jumped into the car before it
had even settled. I wanted him out of there. But Danny wasn't
through. Leaning out his window, he cranked up his loon call
and I could see Batcha's furious face press against the glass. She
was black against the coal oil lamp beyond, but her eyes seemed
like holes in the silhouette, sparking through. Poppa came and
stood behind her with his braces down off his summer longjohns
and, instead of shaking his fist as I might have expected, waved
to Danny like he hated to see him go. I could never understand.
He would have booted my butt back upstairs to bed. Danny he
would have bear-hugged.

Danny was already half-corked. He drifted out the lane and
bounced through the far ditch, running his undercarriage across a
large rock and back onto the road, all accompanied by "ugga-
buggas!" and the loon call. Down the road he tore, the dual
exhausts grumbling, the Chevy weaving and fishtailing from side
to side, the summer dust rising like a rooster's tail behind and
the idiotic record player sounding like it had thrown a rod itself.

"Slow her down!" I yelled.

"Fuck off!" Danny shouted back. He slapped off the record
player.

I wanted to grab the wheel. I had a flash of horror: a big maple
by the creek, maybe, or the creek itself. Suddenly I could see the

vehicle drifting, sliding effortlessly across the sand and into the tree. Just another weekend story from up the Opeongo Line from Ottawa, two nice kids drunk in a high-torqued car. Both nineteen. What a shame. *Lost in action.* Their whole lives before them.

Half right. Danny was already half dead and I had no intention of going the distance with him.

"Slow up!" I said, not loud but firmly. He did, a bit.

"What's wrong?" Danny's voice would have him dropping a hanky at communion.

"I'm not kidding, Danny. Slow down or you'll ditch, okay?"

Danny laughed. A wicked laugh I didn't care for. Perhaps this was his solution. If he didn't have enough confidence in making it and redeeming himself as a hockey player, then why not a car crash that would forever leave the question open.

But we made it out. Danny turned east on the main highway, down the far side of Black Donald Hill and onto the flatlands leading to the lakes.

"Where are we going?" I asked.

"I already told you. Cottage down on Black Donald."

"Whose?"

"You don't know him. I work with him."

"Well, what's his name?"

"Alvin Donovan. It's his old man's place."

"Another fucking Irish."

"I agree. Stupid enough to let a stinking Pole in."

I smiled at Danny. It felt like old times, fine.

We sped across the drag flats with the tangled black tire curls at the start and finish of the quarter-mile mark, down past Reid's cabins, the marina, over past the park campgrounds and the glimmering green rooftops of Poppa's craphouses, past the Indian reservation and then down a graded road which filtered into a rocky path with grass growing high between the tire runs. The Chevy sizzled over the grass, the oil pan and rear axle occasionally clipping lightly over stone. Nearer the cottage the raspberry bushes screeched along the side panels and caught and broke in the windshield wipers, but Danny did not slow until he stopped completely. I gave the car another year at best.

The cottage was lighted up, the yellow thinning out into the parking area where already sat an ancient Buick, a Pontiac, a Fargo half-ton and an Indian motorcycle with its headlight missing. We could hear the party as we got out: a male roar filling the night air with malice and unpredictability, the trademarks of a Pomeranian good time.

We each carried two cases of bootleg beer, tripping over the cedar roots as we made our way to the stoop. "We should have got here earlier if we were bringing the booze," I suggested.

"They got booze. This here's ours."

Inside they sat on kitchen chairs, chesterfields, a fold-out bed and the floor. Two I didn't know were arm-wrestling on a hand-made coffee table. I dropped my beer in the kitchen, already full of cases, a bottle opener hanging on a string from the refrigerator door handle. A transistor radio rode above, sputtering, crackling, fading in and out on the distant Ottawa country station, but no one listened.

"Hey Bats!" Dominic shouted from the floor between the fold-out and the far wall. I waved. He wobbled, a bottle of rye between his legs and a six of large Coke beside him, two already empty.

"Congratulations, pro!"

"So long, John Ferguson!"

"Frankenstein lives!"

They were all here. More Danny's friends than they ever were mine, but all were faded memory. No one new had come to Pomerania since the turn of the century, and no one ever had the guts to wonder why. Dominic Topolski now thick and gutted, a distant memory of the tiny crybaby I once played peewee with, Lacha, Tony, other names I couldn't keep straight. They all knew me. Back home, to their families and girls, we were probably best friends. I liked that, people lying about how well they knew you. When I first went to Vernon it had run the other way; this was simply due balance.

Only one of the gathering seemed reluctant to claim me for his own. I knew him instantly: Donovan, the cottager. I could tell by his look of terror. Poor fool. Chinless, glasses like hydro line receptacles, he was clearly yet another of Danny Shannon's chumps paying the price of Danny's acknowledgement.

Our hands filled with drink, the party drove on, and Danny moved effortlessly to center stage. They even vacated the best chair for him. He talked the loudest, drank the fastest, swore the most. We screwed Maureen the Queen all over again, naturally, and about half a dozen other Vernon girls I'd never heard of. We

had Lucy Dombrowski, Patsy Keswicki, Ruth Barkowitz and Agnes
Palowski — at least until Danny remembered her brother was
there and changed it magnificently into a great practical joke.
Had he not been there, Danny would have had poor Agnes grunting and sucking like she breakfasted on Spanish fly. Poor Agnes,
who would one day become a nun. Her cross to bear Danny's
mouth.

Some of the guys had heard about the Billings fight and wanted
me to go over it again, which I did. And then Orr. Danny kept
interrupting like he'd been beside me all along, but I didn't care.
They listened to me like I was Cassius Clay just returned from
whipping Sonny Liston. I could see it so plainly in their eyes. Fear.
Respect. Fear and respect. The way they looked at me and the
way fresh beer kept flying from the kitchen into my hands made
me open up like I never had before. I told them about Lucille,
which I swore I'd never mention to anyone, only this time she
had tits like Jayne Mansfield. Who knows? Perhaps she had them
sprung down like golf-ball elastic behind that formidable bra.

By midnight Danny was having trouble getting a word in edge-
wise and I noticed him slipping out the door for a leak. I thought
nothing more about it until we heard the explosion.

"What was *that?*" Donovan shouted as he jumped to his feet.
He screamed *dat* so loud at first I thought he was making a joke
of it. It was the first we'd heard from him all night.

We all stood slowly, scared, glancing around. No one knew what
to expect: drunken Indians, the provincial cops firing a warning
before they walked in with the underage drinking warrants? In a
group we headed outside and turned down toward the dock, just
as another blast rang out over the lake, followed by a loud splash.
There was a light on the dock.

"Danny!" I called.

"*What?*" There was resentment in his voice, like I had no right.

It was a floating dock and I stepped carefully out onto the
boardwalk, bothered by the jump of water through the spacing.
The others followed, Donovan right behind me.

"What do you think you're doing?" Donovan yelled, near tears.
Tink — I hadn't taken him for a local. But surely they weren't so
stupid they'd moved here voluntarily.

"Fishin'."

"Fishin'?" Palowski shouted from the boardwalk. I could hear
him and Lacha laughing.

"Watch this," Danny said. He leaned over with the flashlight until we could see the twisting back of a fish, a catfish, foolishly rising toward the light. It seemed to float up from the bottom the way a leaf falls in autumn, swaying as it rose. Just as it was about to break water Danny let the shotgun go again. In front of Danny the lake vanished, a hole dug and the fish gone; then the hole reformed, half of the fish shuddering spasmodically from the tail as its entrails rippled and lengthened in the turmoil of the lake.

"You stupid bastard!" Donovan yelled. He was definitely angry. "You'll have the cops here. I said nothing stupid, remember, Shannon."

"Where'd you get the gun?" I asked.

"I brought it."

I hadn't seen it in the car. I felt I should help poor Donovan before he broke down completely. "That's enough, eh?" I said to Danny.

"One more shot."

"No!" Donovan shouted.

"Tomorrow, Danny," I said.

"Piss off, all-star," he cursed, yanking the gun away from my reach.

The others were all on the dock. It listed badly, the water washing over our shoes at times. Danny ignored us all. He aimed at the floating Javex bottle where the pump intake went up to the cottage, shot and the bottle vanished in a spray of water.

"Those shots'll carry," I said, attempting reason.

"Big deal."

"I'll call the police myself," Donovan threatened. It was a mistake. Danny always operates precisely the opposite of what one hopes. I reached and caught the barrel of the gun and twisted it partly free. Danny held on. I twisted again, knowing it was hurting his wrists.

"You big prick," Danny swore.

I thought I might ease the tension with something we could all laugh at. I grasped the first funny thought that came into my head.

"That's what Maureen called me."

Some of the others laughed immediately, glad for the moment. I felt stupid saying it; I knew I was reaching; but it might work. Danny turned and I thought he was going to let go of the gun. At least he was smiling.

"You know better than that," he said. "You never even got near her. She wouldn't have anything to do with you, you ugly asshole."

A simple act. I twisted the gun and booted, catching Danny square in the gut. He folded easily into my shoe, the air leaving him as if just gutted by a fishknife. There was another splash, a hole, and sputtering, Danny rose to fill it. I simply turned and walked off, carrying the gun. No more laughs tonight.

I awoke to a loon call. Not from the lake but the kitchen. Danny came in in his underwear, grinning ear to ear with a pan full of brown scrambled eggs.

"How's my old buddy this morning?"

"Screw off."

"You want your eggs right away?"

I sat up and smelled them. Something wasn't quite right.

"They're fried in rye," Danny offered encouragingly. "Try 'em."

I shook my head and spun out of bed, thinking for a moment I might lose whatever argument was going on in my stomach. I winced and held it.

"Eat," Danny ordered. "You'll feel better."

I did and I did. Danny poured a beer and half orange juice into a huge glass for me and I got that down too. By the time the rest were up and eating, the party had officially entered its second phase. It seemed the gun and the night before were to be forgotten. Danny was back to his usual charming enthusiasm, planning an afternoon fishing trip on Sabine Creek using his old man's twelve-foot cartop and Lacha's canoe. All we had to do was pick up some more booze and get going.

"Me 'n' Bats'll pick up some two-fours and meet you at his place, okay?"

I turned, mouthing the question, but Danny beat me with the answer.

"We'll need bait."

I nodded. Lacha would be driving, probably, the half-ton I'd seen when we parked.

"Don't honk when you pull in," I warned him.

He looked at me like I was crazy. I couldn't explain. Danny was already packing up with not so much as a thank you to poor Donovan for the use and near-destruction of his parents' cottage. Donovan didn't seem to care. All he wanted was Danny's friendship, and he'd sacrifice anything for it.

All three vehicles raced up past the reservation and the marina and the camps to the flatland drag strip. First one would lead, then the other two would pass, seeing who could come closest to touching. Again, I had shudders about disaster, the career finished before it had even begun, the young star demolished against a thick beech on the far side of the road. When Palowski bore his old Indian out and went past the Fargo with his finger raised, laughing, Lacha threw a beer bottle at him, which whipped across in front of Danny and me in a half-circle, smashing onto the pavement just as we turned into the bootlegger's.

Danny showed no more concern for protecting the booze than he did for his body. We roared toward Batterinski Road as if he thought he could actually catch Lacha, loon-calling out the window and yelling where I could shove my protests. We fishtailed off the pavement onto the gravel and could see the trace of Lacha's wild turn before us, his rear wheels slamming against the footings of the telephone pole. I whistled. Danny laughed, drifting through the turn, down past the rink we once played in, out over the tracks, down along the cattails' flat, up over the bluff and into the turn just before Sabine Creek, Danny slamming the binders so hard that the Chevy turned sideways and stopped barely a door opening from the OPP cruiser sitting idling with the red flashers on.

No one was in the cruiser. As the dust from Danny's spin settled we got out. An officer was walking towards us from up ahead, his hand raised. A second cruiser, also with bubblegums spinning, was blocking the road. He had to cross over deep ruts in the road, snake twists through the hard gravel, where something huge had lost control, bitten into the soft shoulder and sailed over the side into the gully.

I knew without asking that it was Lacha's Fargo.

"There's been an accident, boys," the officer said "I'll have to ask you to — "

Danny cut him off. "The truck?"

"Yes. You'll have to — "

Danny paid him no attention. He ran to the side, staring over.

"Oh, Lord Jesus Christ!" he shouted before pitching down the bank sideways, breaking his slide, jumping again.

I brushed by the cop and looked myself. I heard another siren coming down the road. Not cops, an ambulance.

Two provincials were down below, one putting blankets around one of Danny's nameless pals who was sitting on a stump shaking and crying. The other pal was standing with Lacha, holding his arm at a funny angle and also crying. Lacha was staring down at the ground, smoking a cigarette and nodding at something the second cop was saying. The cop scribbled in his notepad.

I went down the same way Danny did, almost losing my footing and falling onto the undercarriage of the inverted Fargo. The box had snapped right off, clean, against a tree, leaving the cedar skinned and naked by the impact. Steam was rising from the manifold. Both doors were sprung, the cab crushed. The second cop stared up at me.

"Stay away, son! There's nothing you can do."

Nothing I can do? I looked at him and then up ahead at Danny, who was standing beside a fourth figure I hadn't yet seen. But Danny wasn't looking at whoever it was. He was looking at me, waiting.

I ignored the cop and stepped forward. Danny moved as if to say something, but couldn't. At his feet was a lumpy gray blanket completely covering a body. All but the boots, small work boots worn black. At the head of the blanket was a small tin bucket splattered with red pulp. I thought it was blood but it wasn't.

Raspberries!

I looked back at the boots, up at Danny, and suddenly my knees buckled and I was down on them, spinning.

Ig.

The provincial police told Poppa the details. The rest he must have picked up in town when he went in to make the arrangements, because when he returned and walked slowly past my bedroom I could tell from his eyes that he knew I was somehow involved. He stopped and never even tried to speak. Just looked at me and then walked off in his stooped, tired manner. He seemed to have decided there was no point in saying anything.

Lacha had been charged with dangerous driving, I heard that much from overhearing Uncle Jan's and Poppa's talk in the kitchen. Criminal negligence, Jan added, and for carrying open alcohol in the truck and for drinking underage and for no insurance coverage as well. The charges could have gone on forever and they would never equal out. I imagined this moment in Lacha's house, him upstairs feeling sorry for himself, while his old man —I knew the bastard, too, the highway grader who'd probably built up that soft shoulder in the first place —he'd be downstairs comforting his wife by saying it wasn't as if the victim had been a real person, if you know what I mean.

Maybe not, but it was Ig. I pulled the pillow tighter to quieten the sobs. Christ, I hoped he never saw it coming. I prayed Lacha had swept around that corner and picked Ig off the side of the road before he even heard the truck. But I kept seeing him stand-ing there with his shirt off and his pot full of raspberries, his simple little damaged brain trying to figure out what he had done wrong that someone would be so eager to hurt him this way. Ig's natural assumption would be that it was his fault.

I wondered if he saw them through the windshield, laughing as they drifted through the first part of the turn, their eyes sud-denly seeing him standing there with his raspberries, smiling. Him, with a surprise for Batcha. Them, a surprise for Ig.

Oh God, if it hurt him and he had to lie there before he died and wonder what it was that had gone wrong, I will kill Lacha. Please, Lord, tell me, please.

Dear Lord, let Ig have died instantly, unaware, please. The field mouse and the silent owl.

I wondered: would Jaja be waiting for him? Poor Ig, always going on about Jaja being up in the clouds watching over us. So damned simple for him. Ig's heaven was just another floor over this one, something up past my bedroom, somewhere he'd never been, some indescribable paradise where Jaja would hold him in his arms and rock him like he used to when they were both still alive. Where the Nestle's Quik can would be forever full.

How can that be? Father Kulas and now Father Schula with their promises of heaven, St. Martin's with its gawdy sculptures of the angels dancing above the skull, the hell-dwellers scream-ing frantically in the fires below. *How?* Tell me that.

How would Ig recognize Jaja if Jaja is really just some idea float-ing around up there? Ig wouldn't know what an idea was, for fuck's sake.

. . . because thou art lukewarm, and neither cold, nor hot, I will begin to spue thee out of my mouth . . .

Am I one of Father Schula's Laodiceans? If so, I don't care. I'll spit right back.

Poppa had been working on the window, loosening the sashes and head jambs. The window had not been moved since Jaja died, nine years and four months before. He worked slowly, too slowly, and I realized he had been crying while he worked, for he wiped his sleeves across his face several times before standing. I looked down and shut my eyes as if praying; but I could not pray. One prays for answers, Father Schula had taught us in communion class. What could answer this?

That night was to be the lykewake, *pusta noc.* And I remember it clearer even than yesterday. Sophia and Batcha sat all afternoon talking in small voices, and I listened in only so long as I could take it. Batcha claimed she saw *smjerc,* the white woman of death, standing just outside the shed door on Sunday. Sophia moaned, almost with pleasure. I remember I felt like shouting "Bullshit!" at them and storming from the room. Batcha also claimed the chickens refused to eat yesterday. Probably she forgot to feed them. I had seen her in the morning out in the coop yard talking to them. No doubt she had been telling them about Ig; no doubt, too, telling the lilac and the raspberry and the goddamned leek garden. I wanted to ask her if she'd told the minnows, because he sold them, or the leeches, because he had captured them. Would they say a prayer for him?

Batcha made Jan open all the windows in the house except for my room. She wouldn't enter it, thank God, and I guess she hadn't the nerve to ask him. All the mirrors were covered with cloth. The calendars she turned backwards and all the pictures, too, even poor old Paderewski, who was a special invite at Jaja's funeral. She had been at work on poor Ig, too. He had a rosary clutched in one hand and a candle in the other — to find his way to heaven, of course — and one of her silly poplar crosses was there as well, I was positive, though hidden from Poppa. And I'm sure she had put a coin in, perhaps so he could work the bubble-gum machines. And something special of Ig's as well. Batcha would have opted for his prayer book, which of course he couldn't read. I would have suggested his cap, or maybe a spoonful of Quik.

I couldn't bear it. I bolted for my room and sobbed to sleep, and when I awoke it was already dark and I could tell from the smell of fresh rolls and coffee and beer coming up through the register that *pusta noc* had begun. Poppa came up once and asked me if I'd be down. I said maybe I would later; I told him that I didn't feel good, but both of us knew I wouldn't be coming. Down below, their eyes would wrap around me like barbed wire.

I awoke later, at least I thought I was awake, but my eyes wouldn't work right. I had a sense of them being open with my body still locked in sleep. The room seemed blue with new light, and breathing, and then I realized that the room was not breathing but something was moving about in the room. I tried to turn my head to see but couldn't. Then the light changed and something bent down, directly over me, and made the sign of the cross.

Batcha.

She seemed younger somehow, moving freely without her usual sighs and dragging. She seemed to float about the room, black and nearly indistinguishable — like an indoor photograph where the flash has failed — except for the eyes. When she leaned over me they came down like a drill press, ripping.

I could hear a faint murmur, and though it didn't sound like Batcha's voice, it was her. Polish. Chanting. I tried to hear, to understand.

"Bjôj v imję tego, co njebo a zemję stvorził, a nje chodz rechlè nazôd, jak vczora!"

I could make out only a part of it: *"Go away in the name of Him . . . do not return. . . ."*

And another word. *"Vjeszczi!"* Calling me "monster" again.

I tried to move, to speak, but couldn't. I tried to wake out of the dream, but couldn't. I tried to hold my breath, to force something to happen, but couldn't. I was helpless and, suddenly, she was gone.

I awoke and the bedclothes were all on the floor. The sheet was completely soaked and my pajamas as well. I smelled it before I realized precisely what had happened.

I had peed the bed.

I waited until the day after the funeral. Jan and Sophia and their brat had gone back to Renfrew and Poppa was back in the shed sharpening his chainsaw. Batcha lay on her bed with the door open. I passed by once, turned and forced myself back. I hadn't been in her room since I was a child. She stared, expressionless, and I tried to smile and find something for my hands to do. I let them rise and play off the door frame, hanging with my fingers as if I were about to skin the cat the way I used to over Ig's door. I felt foolish, but I had to know.

"Batcha?"

The wolf eyes rose like white flames.

I hurried. "Why were you in my room the other night?"

She blinked. Once. Twice. Three times.

"I saw you," I said.

She shook her head slowly from her lying position. No.

"Yes, Batcha." I let my right hand drop to my rear pants pocket, almost as if reaching for a comb. I had the poplar cross there. I held it out the way Father Schula once held my water gun.

"How did *this* get there then?"

She blinked again, then closed her eyes; I thought she said something. I stepped in, seeing the electric lamp of Jesus on the cross Jan had brought her last Christmas. She kept her eyes closed though she had to know I was inside the room.

"Pardon me?" I said.

"*Vjeszczi!*" she hissed. The eyes opened and fixed me, stopping me dead. Her eyes seemed to widen and fall, shifting almost imperceptibly, like water in a bucket.

"What?" I said, stuttering with surprise.

"*Vjeszczi!*" She almost shouted it this time. I stared down, unable to deal with her eyes.

Vjeszczi. I did not understand.

Vjeszczi? Me, a monster?

I found Poppa throwing out dead crayfish. He had the galvanized tub tipped and partially drained, and the crayfish were tangled in a writhing scramble along the bottom, legs lightly scraping the sides, tails buzzing in what little water was left. He scooped with his right hand, oblivious to their claws, letting the live ones fall free on their own, leaving the dead to be tossed toward the ash heap.

"They're going soft," he said as I came walking up.

"Maybe they're just molting," I said.

Poppa shook his head. "Water's too warm. Too many in here. Shouldn't bother with crabs."

"The Americans are crazy about them for bass," I argued. "We've done as well by them as worms."

Poppa wasn't interested. He tossed another handful. "Shells are soft," he said.

"Poppa, what does *vjeszczi* mean to you?"

He put the tub down and looked up, startled.

"*Vjeszczi?* Children's tales, I suppose."

I knew he was hiding from the point. "But what does it really mean?"

"Where did you hear it?" Poppa looked at me earnestly, as if afraid to hear.

"Batcha."

Poppa shook off a small crayfish that had gripped him. It struck hard on the side of the tub and fell down onto its back, its tail bucking.

"What did she say?" Poppa asked.

"She called me one."

Poppa looked up. "You're sure."

"Yes."

I could see his cheek muscles working. He turned, picked up the bucket of fresh water from the creek and dumped it into the tub. "I'll need more," he said, and walked from the shed toward the milk house. I followed.

"Well, what did she mean?"

Poppa seemed more intent on the water than on me. "She's just an old lady," he said.

"I *know* she's an old lady. Why did she call me that?"

"I don't know. She's upset about Ig, you know that. We all are."

"I've heard her say it before. Before Ig. Before Ig died. When I was little."

Poppa bent down, putting his knee into the muck and letting the fresh water run slowly into the pail. "She's not a fair person," he said.

"You're telling *me* — she's always hated me."

Poppa rose, rinsing the water absent-mindedly until it over-lapped the top. "Not true, son. Not true at all. She's just gotten very old and set in her ways. There's too much of the old country in her maybe."

"But what does it mean to you?"

"What?"

"*Vjeszczi.*"

Poppa stared as if he were hearing the word for the first time. "The same as to you, I suppose."

"Monster?"

Poppa smiled, seemed relieved. "Yes. But it's just children's tales, son. You can't take her seriously. You aren't taking her seriously, are you?"

He looked at me, knowing I was.

"She said it and she meant it."

Poppa let go of a grin. "Well, are you?"

"Am I what?"

"A *vjeszczi?*" He was laughing now, his big brown teeth as dark as his face, his eyes disappeared. "I thought you were grown up, Felix. This morning I find wet sheets in the shed, now this."

"It's no joke, Poppa!"

He wouldn't stop. I couldn't help myself, I started to cry. Tears were oozing out of my eyes and my jaw hurt so badly I couldn't speak. I tried and my throat caught, also hurting. Poppa noticed and set the pail down. He came over and put his arm around me and I fell into his shoulder, wanting to vanish in his gasoline and sawdust and garlic and coal oil. The smells were his strength, and I, the big pro hockey player, needed it. I couldn't believe what I was doing.

Poppa held me tight until I got a hold of myself. I couldn't recall the last time that had happened to me, but I doubt that I had needed him then any more than I did at that very moment. Every time his big right hand thumped into my back it drove Batcha further and further from me, until for a moment I thought I could see the whole thing was as foolish as Poppa believed.

"She blames me for Ig's death, I know. But it wasn't me. You've got to believe me." Poppa's harder pat on the back told me he did. "And she still blames me for Jaja, too. Doesn't she?"

Poppa continued to hold me and thump on my back. But he said nothing. And that hurt more than the hand helped.

I left for training camp a week early. No excuse given, none demanded. Poppa took me out to the White Rose and waited for the Bancroft bus with me; I'd have to make connections to Peterborough. I'd felt I should say something to Danny Shannon and half hoped he might turn up for nothing more than a handshake, but he didn't, and I didn't have the time to tell Poppa to pull over for a moment while I popped into the Shannon house. We wouldn't know what to say anyway. I'd seen him at Ig's funeral, big watery eyes afraid to look, afraid not to look, as the Batterinskis trailed out after the coffin for the burial beside Jaja. Danny wasn't at the gravesite. Nor did he show up back at the house for the wake. I could understand.

Poppa stood patiently waiting with me, neither of us speaking.

It was just going on for evening, the quick shift in temperature full of the hint of an early fall. The air died momentarily while the wind shifted, and the only sound out on the highway the roar of a full logging truck heading down the far side of Black Donald. Poppa kept his hands in his pockets. And with the wind still down, I knew the fabric was billowing with his nervousness.

"Late," he said.

"Yah."

I thought I should say something. Perhaps sum up the years or something profound or at least a thank you and, if I could manage it, a small hint at Ig that he might use as an opening for forgiving me again. I was fairly certain he didn't blame me; he certainly acted no different towards me.

We heard the bus sigh as it crested the hill and then began sizzling down past the church. I picked up my duffle bag and the old suitcase just as the air brakes began, and though I turned and looked at Poppa there was not much to say without shouting. And all my wants were quiet. He stuck out his hand and I dropped the duffle bag again and took it and he squeezed harder than usual and stayed longer.

"We'll pray for you, Felix."

I smiled but could only nod. The door burst open with a wash of cooled air and the driver was bouncing down to scoop up the luggage, anxious to make up for lost time.

I boarded, ignoring the stares of curiosity, the accusing looks from those who felt I was using up their time, and I walked to the last seat, the very place I'd sat when Danny and I left for Vernon and when I left alone for Sudbury. Now I was going somewhere less definite, going, I suppose, to find out.

Poppa looked up into the windows and this time saw me as I ducked and stared out. Self-conscious with the others looking, he raised his hand in a quick Indian sign and dropped it. I waved back, staring at his face. There was nothing unusual in it: just Poppa watching other people's lives unfold. Not overly interested, but there in case they needed him. I felt like blowing him a kiss, but I was nineteen, six-one, a hundred and ninety-five pounds and on my way to the National Hockey League. It just wasn't possible. I waved a second time and sat, just as the bus moved out. Poppa turned and left me a final image, his back.

Down and around the bend and I could feel Pomerania leaving me like my own exhaust. The driver floored it, roaring over the limit, and I wanted him to go even faster. I was certain I would not be back again. I was also wrong.

We'll pray for you, Felix, he had said. Poppa, please do. Batcha, please die.

"Felix Batterinski's grip on hockey was entirely in his hands; it had nothing to do with his mind, his skates, his stick. When he felt himself slipping in Finland, then, it is hardly surprising that he would try and claw his way back the only way he knew how. It was a bitter blow to the many who had stood behind him.

'It was a gamble, sure,' says Alan Eagleson, who probably knows more about international hockey than any other Canadian. 'Sometimes it works out superbly, as it did for Carl Brewer. Sometimes it's a disaster, as it was here. No one is to blame; it just happened.'

'*I* blame him,' says Erkki Sundstrom, Batterinski's boss and the Finnish version of a general manager for Tapiola Hauki. 'He made us ashamed that we ever got involved with him.'"

Excerpted by permission from "Batterinski's Burden," by Matt Keening, *Canada Magazine*, June 1982.

BIG FUCKING JOKE, PEKKA — GO AHEAD, TELL THEM ALL, go on. Big fucking deal. So I'm superstitious. So I did up the belts on all the empty seats — so what? We're still in the air, aren't we? I can see him up ahead — they're all up ahead, I take the last seat, always — and I can hear them snickering and see their flat red faces snap up and down for a look so quick you'd think I was a machine gun and them in foxholes. Sometimes I wish I was. Sometimes I wish I had the whole lot pinned down in front of me: Pekka when he gets this way, that weasel Erkki, the whole goddamn front office of the Flyers, the Jesus Kings too, every fat nearsighted son of a bitch of a sports reporter I ever met, Danny Shannon's gearbox pals, Batcha. Then we'd see who'd laugh at Batterinski. If Pekka thinks the seatbelts are such a joke, why doesn't he get up and unbuckle one? I'd like to see him dare. It'd almost be worth the plane going down just to see the look on his face.

Black as tar-paper out there. And what time is it? Four-fifteen in the afternoon. No sun. No rhyme. No reason. Here we are, off to some Arctic exhibition match in some jerk Swede town I can't even pronounce, all because they got a mill there that supplies the wood for all the damned blue and silver and orange and polka-dotted minnows that are paying for this team.

I almost said "losing team." Not losing anymore, though. We're three for five with a tie since Christmas and a game like this could break our momentum. We don't know a damn thing about this team. Pekka says they're not Swedish *elitserian*, thank God, but who needs to be humiliated by some yumpin-yimminy yokels just when we're starting to click —

— Did I say that? "*Starting to click*"? My mind must be starting to go. I still remember the very day "Hockey Night in Canada" announced they'd hired Bobby Orr to do game commentary. Christ, Orr couldn't analyze his skate laces if they came undone. But true to form, they always go with the guys they can predict.

"Never wake up the big guy."

"Starting to mesh now."

"You can't leave the man in the slot."

"That line's beginning to gel as a unit."

"No question about it."

"Only a matter of time."

"They know there's no tomorrow."

"110 percent."

What's wrong with them? Who needs Fred Stanfield and his all-star teeth? Who wants to hear Jean Potvin use Dave Hodge's name every sentence, whether Hodge is there or not? "Well, Dave, I'm looking forward to a career in broadcasting when my hockey career is through, Dave." It's a lucky thing for some players that their voices are better than their hockey ability. If they announced the way they played, they'd be damned fortunate to get work calling out the bus stops at the Muskoka Hotel.

They should have tried Torchy. I can just see Dave Hodge sitting there with his football helmet of hair, his clipboard and his smug little grin when Torchy comes in with his "Hockey Night in Canada" tie rolled and stuffed down the front of his pants to thrill all the female "shut-ins" and the guts of a grandfather clock dancing in the chest hair of an open shirt, mirror shades on for the camera lights. A cigar.

"Uh, so Torchy," Dave would say, a slight catch in his throat. "what do you have to say about that first period?"

"No question about it, Dave," Torchy would shout, "it *sucked*! But we got some isolated shots of something the kids should be learning out there. Can we run them? Good. There, stop right there if you can. . . . You see that big-titted red-head there, Dave? Eh? She's jumping up on the Gretzky goal — a tip-in, not worth the air time. But this, ain't she something else? Can you just roll that back a bit, fellows: there — now all you youngsters out there pay attention to this. You see there where I'm circling? That's a rock-hard nipple there, kids. You have to look closely but no mistake about it. And you know what that means, eh, Dave?"

Dave, clearing his throat: "Uh, cold?"

"*Cold!* No, dumbfuck — hornnnnyyyyyy! I knew her from when we played here with L.A., eh? Likes the guys to keep their equipment on — even keeps skateguards in her apartment to protect the carpet, no shit, Dave — "

They should have tried Torchy.

But they went with Orr. "They're starting to click, no question about it."

"We'll be landing soon."

I turn to the tap on the shoulder and it's Erkki, his breath smelling of pink Maalox tablets for that whirlpool bath that passes for his stomach. He's been chewing constantly since I discovered the key to Finnish victory.

"What's the name?" I ask for about the fourth time.

"Örnsköldsvik."

I don't even try. In Erkki's mouth it sounds like he's bringing up a green slimy; in my mouth it would probably look like it too. I can't shake this cold. I think Kristiina actually prefers to do it in the snow — but I'd be a fool to complain, even if my knees are starting to crack and bleed.

"What's the team?"

"MoDo."

That, I can say. "MoDo," I repeat, nodding.

Erkki stares, wanting to go on. With his owl face, he always looks like he's pressed up against a plate of glass.

"There's no need for it here, okay Bats?"

"No need for what?" I say innocently, knowing perfectly well. Erkki wants to whisper, wants no one else to hear.

"You know, the bonus."

I stare out the window at a turboprop engine sparking like a hanging exhaust pipe, and answer without looking back. "As far as I'm concerned, this is a game."

"Not one that counts."

I have him now; I turn smiling. "Then why are we playing it?"

Erkki puffs slightly and the eyes narrow behind the wire rims. He is speechless, thank God. I will speak for him.

"We pay. Same as ever."

Erkki squeaks through his two front teeth, turns, nodding, and is gone. I really could care less, but I know the "bonus" makes him uneasy. But hell, we're winning. All he has to face is the board of directors and hear how pleased they are that the team—fire away, Bobby Orr — *is beginning to gel as a unit . . . we're clicking . . . 110 percent . . . Bob's your uncle*. Attendance is up. The papers are full of us. Pekka looks like a shoo-in for the all-star team. What more can they ask?

And so what if it gets a little dicey. What did old Sugar Bowles always say to me? "If you can't face the music, you can't lead the band."

Three days after Christmas in Raumo, with Lukko only two points up on us, I closed the door tight, made Erkki sit down and eat his hands and delivered a speech Sugar would have given his good eye to hear. I talked about how all our salaries were linked directly to attendance and then about how the only way we'd draw more than two thousand a night was if we made people *have* to see us. And we could only do that by being different. Winners are different. But even better than winners are scrappy underdogs. That's what I saw Tapiola becoming — a scrappy underdog.

We'd change our image first. That was easy: all I had to do was remember Schultzy and Kelly and the boys back in Philadelphia.

No more shaving.

No more deodorant before games. Okay after, if necessary.

Same for aftershave.

An end to equipment washes, except in the case of blood, which makes a man look vulnerable.

A chart system to keep track of hits. Twenty-five Finnmarks for solid body contact, double for a hit where the opponent ends up on his butt. I wanted to offer a hundred Finnmarks for a full fistfight, but Pekka pointed out fighting meant an automatic three-game suspension in Finland, so I made do with what was available, offering a special one-hundred-Finnmark bonus for any player dumping five opposing players on a given night. I even told them to keep it clean.

And God bless Timo, my lumbering, philosophical defense partner. I told him my scheme at the Viisi Pennia, our faithful bar, on a Thursday and by our Saturday game with Lukko Raumo he had been to the university library and uncovered just what I needed to make this a true, honest-to-God Sugar Bowles speech in the Vernon arena.

I let Pekka translate. "I know I'm not doing very well with your language," I said, "apart from a few drinks and the word for condoms. But I have been trying to learn some of the fascinating history of your fine country. I've been reading about the seventeenth century and the Thirty Years' War"—Pekka looked at me like I was putting him on, then shrugged and repeated in Finnish —"and I've become particularly interested in a battle that took place at the crossing of the River Lech. April, 1632, if my memory serves me correct." I couldn't resist a glance at Timo here, what a prince; he was looking back at me like I'd just discovered how to get nuclear energy out of a puck. "The great victors of the day were a Finnish cavalry unit called the . . ." — I prayed Timo's coaching was perfect here — ". . . *hack a pelites.* Anybody know why they were called that?"

I looked up as they looked down, Timo as well, the prince. He knew the answer better than I.

"Well, I'll tell you why. Their name they got from their battle cry. '*Hakkaa päälle!*' In my language that translates as 'Cut 'em up!' I think Tapiola Hauki needs a battle cry like that — what do you think, Pekka?"

Pekka looked back, startled. He wanted to laugh but it came out like an air cough, and this he turned into a face-saving nod. "Sure," he said. "Good idea."

"I think so too. And I want to try it before we go out there tonight — are you ready?"

"Ready!" Timo the prince called back.

"*Hakkaa päälle!*" I shouted.

"*Hakkaa päälle,*" about four answered sedately.

"*Hakkaa päälle!*" I shouted, slamming my stick against the wall for effect.

That woke them up. "*Hakkaa päälle!*"

"*Hak-kaa pääääälle!*"

"*Hak-kaa pääääääääällle!*" Some, like Timo and Pekka, were getting into it, beet-red when they yelled.

"*HAKKAA PÄÄLLE!*" I screamed, slamming my stick so hard it splintered, sending the blade sailing like a boomerang across the room.

"*HAKKAA PÄÄLLE!!!*"

"*CUT 'EM UP!!!!*"

"*CUT 'EM UP!!!!*"

"Okay," I said in a calm, steadying voice, the voice Sugar always reserved for the last phrase. "Let's go."

That night we beat Raumo Lukko 4–3 to tie them for last place, and it cost Erkki 400 Finnmarks. The next match, against Lahti, we won 5–2 and it cost 575 Finnmarks; third game 6–4 and 925 Finnmarks with a full 100-Finnmark bonus going to big Timo, who had suddenly taken to screaming "*Hakkaa päälle!*" whenever he slipped over the boards to start a new shift.

Erkki paid out the money from some weird fund he had and by the time we left for the exhibition game in Sweden he was a nervous wreck that someone was going to squeal to the press. I told him he was nuts, that would be like cutting a hole in your own pocket, but he wouldn't stop worrying. Every time I saw him he was scanning a newspaper, and usually he could find something on us, though never quite what he dreaded. Arto Pakola, the most important sportswriter, had already started referring to us as "The Nordenskiöld Street Bullies" in his columns, and I had to explain to poor, trembling Erkki that this was simply a play on "the Broad Street Bullies," which was the nickname the Flyers were known by when they still had Schultzy and me — when they still won, incidentally. There was even an open debate between columnists in the *Sanomat* and Tampere's *Aamulehti* whether such a *kovanaama* as Batterinski was good for Finnish hockey. Kristiina said it meant I was a "bully" and complained in a letter to the editor, which they ran.

Myself, had I been able to write Finnish I might have sent a thank you note. Harold Ballard would die for what we had going here—a team of Finnish rejects and a washed-up National Hockey League cement-head winning for a lousy $300 a night. Harold would have danced with King Clancy at center ice. But Erkki, not on your life. Erkki was gobbling Maalox by the bottle and ripping his nails so badly they were bleeding on his shirtsleeves when he'd fidget. He began walking around wearing little bandages over them. Last game he ate the bandages.

Myself, I'm not so sure it's the money. We got our first point the night after I walked through the park to the Ishallen and thwacked Nurmi's bronzed butt. It might have been that — who can know for sure? Me, I'm not willing to take the chance, so I'm sticking to that route, bum slap included.

Örnsköldsvik, Sweden. Center ice in the ugliest arena of my life, lights like a closet, ice like black cellophane, the public address bouncing off the walls sounding like Danny and I cursing at the rock cliff on the far side of Black Donald, a snotty crowd of whistling Swedes. I'm worried about the new kid, Matti. The weasel Erkki never even asked me, just phoned me and said we'd picked up this great prospect from Helsinki Jokerit for next to nothing. What's that? I asked. Erkki wouldn't say. But once I saw this Matti I didn't have to ask anymore. Next to nothing, indeed. Jokerit dumped him and I could see why immediately: just look at his eyes. A good hockey player keeps his eyes centered, the focus wide as if looking at something buried thirty feet deep in the ice. That way only slight turns of the head are necessary. A player like Matti keeps a fine focus, too sharp, his head always flicking back and forth at something specific. A player like Matti doesn't understand that the game is not the puck, the game is the flow, and that concept you cannot teach. Matti plays out of fear, always looking for the unexpected. I play with near distraction, praying for the unexpected.

I love this moment. Christ, you can take all your orgasms and fine wine and fancy restaurants and movies and music and compliments and financial windfalls and you can shove them where Torchy used to say only the customs agent's flashlight ever shines. I love *this* moment, no matter what anthem or what arena or what country, just me on one side and them on the other, everyone wondering what Batterinski is going to do.

"MoDo AIK" it says on their jerseys. Blood red, they make me think of the Soviets. And they're talking and laughing through the anthem like this game is the perfect chance to stick it to the damn Finns. I feel something I haven't felt since the Pomeranian Peewees went up against Renfrew. We didn't even have a name, for Jesus' sake, and them called the "Millionaires." Them, with their old man's paycheques all over them: forty-dollar Tackaberry CCM skates, brand-new Hespeler Green Flash sticks, oversized pants with the sweater tucked just so in one side only, matching socks with not a single longjohn gap among them, Cooper armadillo thumb gloves — and them laughing the same way these Swedes are right now. The Pomeranian Peewees, with their hand-me-down skates and taped- over toes, undersized pants gaping the pink speckled flesh of underwear, mismatched socks, rings from sealer preserve jars holding in the pads, Tommy Nordowski's pads made by his old man from peeled hemlock bark and sewn together under the knee joint so he could bend, me playing with a wire splice taped around the heel of the stick blade by Poppa and filled in with Scotch pine pitch.

God but I loved that game. Every time I hit a Renfrew player I was hitting his old man too. And when Danny and I skated off together at the end, 5–3 winners, I stared right into their eyes when we walked up the coco matting to our dressing room, sneering when their own stares buckled into their coffees, spitting just before I kicked open the door with my skate toe, ripping a sliver free that they wouldn't dare mention. I had a right to do as I pleased. They, son and father, were beaten.

They can laugh at the start if they like. By the time it ends there'll be something else in their eyes: respect. I can feel it here the same way I felt it in Renfrew twenty-five years ago. I saw the look when we skated around in the warm-up. They weren't laughing at our uniforms — Tapiola makes sure we have the best of everything, even if the front crest does have a damn minnow swimming around on it — no, they were laughing because we were Finns. The NHL laugh when we were WHA. The Canadiens laugh when we were Kings. The Marlie look when we were Hardrocks. The North Bay look when we were Vernon. The Renfrew look when we were Pomeranian.

That look, everywhere, when you're a Pole.

First period over and it's Örnsköldsvik 3, Tapiola 0. With the horn I spin down ice where the scraper is just coming on and skate around slowly, pretending to be checking my sharp, waiting until the rest of the team gets to the dressing room. I come in last, yank the cigarette out of Pekka's mouth as I pass, grind it and then slam my stick into the side of the trash can, knocking it over, rolling.

"Pekka. You translate."

Pekka nods. The room is deathly silent, waiting.

"Don't you *care?*" I say. I am not faking it this time. I am not cribbing Timo's research. This time I come on pure. "I'm ashamed to be in the same uniform as you, do you know that? You're playing like we've come here on some kind of a damn holiday or something. Don't you think there are finer places to visit? Have you no pride in yourselves as professionals? Tell me — don't you care?

"*They* care. You can see it out there the way they're laughing at us. Did you notice? Sure, they're laughing, because to them we're just a joke, a bunch of dumb-ass Finns and a goofy Canuck who doesn't know when to call it quits. That's fine, if that's the way you want it. Swedes are just better than Finns, obviously . . . accept it. Tell me, please, what do *you* think?"

Matti stands up, rubbing his hands along the front of his pads like he's working in a kitchen. He speaks perfect English. "This is just exhibition, surely," he says. "They were playing in front of their families and friends. This is their town. So it means something to them more than just a game. But it is not so important to us. What does it matter who wins?"

I cannot *believe* this! His first game? When Henri Richard went up to Montreal to join Maurice, it was understood that, even as brothers, they would not speak. In the Canadiens dressing room they accepted you after two years, minimum. Then you could talk.

"Do you really mean that?" I ask.

Matti seems surprised. He has his narrow focus on me, unable to see beyond. "Yes. Of course."

"In that case," I say, "you're cut from the team as of this very moment. Get dressed."

Matti stares back, unbelieving. He does not know me well enough to know that I do not joke.

"Pekka," I say. "Perhaps he doesn't understand English. Tell him so he understands."

Reluctantly, Pekka begins, but before he can get into it, Matti cuts him off. "I understand perfectly," he says. "Surely you joke, man."

"Get dressed."

"It's a meaningless game."

"Not to me. Get dressed."

"Do you really mean what you say?"

"Get dressed."

Matti spins around in his nervous, narrow-focus way and finds nothing but heads bowed between knees; fingers on skate laces, taping sticks, adjusting pads; escape everywhere. He looks back at me, blows out some contemptuous air, sits down and throws down his stick and gloves.

"Be cleared out by the time we come in here again," I say.

He doesn't answer. I don't expect him to.

"Okay now," I say, and Pekka translates without being told. "Shall we go out and win this game?"

"*Hakkaa päälle!*" Timo shouts, his timing perfect.

The dressing room erupts.

"*HAKKAA PÄÄLLE!!!!*"

Pekka takes the face-off easily, shouldering their gangly center straight back so he falls and Pekka kicks the puck free. Penalty: interference. No matter. Tapiola Hauki has arrived, one period late. The box impenetrable, the icings sure and easy and delayed magnificently, the forechecking frenzied enough to bring panic to Örnsköldsvik, the panic delivering what we need.

We hold them with Pekka off, and they manage only one long slapper from the point that not one Swede forward dares try to tip with Batterinski and Timo standing guard, sticks raised like lances. Timo gloves it easily as it bounces off his shin and he base-balls the puck off his stick into the corner, where I take it off the boards. Not looking, the focus deliberately wide, I catch Pekka just stepping free of the penalty box this side of center and I send a high, slow floater straight up ice, which he gloves while strad-dling the red line and cuffs ahead so it drops as he skates in, com-pletely clear. Two head fakes and a shoulder drop and the Swede goalie is sliding on one pad straight out toward the face-off circle, staring back helplessly at Pekka tucking the puck into a corner of the empty net.

Our bench empties and Pekka is celebrated as if he has just wrapped up the Stanley Cup in overtime, Timo shouting "*Hakkaa päälle!*" in a sour voice at the still-kneeling goaltender as the arena erupts in angry whistles, a sound I had forgotten since Danny and I used to sneak smokes in the machine shop down at O'Malley's Mill and they'd be sharpening the bandsaws.

I hear my name follow Pekka's as they are ground from the public address system and Pekka gives me a small special tap on the rear as he skates through the octopus of team arms still reaching. I skate away, stick across knees, escaping into the clock, satisfied that he knows what made the goal possible. Let Pekka have the glory; Batterinski wants what lies beneath, what most people cannot see. The respect.

By the end of the period it is a 3–3 tie and Tapiola has played shorthanded for nearly fifteen of the twenty minutes. Timo has a major for drawing blood — he convinced the referee it was an accident, not requiring ejection, and actually apologized to the poor bastard he'd suckered with a butt end — and I picked up three minors myself, though by agreement with Jerkki I will not be claiming for them.

The third period is catered to us. We go ahead 4–3 on Pekka's second goal, a cheap one on a pass-out that goes in off a MoDo skate. Again Pekka is mobbed, the enthusiasm the same as for his first, though the goals are hardly worthy of the same name. But it doesn't matter. Sugar Bowles used to say a scoreboard only counts, it cannot measure.

This goal, the go-ahead that has come all the way, unaccosted, from a shutout, seems to get to the Örnsköldsvik players and fans. We play under constant whistle, if not the referee then the fans, and at times it is impossible to hear the referee's. MoDo presses, sending four men in, and I am reminded of another of Sugar's thoughts — if you want something to break, you need only to push too hard. Sure enough. Timo intercepts a point pass from them and breaks down two-on-one with Pekka on his right. Pekka knocks Timo's high pass out of the air and shifts right toward the boards, sucking the defenseman over as if he had a rope around him. He lips the puck and one-hands it through the lone defender's skates to Timo, and Timo, straightforward, predictable Timo, ignores fakes and shifts and dekes and stuns the MoDo goaltender by simply looking once at the net and rifling a high hard shot straight into his glove hand, the shot so hard and direct that the glove snaps back on the wrist and the puck falls like the top of a child's ice cream, plop on the goal line.

The light goes on, Pekka goes into his little dance, our bench empties and the MoDo goaltender rushes the referee, hurling his cage as he goes. A black-haired, ugly little man emerges, and I don't need to know Swedish to know he is claiming the puck did not go over the line; nor do I need glasses to see that the referee is not interested in arguing. The score is now 5–3 as far as he is concerned.

The goaltender, I think, is right. I like him. I like his rage and his blackness and his ugliness. I wonder if he was made a goaltender in Sweden the same way that boys with weak ankles are made goalies in Canada, only in this case the mark against him is looks. Not pure enough to play out; admissible only if he keeps it all behind the cage.

MoDo presses even harder and closes to within one goal, when I foolishly neglect to freeze the puck, trying to whip it around on the glass without realizing there is no glass, only wire, and the puck hits funny in one of the mesh squares and comes oddly back out in front, where a lanky Swede picks it out of the air and golfs the puck into the short side.

It is my fault entirely. I am angry again, no longer feeling for the goaltender or anyone, and when MoDo breaks down on us again Timo and I fix on the center, knowing he is going to try and split us, using the wingers for decoy. He dumps the puck past and leaps, as we knew he would, and Timo and I bear-trap him, sticks straight into his kidneys. He falls like trash, not flesh, and the puck slides harmlessly into the waiting glove of our goaltender.

Such a play, naturally, is beyond them. The center does not move, but lies where Timo and I have left him. The referee's whistle reaches above the crowd's and aims at me, a police siren sorting the traffic without knowing its direction. I skate off to a hosanna of whistling, pausing only to bow before entering the penalty box.

I realize instantly how spoiled I have become by North American hockey. In Philadelphia I would be entering a bunker, glass on three sides of me, two leather-jacketed city cops with nightsticks and .38 caliber convincers hanging eagerly off their hips. In L.A. one cop, but more glass; in Boston less glass, but perhaps four cops. Here, in Örnsköldsvik, no glass, no cops, the penalty bench simply a red slab behind a swingdoor beside the announcer's seat, nothing between me and the seats but a throng of seething fans, some, for my benefit, trying out North American booing.

I swing my stick harmlessly at them and they break like hay, folding back on themselves. One of them, a puffy-faced man with his neck wrapped too many times in red wool, probably a team scarf, leans forward and spits directly into my face.

Spits.

Spits at Batterinski.

It lands on my cheek just below my left eye, and is cool as it slides down. I do not wipe it off. I wear it.

Those who cannot understand such things will say this is a rash decision caused by an uncontrollable temper. But this is not at all what happens. I am not out of control; I am in control. I step over the bench straight onto the cement, moving deliberately slowly, letting the spit drip under its own power from my face. The puffy-faced man floods with terror and bursts from the crowd. Wonderfully in control, I give chase, my skates ringing and rasping as I step and then run, the crowd splitting like a zipper as I pass in pursuit of the dancing red scarf.

Up the stairs he goes toward the overhead ramp. Up the stairs I go, out through the lobby, the far doors and into the night. The spitter knows by the singing of my skates that I follow, and in the light snow of the parking lot I hear him scream as he realizes his escape is not yet complete.

He leaves tracks, and I do not even have to look up to follow. His tracks lead up the entry road toward some leafless bushes ahead. I cannot see him and am convinced he is gone, but then, above even the sound of my skates, I hear him breathing.

He is behind the bushes, hiding, leaning over onto his knees. His breath is wet, gagging. He cannot even beg me not to kill him.

I do not want to kill him.

I am not even angry.

All I want is for him to acknowledge that Batterinski has taken the spit and put it back where it belongs. Simply, effortlessly, I pull him up by his scarf and then release it so he falls back on his rear end, then push his fur hat so he is on his back, still gasping. The large flakes of snow melt instantly on his face, making it appear as if he is in tears. Perhaps he is.

Gently, considerately, I steady his head with my gloved hands, then lean down toward him and spit mightily into his face.

Flash!

I look up and a young, long-haired kid in a blue pea jacket is standing over us with an expensive camera and flash.

"Fuck off!" I yell.

Flash! He jumps back a step, adjusts.

Flash!

"Perkele!" I shout at him. He laughs and tips his head in acknowledgment.

I jump up from the whimpering spitter and scrape toward the photographer, slipping. He dodges easily.

"Give me that film, you little fag!" I order him.

He shakes his head, no. I grab for him, miss and slip headfirst down into the muck. He slips away and up the path, laughing. I struggle momentarily after him, slip back again and know I cannot go on. I am exhausted, breathing as heavily as the spitter, who has yet to get off his back.

There is a hand on my shoulder. I turn, prepared to swing, but it is a cop. He is young, with a stern look, and tells me in Swedish to stay put while he helps up the spitter. The cop is like oxygen to the Swede, who rises, pointing at me and turkey-gobbling some lie. The cop listens and then starts talking back to the man, and it seems to me that they are arguing, the cop as angry as the spitter. A crowd begins to gather, growing rapidly. Finally the cop grabs him angrily by the arm and pulls him toward me. The cop speaks in English, using a voice the crowd strains to catch.

"He says he will not press charges on you."

If only the referee had the sense of the cop. I come back into the arena, mud covered, my blades as rounded and dull as the spitter's face, and in mid-action, the referee blows down the play. Leaning over the boards, he assesses me a game misconduct.

I can only laugh and walk by the awed leeches on the way to the dressing room, enter and close the door as if a baby sleeps within. One does, but within me. I undress alone, happily, savoring the silence of the crowd and the knowledge that I have led the outcasts in revenge. I pretend this is Renfrew and I am not stripping off expensive, freely supplied Joffa equipment, but the pants Poppa paid a quarter for at the St. Martin's bazaar and sewed together with twelve-pound-test monofilament fishing line, replacing the missing thigh pad with a cedar shingle. I look around at the empty seats, then at the hole Matti has left, and I fill it with Danny. Danny sits, legs spread wide, skates unlaced but not kicked free, braces hanging down off the shoulders like the outlines of wings at rest, his chest heaving with victory.

"Danny," I say. I am not crazy. I know he is not there but I say it anyway. I just want to feel his name in my mouth again and to see him the way he was.

To see me the way I was.

To feel it coming again. Not sure what to expect but success.

Why, tell me why — why is success so much sweeter in the future, where it may not exist at all, than in the past, where there is no argument?

"Ugga-bugga, pal," I say softly and close my eyes, pulling the thuds and cracks and whistles and cheers and moans of this godforsaken arena about me like a comforter.

When the team comes in with a 6–5 victory, I am asleep.

Later, in the banquet hall bar of a squat hotel, I sit nursing a beer, my mood peculiar. A band is on stage, identical straw-haired pipe cleaners in thin black ties, white shirts and black slacks so desperately tapered their toes couldn't tap for choking. And no wonder: a cross between ABBA and a polka band, they manage to make "Tie a Yellow Ribbon" even worse than the original.

But I am quiet, alone. Pekka, drunk first on his hat trick, is now drunk on *koskenkorva*, thrown back neat and then cooled with a beer chaser. Several of the others are staying with him. Never have I seen Tapiola Hauki so — sorry, Bobby — "gelled." We feel completely comfortable together, a unit.

Timo begins strength exhibitions, taking a bite out of a glass and happily chewing it while everyone, me excluded, applauds in astonishment. Timo looks at me and I nod in approval, then stand as the table goes silent. I reach over toward Pekka and pick an empty beer glass. Then I take up Pekka's nearly empty *koskenkorva* bottle and pour out a short ounce, causing Pekka to hoot with derision. I hold up my hand, silently calling for patience. My mood is strange and I am not quite sure what it is that's making me do this, but instead of going for more alcohol to prove the point, I suddenly find myself pulling at my fly as I stand there. In front of the entire table, I whip it out and slowly pee several more shots into the glass. Then, zipping back up, I raise this yellowed, sparkling liquid toward the chandeliers, cut off my breath and quickly drain the glass to the bottom.

"*Hakkaa päälle!*" Timo shouts.

"*HAKKAA PÄÄLLE!!!*" The table, Pekka included, erupts.

I say nothing. Delicately, I place the glass down. Arrogantly, I walk away, leaving their continued cheering and applause. No one can believe what I have done, but there is a rationale to such apparent insanity. There has to be. To them, it looks as if Batterinski has gone out of control, but appearances are deceiving. I have simply taken shock and manipulated it. Those who witnessed the act will be saying that, come morning, I had better not remember it; if I do, I will be aghast. But they are so wrong. I will not only remember it; I will be proud of it.

A rep is not something you acquire and take with you. It is something you must be forever creating. As it suits you.

And this act is not done to serve me in the bar, but on the ice.

Erkki is already aboard the plane when Pekka and Timo and I make it up the ramp, one of us on each side of Pekka, who has thrown up twice on the bus ride out to the tiny airport. I leave Pekka's fate to Timo and the airplane's thin waxed bags, halting in front of Erkki and his empty seat of scattered newspapers. He moves them and I can see by his fingernails how badly he is disturbed by what he has read. As I sit, he drops the best shot in my lap, nearly a quarter page on the front of the first section, of me paying the spitter back in kind.

"Did they get the score right?" I ask.

"It is not so funny to me," Erkki says.

"It wasn't so funny to me, either. That's why I did it back to him."

"The board will not be pleased."

I imitate him: "'The board will not be pleased.' Now what the fuck is that supposed to mean, Erkki? We won, didn't we?"

"That's not the point."

"Tell me then, Erkki — just what is the point?"

Erkki flees to a thumbnail, ripping a thin tortured ribbon free so two small flecks of blood can rise in the whitened crease. Erkki sucks on it, gaining nourishment from his own fears, gathering himself before he dares.

"This was an exhibition match."

"Meaning?"

"Meaning it does not count."

"It seemed to count for them — as long as they were winning, anyway."

"But not so much as to justify your attacking a fan, surely."

"*Me* attack?" I say indignantly. "Who spit first?"

Erkki taps the paper. A blood bud falls from his finger, spreading. "Hauki does not appreciate bad publicity."

The flight is rocky. We seem to be boring straight into turbulence as we head out over the water. We do not crash, but only because when I walked back from Erkki I checked the seatbelts. Pekka does not laugh this time. He lies alone in a double seat, blind drawn, pillows under and over his head, moaning. Matti sits alone as well, near the back of the plane, and untouchable. He is unshaven and scramble-eyed, staring at me like a hungry dog on a short chain. I ignore him.

The flight smooths, a new sky rising clear and bright over a thick mattress of flattened cloud. I set my seat back and close my eyes, imagining what it will be like to be back with Kristiina tonight, whether she will have heard, what she will think.

Something bumps my chair, a sharp jolt that cracks my head against the window.

"Sorry."

I look up. It is Matti, his comment and expression contradicting.

"Fuck off," I say, closing my eyes again.

He bumps again.

"Sorry."

I sit up and turn as he leans over. I can smell the booze. Matti reaches and slaps with an open palm, hand open, and the sting floods my eyes though it does not hurt much. I am startled. I have been hit by a man, kicked by a man, choked, bit-speared, tripped and nearly knifed by a man. But slapped? I can do nothing but laugh.

"You think it is funny, Batterinski?" Matti asks.

"Not really," I say. "That's about what I would expect of your type — a woman's slap."

Timo rises behind Matti, waiting. He puts a hand on Matti's shoulder, gently, suggesting, but Matti shakes free more than is necessary and leans again toward me.

"You fucking Canadian!"

"Forget it, Matti," I say, trying to remain reasonable. "You're off the team. Let him be, Timo. Matti, go on back and lie down. Get some sleep. You need it."

Matti lunges, a nail catching under my eye and stinging off my cheekbone. He is both too weak and too drunk to fight. I grab his hands together like he's a child throwing a tantrum and stand up, throwing him into the empty seat while I still hold on to him.

I look straight into his tortured eyes. "Are you going to settle down now?"

He twists angrily, grunting. I slap his face back.

"Lars," I shout back at the trainer. "A roll of tape — quick!"

Lars has his jacket pocket full of them and tosses a roll immediately. I catch the tape, bite the loose end up and, holding it in my mouth, yank a long squawk of tape free. Letting it drop from my mouth, I work it loose with one hand until it catches and then wrap it tight, around and around and around Matti's arms as Timo pins him. He barely bothers to struggle but begins to curse me in Finnish.

"Kovanaama!"

"Perkele!"

"Vittu paska!"

"Bully, bastard, fucking shit — he has exhausted my own Finnish comprehension by the time I decide to finish off the roll of tape by doing Matti's mouth as well.

"There," I say gently into Matti's burning ear. "That should hold you until we get home."

Timo carts him off to the applause of the team and by the time we land I have forgotten Matti. There are far too many other concerns. Erkki is waiting smugly by the luggage carousel, lightly slapping the afternoon *Helsinki Sanomat* against his palm as if waiting for a fly to light. The front page belongs to Batterinski.

He hands me the paper and turns away, waiting for me to read. As he rocks on his feet, hands rip nails behind his back. For comfort he stares into the deep hole of the carousel, closing his condemning eyes only when they settle on the arrival of the first luggage: Matti, taped, twisted and terrified as he rises on the rubber treadmill and rolls down the steel plates, circling twice before Erkki, alone, hauls him off like a flopping, massive muskie. No one moves to help as we gather up our equipment and depart, for the first time a true team.

Kristiina was not home. I called fourteen times from five o'clock on but no answer. Finally I showered, shaved and dressed anyway and walked from the hotel over to the Viisi Pennia for a few brew and compliments, but the evening did not sit well with me. I talked while silent inside, laughed while sulking beneath, drank but was dry to the pit of my gut. Three times more I called, but still no answer. No Kristiina.

Midnight and I think I see her through the smoke. She stands at the front door, swaying as she winces through the bad air for me. She is not alone. Her hand uses a man's arm like a pole to swing from as she searches, the other hand pressed to her silken bangs, scouting. I want to shout but I cannot; I cannot even look at her properly because of him—who is he? *what* is he? He stands tall beside her, nearly my height, and it is difficult to make out his build for all the bulk, lamb jacket, scarf, black Russian hat. He grins the smile of the horribly uncomfortable, teeth like a clamp on a pipe so curled and whittled that I wait for a soap bubble to drift across the bar and burst on my table: this late-night, late-drink, late-thought nightmare finished.

But it does not burst. She sees me seated with the usual leeches, waves frantically and heads through the crowd, tugging her uneasy giant behind. It is clear he is not used to bars. He smiles a welcome the way frightened dogs expose their bellies, unaware that others turn not to greet but to leer. On other nights, with Kristiina on this same walk, picking up imaginations the way Poppa's magnet pulls nails from the laneway, I have been proud, knowing they all see Batterinski between the hard thought and the soft comfort of her body. But not this night. I stare as well. But not at her. At him. *Who is he?*

"Hi," she says, the tone tentative, hopeful.

I am glad she spoke first. Sensing defense, I am free to lag the puck, letting her commit herself first. I pick up my glass and raise it in a toast which says, and is supposed to say, nothing. The leeches clear out, knowing Kristiina; from their hands on my shoulders and back I know they are wishing me well and content just to touch. I am to them what Paavo Nurmi is to me: a charm. And I am as aware of them as the statue is of me. Kristiina, though, is another matter.

She smiles enthusiastically. "Felix. I would want you to meet a friend of mine from where I work. This is Jorma. Jorma, I would like you to meet Felix Batterinski, please."

I rise not out of good manners but to show him my size. Yet it does not work. He is not as tall, he is taller, and when his hand comes down off the pipe — white clay, the bowl like a full-breasted woman with vents for nipples — and reaches for mine, it is as if I am putting on a hockey glove. His grasp is huge, the fingers long and strong, and if the flesh seems soft it is only a false covering over hydraulic bones. We both grip hard and shake once, up and down. An egg held between would have splattered to the ceiling.

"I have read much about the Great Batterinski," Jorma says. His voice is soft also, equally deceptive. It does not sing like most of them. He sounds like an Englishman, one of the snotty ones. Behind the voice I look for sarcasm, but cannot be sure.

"We have all today read so very much of the Great Batterinski," Kristiina says, her sarcasm open, obvious.

"Sit down. Sit down," I say, suddenly the perfect host. I signal to Thomas to bring over a round of beer.

We sit and Jorma immediately begins to clean his pipe with a large, elaborate jackknife, the blade left exposed and threatening on the table between us. Kristiina catches me staring at it as Thomas sets down the beer.

"Jorma is one of the architects for your new ice hockey stadium," she says.

"That so? At Tapiola?"

He relaxes visibly, comforted by his work. "We are doing what we can, you see, considering the laws they have there concerning what you can or what you cannot build. If they had their way, old man, your center-ice line would be a bicycle path —very difficult to deal with."

"When will you have it completed?"

"With no strikes, maybe we shall see progress by this time next year."

"How many seats?"

"How many seats do you want, old man?" he says, smiling from behind the pipe.

"One."

Jorma is not sure whether to laugh. "*One*?"

"One." I nod toward Kristiina. "For her."

Kristiina blushes. Jorma laughs, pulls his pipe free and reaches in through several inches of sweater wool to drag out a leather tobacco pouch. He unzips it and loads up his pipe, staring back and forth at Kristiina and me as if we are a tennis match.

She serves. "I am not so sure I should want to be there after this."

I return. "After what?"

"They are talking about you all over Finland. Do you not know that?"

"Good," I say, turning to Jorma. "Better go for twenty thousand, anyway. I'm a draw."

Kristiina is not finished. "The radio station has started a petition against you."

"A what? A *petition* against me?"

"Anyone who thinks you are wrong for Finnish hockey is supposed to go down and sign."

"Let them go ahead. They have no idea what happened."

"You, you — " she looks at Jorma, "*sylki?*"

"Spit," he says, smiling.

"Yes, you spit in that poor man's face."

"He spit first."

"Must you always be the person to react?"

"What would you have me do, kiss him?"

Jorma is beaming as he follows our rally. I am suddenly aware of what is in this game for him. He will be the true winner. If I go too far he will be leaving with Kristiina even more confidently than he came. I soften my shots.

"It was unfortunate," I say. "I had no idea anyone would be there with a camera."

"I thought it was great, old man," Jorma says, putting away

the knife. "It's not every day Finland gets to spit in Sweden's face on the front page."

Kristiina is not amused, and deliberately changes the subject, talking directly to Jorma. I tune out, staring: she looks so lovely tonight, her teeth white as surf as she speaks.

This Jorma's agreeability does not fool me. I scare him. I have him. I look around. Viisi Pennia is winding down, the smoke snaking about the room as the front doors open and close on red-faced, staggering patrons, each door swing silencing the bar a little more.

"I'm sorry?" I say, dipping back into the conversation. There was something there I didn't quite catch.

Jorma stops in mid-sentence, eyebrows flexing, pipe smoking, the talker idling. He pulls out the pipe and stares, questioningly.

"I don't understand what that is," I say.

"What what is?"

"This Amisty thing."

Jorma smiles, grateful. "Amnesty International," he says loudly, as if the word should be as familiar to someone like me as "unsportsmanlike conduct."

"That's where we were," Kristiina says, her smile encouraging. "We had a meeting."

"Well," I say, a touch belligerently. "What is it?"

"You must have heard of it in Canada, surely," Jorma says. "It is a world-wide organization to fight repression. Communist. Right wing. You name it, my friend, we fight it. Kristiina and I are both members. I am the national director, I think you would call it in your language."

I am not listening. I stare at Kristiina, who hides her awkwardness behind a sip of her drink.

"What can *you* do?" I ask sarcastically. "You got guns in the closet or something?"

Jorma thinks this a huge joke and laughs the laugh of those who enjoy through imitation rather than creation. It comes across false.

"We have something much better," he says, and winks at Kristiina. I clench my fists, wanting to lunge. I wish I were in full uniform and we were sitting in the penalty box, not here. There would be no winking there; a closed eye for Jorma, perhaps, with my blessing; but no winking.

Jorma goes on: "There is an English saying we use here, as well. 'The pen is mightier than the sword.' We write letters, you see. We have no use for guns, believe me. They solve nothing, obviously, otherwise there would be no need for us. We write reasonable, persuasive letters."

"Who to?"

"To whom?" he repeats, deliberately stretching the "m." I want to kill him. "We write to the leaders of the countries like Pakistan and Guatemala, places where people are being tortured, where they are being detained in prison without charges, convicted of crimes without trials, where they are, in many cases, being executed at the whim of the ruling party. We fight against all of this everywhere."

He leans back, deliberately staring down his nose at me. He thinks I don't understand. The prick.

"Fight?" I say. "In letters?"

"Yes. We apply enough pressure, we hope, to force them to release their political prisoners."

"Through letters?"

"Yes."

"You ever write Idi Amin?"

Jorma shrugs, now distinctly uncomfortable. "Yes, I have."

"Did he write back?"

"Of course not."

"Did he get your letter?"

"I assume he did."

"Did he do anything about it?"

Jorma only shakes his head. "We are satisfied if we win even a small percentage. We believe we've caused over a thousand prisoners to be released in the past year, you realize."

I turn to Kristiina. "And you write too?"

"Yes."

"Who to?" I ask, emphasizing the lack of "m" for Jorma.

"Different regimes," she says hesitantly, "all over the world, really."

"A waste of stamps," I say.

"I'm sorry, really," Jorma says, lighting up his pipe for support, "but I can't agree with you. Amnesty has a fine record—we won the Nobel Peace Prize, you know. We are simply — "

"Kidding yourselves. You can't change the world."

Jorma shakes out his match. "We can try."

"It won't do any good. Writing letters? Come on, man, use your head. You're being laughed at."

Jorma eyes Kristiina for further support. "We believe we are taken very seriously. I can show you the statistics — "

"I can show you statistics, too, fellow."

I leave it at that, standing up and walking through the smoke and away from Kristiina's uncertain call. I do not even turn. A hundred-Finnmark bill tossed at the bar, my coat lifted from the rack and I vanish into the night, leaving them to wonder how they can best deal with the island known as Batterinski.

Let them write. Let them see firsthand how useless it is to fool yourself like that. Imagine, believing their idiotic letters mean a fucking thing to someone like Idi Amin or the Russian pigs. The fools.

Outside, during the long walk back to the hotel, I imagine my letter to Tiger Williams:

Dear Tiger,

It was brought to my attention the last time we played that you don't like me. Seven stitches and a fat lip, thanks to your repressive activities. This has got to stop, Tiger. I don't care whether you're right wing or left wing, I'm telling you right now that the Philadelphia Flyers will no longer tolerate this treatment. Putting Batterinski in the slammer solves nothing — surely you can appreciate that. Batterinski is merely expressing his right to play, his freedom to check as his conscience tells him. You're not fooling anyone when you blab in your hometown press that Batterinski sharpens his butt end or kneed you in the face. Search yourself, Tiger. See that there is more to this life than cheap shots.

Someone else will be writing to you in Pig Latin in case plain English isn't your first language.

Yours in hockey,

F. Batterinski

She wants to talk.

How many times have I been through this same idiocy? She

wants to talk. Talk, in all the years of Batterinski's experience, has yet to solve a single goddamned thing. Talk has both caused my problems and finished them off completely. Talk I can do without.

But she wants to talk. She says we *have* to talk.

Why can't people just screw until they solve things?

It is Sunday and I am no longer Batterinski, I am Christ, walking on water. We are approaching Helsinki from the sea, walking; fortunately, the harbor has frozen solid. When I breathe in too fast my nostrils solder together and my lungs cringe. I love it.

The walk, that is, not the talk. We met at the market, walked up through the Kaivopuisto hills and down onto the ice off the island fortress, then on toward the harbor. The conversation seems to have raced ahead of us, all sorts of meaningless talk of Tsar Nicholas and hot baths and armed Russians at the city gates, but I have not even bothered to chase it. My mind is caught between leather and wool, aware only of the life in the small mitt I hold in my glove. Kristiina has a ski jacket so white she stands out startlingly even in the new snow. She has her Lapland toque on, reds and yellows like an electrical circuit, and carries a birch sucker with yellow and pink dyed ostrich plumes dancing from the tip, a purchase she forced on me in the market.

The mitten loosens in my hand. It is time, obviously. She pulls it free and pretends to adjust the ostrich plumes, an unnecessary act for the plumes but necessary for her tactic. She steps away just enough.

"I think you did not have any reason to embarrass me in front of one of my friends," she says at a reasonable level.

"I thought *I* was your friend," I say unreasonably.

"Jorma was very good about it I thought," she says. "He behaved admirably where you did not. Why did you just jump up and leave?"

"I had a practice next morning."

"You could have said goodnight."

"I forgot."

Her mouth curls into a frown. "He is a good friend of mine and I would appreciate you treating him this way. Do you understand?"

"How good a friend?"

"A good friend. Why — are you jealous?" She smiles.

"Should I be?"

"No. You should not be. My friends are *my* choice, not yours."

"Ever sleep with him?"

She stops, turns. "What?"

"Did you ever sleep with him?"

"Why would you ask something like that?"

"I want to know."

"It is not for you to know, I think."

"So — then you have."

"I did not say that. What if I have, as you say, 'slept' with him? What difference does that make?"

"A big difference."

"*What* difference, please?"

If she were only in hockey uniform I would hit. But I am helpless here. Talk — always goddamned *talk*. She should know the difference without having to ask. She should feel the same things as me.

"Please, Bats, what difference would it make?" she laughs, but not with amusement. "You don't own me, you know."

"That's not what I mean."

"Well, then, what *do* you mean? If I cannot have the friends I choose and I cannot make love to whom I choose, what are you doing then but possessing me?"

I feel a turn, in my favor: "That's the point — I want you."

She laughs: "You have had me."

"But I want you for myself. Just the two of us."

"You want to own me."

"No. I want you to feel the same way I do. Just me for you and just you for me."

"Isn't that what they call 'going steady' in your country?" Again, the laugh.

"We're a little old for that," I say with heavy sarcasm.

"Then you want marriage," she says.

I say nothing. I cannot say anything.

She picks up on it, giggling. "You *do* want that!"

I feel like I am in a movie, the lines beyond my control. "I care a great deal for you, Kristiina, you know that."

Laugh. "How much?"

"Lots."

"Well, how much is lots?"

I am being played with here. I feel almost giddy with finally talking about it. Again, it is like a movie, the two lovers oblivious to the world going on around them. But I am not. The harbor is the reverse of summer: no white sails wedging through the colors, but colors cutting everywhere through the white. Skiers are passing us. A young family has a youngster on a toboggan, the rope around his waist and a second rope trailing from the toboggan to a ribbed sled, where a baby sleeps.

"*I love you!*" I shout. I imagine everyone coming to a dead halt, applauding while the young lovers fall into each other's arms, but they merely look at me as if I'm mad and the father of the children says something in Finnish to his wife, making her laugh.

Kristiina is also laughing.

"What's so funny?"

"They do not understand what it is you have said. He told her he thought you were calling for help. He believed the ice was breaking."

"To hell with them! *I — LOVE — YOU!!!*"

God, it feels good to shout this. Kristiina dips down for some snow, pushes it into my face and walks away laughing. I hurry to catch her and my feet slip in the glaze of the ski track. When I catch her it is as much for support as explanation, but when I get my balance I see she is still only amused, not moved.

"What do you feel about me?" I ask. I hate to beg but am forced: again, talk has set my own ambush. It is too late to act as I should have, by shutting up. The solution is talk, but the problem is also talk. I have yet to learn that the only reliable answer is not to begin.

Kristiina leans forward and kisses my cheek. Her lips are cold, making me suddenly aware of how much blood has flooded my face.

"I care for you very much, Bats," she says.

"But you don't love me?"

"I'm thirty-two years old. I'm not sure what love is."

For Christ's sake — we're starting to sound like a movie again. "Well, I'm sure," I say. "I love you and that's that."

"How do you know?"

Jesus, Jesus, Jesus — what the fuck is going on here. What did Ali McGraw say to Ryan O'Neal? Why didn't I pay attention then?

"I don't know," I say, trying to sound philosophical, as if I've given it a lot of thought. "It's just something you feel inside. You know it's there."

"Then I must not feel it," she says, turning away, "because I don't know what it is I'm supposed to feel."

Talk! Goddamned piss-cutting shit asshole *talk!* If they want to
play with me let them put on skates! Batterinski was not made to
talk but to act! *Don't they see that?* Do I have to beat her head
against the ice to get my point across?

I stomp away, moving faster so she must run to catch up. I
hear her slip and fall but do not turn to help; nor, however, do I
take the advantage. I slow down near the summer ferry docks
and let her catch me. She grabs my arm from behind and pulls
back, shouting:

"Bats! What is wrong with you?"

I turn and simply stare, making my first point properly,
wordlessly.

"I have hurt you, yes?" she says.

I say nothing, saying everything.

"But I do like you, very much. Please understand that."

I cannot do as I should; I talk: "Why?"

"I like being with you."

"Why?" I repeat.

"You're fun."

"Amusing, you mean."

"Fun."

"You laugh at me."

"Of course not."

"You think it's a great joke being around the Canadian animal,
don't you?"

"Don't be silly, Bats."

"I'm not being silly. Look at you. You're a goddamned architect.
I'm a washed-up player who hasn't got enough schooling to pump
gas. You have all these highbrow friends like that Jorma asshole
and you sit around and write your fucking letters to this International thing, whatever it's called, and I wouldn't even know
what postage to put on, let alone what to say. We don't talk. We
just screw. When we do talk we just get worse off. So what is it,
eh? What?"

"You're different."

"*Different* — well, that's just fine. Like something from the zoo,
is that it?" I feel anger akin to hockey anger rising and it fright-
ens me. Her I must not hit, no matter what. But is *that* what it is?
I'm *different* — like something she might collect. Is that all that
attracts her: surely to God . . .

"No, silly. Different in a nice way. The men I know here in Helsinki are all so predictable. Like Jorma. There are no surprises in him. I know what he thinks, what he will say, I know what books he reads, where he has been, even precisely when he will start rooting around in that foolish pipe he smokes. You should not worry about Jorma — he's nothing to me. But you mean a great deal. I care very much for you, Batterinski."

A reprieve! I have never come so far in such a conversation and saved anything. I look down at her and there are tears in her eyes, clear beads hanging but not dropping from the blue; her pupils are as small and stabbing as pins, and they have caught me completely.

She sees what I am looking at.

"The wind," she says, brushing the tears away with her mitt.

I say nothing. This I cannot destroy with more words. I take her mitt and we walk away, back toward the hotel. I feel her hand in mine, no longer accepting but taking, and the tightening grip feels as fine as any victory I have ever known. I must hang onto it with silence.

"Are you still mad at me?" she asks in a small voice, as we board the tram for the ride back.

I shake my head, no, and she misinterprets my silence to mean I am in fact still angry. And perhaps she is right. Not angry, but hurt by the fact that I have fully committed myself while she has not. A cardinal sin in hockey and, I fear, as bad or worse in love.

We arrive back at the Inter-Continental with me still silent, talking only through the pressure of my fingers. There is a message shoved in under the door for me to call some radio show called "As It Happens" back in Toronto, and I immediately crumple it and throw it in the waste can. Let them get someone else to tell the world how a crooked agent can dupe dumb hockey players.

I go into the bathroom for no more than a minute and when I come out Kristiina is lying on the bed, naked. There is something pathetic about all of this, but I cannot help myself: my sulk has become a magic wand. I do not smile or even speak. I lie down on the bed with my hands behind my head and stare at the ceiling while lovely Kristiina unbuttons my shirt and then my belt and pulls down my zipper. It is like I have become separated from my own body, my head lying there sad, feeling sorry for itself, sulking, while below my body leaps up like a volunteering soldier, a keener. *My assignment, sir? Yes sir! Right away, sir!*

There is something sick about this. Only Batterinski could lie in bed with a naked, incredibly, exquisitely beautiful Scandinavian blonde and still feel like the most hard-done-by creature on God's earth.

But so be it. I have never before had all things working in synch, so why now?

I can't be that stupid. Anyway, I know that I think on a higher level than most hockey players simply because I can prove I have had some thoughts. Even one would put you in hockey's Mensa, Torchy used to say. I was much too hard on myself out there on the harbor ice. Besides, by dawn when she got up to head back to her apartment to get ready for work, we were carrying on as always, as if there had been neither hurt nor healing, as if there was nothing but what had always been: pure raw passion.

The phone is ringing. The line is distant, crackling, the voice slightly echoed.

"Felix Batterinski, please."

"Yes, speaking."

"Mr. Batterinski — is that you?"

"Yes."

"Could you speak up, please?"

"It is me, yes."

"Good, great. My name is Matt Keening, Mr. Batterinski. I'm with the *Canada Magazine.*"

"A reporter?" Not bad news, please.

"I'm sports editor." The connection fades, then clicks into a higher range. ". . . the magazine insert, you know, the one that comes out with the papers. We've got the largest circulation in Canada."

"Oh, yeah. What's up?"

"I guess you know your picture turned up over here."

"No. What picture?"

A giggle. "You and the Swedish fan."

"Oh, no — how?"

"Reuters picked it up. The *Globe* ran it front page — with an editorial. I won't read that to you. Montreal had it. Ottawa. Others probably. It's big talk over here. 'As It Happens' did a number on you last night. They said they were going to get you on but never did. Harold Ballard was the only guy who defended you — "

"Ballard? Good on him. The Swede spit first, you know. Anybody report that?"

"No. That's what I wanted to talk to you about. Nobody got your side of the story."

"Well, tell them that, then. The Swede spit first. It was self-defense."

"Well, I'd like to tell them much more than that."

"And put the score in too. We won 6–5; they had us 3–0 at the end of the first."

"Much more than that too. I think there's a much larger story here. We're talking at *Canada Magazine* about a full cover takeout, with you having your full say inside. The works, eh?"

"He spit first. I spit back. That's all there is to it."

"But people don't see it that simply. They can't see it the way it was. You've become a symbol overnight for what's wrong with Canadian hockey. Some New Democrat even tried to push a motion of censure through Parliament, did you know that?"

"Did he?"

"It got shouted down. But you were debated in Question Period. It's a bit unfair, I'd say, you not having a chance to explain — "

"You're goddamned right it's unfair!"

"That's why I think we should do something about it. We're the best forum, by far."

"What did you have in mind?"

"A full-length article. We take the picture and all the crap it's raised and then I do a full-length sympathetic treatment of just who Felix Batterinski is and what he's about and by the time I'm done they'll be standing up in Parliament to award you the Order of Canada, mark my words. Now what do you say?"

"To what?"

"Me getting together with you."

"How?"

"I'll come over. Hang in with you. You know, do it right."

"It costs a fortune."

"Don't sweat it. Magazine pays. We'll have a few top meals. Expenses, eh? I'd even like to take in a road trip."

I recoil instinctively. "I don't know."

"Listen, Bats, I'm a fan. You gotta have your say or they'll lynch you, you understand?"

"Yeah, well. I still don't know."

"You wouldn't regret it. I promise you that. You set the ground rules. I come when you say, listen when you say, get lost when you say. You want to go off the record, that's fine, anything — it's your show."

"Well. I can't say right now."

"Take a couple of days. Think it over. I'll call back on, say, Wednesday, okay?"

"I guess."

"Good. Remember, this is your chance to stick those bastards back, eh? It's perfect."

"Ummm."

"Okay, Bats. I'll call Wednesday. Take care now."

"Yeah."

There is a letter from Poppa at the front desk, a letter so thick they couldn't fit it in my slot. I take it, pleased he has written before hearing about the spitting incident. Most of Pomerania would be proud; Poppa, I know without asking, would be disgusted. Perhaps I should let this guy do the story on me, for Poppa's sake.

January 5, 1982

My dear son,

Well, here it is, another year. January is always the most unfamiliar month to me, what with the cheques and the taxes and the like, and you find yourself writing down wrong numbers or else some number you can't believe you've lived so long to see. I'm turning seventy-seven this year, son. If it shocks you, you ought to be in these shoes. That number I put down for my age is some dried-up old geezer, sure as hell ain't me. (*That I'll vouch for — Marie.*) I feel forty, you know. You're damned near forty yourself, you know, and not even married.

Batcha just got back from a four-day stay in Renfrew Hospital where they did all kinds of tests on her, so we've got a better idea. She still has none herself, poor dear. At least not officially. But she knows, the way Batcha always knows everything, and that I don't have to explain to you. (*Nor me! — Marie.*) She hated it there. Your Uncle Jan and

Aunt Sophia and Aunt Jozefa visited every day and I came twice but she wouldn't even speak to us and us her own flesh and blood! The doctors found leukemia, that's a blood cancer, and this young dark doctor (*he's Pakistani and very good, I hear — Marie*) he says it's a matter of months is all. Anyways, I'll keep you posted.

Going down to 45 below *Celsius* tonight, whatever the hell that means. Damn radio won't give out the real temperatures at all anymore, since the New Year. But the thermometer on the bait shed darned near disappeared last night and that's 50 below Fahrenheit, so you have some idea what kind of spell we're up against. There's even frost on the north wallpaper and poor Marie's sitting here in her ski jacket taking notes. (*It's not so bad — Marie.*) My secretary, ha, ha. (*My boss, ha, ha — Marie.*)

Transport made it in through the Park from Vernon the other day. Jazda's got a new chesterfield from Eaton's and Marie remembered you were asking for any news about your old coach, so I'll let her fill you in, okay? (*Felix, he's apparently been in hospital since before Christmas with pneumonia. Mr. Cryderman, the driver, he said he thought your Mr. Bowles was improving. Said he'd been in to see him and asked about you. But Mr. Cryderman didn't seem too hopeful. — Marie.*)

Cryderman? Does she mean Bucky? Old Bucky with his old man's Edsel that we picked up that Maureen slut in? Is that what he's doing now? Riding transport? Jesus H. Christ. He's probably married and feeding six brats, living out on the town line with a Skidoo, a gun rack, a belly like a tractor tire and no hair. I bet he can't even skate anymore. Poor old Bucky — he always wanted to be me, the poor bugger. I wouldn't trade him for a second.

Anyways, we've been going pretty well steady on Jaja's boxes. Nothing else to do. I must say son, I do love this. I'm learning things about our family I'm almost too old to appreciate. Old Jaja used to tell me these things but we'd be working and maybe I didn't pay too much attention, eh? But now it's all written down permanent. Like a history book they could study, kind of. And that's why I'm shipping so much of it off to you, so you'll have it at an age when it matters to you. You'll see just how important it is to you to continue Jaja's good name. Look at your Uncle Jan, just one girl, and you know yourself she took off last year and her only sixteen. Some thanks. She ever comes home she'll probably marry a Kulas or Betz or Hatkoski and our name will be lost forever. It's like thinning coal oil, eh? —eventually you can't even get it to light. Now you've done all us Batterinskis damn proud, son. Stanley Cup — nothing'll ever beat that, getting our name put on there with Howe and Apps and Beliveau and Armstrong and all them other class gentlemen. But please, don't let it stop there.

That's why I was tickled pink to hear about your Kristiina there. Some might call her a D.P. over here, but we were all D.P.'s once. She sounds to me like a very fine person and, knowing you, I'm sure she is. You probably forgot, but you didn't say whether she was Roman Catholic or not, son. If she isn't though, it's not the end of the world as far as I'm concerned. She can always convert.

One thing about your Poppa. I'm not of the old school, eh? Not like Batcha and old Dombrowski and poor dead Father Kulas (*prosie zdrovas*). There's a list of old Polish proverbs in Jaja's notes and one of them says, "A woman must be constantly reminded that she is incapable of ever having any wise or important thoughts or opinions." He just wrote it down. I doubt he believed in it. But that's still the way the old fuddies like Dombrowski think, eh? (*And — excuse me, please, Felix — old fuddies like your Poppa, eh? — Marie.*)

Anyway, enough of that. You'll mind we left off your grandfather's memoirs with the tragic death of your great-grandfather in Warsaw on February 27, 1861, killed by the cursed Russians. After that, Jaja wrote 468 pages of history before he once got back to the family proper. I'm not going to bother you much with that, but Marie and I have worked through it steadily, but it's all here for the day you *or your children* want to know what it was the Batterinskis experienced.

Your Jaja went into incredible detail, page after page after page on the martial law the Russians forced their phoney Polish government to impose in October, the hanging of Romuald Traugutt on August 5, 1864. (Traugutt was young, like Lech Walesa, and had the same following—God forbid the same fate awaits Walesa, eh?) Jaja even gives a full chapter to the Polish philosophy of Positivism, which managed to bore even your old Poppa.

That reminds me of something Hatkoski was saying down at the barber shop Friday, son. He says the only country in Europe where they aren't marching against nuclear weapons is Poland. Hatkoski's convinced there they pray for such a war. It's the only sure way they can see of clearing out the Russians. In a way, I guess, that's Positivism.

You know what the so-called great "friend" of the Poles, Tsar Alexander II, said in 1865, son? *"Pas de rêveries."*

No more dreaming, according to Jaja's translation.

He said that 118 years ago and look what's happening right now in Poland, eh? We are truly either God's chosen people or else the biggest bunch of fools the earth has ever seen. What do you think?

That's about it, Felix. Marie is including some of Jaja's work here and it's all stuff you should be interested in, I hope.

One last thing. There's talk on the television that this Gretzky could score 100 goals this season. Can you imagine that? What does it mean for the NHL? Is he that good or has it gotten that bad?

Do take care and remember that we love you and pray for you.

Your father,

Poppa.

One hundred goals in a season . . . Gretzky makes me puke.

I have a dream about Gretzky. He develops early as an athlete, late as an adult; working on his seventh straight Hart Trophy he mysteriously becomes afflicted with pimples; 7-Up dumps him because he is suddenly living proof that the carbonation in pop eventually bubbles to the surface; Levi's buys out his promotional contract because someone who looks like that is not likely to get into anyone's pants; skate manufacturers drop off, stick manufacturers aren't interested; garbage collectors throughout North

America report a dramatic increase in discarded posters; and in the final game of the season Gretzky tries to split the Islanders' defense and Potvin and Morrow wedge him so perfectly that the Kid — now nothing so much as a white head on a red blister — bursts. Gretzky's final play is etched forever in hardened pus on the roof of the Northlands Coliseum. They burn his sweater.

Dream on, Batterinski. I am as much a fool as old Jaja, only I dream about what might happen while he imagined what might have happened. I am forever proving myself in the future, getting back, suckering, nailing, shafting, shouting the magnificent comeback I couldn't find at the time of the insult. Jaja's proof is behind him. He looked forward and saw nothing more than another spring of knocking pipes together to break off the soot, more cedar to cut for kindling, pulp to cut in another swamp, two dozen more identical brown and green crappers for the city bastards who can't manage a single day in the wilderness without Delsey Super Soft. No wonder he turned to this ridiculous reinvention of himself. Only in the past can things not get any worse then they are right now — the perfect philosophy of a beaten-down Pole.

But such a lovely man. When I think of him I do not see his face, but I smell him. Jaja is gasoline and kerosene and coal oil and lime and ashes and spruce pitch and cedar chips and chicken molt and sow slop and rotten worms and rolled oats. I see the mole on the back of his neck as I hang on from behind, feel the squeeze of his thighs as he tricks me nearer the desk where he works, trapping me for a quick tickle.

Where have those nights gone when I lie full out on the back seat of his old Plymouth, his coat over me, the rare headlights of an oncoming car sliding along the telephone lines to warn us, the honk of a horn at a tight corner, the feel of the floating shocks on the potholes, the soft voices of Jaja and Poppa and Ig in the front seat going over the bingo calls as if they were baseball plays and might have been different if only . . . ? Where are those nights? They are not here. They are not the nights of Batterinski, where too often the glass goes up until the eyelids go down.

Whatever became of Jaja's big coat? If I had it now I would curl until it fit over me. I would raise my knees to my chin and fold my hands in the warm muff of my own body. I would close my eyes and call out the bingo . . . four corners . . . elimination . . . under the "B" 13 . . . "B" for Batterinski . . .

The Batterinski History
by Karol Batterinski

I cannot remember my valiant father. I have not so much
as a picture of this great hero of Poland, though it may be
that one existed. Daguerre's invention was to be found in
Warsaw as early as 1839 and there were more than a
dozen photographic studios in the city by 1861, the year
of his death. I have always had a feeling a picture of him
did exist, but I have also always had a fear that the picture
of him was of his death and that perhaps it served to
warn other Poles what they could expect for denying the
Russians. I prefer to think of him alive, even if I cannot
see him. I see easily what he stood for, and that is enough.

My mother I certainly remember. She was a
melancholy good-hearted woman with thick black hair
severely parted down the middle. I have her nose, slightly
hooked, but not her face. It was round and grew ever
rounder, a characteristic I seem somehow to have passed
on to my beloved second son, Ignace.

That she was tough of mind there can be no question.
With the revolution squashed there was a great exodus
from Poland and her family pressed her hard to leave. We
stayed, however, because the movement, what there was
left of it, felt responsible for Father's death. In any other
circumstances a thirty-year-old woman with a small child
might have starved or barely survived by begging, only
by incredible luck being taken in by another family as
kitchen servants. But not the family of the hero
Batterinski. We were taken in by the Mickiewicz family,
cousins of the great poet, and they put us up in a
comfortable home with a slight view of the west harbor
in Gdansk. I still very well remember important men
coming around and the sounds of argument and serious
talk from below. Always there would follow a summoning
of Mother and me from the third-floor attic. I would be
questioned and tested by gruff, cigar-smoking men in
work clothes but who were always to be called General or
Colonel or Captain whenever I spoke to them. I
remember them all not for their beards or walking sticks
or the strong smell of drink, but for their eyes. They had
tired eyes with sad, sad messages in them. I never seemed

192 The Last Season

an intrusion to them; it was more like I was being sized up
in some way.

Scouts. Jaja and I are not so far apart. I remember the Bantam
"A" finals in Collingwood when Sugar came in and closed the
door and spoke like Father Schula about the scouts who were
coming to the final round-robin. You would think the Holy Ghost
himself was coming down with a clipboard and plus-minus figures to see if you were worthy of the call. Sugar's good eye shifted
between Powers and me, and though he spoke to the whole team
the words couldn't hold a candle to the stare.

His voice said: "Just forget they're there. Play your game as
you know it. If anything comes of it, it was meant to be. Nothing
you can do out there today will change all that, okay? So just
forget they're there watching."

His eye said: "Batterinski! Powers! You two bust your asses out
there like your life depended on it. If the scouts don't say anything to you, then neither will I — ever again. So don't fuck up,
understand?"

We lost in the finals to, naturally, Parry Sound. But after the
scouts were through sucking around the kid Orr — Christ, he
wasn't even legally a bantam yet! — two of them, Bob Davidson
from the Leafs and an old fart from the Boston organization named
Dempsey, came and asked Powers and me to come to this little
room for a chat. It turned out to be the room for the skating club,
and we sat in a perfumed dressing room surrounded by crino-
line and tutus and a glassed-in portrait of Barbara Ann Scott side
by side with a glassed-in portrait of Queen Elizabeth II.

"How old are you, son?" Davidson asked me.

"Fifteen."

"How much you weigh?"

"One-seventy."

"You ever go to hockey school, son?"

"No."

"You should, son. Your skating needs a lot of work."

They did not ask what number I wanted on the Leafs or Bruins.
They did not ask who I'd like for my defense partner. There was
no mention of junior, of the minor leagues, of anything. Same for
Powers. They did not ask whether we had any interest in playing

professional hockey. It was a given. They did not once mention school. In its own way, I would later realize, it was also a given.

Sugar was delighted. All the way home he kept slapping our backs with his knobby hands and calling us "prospects." I sat with him later and tried to explain that it wasn't that big a deal, but he cut me off with a stab of the eye.

"You wouldn't know," he said.

Same with Jaja, I suppose.

In 1875, when I was fourteen, I went through an experience that has stayed with me to the present. One of the bearded generals who came to dinner at the Mickiewiczes' convinced my patrons that I should be sent on a pilgrimage to the Jasna Gora basilica in Czestochowa. I was sent alone, and how I made it I can barely believe, now so many years later. The distance must be well over one hundred miles, and while I do remember rides from other pilgrims in mule-drawn carts, I also remember frost in the beginning and then the sound of crickets so loud at times I could not think. So I must have walked from early June until sometime in August.

I slept in barns and fields and trees and wagons. Because I was a pilgrim and also because I had a letter of introduction from the general of that night, I never went hungry, and most farms I left in the morning with my sack heavy with *kielbasa* or some sweet *paczki* for lunch.

When I arrived in Czestochowa the village was filled with pilgrims and I had to wait three days just for a place at a pew to pray. I waited, was admitted, but I could not pray. I could only stare. It is the same face we have in our beloved St. Martin's here in Pomerania, but I cannot possibly explain the difference between the real thing and an imitation, even if our imitation is still something to be proud of. But there, the painting of Our Lady looks down on you with a power so unnatural that I feel it still, just writing about it. She had the same long and sad eyes that I had come to believe was the secret code of the movement. And of course she was wounded, twice slashed on the right cheek by a man who, it is said, fell instantly dead when his blasphemous deed was done.

Before I came to Jasna Gora I had trouble believing

what I was taught. The historian in me said it was not likely. But now, in the church, the believer in me argued that it was indeed true. Sitting there, caught in her stare, I knew absolutely that 330 Poles had repelled 4,000 Swedish soldiers in the year 1655. How? Simple: Our Lady fought with them. If the Swedes felt half the power I felt, they would have dug their own graves and lain down in them to help the Poles out.

No, I did not pray, but I carry no shame for that. When I stood to make room for other pilgrims I felt myself different from them. I felt that because of my father and Our Lady's stare that I, Karol Batterinski, had been chosen to do something for Poland.

But what? When I arrived back in Gdansk I felt different, no longer the child living in the attic with his mother. I had no one to talk to in the family. Not mother, not the Mickiewiczes, not the men who came to dine. I had only poor nervous, nearsighted Mr. Kopernick, the tutor the family retained for their eldest son, Casimir, and who was allowed to teach me in the afternoons. The poor man claimed he was a descendant of Poland's greatest scientist, Copernicus. He used to read aloud from *De revolutionibus orbium coelestium* and he had an irritating habit of tying all knowledge and thought to Copernicus's theory. I should have known that he would twist my feelings of Czestochowa to suit this purpose. When I told him how I had felt chosen, somehow more special than the other pilgrims, Mr. Kopernick argued that it was evident from Copernicus's teachings that man is incapable of perceiving correctly. Man's eyes tell him that the sun revolves around the earth. And each day this self-evident truth is repeated as the sun begins in the east and rises into the sky and falls in the west. The actual truth, as Copernicus proved, is precisely the opposite of what man naturally believes. Man revolves around the sun.

We are part of the plan, Mr. Kopernick argued, not the planner. As a true believer, then, what I felt in front of Our Lady was *her* power, not mine, but since the sensation was within it was only natural I should mistake it for my own creation. He seemed mildly amused at my arrogance.

We had this discussion in the late fall of that year, 1875. It was a wet, cold fall with no snow and no wind to dry up the rainfall, and everyone came down with severe colds which we were several weeks shaking. And one day Mr. Mickiewicz called on Casimir and me to join him in his study, where he told us Mr. Kopernick would no longer be tutoring us. He had been found dead in his bed that morning.

It left me with the most peculiar sensation. I was sad because I had been fond of him, but I was also all the more puzzled now. Was Mr. Kopernick right? Are we merely part of the overall plan and not the planner, and that luck of the draw had felled him? Or was I perhaps closer to the truth and was it his denying of the power of Our Lady that had caused his own weakness? By not being a solid believer, as I was, he wasn't fully armed.

I would never know. When I came to this blessed land in Canada, what was I doing for Poland? I worked hard and I had a family and prayed and I loved Poland always, but I must here confess that I might have failed Our Lady's message to me because I did not have the courage to trust in my own judgments.

Part of why I write this is to fix that, even if only to paper it over the way I might a broken window in the house. I believe I have served Poland, however insignificantly, by carrying Poland to my family now in Canada, forever in Canada. It is in Jan's children and in Walter's Felix that the Batterinski name continues, the name of Tadeusz Kósciusko Batterinski, our father who died for Poland.

What I can do, even if it is now late, is to make sure they remember his death. And when they remember his death they will think of Poland, and when they think of Poland they will feel the power of the blessed Black Madonna, Our Lady. And if Felix has a son and one day when I am dead this boy reads of his great-great-grandfather and the country he comes from, then I will be content and, perhaps, Our Lady will be content as well. Her message I received in 1875 I will have passed on.

Mother of Jesus, if Our Lady has any idea what I've been using

her *power* for, St. Peter is going to whistle me straight into the
penalty box forever. I'm sorry, Poppa, but I can't buy that. Love
Jaja, yes, but accept that we are all part of some master Roman
Catholic plan to make sure the Batterinski name doesn't have its
last fling as an asterisk in the *1992–93 NHL Guide* is a bit hard
to take:

> *The 62 minutes in penalties Felix Batterinski accumulated in a
> single game (February 23, 1979, Los Angeles at Pittsburgh) is the
> most any player received per game, though Batterinski's season's
> total of 254 minutes was less than Toronto's Dave Williams's 298
> minutes.

I am simply not in the mood for this. First Poppa, now Jaja, and
what I need to think about is Kristiina and what is going wrong
with us. I can read us easier. We have had our fight; we have had
our talk; we have made up; she will call soon for another talk; I
will get mad; I will call it off before she calls it off; she will win.
The same pattern, always, my love life as predictable as a Toronto
power play. This time, however, with Kristiina, I have never had
possession so long. In the past — Carol in Philadelphia, Miranda
out in L.A., how many others? — I have usually been checked the
moment I began the rush. Tripped by my own tongue. Checked,
always, by them.

There is no insult intended to Jaja, but it is all I can do to leaf
through the next thirty pages:

> As if the Russians were not bad enough, we now had the
> Prussian *Kulturkampf* to deal with. There was, of course,
> no Poland in political fact, just in our dreams, and what
> the Russians didn't control the Prussians did. Bismarck
> began his anti-Polish campaign in 1872 and its intention
> was to wipe out Poland in wish as well as actuality. The
> Germans changed the Polish place names, forced Poles to
> sell whatever little land they owned, and even attacked
> our language. . . ."

What's this? Yes, Jaja said he had been a teacher but I hadn't
believed him. Teachers were nuns, not old men who worried about
whether white bread would attract more minnows into the traps
than rye. But here it is:

. . . It gave me great peace of mind that Christ was also a
teacher. But there the similarity ended. Jesus saw
inequity and he set out to equalize. He saw the outcasts
and he embraced them. He gave food to those who were
hungry, comfort to the ill, miracles to the lame. I shut my
eyes, I admit it. The children scratched head lice all
winter and I would not ask for a doctor, for fear the
Prussian administrators would conclude the parasite
originated in the Polish teacher. I saw them at lunch
hunched over small cloth bags, their mouths pressed to
the hole where small hands fumbled as they rolled their
tongues in their mouths and made the Prussian
inspectors think there was actually food in their bags. . . ."

Poppa, Poppa, Poppa — as if I'm not depressed enough! I cannot
read all of this, not now. Jaja's memories I will place with the
others, not in the dresser where Kristiina might see it and ask,
but in the satchel section of my traveling bag, zippered up, locked
in the hotel closet.
  That way we'll leave each other alone.

It is only a week since the so-called "disastrous" Swedish trip
and Turku was sold out last night. They were hanging from the
rafters to see the big stud who spit in the face of Sweden. Some
disaster, I pointed out with great pleasure to Erkki the Jerkki.
And we won, as well, a fluke 3–2 thanks to Turku losing out on a
protested goal that I'm forced to admit was over the line before
my big paw hauled the puck back and tucked it in under the
goalie's pads. Pekka actually scored one with his teeth when a
shot of mine from the point was tipped into his face and then the
net. He's sitting on the back of the bus right now trying to suck
cognac through a straw so he can kill the pain of the stitches. But
even he's not complaining.
  Not like Erkki. Erkki's still having his hissy fit about the Swedish incident and he won't let up on it. Says the board's on his
back and that Hauki's been internationally embarrassed. What's
going to happen — will people boycott their goofy little wooden
minnows the way France won't have anything to do with Canadian
seals? Cruelty to balsam, perhaps? I asked Erkki this and he says
that's not the point. He says my actions aren't in keeping with
the Hauki image. I felt like asking him what the board wanted me

to do, attach a treble hook to my belly button, but I just walked
away instead and left him to chew out his nails.

The bus gets us back from Turku at noon the following day, and
the telephone is ringing when I reach the hotel room door. I rush
in, worrying, hoping, praying that it is Kristiina. I am uncomfortable, tired and nervous after the long haul home, and I am
afraid the call will make me feel even worse. But I am not certain.
I take it tentatively, half wishing I'd merely let the phone ring
itself out.
   "Hello."
The line crackles badly. Someone sounds like they are shout-
ing into an empty pail.
   "I can't hear you!" I shout.
The line goes dead and I place the receiver back. In a few
moments it rings again, the line this time clear and loud, as if I am
getting a call from the next room.
   "That you, Felix?"
   "Yeah."
   "Matt Keening here—from *Canada Magazine*. I said I'd give you
a shout back today."
   "Oh yeah." *Damn.*
   "Have you given any thought to my proposal?"
I lie. "Some."
   "And?"
   "Well, I think the timing's not so good right now, eh?"
   "But it couldn't be better, Felix. We should nip this thing in the
bud, I say."
   "What's been happening?"
   "There isn't a columnist in the country hasn't taken a run at
you. Fotheringham was so hot you could have fried an egg on the
back page of *Maclean's*."
   "Well, I'm not so sure I want to do it. Not right now anyway.
We're going into the stretch for the play-offs right now and coach-
ing needs my full concentration. You can understand. That's what
I'm paid to do. I just like to hold off for a bit, okay?"
   "How long?"
   "Until I see how things are going."
   "But you're not saying no."
When I finally shake him and hang up I realize that I have not

said no, though I had meant to. Perhaps I need my say. Would Jaja be comforted to know that the name has indeed been remembered, but as something they hold up to children as a bad example?

Just maybe there's something to be said for one final full-color story to close out the scrapbook. A final correction.

Pekka sure doesn't look any hell, his lower lip rising like a water-ski ramp, but at least he's game. When Kristiina called I figured for sure it was time for a quiet heart-to-heart, but when she suggested we invite Pekka and Pia along to the cottage, I knew I was Scot-free for a while: Pekka wouldn't allow an undertaker a serious moment. Kristiina couldn't possibly be going in for the kill. At least not yet.

"Don't dock do me," Pekka mumbles as we're hauling the booze and fishing gear out of the trunk.

"Huh?"

"Don't dock do me."

"I never said a word."

"Well don't. My deeth hurt like hell in dis cold."

Dis. I have not heard *dis* or *dat* or *dem* since the last time I talked to Poppa. It doesn't even sound right in my brain any more, though it's still my first language.

When we cut through the spruce there is already heavy smoke rising out over the lake. The girls have gone ahead and fired up both stoves, the cottage and the sauna, and I imagine them already busy inside, turning down beds, setting the lopsided little table, melting down snow for the coffee.

They come out onto the porch as we ease the toboggan down the slope. When I turn she waves a hand mittened in pink angora, and the innocence of the action almost causes my knees to buckle with need. She has on her white ski pants but has removed the top. The braces ride over a black, gray and white test pattern of a sweater and form convenient brackets around her breasts. The air has heightened her color as if she had on make-up, though I know she wears none; it is precisely this freshness and purity that makes her so precious. Pia stands beside her, less committed to the excursion than Kristiina; Pia is there for the drinks, the laughs, the sex. With her red hair tangled by the wind and her eyes dark from the sleep on the way up, she stands like the saucy opposite of Kristiina, awkward, as if out of her element. Surrounded by wind and cold air and sunshine, the trees, the frozen lake and the smell of burning birch, Pia seems discontented, as if longing for a more suitable natural habitat for herself. A bar, maybe. Perhaps the bedroom. Kristiina, on the other hand, seems as much a part of the setting as the snow itself.

"All we need now is the fish," she calls.

"Grease the pan!" I call back, laughing.

"Are you going out right away?" she asks.

I look at Pekka. He nods, unwilling to speak.

"Sure. Why not?" I say. "We'll leave you two here to warm up the place."

"No, we'll be shoveling off the roofs," Kristiina says.

I hear Pia groan. It is nothing compared to what I feel. The snow she should leave for us, when we're through fishing. She should be in the kitchen, waiting for us with hot drinks and a snack, her voice drifting out as pleasurably as the lines wind in — "Did you catch any fish?" — with us saying nothing but dropping the catch at her feet while she ohhs and ahhs in appreciation. This is unnatural.

"Leave it," I say. "We'll do it after."

This time Pekka groans.

"Don't be silly," Kristiina says, laughing. "We've nothing else to do, have we, Pia?"

Pia agrees half-heartedly. "Sure."

I say nothing, trusting in my eyes to express my anger. But when I look there is no eye contact to be had. Kristiina is booting the ice from the shed door, muscling it open to get at the shovels. There is nothing to do but deliver the toboggan to Pia's feet, swoop up the auger and bait box, and stomp off through the drifts to fish.

The ice is thick. We select a place just out from the point where I figure a rock shoal should run out toward a near island, and Pekka and I take turns on the auger, finally cutting through at a point near the end of the tool's potential.

It is numbingly cold out in the open. There are no trees or knolls to break the wind and we end up with our backs to it, jigging the lines just to keep warm.

"I hab one!" Pekka shouts.

I try to remain calm. "Let him take it. Easy now!"

But Pekka is too excited. He jerks the line and the line slackens, the fish freed.

"You've got to give them line," I say. "Let them take it right down, okay? Then when you hit you'll set, understand?"

Pekka nods.

I feel something at my own line, delicate as a mosquito on a shirtsleeve. I loosen the line, picturing the fish below as he nudges up, perhaps a poke with his nose first to see if there's any life to this twisted, dead minnow. Silently I count ten and then yank upward, fast, short and very hard.

"I've got him," I say quietly.

Pekka shouts and drops his own line to watch. I would never watch, at least not directly. I take my purchase in carefully, making sure I don't tear the hook from his mouth. The fish turns slowly, exhausting quickly and conceding. I see him rise. He enters the hole defeated and arrives on the other side to my victory.

"Fantastic!" Pekka shouts, then grabs his mouth in pain.

"It's a goddamned pike!" I say. "Isn't it?"

"Bike?"

"Pike!" I repeat. "'P' — *p*ike!" And then realize Pekka can't pronounce it anyway.

He shakes his head, confused. No matter. I can see by its snarl it is pike: the snake has followed me even here. Danny or Poppa would shoot it or take an ax to it.

"*Hauki!*" I say, suddenly remembering that this is what our team name means.

"Ah," Pekka says. "*Hauki.* A good one."

"A damn pike," I say.

"He's good."

I say nothing. I set the line again and return to jigging, praying for a whitefish. This has not gone the way it should. When the wind shifts I can hear the sound of shovels scraping on the cottage roof and from time to time the gasp of heavy snow falling down onto itself.

The shoveling eventually stops and I am pleased, but no more fish bite and I am distraught. What man ever returned home triumphantly with pike? Pekka is beginning to freeze. He beats his arms against his sides and has pulled his sweater neck up over his mouth.

"Let's quit," he says finally.

I have been waiting for that. The pike I can now blame on him; Pekka didn't have the patience for whitefish.

Our silent walk back is broken by the crack of the cabin door. The sound bursts into the bay like split firewood and Pia's head hangs sideways out the partly opened door, her long red hair falling, nearly touching the snow.

"Hey! You cold enough?"

"You bet!" I call back.

"Catch anything?"

"Bats caught a bine one!"

I wince.

"Great!" Pia calls. "Shall we have a sauna first to warm up?"

Sounds marvelous. "Sure!" we both call at the same time.

Suddenly the door bursts fully open and Pia, laughing, runs naked out onto the porch. The cold hits her like a groper and she unsuccessfully wraps her arms around great, bouncing breasts. Behind her I hear the unmistakable giggle of Kristiina, and then she follows, also naked, jumping off the porch into the knee-deep snow and then brazenly high-stepping in a flush-faced march toward the sauna house.

"*Haakke päälle!*" Pekka shouts, forgetting his lip. He buckles and hangs on to it, cursing. "*Paska!*"

When I see that it is Kristiina he stares at, I have to hold myself back. I should deck him. That goddamned Pia! She talked Kristiina into this, that little tramp — making a fool of her best friend. They must have been into the booze.

Pekka doesn't even act as startled as I would expect. I myself am too stunned to speak. I have never seen Pia in anything other than a clinging dress or tight jeans before, and though my mind has tried to imagine, it has clearly fallen short. I am afraid to look again. Pekka, however, stares at Kristiina as if she is in a magazine. He tries to whistle but can't. He tries to make a snowball but the snow is too cold and won't pack. He gives up, giggling closed-mouthed, and hurries after them toward the smoke of the sauna.

I do not know what to do. Cursing Pekka, I lean down and gather up the equipment he has dropped and the board-stiff pike.

When Pekka goes through the sauna door and the giggles are shut off, it is as it has been so many times in the past: me, alone, cleaning up after a day's fishing. I have half a mind to simply walk to the cottage and gut the fish, just to let them know Batterinski takes the outdoors seriously, unlike them.

But while I can imagine, I cannot follow through. If I was just out fishing alone and this scene happened in my mind, I would follow through in my mind, ripping off my clothes as I raced to the sauna and bursting in on the heaving-breasted, saucy redhead and her lithe angelic friend while they squealed in delight and spread their legs in greeting. But no, this is not in Batterinski's mind, and in reality I am standing here with a toothy, useless fish in one hand and a basket in the other.

There is laughter in the sauna. It had better not be at me. But what then? No, it had better be at me. Those bastards, leaving me out here . . .

The sauna opens and Kristiina's head leans out. She shines with sweat and her entire body bursts with fog as it slides further out. She is giggling, unable to speak, and I imagine right through her, right through the door and the dry wall and the birch and see a puffing, fat-lipped Pekka tickling her from behind with his erection.

"Get in here!" she commands.

I drop the fish and basket, walk over slowly as if we have not met.

"Hurry up! It's cold," she laughs. She reaches out and grabs my arm, pulling me and yanking the door open with her other hand. Pekka is not there. His clothes are neatly hanging from the wooden peg.

"Take off your clothes, silly man!" she orders.

I do, only shucking my jockey shorts at the last moment when I decide it would not make the point intended. Pia would think I was ashamed of my size when in truth I am ashamed of Pekka. No, outraged—outraged that he is in there naked and my woman is also in there naked.

Inside I do not focus quickly, but when I do there is no grunting and slipping and sliding on hot rocks, no tongues and missing fingers and steaming pubic areas. Pia and Kristiina are sitting on the top bench, their heads lowered and hair falling and sticking on their faces as they lean forward intently toward Pekka. But he is not standing there waving an erection at them. They stare at his back, and he sits like them, only one step further down.

No squeals. No sucking. Nothing. You'd think we were at a church social were it not for the fact that all are naked and the two women have shapes that should have creases in their bellies where the centerfold fits into the magazine. But it is neither church nor magazine. It is real and, for them at least, natural.

"What's going to happen to Walesa?" Pia asks me.

I pretend not to hear; there is no need for them to include me just out of courtesy. And how would I know anyway? But she is waiting. I pretend to be mulling it over, and then answer as if it is all well thought out.

"It's hard to say."

"Your *Time* magazine has made him their 'Man of the Year,'" Pia says.

I nod. Didn't Poppa say that in his letter? I can't remember. I should have paid more attention.

"It is so pathetically ironic," Kristiina says, "Karl Marx's great prediction finally comes true, Walesa leads an honest-to-God authentic revolution of the proletariat and what happens — the communist party puts down the revolution."

"Dey say nineteen died," Pekka says.

"They *admit* nineteen died," says Pia. "Who will ever know?"

"Such a sad, sad story," Kristiina says.

I can feel Pia's hand on my back, comforting me; it sends a shiver down my back that has nothing to do with comfort.

"You must feel very strongly about what is happening, Bats," she says.

"I do. Yes."

"Walesa gets his strength from his religion. Where do you turn?"

"I try not to think about it," I say with total honesty. Her hand pats along my back as if burping me.

"Your prime minister says Solidarity's demands were excessive anyway," Pekka says, laughing.

He is staring at me. *My* prime minister? Trudeau?

"How did Canadians react to that?" Pia asks.

"They think he's a jerk," I say, again with complete honesty.

I am scouring my mind for some remembrance of what Poppa or Jaja might have said. If only I had read the letter more carefully; if only I had paid attention. Why should they, Finns, know and care more about Poland than a Batterinski? Can I really be that ignorant?

"It has happened so many times before," I say gravely. "And it will happen again. My great-grandfather died fighting, you know. There was a revolution a hundred years ago or more and he was a great general and the Russians tortured him but he would never talk. He died and we came to Canada. Even now I would not be allowed back in Poland, you know, not with my name. It is the same as his."

Pia's hand rests in respect. Pekka leans forward and shakes his head. I am afraid to turn, so I imagine Kristiina, staring at my back, listening and then going over my words, so moved she can only sit and let the tears fall, imagining what wonderful, special thing she can do to me to ease the enormous pain of my past.

Bless you, Jaja.

My stomach sloshes with wine. When I turn in the bed, I listen to supper. Parts of it I can still find in my teeth where the goddamn pike bones have anchored like tent pegs. We have made love, formal as missionaries but with the climax of heathens, me riding above on the sole support of my forearms and toes, our bodies touching in one area alone, slowly, silently, tensely, as if the organs have gone off alone to do whatever pleases them and the lovers are merely politely smiling at each other from a respectable distance, unaware of the lust below.

We were so quiet in our lovemaking that I could hear the wood stove and the wind outside. I have mentioned the wind and Kristiina has said that the sounds of the elements are so vital to Finns that there are even different names for separate winds. *Humista* for the whisper in the pines. *Kohista* for the slight rattle in the birches. And so on. It strikes me as the work of people with too much time on their hands. I think of the bleak farmhouses on the way up here and the madness I imagined beyond the curtains. I see Finns inside cowering in the corners as armies of wind attack, some slipping in lassoes across the fields, great sheets roaring in off the roads, wind sneaking through the trees, wind full of the kind of voices even screams cannot silence.

I tuck in close to Kristiina, grateful for her warmth and smell.

"Can't sleep?" she says very quietly, her eyes still closed.

I nibble at her ear. "Uh-uh." I bite, hoping it will lead to a full meal.

Her eyes open. She turns full on me, smiling. "Something's been bothering you since the sauna. Is it Poland?"

"No."

"What then?"

"I don't know."

"Come on. You can tell me."

I control my voice, lowering it to a bare whisper. "I don't care to have Pekka see you like that."

"You saw Pia 'like that.'"

"Yes. And Pekka should be upset too."

"Pekka upset — but why?"

"Pia is his woman."

"Pia is her own woman." She seems cross. "You think Pekka has never seen *me* naked before?"

I hadn't thought of that. For a moment I am angry, then realize I am probably acting like an ass.

"The sauna?" I say.

"Yes. That's one place."

"Just the two of you?"

"Yes. And others. Like today."

"What do you mean 'That's one place'?"

"Bed," she says in a small voice.

"Bed?"

"Yes. Bed. Just the two of us."

"You and Pekka?"

"Me and Pekka."

"In bed?"

"Yes. I thought you knew."

I can barely speak. "How could I know?"

"Pekka introduced us. I thought he might have said so to you."

"Said what?"

"We were lovers once, you know. Pia and I were roommates and when Pekka and I broke off they moved in together. They make a much better couple than Pekka and I ever did. All we did was fight and make up. It was awful."

I say nothing. I cannot.

I turn my back to her. She kisses my neck and runs a hand down my side and begins working around toward my pubic hair, and though I can feel myself growing I carefully lift her hand away. She sighs, accepting this, and after a while I can hear her breathing deeply, asleep.

But I cannot sleep. I stare up at the ceiling rafters, now fully formed in the glancing light of the moon. The room is shadowed, the furniture clear and black, the windows light blue with a slight glow. I can hear the fire, the heat in the pipes, the wind beyond, and as I lie staring another sound comes, faint and slow at first, but soon accelerating. It is the sound of a bed and soon it is the sound of the entire cottage, a grinding, knocking beat of old springs and headboard, and through it all their breathing, moaning, quick Finnish phrases.

I lie listening, and it is no longer Pekka and Pia but the sound of Pekka and Kristiina making love in the past. I can feel her pressing spoon-fashion to me, but it is still her, not Pia, in the other room thrusting herself upward to meet Pekka's arrogance. He knew her before I knew her. He perhaps knew her better.

I think of the fish knife in the basket, a long, thin tapered knife for filleting, with a blade so thin it bends like plastic but so sharp it can remove skin from flesh so cleanly that the scales and outer skin are left lying on the board like a book cover. There is one enormous burst of air from the other room and then silence, nothing. I imagine Pia waking up in the morning to find a perfectly filleted Pekka beside her, the flesh removed from the skin the way Poppa taught me, the shell of Pekka left beside her, empty and useless and deserving what he got.

The fucking bastard.

So this is the way it is. Outside the various winds work in off the lake and inside I dwell in madness, full of bad *sisu*. No longer Pole, or even Canadian, but Finn. I should cut out his heart.

I listen to the wind and try to sleep. The wind works in along the sauna and up onto the porch, singing in the support beams. The wind trills along the window, then bumps angrily in the eaves. The wind moves in the moonlight, little soldiers advancing.

And from down near the upturned boat comes the old woman's laugh, teasing along the tracks and past the skis and straight up to the window where Batcha stands staring in. I feel the wolf eyes burning along my neck, cutting straight into Kristiina so she opens like a gutted pike and her insides spill along the bed and down my stomach, covering my balls. Something is pulling at her neck and she breaks like gills from the throat, the air popping from her bladder, sending her spinning down into the water until I can no longer see her. . . .

"*KRISTIINA!*"

I sit up and feel the sweat ice along my entire body. The bed is soaking. Kristiina is reaching for me, half kneeling in bed, holding me. She is not torn; she is not with Pekka. She is with me, holding.

"You had a nightmare," she says.

I cannot speak. I want to cry but dare not. Batterinski does not cry from nightmares. There are sounds from the other room.

"*PIA!*" Pekka shouts, in mock imitation of my own yell. Muffled laughter comes from their room, followed by a "shave-and-a-haircut" knock from Pekka, then silence.

"Come here," Kristiina says, opening herself to me.

I fall into her fortress, smothering myself in her breasts. I grab her about the waist and hold tight so she cannot escape, a hockey hold, really, so they cannot land punches. But it is not fists I am afraid of. It is dreams.

I saw Batcha at the window! I *thought* I saw Batcha at the window. I *dreamed* I saw Batcha at the window.

Dreams . . . I must remember what it was Poppa said in his letter. It was about dreams . . . something about a Tsar or some other goddamned Russian . . .

Pas de rêveries.

That's it. No more dreaming.

No more dreaming.

Please.

"With Philadelphia's Stanley Cup win over Boston in '74 and then a repeat in 1975 over Buffalo, winning through intimidation was no longer seen as a fluke. No one wanted goal scorers now; the ideal draft choice was six-and-a-half feet tall, close to 220 and able to bite the head off a live chicken without first putting his dental plate back.

Even the law was getting involved. When Ontario Attorney-General Roy McMurtry charged Detroit's Dan Maloney with 'assault causing bodily harm' for smoothing out the ice at Maple Leaf Gardens with Brian Glennie's head, Leaf owner Harold Ballard reacted not with congratulations to McMurtry, but with his own commitment to violence. 'We've got to get a line-up that can take on a bunch of goons,' Ballard announced. 'I'm looking for guys you toss raw meat to and they go wild.'

Ballard got an American, Kurt Walker, a giant who looked like a Pittsburgh Steeler lineman and seemed, on the ice, like he was still waiting for the play to be sent in from the sidelines. In the play-offs of that year, Philadelphia's Dave Schultz dropped Walker with a single punch. And soon the Leafs' play-off hopes were history.

In the World Hockey Association it was as bad if not worse, with Winnipeg Jets' superstar Bobby Hull even sitting out a game to unsuccessfully protest against the violent attacks on his Swedish linemates, Ulf Nilsson and Anders Hedberg. 'If something isn't done soon,' said Hull, 'it will ruin the game for all of us. I've never seen so much vicious stuff going on.'

The effect was absolutely zero. Philadelphia, thanks to the likes of Batterinski, continued to win and others continued to model themselves on the Flyers' formula for success.

'If it's pretty skating the people want,' said Philadelphia coach Fred Shero, 'let 'em go to the Ice Capades.'"

Excerpted by permission from "Batterinski's Burden," by Matt Keening, *Canada Magazine*, June 1982

CANUCKLEHEAD . . . IT HAD BEGUN THE WEEK BEFORE IN the *St. Louis Dispatch* after I took a run at the Blues' prettyboy, Garry Unger, and now it was all over the Spectrum's walls. Two huge posters were up along the east wall, and on the south side a massive queen-sized sheet had been painted to show a hammer and sickle being bent double under the skates of a raging Flyer who was wearing my number. Thirty-two. I know, I know . . . but Bill Barber had dibs on 7 before I got there from Pittsburgh and had already made the number less than what it was, if that's possible. Not that Barber wasn't a fine player, but his reputation around the league was precisely the opposite of mine: if Barber took dives, then Batterinski was the hidden rock in shallow water. One predictable, the other not for a moment. So 32 it was. At least it was distinctive. Over the bottom of this cartoon of Big Number 32 the sheet was spray-painted red for blood. And over the top, in magnificent Flyer orange, four words: "CANUCKLEHEAD JA, SOVIETS NYET!"

Everywhere there were American flags or posters going up. "END THE RED PLAGUE!" "BORIS IS BORING!" "THE BELL OF FREEDOM WILL RING SOVIET SKULLS!" "THE FLYERS ARE COMING, THE FLYERS ARE COMING!" "BROAD STREET BULLIES 10, LENIN SQUARE COMMIES 0!"

Central Red Army was in town for the final game in an eight-game NHL-Soviet series, the first since Paul Henderson had salvaged Canada's pride in Moscow back in '72, with a lousy 34 seconds left. The two touring Soviet teams had already taken the series in a walk, easily defeating the Islanders, Rangers, Black Hawks, Bruins and Penguins, tying the Canadiens on New Year's Eve and losing only once, to Buffalo. But since we were the defending Stanley Cup champions, the NHL was expecting to avenge each and every insult in the final match. Schultz, Kelly, Dupont, Saleski and Batterinski were suddenly white knights riding out to meet the forces of evil. We were going to war, and all Philadelphia was at our feet.

Poppa even called, the first time he'd ever done so, with the exception of Christmas and Good Friday. For some reason I thought it was the press, somehow finding out my unlisted number, and I tore into the poor bugger for daring to use my Christian name.

"Hello, Felix?"

"Who's this?" I yelled.

"That you, Felix?"

Dat. Dat.

"Poppa?"

"That you, Felix?"

"Yah, it's me. Where the hell are you, Poppa?"

"Home. Right here in the kitchen. I'm sitting in your old chair, son."

"What's up? Everything okay?"

"Sure everything's okay. I'm calling about you, not me, eh? They're all talking about you up here. Danny and all the rest of the lads. I hear 'em."

Duh lads.

"Yah, what about?"

"Tonight. You boys are going to send them Russians packing. It's going to be on the television."

"So? You haven't got one."

I could hear Poppa's laugh, a hiss above the constant hiss of the line. "I got one now, thanks to you."

"What do you mean, 'Thanks to me'?"

"I used the money you sent to get one."

"I told you to trade that old shitwagon in on a new truck, Poppa."

"Old truck's perfectly fine. I got an overhaul down at Betz's and Jan found an alternator for her over at Renfrew, so she's good for some yet. Besides, Batcha can't enjoy the truck. I got the television for her."

"*She'll* be watching tonight?"

"She won't watch much. Says it hurts her head, not knowing where the lights are coming from."

"What lights?"

"She's old. She doesn't trust it. She won't even use the telephone."

"Who'd she call? She's got no friends."

"Now, now, son. There's no need for that, eh?"

He was right. No need for *dat.*

"You're going to watch, eh, Poppa?"

"You bet. You play your heart out against them Russians, understand?"

Poppa seemed so serious. Did he really think Batterinski needed a pep talk?

I couldn't resist teasing. "Why, Poppa?"

"You're a Pole!"

I could feel his anger through the wires.

"What's that got to do with it?"

"The Russians are the root of everything bad that ever happened to Poland. Don't you forget that!"

"How could I?"

"You'll have God on your side, you watch."

"God?"

"Damn right. You watch. Look, we're almost up to three minutes. I better go. You play well, son. We'll be watching."

"Okay, Poppa. Thanks for calling."

"Goodbye, Felix."

"Bye, Poppa."

I hung the phone up slowly. *God?* What could He do to help? Center a line between Hound Dog Kelly and Hammer Schultz? Okay, Poppa, He's got experience, so we'll let Him handle the floods.

Clarkie put a knee into a Russian right at the face-off, and before much more than ten minutes were played Eddie Van Impe had elbowed a Soviet forward, Valery Kharlamov (the very one whose ankles had been busted by Clarkie in '72) so hard those of us on the bench thought the crack had been the poor bugger's neck, but ended up being only his suck helmet hitting the ice. That caused a whistle; it also caused the Soviet Red Army to skate off the ice, lock the dressing room door and refuse to come out until Eagleson promised them we'd settle down and try, at least once in a while, to put our sticks on the puck rather than Soviet flesh. We knew the moment they skated off they were beaten. Returning to the ice was merely a formality to run out the clock and accept defeat.

Near the end of the first period Freddie the Fog touched my shoulder and I sprang over the boards into a grenade of applause. They stood; they cheered; they whipped American flags back and forth; they screamed, blew horns, whistled, stomped Dixie cups, threw toilet paper, punched the air and partners and waited: for me. I skated to my position for the face-off as if the rink were empty, my legs closed, blades drifting, head down as if I were weighing myself on a bathroom scale. When I looked up it was just once, and then to see what the airhead with the signs had to say behind the Soviet goal. He held one high, dancing in circles, and when it came around to me I spat on the ice. "NUCLEAR CANUCKLEHEAD!"

The face-off was in our end to the left. Torchy would take the draw; Saleski stood to the right, snorting like a workhorse, Kindrachuk on the other side, staring with eyes you see at deer hunts when the booze starts working into the trigger finger. Beyond Kindrachuk stood the closest Soviet to me, Kharlamov, who less than half an hour ago had seemed on his death bed, courtesy of Eddie Van Impe. Kharlamov was looking right back at me, also aware of the crowd chanting my name, and he was smiling.

And then he winked.

Winked!

It caught me so off guard I blinked myself and he kept smiling and nodded at me. I looked down at my feet and felt the old heat rising in my ears. Not the old heat, a different heat; this warmth was not comforting, but disturbing. How many dozens of incidents had set Batterinski off before? That blown kiss in Vancouver . . . the geek who called me a "Polish sausage" on Long Island . . . the fan who threw a bag of used Tampons over our bench in Boston . . . dozens of fool's plays, and all of them ending with blood and Batterinski skating away in his stalled-time, distracted manner.

Kharlamov saw: here I was a journeyman hockey player, at best a man who had completely ignited the crowd by doing nothing other than skating slowly, without falling, from the bench to the face-off circle. Players like Kharlamov and Lafleur could only turn the crowds on that way through realization. But I did it through expectation. And in Philadelphia, where the good play was seldom realized but violence always expected, Batterinski was the largest draw.

It stunned me that Kharlamov understood this and was amused by it. Not only did he see the absurdity of the crowd from his elegant side of hockey as clearly as I saw it from the animal side, he had the nerve to share this insight with me. This guy had guts, taking a chance like that, and I had to admire him for that. I found I couldn't look up. Afraid I'd return his wink.

The puck dropped and it squirted to Kindrachuk and then back to Torchy, who put it behind the net to me as I swung quickly toward the far corner. Christ, but it was good to be back playing with the only guy who never had to look to find me. As soon as Torchy dropped me the puck he took off in full flight for center and I sent a high, quick one, leading his chest so he could glove it just before the center line. The perfect play: Torchy Bender's breaking speed, Batterinski's thread.

But the puck never arrived. Sent out in perfect flight, it was intercepted straight out of the air before it even reached the blueline, a heavily taped stick snicking it as clean as a cat would a floating Kleenex.

Kharlamov!

The puck seemed to rest on his stick as he brought it down into his skates. I dove to poke-check it, convinced he would be tied up momentarily, but the drop into his skates was deliberate. The puck moved like a pinball, left blade onto the stick, and me skidding out over the blueline like a curler who's just found Krazy Glue on his rock handle.

Then I felt the familiar heat rise. I rose on one foot and hopped back, just in time to see Kharlamov cut in front of Moose and drop the puck perfectly to another Red Army stick for a clear shot, which fortunately caromed off the far side of the post and up against the glass. Kharlamov immediately turned to set up their forecheck pattern, but as he came out toward the blueline his stomach met the same fate as my lead pass to Torchy. I caught him full blade and turned, twisting. No cat with a Kleenex here; the lion with his kill. Kharlamov went down heavily, rolling, but I was immediately blindsided by Petrov, the big forward, who pushed me back toward Moose. I turned and threw down my stick, but not Petrov. He stood shouting something, whether to me or to the referee I couldn't tell, but it didn't matter what it was: I had moved into my fighting time zone. All I needed was for him to drop his stick.

I charged Petrov but he turned his back and both linesmen caught me and, holding an arm each, forced me back toward the boards. I'd never been held this way before. Where was the mutual restraint? Where was the tug and release of so many previous battles, the opponent with his personal linesman, me with mine, the four of us sure of our roles, what was allowable, what not, when to lunge and when to retreat, when to quit? Where was the old pattern?

I twisted, but they did not release and then grab. Both held fast. They pressed me up against the glass while Mikhailov moved in, and through the reflection I thought I could see him talking to the referee like they were meeting over lunch. I put my knee to the boards and tried to force the three of us back, but they just pressed tighter. My face went flush against the glass and I could see the crowd pressing back, wide, gaping, outraged mouths all screaming in protest. They were on my side. They wanted me freed. They wanted Batterinski alone in the ring with the Russians.

A hand-held camera moved in on the other side and I could see the cameraman duck down on one of his knees to get an angle on me. I cursed as loud as I could, hoping he might have the pick-up mike on, and stared straight into the camera. There was a small red light on over the lens, but inside the lens was black, with a small white core at the center. It looked like an eye staring back.

Batcha's eye. Cursing.

I tried desperately to wrench free, but they held fast. The fans were leaning and pounding fists against the glass now and I could feel their punches on my forehead. Punches given in sympathy, pounding mercilessly. The cameraman panicked and stepped aside, letting the crowd crush fast to the glass. We were less than a quarter of an inch apart now, fists pounding, mouths silently screaming toward mine, eyes bulging with thrill and desperate terror at the same time.

All I could do was stare back, helplessly held by the two linesmen.

I'd never been this close to my fans before, never seen what they looked like. Never cared. But I saw now, and I knew finally that I was not Batterinski.

They were.

Two weeks later, our 4–1 victory forgotten by every Flyer but me, who saw it as a personal loss — but of what I wasn't sure — I was having a beer with the boys out at Rexy's. Torchy had a piece of paper unfolded and pressed flat on the table, an empty Miller at each end anchoring it, and we were trying to make out his scribbling. He'd had to hurry. He didn't want Freddie the Fog to catch him taking down the day's thoughts, but this one had to be saved. It was in a class by itself.

"*We know that hockey is where we live,*" the Fog had written on the dressing room blackboard, "*where we can best meet and overcome pain and wrong and death. Life is just a place where we spend time between games.*"

Kelly giggled. "I thought Rexy's was where we spent our time between games."

"What's it mean?" Torchy asked. Only Torchy would have the nerve.

"I don't know. Where's Clarkie? — he'll know."

"He fucked off home."

And so they sat, wondering. Kelly finally called for one of the waiters, and Torchy and the rest began scouting around for action, settling on a foursome of pancaked, fidget-eyed, chain-smoking bleached housewives in the corner: Torchy claimed he was responsible for more kids in Cherry Hill eating casseroles for dinner than Kraft was — they put it in at three, he put it in at four, he pulled it out, ate, she pulled it out at six and the family ate. "I sometimes wonder if they can still taste me when they're saying grace," he used to say.

I sat nursing my own beer, still not in a proper frame of mind since the Russian game. They left the paper on the table when they left for the housewife table and I tried to read it again upside down . . . *hockey is where we live, where we can best meet and overcome pain and wrong and death.* What would Clarkie say if he was here? I remember when we won our first Cup in '74 and just before the final game the Fog wrote: "*Win today and we will walk together forever.*" Clarkie thought that wonderful; he'd repeat it to the rookies, use it again and again in the dressing room until we all got sick to death of it.

I felt uneasy inside. I wanted someone to tell me how hockey could overcome pain and wrong and death, death in particular — how did the Leafs overcome Bill Barilko's death if it took them more than a decade to win another Cup? Explain that one to me, Fog?

As far as I was concerned the sayings of Freddie the Fog Shero were utter crap. On the night of May 19, 1974, the day we beat Boston 1–0 at the Spectrum to win the Stanley Cup, the Fog wrote down, "We will walk together forever." We won.

On January 29, 1976, the Fog decided he was tired of walking with me. He didn't even have the guts to tell me himself.

"Felix Batterinski?"

It was my phone but I didn't recognize the voice. Was Torchy handing out my number again?

"Yah, who's this?"

"Phillip d'Atillio of the *Enquirer* here. We've received a tip that you've been put on league waivers. Any confirmation?"

Surely it was a wrong number.

"Hello?" the voice barked. "Are you there?"

"Where did you hear that?"

"A tip. Has anyone at the Flyers told you you're up for trade?"

"No."

"Well, we hear you are. We're going with it in today's paper. Any comment?"

"Like what?"

"Well, how does it feel?"

"I don't know whether it's true."

"It's true, believe me. How does it feel?"

"How would you feel?"

"I don't play hockey."

"Then you wouldn't understand, would you?"

I slammed the receiver down and then picked it up again quickly, welcoming the dial tone. I let the receiver rest while I poured rye halfway up a beer glass and then filled the rest with Coke. I gulped it down in quick swallows, my eyes burning wet, but it did no good. Batterinski was on waivers. *Waivers.* For the first time in his life.   I stared at the wall unit over a second, stronger drink. A half-dozen team pictures — some magnificent, like the million and a half Philadelphia fans spread out over Broad and Walnut and Chestnut and the parking area around the Spectrum, Torchy and I riding in the back seat, both of us covered in confetti and champagne. The goofs in the minors — Saginaw, Wichita, Saint John, Rochester — faces and places I'd love to forget. My first training camp just before Pittsburgh claimed me in the expansion draft. Pittsburgh, the town that makes Sudbury look like Paris. Erie. Hershey. My fling in the World Hockey Association: the Ottawa Nationals before they became the Toronto Toros before they became the Birmingham Bulls. To Philadelphia and back together with good old Torchy the following year, Torchy picked up from Detroit for two stinking draft choices. Some of the faces I could barely remember. Swoop Carleton, Pelyk, Harris, Hampton, poor damned Bill Masterton with his fractured skull and a trophy for his memory. Hockey, where *we can best meet and overcome pain and wrong and death*. Tell it to Bill Masterton, Freddie.

Walk forever, my ass —I broke the glass setting it down, pulled on a shirt, shoes, and raced in to the Spectrum, petrified to turn on the radio in case I turned up as a bulletin.

Freddie wasn't there. I ran over to the general manager's office and could hear Keith Allen's voice soft as pussywillow as he thanked someone for their "unselfish effort." I was stunned to discover he was talking to Torchy Bender, dressed in what he called his best "screw suit," the orange three-piece, pink silk shirt open to the navel.

"There he is!" Allen called out to me.

I nodded. Torchy turned in his seat, smiling as if he knew something I didn't. Like everyone else around here.

"Come in, Bats, come in!" Allen ordered as he stood up. He seemed to be welcoming me rather than knifing me in the back. I went in hesitantly, suspicious.

"The *Enquirer* call you?" Allen asked.

I nodded.

"Damn. I'm sorry."

"Is it true?" I asked.

"It's true," Torchy answered for him.

I looked at Torchy, wondering.

"It's not all so bad," Allen was saying, trying to pull a seat over toward me. I wasn't in any mood for sitting and refused, staring straight at him.

"Then it's a lie," I said.

Allen was glowing. "Well, not exactly, Bats."

"They're dumping you, Bats." Torchy said. He was still smiling.

"Not dumping," Allen argued, frowning at Torchy. "We're a changing team, that's all, boys."

"You just won two Stanley Cups," I said.

"Yes, and no small thanks to you, either. But a team can't sit fast, son. We need new blood all the time. You —"

"You're old blood, Bats," Torchy butted in.

Allen pulled in his air and scowled, wishing Torchy would leave or shut up.

"We have a good opportunity, Bats. We think it's best all around."

"How can it be best for me?" I asked.

"Ever been to California?" Torchy teased.

I stared at him.

Torchy smiled back. "We're both going."

Looking back, I came to see that Los Angeles was a godsend. For me, if not for Torchy. It had been necessary to have my face pushed to the glass before I could see that the Batterinski rep existed more in the crowd's mind than my own. At thirty-one Batterinski had peaked.

Tough shit. Hockey meant nothing in L.A. Not only were the Kings nobodies up against the Lakers and the Dodgers and the Rams, but who could possibly compete for notice with The Fonz and Suzanne Sommers and *Charlie's Angels* and, more precious yet, the true Hollywood stars. The Los Angeles Kings made as much sense as turning the *Queen Mary* into a hotel. We were the London Bridge in Arizona; the magic mountain in Disneyland was more real than a bunch of half-talented Canadians charging around on ice after a forty-five-cent piece of black rubber in a replica of the Forum in Rome, all for a mere $12.50 a seat. They even sold margaritas and tacos in the tuck shop at the Fabulous Forum. No fat men with runny noses peering knowingly through the steam of their Styrofoam cups; in California there might be foam cups and heat but it began with cleavage and ended with skintight acrylic pants.

Torchy and I rented a huge house out at Rolling Hills Estates, a twenty-minute drive down the San Diego Freeway and out towards the Palos Verdes Peninsula. We had a massive ten-year-old mansion with cathedral ceilings, black leather furniture with Tex-Mex design, bull horns over the bar and a spring-loaded, embroidered saddle seat in the television room which Torchy like to ride nude while watching *Sonny and Cher*. Outside we had a huge, clover-shaped pool, a hot tub, a eucalyptus grove and a small garden of hibiscus, morning-glory and — Torchy's favorite — scarlet passionflowers, all cared for by a nattering little Japanese man he took to calling Hirohito. The next house was a hundred yards away, past our purple morning-glory fence, past their stables, grazing Morgans, jump range and tennis courts. Another house beyond that and we had a view of the Pacific, great breakers rolling white and silent in the distant blue. Ugga-bugga.

It took Torchy about twenty-two seconds to forget he'd ever come from Kirkland Lake and that once, when we were in Sudbury, he had actually asked Lucille if she was serious when she said he should stop making a fool of himself with white T-shirts under his red shirt. Torchy became an instant minor Hollywood celebrity, except he didn't make movies, just stars. He made the gossip pages almost as often as the sports pages, pictures of Torchy in his new hairstyle from The Clip Joint and his aviator glasses and his white silk bandannas and pink suits making his hair stand out like a devil's paintbrush. And of course, the large-breasted, hopeful starlet of the week. He even got his teeth capped — which turned out to be weird because he also suffered his first major injury: two lost teeth. But it had nothing to do with hockey. Torchy grabbed a couple of rookies, bought a water gun and some thick cream, loaded the gun and the rookies and took them all down to the Bare Bottom Bijou, where he emptied the joint by squirting cream over the necks of the entire front row at the precise moment of the first penetration. Unfortunately, three of his victims turned out to be football players from Houston, and failed to see the harmless fun in it.

Not that this incident fazed old Torch in the slightest. He talked the team dentist into recapping the two and putting the bill through as a blocked shot in practice, something that Torchy Bender had never done in his life. But then, Torchy was trying a lot of new things.

"Face it," he told me one night when we were screening some of his recently acquired hardcore for an upcoming team bash. "We're just hanging on by the skin of our teeth now anyway."

"What do you mean? They're talking like we're saviors, man."

"We're fillers, son, and you better come to grips with it. I got maybe two, maybe three more years in these legs. What have you got left in your fists?"

I was hurt, though I knew he was right.

"They didn't get me for that."

"The fuck they didn't. I'll give you one more season beyond me 'cause you don't need the speed. But that's it."

"Maybe."

"No maybe. And since I'm not here for a long time, I'm sure as shit going to be here for a good time."

As it turned out he was going to be there for a time he couldn't possibly have imagined, good or bad or long. But for the time being, he was Torchy Bender in all his California glory, now so far away from Kirkland Lake that he could wear a white T-shirt under a red shirt and by the weekend a dozen Hollywood hangers-on would be following suit.

Torchy and I were going to a team that had just come off the best season in its history, 105 points and a record of 42 wins, 17 losses and 21 ties. At the start of the season the know-it-alls had predicted a first-place finish for the team and the Kings were supposed to be a Stanley Cup contender. Coach Pulford was called a genius. Rogatien Vachon was called the game's greatest goaltender. It was, however, nothing but a fluke.

Torchy and I tried, but we could not do everything. The only category the team improved in was they had less ties, nine compared to twenty-one, but unfortunately they also had far more losses, sixteen more to be exact. Still, Torchy and I did improve the team for the stretch, and whereas the previous year the Kings had been beaten out in the preliminaries, this time we took them to the quarter finals. Torchy ended up with 33 goals and 40 assists and I ended up with a new team record for penalties, 218 minutes.

Personally, it was not so bad, even if the team flopped. My coming to L.A. was considered a great success, precisely as intended. Dionne had more freedom to wheel; little Goring wasn't beat on; and, much to Jack Kent Cooke's delight, the attendance didn't falter as badly as the team, a fact he attributed directly to my presence. No one blamed the losses on me.

But it was false and I knew it. From the day I arrived in Los Angeles I'd been obsessed with my rep, for the first time seeing directly through my own eyes rather than examining myself through my image. I was like the water spiders on Black Donald Lake. Ig and I used to find the spiders by first scanning the lake bottom for their shadows, the shadows being considerably larger than the spiders themselves. That's the way Batterinski was. Players knew me by something larger than I was myself, and that was the rep. My stats formed the shadow, and the shadow alone spooked them. But they were not seeing me as I truly was. Not at all.

But I am not stupid. Nor was Vincent Wheeler, my New York

agent since the first call to the pros. The Flyers had dumped me on the last leg of my contract and L.A. would have to renegotiate, so I couldn't have changed teams at a better time. Nor could I dare change the rep, since that was what they were buying.

Wheeler flew out and began his pitch to management. The Kings were interested in three years, offering a contract that would pay $100,000 the first year, $150,000 the next and $175,000 the third. I was all for jumping at it, having never made more than $70,000 in a year in my life, but Wheeler was convinced they'd go for five years and even more cash. Why? I don't know. We both knew in five years I'd be in the minors, if anywhere. But he convinced me to let him try, anyway.

For three days they met at the Forum, and when Wheeler finally came out to the house it was to tell me they'd struck a compromise.

"Four years. If you collect your bonuses, $700,000."

I knew better than to ask what the bonuses were. "Sounds good," I said.

"Good! You've struck gold, man!" Vincent shouted. He was already turning California: burnt like a rash, polo shirt, open, enough neck metal to put him in traction, mirror shades. Every time I looked at him I saw myself. But as he was my agent, I suppose that was proper.

"I'm telling you this is a super deal, Felix."

"Yah, well, thanks."

Vincent smiled, seeming to pull harder on the left side to show off the gold cap on the eye tooth. "Not me, you did it."

"You negotiated it."

"You were my trump card."

I was bored already. But Vincent showed no signs of leaving. Torchy had gone up to San Francisco and didn't plan on returning until just before camp, so Vincent suggested he might take over Torchy's room for a couple of days and soak up some sunshine.

"You won't like it," I warned.

"Me? Fuck, man, I feel more 'me' out here than I do back in New York."

"I mean the bedroom."

"Torchy's? Gwan with you."

"Go look for yourself."

Torchy's bedroom had an expensive pewter handle on the door rather than the customary knob, and he had immediately replaced it with his own version of a "knob," a twenty-one-inch black monster made of plastic flesh gel and advertised in the back of *Cheri* magazine as the "mule." He pulled it over the pewter handle and adjusted the setting so the only way the door could be opened was if the plastic penis was moved to the erect position.

Inside, he had a trapeze over the bed, an RCA home video complete with camera, sound, videocassette capability on a special television "sports" screen that took up most of one wall, a shelf of the latest porn movies — *The Devil in Miss Jones, Deep Throat, Debbie Does Dallas, The Horizontal Secretary*, several dozen more — mirrors on the ceiling, centerfolds completely covering the closet doors, an entire five-drawer dresser devoted to sexual aids, from BenWa balls to blow-up dolls you could penetrate without bursting to a box of Licketty Dick's edible condom, in four tantalizing flavors: mint, passionfruit, banana and, of course, cherry.

"I can't believe this shit!" Wheeler said when he saw it.

"I didn't think you would, but I figured I'd show you anyway. You wouldn't want to stay here."

Vincent's eyes bulged. "Are you kidding?"

He stayed four days. I hardly saw him. He'd come out to the pool looking like the old men we'd see in the hospital corridors when Clarkie made us go see the sick kids. He'd hobble out, blink, dive in and excuse himself, saying he must be suffering "delayed jet lag."

And yet, between bouts in Torchy's fantasyland, Vincent hammered out the fine details of my financial status. There would be $80,000 up front to put into the drywall business Torchy and I and three other Kings were forming. Every month I'd get a check for $3,500 just to cover living expenses, and since half our time was spent on the road, that would be more than enough. Vincent had invested for me in a condominium complex out on the island — several Islanders were already in on it, he claimed — and there was also a $400,000 annuity that Vincent was purchasing through my holding company, PIM Inc., which would be paid for as the money rolled in and which would allow me to spread my tax base out over the next twenty years. At age fifty-five the annuity would begin paying me an annual dividend of roughly $50,000 a year income. All on top of my NHL Players Association pension fund, which would, all combined, make Batterinski a well-off man indeed.

But what I liked best of all was the clause in the contract that forced the Kings to lease me a brand-new Corvette each and every year of the contract, with a gasoline credit card thrown in for free. The car was ready to be picked up.

And I was going home again. To show Poppa. In style.

A more sensible man would have flown Los Angeles to Toronto, Toronto to Ottawa and then rented a car and driven back up the valley. I drove all the way, air conditioner blowing full against a late August heat spell, up across the desert flats, past the Grand Canyon, through an endlessly boring midwest of green corn, up through Detroit and onto the catatonic Highway 401. At Toronto I turned north on Highway 400 and then onto 11, one eye in the rear mirror for provincials and then quickly into the looping cut-off for Vernon. I had not been here in nearly fifteen years. Several times, back in Pomerania for Christmas or a quick visit with Poppa, I'd thought to drive over. But I hadn't. And I wasn't sure why.

I remembered Sugar's place painted yellow, but it now looked baked. There was a dog now, a part-hound, part-Labrador chained to a makeshift doghouse, and she nearly ripped her throat out when I pulled into the rut that served as the driveway. A face appeared at the window, wiping at the grime. It was Willy, Sugar's wife. Three o'clock in the afternoon and she was plastered, just as she'd usually been when she'd sat in the stands ringing that cursed cowbell for Danny and me and Powers and Cryderman and a half-dozen names I can no longer even remember. She had her housecoat on, a red- rose acrylic, one sleeve caught up to reveal a bone-thin left arm. In her hand she held a cigarette that shook so badly the smoke rose in small loops.

"Hello, Willy."

"Who the hell are you?" she asked. Her voice was an old man's, cracked and rough, the vowels thick.

"Felix. Don't you remember me?"

She shook her head and frowned, holding the door closer to the jamb, as if I had come to rape.

"Batterinski," I said.

She sniffed deep but continued to frown.

"I used to play for Teddy, eh?"

"Everybody used to 'play for Teddy,'" she said angrily, imitating my own voice. "But not me. I never played nothing for that no good bastard. Who are you?"

"Batterinski. I play for the Los Angeles Kings. I used to be with Philadelphia."

"Good for you."

"The NHL, Willie. Come on, get with it. Where's Teddy? I wanta see him."

"I wouldn't know. He never tells me."

I was losing my patience. "Any ideas?"

"He fishes down by the dam."

Sugar had hipwaders on, their dark green streaked pink where he had used nail polish to mend the tears. In the distance he looked unchanged, same stocky build, same swollen head, perhaps a bit gray now but Sugar all the same. He stood on a rock well out in the water just below the dam and was working a taut line through the deep sworl, playing the current edges for rainbow. He had a roll- your-own tacked to his upper lip but not lit, and when he cast with his line and tongue, the cigarette bobbed as if it had its own strike.

I came onto him from the hill, where I could overlook the locks, the picnic area and the dam beyond. I scooped a small rock from the parking area and tossed it so it splashed just under a leaning cedar on the near shore. Sugar immediately reeled in and cast toward my splash. I threw another, this time to a pool upstream, and Sugar chased that one as well. I threw again to the tree and when Sugar's head turned toward the sound he suddenly thought to look up. I could see him tilt the good eye, could see anger wash across his face before recognition, but then his mouth opened and stayed open, the cigarette jigging in uncertainty. He mouthed my name, the dam drowning any sound he might have made.

I waved.

"*Batterinski!*"

The cigarette fell from his mouth, darting into the rocks. Sugar jumped off the rock, sinking in to his waist and slipping slightly in the current. His footing salvaged, he held his rod high and babywalked to the cedar, where a bone-white root formed a convenient and much used banister out. I could hear him laughing.

"Here, you old bugger, let me take that."

He handed me the rod, a shredding fiberglass model with broken lashing and a tip repaired with black hockey tape. Just as I'd expect.

Sugar stared but did not speak, nor even smile. The seventies had had no effect whatsoever on him. He still wore a thick, blunt brushcut, though it was now gray enough that his bulldog head looked wrapped in cement. He was pinker than I remembered, but this was undoubtedly because of the summer sun and I had known him in airless, lightless arenas. His bad eye seemed clouded out completely, the useless pupil swimming aimlessly in milk. The other eye, the good eye, was wet.

"I had a dream about you."

I laughed. "A dream?"

"Yah. You and me and some of the other lads. We was a team again, Bats."

His eye was running. I tried to lighten things. "Here or in L.A.?"

Sugar spit on the ground. "Not here. Not there neither. I don't know where we was. But not here. This fuckin' town's gone to the dogs since you were here, son."

Son?

"Yah, well, things change, eh?"

Sugar fixed me with the eye, looking for something. "You talk different, eh?"

"Me?"

"Yah, you. Who do you think I'm talking to? Maybe I don't always look at the right person but I talk to who I'm talking to — you! And you talk better."

"Well thanks," I said, concentrating on the "th" so deliberately that it almost turned into a lisp.

Sugar smiled finally, the big scarred lips rising over a vandalized graveyard of gray, broken, missing out-sized teeth. "You used to say 'tanks,'" he said, lifting an eyebrow in reminder. I hardly needed it.

Sugar examined my clothes: new Nikes, soccer socks with blue and red rings, Adidas shorts, John Newcombe tennis shirt with flared armpits for backhands and the mustachioed insignia winking from my heart, single shark's tooth on a thin 14-karat gold chain.

"I'm surprised I recognized you," he said.

I smiled, reassuring him. "I'm still the same Batterinski."

Sugar nodded, unsure. "Well, if you are then you're the only fuckin' thing that hasn't changed. You want a brew, son?"

Son again. "Sure. Where'll we go?"

Again the smile. "Don't have to go nowhere."

Sugar turned, pulling off his straps and stepping awkwardly out of the hipwaders. He went to the overhanging cedar, knelt down and untied a line from the root. On the line was a burlap sack. When Sugar pulled it up, the sack spoke of cold beer and plenty.

"You're still coaching." I said it as a fact, though I suspected it wasn't.

Sugar shook his head and hid behind his second beer. I waited. Finally, unable to look at me, he told the river: "I can do house league. That's all they'll let me touch."

We both waited. I knew he wanted me to lead. "What happened?"

"I got burnt, that's all."

"How?"

"You remember Des Riley?"

"Of course I do. I lived there, remember?"

"He worked his way into the association until he got president. Then he went after me. Why I don't know, but he was bound I wouldn't handle the bantams no more. Passed a ruling that coaches all had to pass some fuckin' level III shit coaching courses. Had some fuckin' four-eyed bearded sports 'psychologist' or some shit come up from Toronto to teach it. I refused to go."

"So you're out?"

"I'm out. Except house league. Such a challenge, too — I have to wait until the mothers finish tightening their skates before I bring out the chalk."

"But you keep doing it."

"It's hockey. Kind of. It's all I got."

I finished my beer in idle talk, my mouth covering up for my thoughts. Only two coaches had ever touched me in ways I could never quite understand. One was Shero, the Fog, the man who promised we would walk together forever and led two of us straight down the garden path. The other, of course, was Sugar. To me Sugar was a far superior coach, a man who made you play your heart out for sheer love of the man and the game. Shero used an element Sugar would never resort to: fear. With Shero you always knew that a bungled pass or a half effort meant the bench or the press box until he figured your pride had been bent far enough to rebound to his advantage. Sugar worked the opposite, getting you to give your best out of sheer *respect*. But still, they did have much in common. Hockey was where they both lived.

All he wanted to talk about was the team from that season, where the players were and what they were doing. Tom Powers had worked his way through college on a hockey scholarship in the States and was now back in town selling cottage real estate to all the contacts he'd made at school. He even owned a trucking company, and Bucky Cryderman was delivering freight for Tom now. Sugar asked about Danny and when I told him about the mill job and Danny's marriage to Lucy Dombrowski and the two kids, he just nodded as if he'd known all along.

"I seen you against Toronto in March."

"National?"

"Sure. I had a good look at you, son."

"I was thrown out in the second period."

"I seen enough."

Sugar said no more. I waited but he said nothing. Finally, as he knew I would, I asked.

"You saw something. What?"

"There was no reason for you to fight Lalonde."

"He's a goof."

"So he's a goof. You're a hockey player. You played like a goof too."

"That's what I'm paid to do."

Sugar nodded. "I was afraid of that."

I looked at him. "You shouldn't act surprised. You were the one who told me I'd only get ahead if I went with my strengths."

"I did, yes. And I meant it too. And I think I was right. But your strength has become your weakness, son."

"What does that mean?"

"You know better than me. Think about Teddy Roosevelt."

The name rang a bell, but only lightly. Not someone we'd played against, but something he'd said. I thought I'd caught it, but felt it slip and could not ask.

Sugar finished the conversation with his good eye running over my face like he was tracing a coin with a pencil. I knew I was blinking. I felt as if I understood, but if I did I could not articulate it. I stared back at him and he smiled.

"Don't worry about it. It had to, you see?"

No, I didn't. Yes, I did. I didn't know. I just knew that if Sugar thought he had seen some change and I thought I had felt some change, then there must indeed be change. Batterinski had created the rep and the rep was destroying him.

Sugar stood and gathered the beer bottles and his fishing rod. I carried the tackle box. Up the grassy knoll, slippery from the spray, over the foot bridge, past the locks and on up to the car.

"I'll give you a ride," I said.

He pointed to the Corvette. "In that?"

"Sure."

He shook his head. "I'll walk."

"It's no problem, really."

"I'll walk."

I stuck out my hand and he took it, gripping tight with those gnarled, stubby fingers. He seemed uneasy, unsure, and then he grabbed my shoulders and buried his head into my chest. I held, but awkwardly so. I could hear cars on the highway above, and wondered if they could see. But then I felt Sugar's hold still tightening and I realized how much more difficult it was for him than for me, and I didn't care who saw. I held back, just as tightly.

When we broke there were tears in both of Sugar's eyes and small drops falling off his stubbled cheeks. He tried to laugh them off but couldn't and turned instead to pick up his tackle box. But as he reached he stopped, and stood back up, now smiling.

"Still good for that ride?"

"Still good, old friend."

Sugar nodded, calculating. "Up and down Main Street?"

"Anywhere you like," I said.

We did both sides of Main Street twice, with Sugar shouting, screaming, laughing at every pedestrian and driver he knew or thought he might know. He leaned out and slapped the side of the Corvette like it was a pony express as we hurtled down from the theater past the old Muskoka Hotel. He made sure there wasn't a soul in all of Vernon who didn't know the house-league squirt coach was being chauffeured about town by a true National

Hockey League star. He wanted them all to know Ted Bowles was good enough for me, if not for them. And when I turned the corner by Riley's hardware store, Sugar leaned as far as he could out the window and honked his nose at Des Riley, who was standing by the jackknife display watching his precious town parade before him. I goosed the car and we squealed up past the hardware store and out the Lock's Road toward Sugar's home and a passed-out Willie.

I ate at the new steakhouse by the Canadian Tire, where a massive waitress came to my table with deliberate slowness and contempt, chewing gum and reaching slowly for the pad tucked into her apron.

"Youse want a menu?" she asked.

"Please."

She turned to remove one from another table and I tried to fix the face. It was like an advertising balloon that had been blown up too far, making the message illegible. Shrunken, the face would be beautiful. But the body below was so fat you'd have to roll her in flour just to find the wet spot.

I wondered all through a hot beef with peas, puzzled through the coffee. And the answer came only when she slipped the check onto my table with the bubblegum popping "Thanks." The price was $8.79, the party was one, and the waitress was Maureen.

Maureen the Queen.

I left no tip.

Poppa came to the door expecting a worm sale. With the sun flush on the screen, he seemed drawn on graph paper in a scale smaller than I remembered, though I had seen him at Christmas. No, I'm mistaken. For a day and a half the previous spring after the play- offs. So it had been more than a year. He was in his seventies and beginning to stoop. His hair was finally graying, and longer, meaning he was not going to town much. His eyes were failing. For a moment he danced behind the screen, feinting like a boxer as he tried to shield the sun and make out who it was in the yard. He opened the door tentatively, and by the time it slammed shut he was already at the car.

He grabbed me exactly the way Sugar had, almost as if we were wrestlers waiting for the referee to slap the mat to begin. But he was so much taller than Sugar. Even stooped, when he came into

me it was my face, not his, that found the shoulder. I breathed
deep: all the sweat oil and gasoline and pine pitch and cedar chips
and sawdust and dead minnows and cooking grease and lime of
my childhood. He smelled the way I remembered Jaja. He walked
the way I remembered Jaja walking, the slight stoop, the delicate
step that said all was not right in the privates.

Poppa had grown into Jaja, but I had not grown into Poppa. I
had grown into Batterinski, Frankenstein, *Canucklehead* — and
now I sensed I was retreating. But where?

"Batcha! Batcha!" Poppa called as he held the screen open for
me with his knee. "Look at who's here!"

Batcha did not answer. Poppa turned, apologetic: "Sometimes
she doesn't hear so good."

I nodded. Poppa did not call again.

Inside, the house was exactly as I had left it: a calendar on
every wall, one from 1967 but with a picture of Queen Elizabeth
II that never went out of date; the pots hung on nails over the
sink; the hand pump. Poppa saw me eye the stairs.

"Nothing's changed. Your room's exactly as it was the last night
you slept here. Haven't even changed the sheets."

Da sheets. I was indeed home, exactly as it was.

"You still got the minnow setup?"

Poppa looked cross. "Don't you think you should see your
Batcha before the goddamn minnows?"

I can see her as perfectly today as I did that day, because she
left me something that makes me shiver to this day to think of it.
Batcha was in the sitting room, dozing in her rocker with the
blinds half drawn. She wore her black uniform, long sleeves with a
white Kleenex tuck, buttoned shoes, thick brown cotton stockings,
wrinkled. Her hair was blacker than Poppa's and healthy, but
her face was far *thinner*, giving in more and more to the skull
beneath. Her cheeks were sunken, her mouth parted, her eyes
deep and shrouded by black heavy brows. But when they opened
and settled on me, they burned with all their old strength, recognition settling into memory, forming hatred.

"Hello, Batcha," I said with forced sincerity. "How are you?"

"Hello, Felix," she said. Her voice was full of air, empty.

"Batcha's ninety this summer, you know, Felix," Poppa said,
knowing he would have to force the conversation. "She tires easily,
but she's glad you're home."

Poppa said this just so it would be said, officially.

The white eyes stared at me and then rolled away, Batcha drifting back to sleep. Poppa shrugged and pulled the blinds down
quietly, taking my arm as we left the room where Jaja and Ig had
lain before burial. The closed blinds turned the room ink black
and I stumbled, my eyes slow to adjust, and when I reached to
catch myself I caught on Batcha's rocker arm and her hand. The
hand ice-cold, recoiling like a snake. It was a sensation I would
not forget.

How strange to be back in my old room, the smell of must rising
from the mattress. Poppa's stolen lumber-camp blanket was folded
carefully at the foot of the bed so the moth holes wouldn't show;
the pine dresser had new linoleum tacked on it; the blind was
now permanently rusted and rotted at half-mast, the exposed
portion bleached near white, the rolled half as green as Poppa's
new aluminum siding. Dead bluebottles were so thick between
the storm and the inside window that the flies formed a mass
graveyard deeper than the frame. I opened it, swept them out
onto the shed roof, and propped the storm open with a boot for
air. The air that entered contained Poppa's chainsaw and the
outside, but at least it was new air, something my room hadn't
seen in years.

I lay there in brand-new silken B.V.D. pajamas. In the rough-
cut doorless closet, on four of the only unraveled coathangers in
the house, were a light houndstooth jacket from Lou Myles, a
blue serge sports jacket, two light-blue and a single light-brown
pair of slacks from Lou, a white pair of painter pants that flat-
tered my thighs, several polo shirts and a couple of Newcombe
tennis shirts. Below, on the floor, sat my Nikes and a hundred-
and-twenty-dollar pair of penny loafers. And that didn't include
the ties, the running shorts, the thigh socks, the underwear still
sealed in plastic, my leather cowboy hat or the several L.A. Kings
caps I'd stashed in the drawers of the dresser. I had more invested in the contents of my suitcase than Poppa had in the house.
Absurd, I know, but he would hear nothing of my suggestion that
we tear it down and I pay for a new one.

"That siding cost me $750," he said, settling the issue forever.

In the morning I found him just beyond the shed, to the side of
the ash dump. He had an old, blackened and torn camp blanket
out and had assembled the parts of the kerosene engine for the

washing machine on it while he washed everything down with gasoline.

"What's wrong?" I asked.

"Goddamned carburetor's gone. Worn out. And I can't get any diaphragms no more so I cut my own out of leather. I don't know whether it'll work or not."

"Forget it!"

"Forget it?" he said, still scrubbing. "The tank's good. The roller works perfect. It'll work perfect if the diaphragm sets."

"You've electricity now, Poppa, get a proper machine."

"Not too fussy about electricity. Somebody else can put it out on you. This I can bugger up or fix on my own."

"You don't have to tell me you're not fussy about it. There's hardly a light in the house."

"Batcha likes it that way. We don't need any more."

"But Poppa, that's why I sent you that money. So you'd have things like that."

Poppa looked insulted. "I got the siding up, didn't I? You never even said anything about it."

"I noticed right away."

"Well, there. See. It's darned nice too, isn't it?"

"Lovely."

Poppa grunted his approval and returned to his scrubbing.

"Look, Poppa. Isn't it about time you let me pay you back for a few of the things you've done for me?"

Poppa put down an idle valve and looked up, smiling. "I don't want your money, son. You keep it."

"Not money. I want you to have a few things around here, things you should have."

"But I've got everything I want."

"You're half a century behind the times. I like a shower. I can't have a shower here."

"Batcha and me wouldn't even know how to have one."

"Well I don't care what you say, Poppa. I've got good money now and you're going to enjoy some of it and that's that."

Poppa looked up and blinked once. "Save it," he said harshly. "You might need it."

I laughed, savoring the moment. "Poppa. Don't you understand. I'm set for life."

Poppa went back to pouring gasoline on his scrub rag. "No

one's ever set for life, Felix. They only set you for death."

"Very funny, Poppa. I'm going to town. You're going to have some changes around here whether you want them or not."

Poppa spit to the side of the camp blanket, but whether to clear his mouth or speak his mind, I couldn't say. By week's end I had had an electrician out from Renfrew to put in some proper lights and do some upstairs wiring, a plumber from Vernon over to put in a proper toilet, a front-end loader and three trucks of gravel from Eganville to set a septic tank and make a weeping bed, a hot-water tank, hot-water piping and a full tub and shower enclosure for what used to be Ig's room. I also bought a new electric washing machine, a new double stainless steel sink for the kitchen, faucets, traps, electric baseboard heaters they could plug in to supplement the basement wood furnace in winter, and two fire extinguishers to ease Poppa's fretting about all the new wiring.

Poppa said nothing, which I took as acceptance, but the old bitch was outraged, particularly over the invasion of Ig's room. She stopped speaking to me completely. The day the electrician wired she refused to let him come into her room, locking herself in by working a butcher's knife across the frame. I was about to boot it in on her when Poppa came up and put a hand on my shoulder.

"I'm going for a walk," he said. "You want to come along?"

Our second "walk." And even hotter than when Poppa had chewed me out for chopping down the bitch's goddamned aspen. Poppa walked in Kodiak workboots so stubbed the steel toes had worn through. I wore my wedge-heeled, suction-cupped Nikes. Poppa was in his summer longjohns and green hydro pants. I had on my white painter jeans and a fishnet blue tank top. Poppa was bareheaded. I wore my stiff, ten-pound leather handcrafted cowboy hat, and felt like a damned fool.

I took it off and stared at the brim, already blackening with sweat. I danced to the side of the road, lifted a spruce bough and laid the hat carefully under the apron, concealing it.

Poppa laughed. "I don't blame you."

"Nobody'll see it there."

"A porky finds it he'll eat it."

"Porky finds it he can wear it."

We walked on a bit, almost to the creek, before Poppa spoke again.

"You must go easy on Batcha, Felix. I don't think she's very well anymore."

"Then get her to a doctor."

Poppa laughed. "For fifty years they've come to her as a doctor. She thinks medical doctors are as trustworthy as they think she is. She won't hear of it."

"Then tell her to cure herself."

Poppa clicked his tongue in condemnation. "Son, son, son — you must change your attitude toward her. Batcha loves you as much as me. She just can't say."

We stopped on the bridge and stared upstream. A crane flushed at the sound of the gravel we turned, falling through the scaffolding; we could hear the wings slowly pushing through the air as it rose, the sound and speed of a sleeping baby's breath.

I didn't want to hurt Poppa, but I had to let him know how I felt. "How can you stand her living there?"

Poppa spit into the river, watched it vanish beneath his feet. "I never think about it that way. She's there and I'm there and that's the way it is."

"She must drive you nuts."

"No. Not at all."

"How can you put up with all her hocus-pocus?"

"How has it hurt me?"

I kicked some gravel into the river, turned and walked on.

Poppa wasn't finished: "Her ideas are no worse than Father Schula's, as far as I'm concerned."

I had to laugh. "Aren't you speaking heresy, Poppa?"

"No, I do not. Batcha is as good to that church as the fathers are themselves. Who's to say what they read out of their books — not the Bible, but their church books — is any more right than what she was taught by respected elders in the old country? Her type is very highly regarded back there, son. It's only over here, with television and all that, that people stop believing. And I ask you, is the world any better for that?"

I couldn't be bothered answering. "Why couldn't Jan take her?"

"Jan has asked her. She says this is her home and it is, no one can argue about that."

I stopped. "Well, I can, Poppa. It's my home too, and she makes me feel like some sort of disease that snuck in through the cracks in the floor."

Poppa seemed weary of it all. "She loves you. Believe me."

"I can't. Because she doesn't." My voice was sharp, hurt.

"You know that's wrong."

"I don't know how Jaja ever stood her, I don't."

Poppa's voice went hard. "That's right. You don't."

We walked on further, not speaking till we reached the cedars at the far end of the flats. I felt badly that I had angered Poppa. My fight was with the bitch, not him. "How far you planning to go?" I asked, pumping enthusiasm into my voice.

"I might see if that jet pump is in at Betz's."

"You're going to *walk* all the way to town!"

"Of course I'm going to walk. Can't you do it anymore, big hockey player, eh?" Poppa laughed, the distance between us vanishing.

I laughed back at him, glad for his company.

"Of course I can do it. I just wonder why, when there's a perfectly good car sitting back there."

"Let it sit. They see me in that thing and they'll be saying your success has gone to my head."

"No they wouldn't."

"Why did you get it?"

"It's a great car."

"People look at it, am I right?"

"Sure they look."

"Well, there you go."

Der you go. What did that mean?

"Where I go?"

"You didn't buy it for its machinery. You bought it so you could wear it, like them Fancy Dan clothes of yours. If Walter Batterinski could drive to town in a vehicle that looked like him, he'd come in a chainsaw."

"You're being crazy, Poppa."

We walked on, content to be silent. I, too, was happier walking with Poppa than I would have been alone in the Corvette, but I was also dreading our coming on Shannon's, hoping Danny would not be visiting his parents. When we crested the cedar turn I could see only the gutted cars in the yard. Not the truck. Not the big Packard Poppa said Danny was driving lately. Old Mrs. Shannon would be inside, but she would stay there even if she saw us. A woman in Pomerania does not presume anything unless her husband or sons are there. She would take note and report, and hope that the next time we passed, Martin would be there to haul us in for a drink or two and a few blessed moments away from her eternal drudgery. No wonder the church ran thickest in the veins of the women. Prayer was like talking to a fresh face.

"You got rats in California?"

Rats? "You mean like big mice?"

Poppa impersonated me. "'You mean like big mice?'—Of course I mean like big mice. You got them?"

"Well, I suppose so. Not at our place though."

"We got 'em at the house. Can you hear them at night? They gnaw in the back shed."

"No, I haven't."

"Damn summer's too wet. No berries. Too many snakes. Too much muck for holes. They've been coming in since June. I can't get rid of them. Catch maybe one a week by traps. But I gotta get some proper poison."

"Betz's should have some."

"I tried theirs. Didn't work. Maybe I'll have Batcha mix up some. She's done it before, but it's hard to get the chemicals these days with all them regulations."

"How can she make better than what they sell?"

"I can hunt better meat than what they sell. Why couldn't she make better rat killer than what they sell? I already tried what they sell and it didn't work."

"Why don't you just set traps? We used to."

"They're too smart. It's like setting a table for them. I get some but not enough."

We passed by the corner where Ig died and Poppa never mentioned the accident. There were guardposts up now where the half-ton had drifted over the embankment, and below it was all overgrown with maple saplings and poplar, and just to the front of the saplings a great, luxurious raspberry patch. Ig's raspberries. His monument.

The pump wasn't in. Poppa ordered his rat chemicals from old Betz and then suggested we hike further on up Black Donald Hill towards St. Martin's. Twice half-tons stopped smack in the middle of the highway, the drivers riding their clutches while they leaned unconcernedly out the window and laughed with Poppa and welcomed me home. Both said they were Kings fans as of last January and I told both — Jerzy Palowski and Donny Betz, both from the mill—that they'd have to come out to California to see a game live. I'd get them tickets, I said, even put them up.

Both pulled away, delighted with the invitation, petrified by the possibility.

"You glad to be home, eh, Felix?" Jerzy had asked in a voice like a panting dog.

"Sure."

He looked beyond us, toward the church spires. "No place like this in California, eh?"

I answered honestly. "That's for damn sure."

Jerzy seemed even more delighted with this than with his invitation. His — and probably Donny's — dedication to the Kings was merely a formality. My real worth to them was if they could wrangle some reinforcement from me that their petty Pomeranian lives were indeed worth living. They weren't envious of my life; they weren't even much interested in the Kings or California. What they cared about more was that Batterinski, who had seen both Pomerania and Los Angeles, believed Pomerania to be the superior place.

"This here's God's country," I said to Jerzy, stressing the *dis*.

I wasn't lying. Pomerania suited God perfectly. Filled to the brim with suffering and true believers.

We passed by one of the old railway houses, where a man hailed Poppa from an upper window where he was scraping paint. He had a cap on, but not pulled low enough that I couldn't see the large dent in his forehead. Old Sikorski, from down at the lake. From the cartons and full half-ton in the yard he must have just moved in. He worked with the wire brush as he talked, many of his words indecipherable for the rasping, but it didn't matter. We needed very little of what he said —". . . Leafs stink . . . you'd think Indians had been living here . . . goddamned tourists fucked the speckle fishing . . . Trudeau's a fucking communist . . . no one's shoving French down this throat . . . "—to stand and nod in sympathy.

A woman appeared in the window frame behind him, holding a new brush and a purple-stained paint can. Thick with the Pomeranian look, there was something about her I couldn't fix on, and waited till we'd all cursed the tax department a few more times and taken our leave before I asked Poppa about her.

"It's the same wife," Poppa said with a look of surprise.

"But she was dying of cancer." I saw the thin, crying woman at the kitchen table, waiting for Batcha.

"Well, she didn't."

"What happened?"

"How should I know? I never asked. She got better. The cancer went away."

Poppa didn't seem interested in talking about it. And I couldn't ask. Was Mrs. Sikorski saved by doctors? By prayer? By the bitch Batcha? By cutting the heart out of a poor cat? Poppa would laugh if I asked.

"You're sure it's the same woman?" I asked.

Poppa blew his nose against his finger, disgusted. "This isn't California, Felix. People don't get divorced here, remember?"

"Okay, but maybe she died and he remarried."

Poppa looked at me like I'd taken leave of my senses. "And nobody noticed?"

I let it drop. The sun beat against my back and my fishnet shirt was stuck to me like Saran Wrap, but not stuck tight enough to prevent the shiver. Last night there was wax in my bedroom door keyhole again. I poked it out with a coathanger, knowing it would be useless to complain to Poppa. I knew also it would be in place again when I returned. The bitch at work.

Poppa led the way up the hill and through the church parking lot, on up past the newly split winter wood and into the graveyard. I followed silently. Some grass was thick, with grasshoppers snapping off in long arches about us. The grass was freshly scythed and raked into a corner, where it was drying yellow. There were careful paths about the stones and wooden crosses, and where the end path petered out in the far eastern corner there was the Batterinski family plot.

Poppa stopped in front of Jaja's marker, carefully removing his straw hat. Jaja had a cross with flaking white paint, small diamonds whittled at the three exposed corners, his name chiseled in Polish and painted black, his dates, 1861–1955, and, at the end, *prosie zdrovas:* "He beseeches a Hail Mary."

"Here's Ig," Poppa said.

I looked over. He was pointing to a settled, worn area marked only with four corner stones. At the head of the grave was a small, cracked encasement of plastic flowers. They were doing precisely what they were invented not to do: wilt. The colors were washed out, the stems sagging and the flowers folding in on each other to form joining globs. It must have been the heat and the years. But Poppa made no move to remove the case.

"Batcha misses him terribly," Poppa said, his voice uneven.

"We all do," I said.

"But her most of all. She thought he was hers, to protect."

"And then he got killed."

"And then he got killed," Poppa repeated.

There was nothing to gain in saying so, but I couldn't contain it. "And she blames me."

Poppa shook his head. "She blames herself. It was her suggestion that he go after the berries."

"It was my friends."

"But it was not *you.*"

Poppa moved beyond Ig's grave. I tried to follow, but couldn't. I stood over the grave and bowed my head, unable to stop my hand from instinctively making the sign of the cross over my heart. I hadn't done that for years. I hadn't even prayed since Clarkie had had the dumb idea that we should all attend a nondenominational service as a team, something that turned into a once only disaster when Torchy let squeak a silent stinky that had us shaking like boiling kettles when the preacher announced "The Lord is all around you!" and Torchy sniffed loudly and answered with, "Is *that* what that is?"

Poppa dropped to his knees and kissed the earth carefully. It was another plain marker like Jaja's, again with plastic flowers but also with a small, encased box containing a plaster cast of Jesus' head and upraised arms, looking pained and, unfortunately, half-buried in the grass.

Poppa stood back up. "Your Matka," he said, his voice slipping.

Poppa's eyes were shining when he stepped back, and turned toward the church. He walked with his hands behind his back, playing with the brim of his hat; his eyes worked along the markers, reading, recognizing, remembering. I stared at my mother's marker, leaning forward but afraid to step on the grass over her. The dates were difficult to make out, the weather having eaten away much of the black paint and leaving only letters formed by shadows in the chisel work. Her birth was clear, 1914, but not the final date. But that I knew by heart: my birthday.

I felt sick. I went down on my knees — to hell with the grass stains — and I simply waited for the tears to come. They squeezed out of my closed eyes, around the corners of my nose and dropped off my upper lip. I wanted to hit something. I wanted to take my two hands and pound them into the soil until I, too, was gone from the face of the earth.

Had Poppa brought me here deliberately so I could see my conscience laid out before me in perfect rows: Jaja, a heart attack doing my chores — so I could make Father Schula's useless hockey practice; Ig, mowed down by my so-called buddies; Matka, dead because Felix Batterinski was too much to bear.

Too much to bear — even then! *What in God's name was happening to me?* Two weeks after I sign the best contract of my career I'm acting like *this?* What kind of an idiot am I? Why have I come here?

I belong in California with the sun tonguing my back, not here. Batterinski's record is written up in the NHL *Guide*, not some spooky graveyard in a village that has nothing more significant going for it than a goddamned road kill on the side of a tourist highway.

God's country indeed!

Poppa and I walked home together with our own thoughts, me thinking of going in to see Danny and Poppa thinking God knows what. We passed by the spruce where I had hidden the leather cowboy hat and still not a word was said. We both knew better than to mention it. It could rot, for all I cared. It would serve a porcupine better than me.

I washed my pants when we got home, but the stain remained on the knees. I tried bleach and the grass faded, but only slightly. More bleach but still the stain would not go. Matka's stain. The mark of my mother's grave. I buried the pants out in the ash dump, overturning several dead rats as I dug, all with their mouths broken up and tongues leaping from the crush of the trap. I felt they were sticking out their tongues at me, laughing at the California I was trying to bury.

Danny sat waiting on the steps of his house. He and Lucy had taken over one of the square railroad houses that had been tacked onto the hill like coathangers, which is all they were intended to be, a place to put the line workers up for the night, and then abandoned by the railroad when the idea of a grain line from the Great Lakes through to Ottawa seemed as likely as sending fresh water back. Danny's was newly painted pink on three sides, black tar-paper with the Johns-Manville factory stamp providing a little relief on the east side, where the wind blew least. The Packard was in a drive someone had forced onto the hill with crib support, fill and enough stolen planking from the mill to finish off Danny's east side four times over. The car was massive, longer than the drive, blacker than the tar-paper. Had there been a wreath on the back window I might have crossed myself.

Danny was glowing. A single-stranded shaft of yellow light was slipping through the white pine further onto the hill, a light that seemed cleansed and crisp and angled, and it settled on Danny like an ill-exposed photograph. He sat, knees spread wide for his gut, cigarette as comfortable in his fingers as nails, a half-empty, glowing brown beer bottle at his side, and he was wearing an Ottawa football jersey. When he saw the car was the Corvette he'd been expecting, he stood, stretched and stepped off the steps like a Buddha descending.

"Here it is, ladies and gentlemen, straight from Hollywood, U.S.A." The voice had somehow remained thin as Danny had thickened.

I winced. "Cut the shit, Danny. How ya been?"

Danny surveyed his property. "Fine. Good." He scratched his belly, lifting the jersey so a great bellybutton could smile silently through its thin beard and then vanish.

"Where're your kids?"

"Inside. You want to see them?" *Dem*, of course. As bad as Poppa. Danny asked this as if I'd come to inquire after some used tires.

"Of course I want to see them."

I got out of the car and Danny, still smiling, looked me up and down, again scratching his great belly. "You look like a goddamned movie star, Bats."

I smiled. "They won't let you stay in California unless you do this, did you know that?"

"Why all the jewelry? You gone fag on us, lad?"

I cuffed my own throat, as if just now aware I was wearing anything. "Ah, they all wear it. All the guys."

"Real gold?"

"Some, yah."

"Ugga-bugga, man. You're doing all right, Jack."

"Yah, I guess so. Where's them kids?"

Dem. I said it deliberately, hoping to tarnish the gold a bit.

"Come on. I'll get us some beer for the road."

Danny pulled the screen door back and I noticed that the bottom portion bulged like a sail and was split all up the latch side. Danny saw me look and punched it straight. "Fuckin' kids," he said.

"Lucy!" he shouted up the stairs. "Get down here and see who's here!"

The answer was the kids shouting and scrambling over the floor, with a woman's drill-sergeant voice ordering them back into their beds. Danny waved me forward and I followed him, thinking of my own pants and the double fitting Lou had forced on me even when I assured him they fit perfectly; Danny's jeans fell flat off his rear, bagging in and out as he walked, grayish underwear offering a two-inch trim above his belt, bisected perfectly by the top of a hairy crack that snaked slightly as he walked. He went through the hall with the lines of pegged coats and corners of boots, through the kitchen with the dishes drying in the rack, the usual triple calendars, the fading Santa that wished "Merry Christmas" to anyone who could run a thumbnail fast enough down the plastic tape hanging tongue-like from his mouth, out through a badly suspended door with an inner tube for a latch and into the back shed. The case of beer was in a corner, piled on case upon case of empties, the recent history of Danny's gut.

As he loaded up a grocery bag I looked about. The shed was as crucial to Pomeranians as the hot tub to Californians. The smell was the same as Poppa's, though Poppa had said he'd not yet been to Danny's. Coal oil and wood chips and oil and cleanser and lime and fish scales and skinned rabbit and old leather and rotting wool and musty boxes. Cables, hubcaps, license plates, used air cleaners, empty Javex bottles, makeshift anchors, water-logged life preservers and sun-faded cushions, broken snowshoes, tangled fishing line and bulbless light receptacles wired onto extensions with Band-aids and hockey tape. The light was not good, but I saw on a far spike Danny's old skates, the leather shanks hanging tired, dust over the boot, the blades barnacled with rust.

I pointed to them. "You ever use 'em anymore?"

Danny had to follow my finger. "Skate? No way, lad." He slapped his gut. "I'd turn a rink into ice cubes in one shift."

I laughed, because it was easier. Danny was ashamed of his skates, ashamed of his gut. I had seen the rust; I had proof before my eyes that he no longer skates; but yet I had to ask. Could it be that I was rubbing it in?

"Hi Daddy," a small, flat voice said from behind.

I turned. A small boy, four maybe, was standing with a tattered pink — or once pink, anyway — blanket, his other hand on the inner tube latch.

"You're supposed to be in bed," Danny growled.

The boy said nothing. He was staring at me, looking directly at my neck and the lunacy hanging from it. He was thin and brown, with black curly hair like Danny's once was, but with a thin face and small eyes, unlike Danny. He smiled. I smiled back.

"You know who this is?" Danny said to the boy. The boy shook his head. "This here's Mr. Batterinski. You know what he does?" Another shake. "He plays hockey in the NHL. You know what that means?" Shake, no. "It means Mr. Batterinski is one of the finest athletes in the world. Now mind your manners and show Mr. Batterinski some proper respect, understand?"

The boy looked awestruck. "Hello," he said in a voice as small as Danny's was large.

"Hi there, what's your name?"

"Tommy."

"Hi, Tommy. I'm an old friend of your dad's."

Tommy said nothing. The hand came off the inner tube and into his mouth.

Danny lunged for the hand, pulling it out so quickly Tommy's mouth popped like a burst bubble. "Get that outa there!" Danny shouted. "And you keep it outa there or I'll burn that damn blanket when you're asleep, understand?"

Tommy sniffed and nodded. He turned his gaze back to me.

"You play hockey, Tommy?" I asked.

Tommy shook his head.

"He will, he will," Danny said. "He's a tough little squirt too. Just look at him."

Danny scooped up his son and thrust the boy at me. When I took him, Tommy grabbed back instinctively for his father, but curiosity overcame him and he came into my arms and stared fixedly at my neck. He smelled of flannelette and dried urine, the smell of my childhood. It didn't offend me. I wanted to bury my face in his pajamas and remember, to know if I only could that the glory was all ahead rather than falling further and further behind. I breathed deep.

"Tommy! Get up here!" It was the woman's voice again, edgy, exhausted.

"He's with us!" Danny shouted back.

Danny went back into the kitchen and I followed, waiting while he looped the rubber latch tight for raccoons and porcupines. Tommy showed no eagerness to escape. He rode my arm comfortably, hanging on to my shoulder with one arm, the torn, smelly pink blanket with the other, and staring still at the vanity about my neck.

"Tommy!" the woman shouted. She was halfway down the stairs, leaning over the banister so she could see into the kitchen. Tommy cringed back into my arms for protection. I tightened my grip.

It was Lucy. At least I was pretty sure it was Lucy. The marvelous, churning butt that used to drive Danny and me to the point of self- mutilation had turned from cream to fat.

I could barely recognize her as the daydream I had carted around for the past fifteen years, me always trying to imagine what might have happened if I'd gone on to the majors and Lucy had stayed at her peak. I would be maybe thirty and I'm wearing my gray and silver pinstripe, an open powder-apple silk shirt, Texas handcrafted cowboy boots, gold-plated razor blade around the neck, California tan and mirror-backed aviator shades, and I'm dusting along in the silver Stingray with the mag wheels, and suddenly I shoot through a time warp straight onto Pomerania's Old North Road, where I come out of a controlled drift straight toward the chewing cheeks of her pert little bum as she hums toward town. Like a lift? I say, and she recognizes me instantly, no questions asked, but it's obvious I've got it made and my face has cleared up. Before we've gone two turns down the road she's screaming at me to turn into the gravel pit, and fast . . .

But now, she herself had turned into the pits.

"Pet, you remember Felix Batterinski, don't you?".

"Hi, Lucy. Good to see you."

She looked at me and smiled. Even her teeth had faded. But in her look I saw the old Lucy Dombrowski smoldering still, the embers of the fire that had soldered the image of being naked with the young, luscious Lucy forever in my mind. I felt awkward, as if this was a Saturday night Legion dance in 1963. And I could see in her eyes that she, too, was seeing the old Batterinski with the pimples and the Frankenstein haircut and the crummy clothes from out Batterinski Road. And I saw that she had known all along that my secret passion for her had been something she had been aware of always.

"You've certainly done well for yourself, Felix," she said.

"I can't complain."

"Great kid," I said, indicating Tommy.

Lucy smiled, agreeing. But her voice argued. "He's supposed to be in bed."

"I don't want to go to bed," Tommy said, clinging closer.

I looked at him. "Would you do as your mother wants if I gave you a present?"

Tommy smiled and shut his eyes.

"Shit, you don't need to give him nothing, Bats," Danny said. "*I*'ll put him to bed so he stays."

Danny reached for the boy but the boy burrowed into my neck. "Hey, wait," I said, trying to laugh away the tension. "Here, I want to, okay?" I said to Danny, who shrugged. I handed Tommy to his mother and then looped the first neck chain off—the shark's tooth—and ceremoniously put it around his neck. The boy's tiny eyes bulged as he grabbed at the prize.

"Jesus Christ, man—you don't have to do that!" Danny railed.

"I had it given to me. Some fan. Let him have it, okay, from me?"

Lucy was agreeable. "What do you say, Tommy?"

"Thank you," Tommy said shyly.

"You take that thing off before you get into bed," Danny warned, "or you'll strangle in your sleep, sure as shit, and I can't afford no funeral."

"I will," Tommy said.

I leaned over to chuck his chin the way Clarkie always did in the hospital visits, and Tommy surprised me by leaning out from his mother's arms and kissing my cheek. It embarrassed me and I handed him back, laughing, as if he was going to fall. The kiss was wet, at first warm then cool, and I let it dry on its own, delighting in it.

"Where are you two going?" Lucy asked.

"Out. A few beers, that's all."

Lucy nodded.

"Drive carefully," she said. A reflex.

"Give her shit!" Danny shouted as we moved up the hill and past St. Martin's, cresting to the downslope — "Trucks gear down" the sign warned — that led down onto the drag flats. I double-clutched up into third and popped, the engine soaring and the rear wheels screaming blue smoke. The tachometer hit 6,500 and I slapped down into fourth gear, a tiny squeal saluting the speed of the shift. We passed over the black tire marks of the quarter-mile mark doing 110 miles an hour.

"UGGGGAAAA-BUGGGAAAA!" Danny screeched out the window. The air rushed in cupping my head forward, blowing my mirror shades off my hair. I placed my beer between my legs, gripping the wheel with both hands.

"Roll that up!" I shouted, but it did no good. Danny leaned out like a spaniel, eyes closed, thinning hair and thickening flesh bending back from the force, smile hanging onto his teeth so his entire face didn't rip free and go rolling down the embankment like a lost hubcap.

We pulled off the highway at the first village east along the line, parked just down from the hotel and walked up a backstreet that smelled of the desperation and vomit of closing time. There had been improvements, most obvious being the single, dripping air conditioner that had been cut into the ledge above the door with the faded "Ladies and Escorts Only" sign. Inside, the coolant was immediately canceled by a hundred or more sweating bodies, cigarettes, pipes and hot-air talk.

"Hey, Dans!"

"Shannon, you old fart!"

"Hi, Danny."

"*Shannon!* Over here!"

Danny returned a little smile here, a finger, a wink, a few famous Shannon grins, a half-dozen punches to eager shoulders. He moved through the room like the Pope in St. Peter's Square, and I simply trailed behind, awestruck by his popularity. Some of the faces I recognized, and a few names came easily; but though I sensed many recognized me, nothing was said. No *Batterinski, you old fart*, no *Bats, over here.*

Danny refused all offers of seats. We got our own table near the back and Danny held up four fingers and instantly a waiter with slicked back hair and a rubber apron was slapping down four draft and a small opened can of tomato juice.

"Missed you last night, Danny," the waiter said.

"Ball practice," Danny said.

I looked surprised, seeing Danny going down for a hot grounder and rebounding off his own stomach as the ball scooted safely between his legs. "*You* playing?"

Danny looked hurt that I would ask that way. "I'm leading the league in average, lad."

I shook my head and looked at the waiter, expecting he, too, would be amazed; but the waiter was looking for another kind of statistic. He wanted money. I pulled out a twenty, collected my change, tipped well and we drank. I paid for the second round, the third, the fourth and gave up caring or counting on the fifth.

When the music died, which was seldom, we talked. But mostly the music poured out of the juke box as steady as draft from the taps: the Eagles, Waylon Jennings, Elton John, Conway Twitty, the Stones, even the Rovers, with the young crowd dancing eyes closed and rubbing together in the section leading toward the toilets, the oldsters center stage, generally moving about like so many pogo sticks as they desperately sought to adapt this strange music to the polka. How different from Thighs up at Burbank, where Torchy was current, where the skinny Italians and Mexicans danced like the place was a continuous, wrap-around mirror. There were none of those here in the Opeongo Hotel. Nor were there any painted women slinking about like one foot was shorter than the other. Here, the best way to tell the men from the women was that the woman generally had the hockey windbreaker on, too long in the sleeves but hiking up in the middle.

It took Danny only two drinks to start rooting around in the old ground. Nothing about me unless the story also included him. I was just about to tell him about finding Maureen the Queen when Danny's mill friends arrived, pulling up several chairs without waiting for an invitation. Two tables were pushed together and a flood followed. Like wolves, they had been waiting for the first ones to risk the hooves, but now that one was in, they all wanted to feed.

And feed them I did. Some of the faces I knew from past experience: Donovan, from the drunk at the cottage, which made me think of Ig, Tiny Fetterly and one of the Lacha boys, but not, thank God, the driver of the half-ton that day, a couple of the Palowskis, one I think being little Dominic from our old days on Father Schula's church team.

Naturally, they wanted to talk hockey. We went quickly through the standard beer talk, me sleepwalking through their so-called "inside dope" and Danny paying very little attention at all until I made the mistake of pausing to order some more draft.

"Bats," Danny said, suddenly attentive. "Do you ever think of Maureen the Queen?"

I was tempted to tell him about her as she is today. But he was already stuck in Vernon, yesterday. "Constantly," I said.

Danny took over then. He told the Maureen the Queen story in a version that made me sound like Henry Miller and him like the Marquis de Sade. From that he slipped easily into his glorified history of our hockey days in Vernon, leading naturally to: "What do you really think, Bats, could old Shannon have made the big leagues if he'd kept at it?"

This was no place to discuss Sugar's concept of "heart."

"You might," I said.

"*Might?* What kind of answer is that, *might?*"

"Well, it depends."

Danny was drunk. "Depends on what?"

"I'm no scout."

"You played with me. Come on — was I any damn good at all?"

"Sure you were good."

"How good?"

"I guess."

Danny sat back, satisfied. He had what he needed for the table, however vaguely I might have put it. By tomorrow it would be *Batterinski says Danny might have made it.* By next week it would be *Danny threw away a career in the NHL to stay here.* Danny would not even have to work on it himself; the others would do the work for him, all of them just as eager as Danny to agree, to believe that Pomerania had something to offer that the National Hockey League did not. Danny, after all, had *chosen* to stay.

How could I say what I was really thinking: that both were dead ends. How could they possibly believe a guy who had a brand-new $700,000 contract in hand, a new Corvette parked outside, clothes, friends, California, did not have it made forever?

"You guess what?" a thick, deep voice said from the far side of the second table. I leaned and looked. Almost out of view, a thick, dark man in a Renfrew hockey jacket was staring at me, his eyebrows challenging, his mouth open and wet with drink, and surly.

I smiled. "I guess he could have played," I said.

"Danny Shannon's too fat to have played in the NHL," the man said contemptuously.

Danny laughed, once.

"Danny didn't used to be fat," I said.

The man responded with his nose, an arching, accusing snort, his eyes closed. When the eyes opened again they seemed to have gathered more ammunition and were ready to attack again. I felt defensive about my old friend, even though he had put me in this awkward position. "Danny Shannon had moves like you wouldn't believe, pal," I said, my own voice a little surly.

The eyes tapered in on me, testing. From the side Danny spoke: "Forget it, Bats. It doesn't matter." He spoke with a tone old and familiar: beware.

I left it alone. There was a mumble from the other table and then silence. Danny picked up the slack by moving into the Orr stories, but thanks to a few minor revisions, this time Orr was invariably flattened as he crossed the blueline, either by Danny's stick or my hip. Danny even had a new story worked out, this one about his shot, which now seemed somewhere in a special league reserved for the Hull brothers. Danny claimed to have taken a slapshot—"Now this is before Mikita and the curved blade, eh?"—in a game against Parry Sound that struck square against the crossbar, shattering it into fifty pieces or more. I knew where Danny had taken the story from—I did it myself, with an overly frozen puck at a bitterly cold Vernon practice—but where the gall to take it for himself came from I couldn't imagine. The way I remembered it, Danny had a shot you could time with a calendar.

But I let him have his lie and took time out to survey the growing faces around the tables. The bitcher was still there, his brow nodding helplessly down toward an empty beer. He sat with his hands folded on his chest, coffin-like, but looked anything but dead: the arms were powerful, the hands thick and calloused and heavily scabbed around the knuckles from his last argument. If we were lucky, he'd pass out soon.

Not counting me, sitting dead center, there were twelve gathered at the Opeongo Hotel. Nine guys and three women, but it may just as well have been nine men alone. Not one of the women had said a single word, though two were animated in their laughter and one, in particular, kept looking at me with that stare I usually find in the anxious distance between arena side doors and team buses. Whether the three were wives, girlfriends or simply strangers who could find no table space anywhere it was impossible to say. They sat there and the men talked to each other, leaning back to speak around a woman, at times shouting right through them like they were thick underbrush. When the men laughed, the women laughed, though I suspected at the cue rather than the joke. They were allowed at the table the same as the salt shakers were, though the salt shakers received more contact.

I had almost forgotten how women were treated in my old world. No one in Pomerania was arguing about whether God was "He" or "She." God here was "Force," and the only sexual connotation a Pomeranian could count on was that every once in a while this force was going to throw a fuck their way. There was no Californian "I can see where you're coming from" in this room. No empathy, support for the Equal Rights Amendment, marches against rape, lesbian press conferences . . . in Pomerania women were just another form of wildlife, yours to do with as you will. Worship, screw, beat, ignore — it's your business alone.

"How 'bout *you?*"

"Huh?" I turned quickly to answer the hand on my shoulder and the thick voice, the same voice that had challenged Danny's revised hockey career. He was staring at me like I was someone else's newspaper, just out of sight. His eyes seemed unfocused, filled with nothing but barely controlled rage.

"Arm wrestle?"

I looked behind him. While Danny had been lying and I drifting, a table behind us had been cleared off and several burly men, some with cut-off jean jackets and cheap tattoos, most with sixties haircuts that had been last washed in that decade, were all waiting for my answer.

"Well?" he growled.

I shook my head. "No thanks."

"Chickenshit."

I looked at Danny. Subtly, he shook his head in further warning.

252 The Last Season

"I'm just going to have a drink with my friends here," I explained to the man, careful to smooth any possible edge from my voice.

"You're supposed to be the tough hockey player. Let's see what you're made of."

I again tried patience. "Sorry. I don't need that."

"I got five bucks says you're nothing, Batterinski."

Patience gone, I slapped my hands on my thighs and stood. "Let's get it over with," I said.

As quickly as I stood, the tables emptied and formed a circle around us. A bull terrier pit. I sat and steadied my hand, waiting for him. He sat, surly mouth twisting into a sad victory smile, and as soon as he reached to take my hand I knew I had him.

"Any time," I said, deliberately filling my voice with boredom.

He hit hard and fast, a bass trying to break a lure against the current. I let him have some line, too, allowing my arm to sag back and fool him into putting full force into his lunge for a lucky, fast victory. He poured his rage into the arm, practically rising out of his seat as he went full out of it. But I held. And when I looked up at him I saw his brow folded into itself, his face popping with blood, the tapering eyes retreating in panic. I smiled.

Slowly, deliberately, I brought our arms even by fractions. When we steepled I smiled for everyone and winked at Danny, then surged once through my arm and flattened him instantly, the back of his wrist cracking loudly against the table, just in case anyone had any doubts.

"Five," I said, and held out my hand.

His second handed the bill to me quickly. I took it and, anxious to avert any return match or second challenge, turned back to our own table and raised my hand for another tray of beer, throwing the five into the dwindling pot.

Danny continued to drink heavily until he was so drunk I was sure I'd have to carry him home and tuck him in with Lucy. I was not in such good shape myself. A rolling wall in the washroom convinced me it was time to quit, and when I came out Danny was face down on the table, snoring. I picked him up from behind, shook him a bit to wake him, and then helped him hobble out onto the porch, where he stood singing and pissing the length of the steps. He finished, half put himself away and took a step into space that would have ended with a broken neck had I not caught him. I hadn't expected him to be so heavy, and he dragged both of us, stumbling, down five steps, but I managed to get his arm up around my neck and, lifting and dragging, down the steps and off toward the car.

I thought it was Danny's hand at my neck. But then the voice.

"I'll have my five back, asshole."

Danny straightened up, suddenly capable.

"Fuck off, Patterson," Danny said.

"I want my money."

"You bet it. You lost it," Danny said.

"I got fuckin' tricked."

I had said nothing. The arm wrestler, Patterson, was reeling on his feet. He was not after his money, but his pride.

"Go home and sleep it off," I advised in as rational and comforting a voice as I could manage. I pulled out my wallet and searched a five out in the moonlight. "Here," I said, crumpling the money and pressing it into his hand. "Take it. I sure as shit don't need it."

Patterson let the bill drop, kicking it away, and then rushed me, using his thick head like a football helmet on my ribs. The blow knocked me staggering, and when I stepped back I saw that Patterson's friends were moving out from behind the cars and hotel. They again formed a ring.

If I struck fast, I thought, they might panic.

Patterson was watching me with contempt, hoping the head butt would be enough, that Batterinski would slink away with his useless friend, and one day Patterson's brawl would take on the same magic as Danny's short hockey career. *You know that Batterinski that used to play for the Flyers, eh? Tough cop, eh? Patterson cleaned that asshole's clock right here, right outside this very hotel. I seen it, eh? Batterinski was never the same after that, eh?*

With Danny shaking his head at me I shot right through his warning and landed a boot — loafers, for Christ's sake! — in his gut. Patterson bent double and I hit him with both hands together right across the face, spinning him backwards onto his back. I leapt so I landed on him, kneeing his shoulders back against the ground, and grabbed his hair in one hand and raised the other in a fist. His eyes focused clearly now, the rage buckled by terror.

Time slowed marvelously, the warmth surging through me and the sting in my hands as sharp as freezing rain on the cheek. I could see he was bleeding heavily from the mouth where his teeth had gone into his lower lip. When he tried to talk the blood bubbled and he had to spit first.

"Lay off," Patterson begged. "I'm hurt, okay?"

I stepped off slowly, watching his friends. But no one moved. Danny was steadier now and we backed off quickly, me with both hands out so they would know I was ready for anything they might care to try. Batterinski was leaving as a favor, not in panic. Batterinski had complete control.

When we turned at the corner and vanished toward the car I lifted my face into the night air and drank deep from it. I felt better than at any moment since I had entered the tunnel at Detroit.

I helped Danny into the car and shut the door on him, and by the time I came around to my side he was already screaming from within. I opened on: " —fuckin' showed him, man. Oh shit, oh shit, oh shit it was beautiful, Bats! That asshole finally got his. You're a fuckin' hero, man!"

All the way back to Danny's I wondered. By the time I helped him in through the front door and closed it after him I believed otherwise. I stood for a moment staring up at the quarter-moon and the stars and I knew that Patterson, whoever he was, had simply taken a run at Batterinski for every person sitting in the bar. Probably Danny Shannon included. Perhaps even for Batterinski himself.

After that I stayed away from Danny and the bars and even the village itself. I ran every morning, always five miles, and usually down the other direction on Batterinski Road where it entered the tamarack swamp and quickly faded from a washboardy gravel road to a one-vehicle-wide path with a high mound of fractured grass in the middle.

I ran before breakfast, the late summer fog clammy on my face and hands, and then the sun, when it burned through, like a comforter in the personal hours of a sleepless night. It was a most peculiar feeling to be a shadow slipping, slapping, grunting along in the fog, my skin defining the limits of space, the trail seeming to run at me rather than I at it. I could not tell where the fog would end and the sunshine begin, and entering sun patches felt much like bursting through a wall.

Several times I frightened myself, twice coming across partridge scratching gravel in the fog and having them explode in my face, twisting toward the spruce, and once I almost landed on two fox kittens who froze in terror as I materialized suddenly and then was gone, re-entering the fog.

On the final morning of my ten days back home, the fog lay stubborn along the swamp trail. But I had come to like it this way, the fog like a defender hacking away at me as I picked up speed to stay just out of reach, eyes alert to whatever might spring from the fog, knees ready to pivot instantly, no matter what the surprise. It was hockey. I had to have my arms alert to push off spruce and drooping raspberry. I fancied I might come across a mother bear ready to swat me away from her cubs, perhaps a wolf standing over a rabbit, thinking I had come to swipe the kill. This unknown gave what would have been an otherwise boring run the dimension it lacked: a test of reflex. Rather than running, as others did, to raise my heartbeat to some ridiculous number minus my age, I ran to keep up with my heart.

Your strength has become your weakness. Wasn't that what Sugar had said? What did it mean? And Teddy Roosevelt? Something about a big stick. *Walk softly and carry a big stick.* Is that what it was? What did Sugar mean? If my strength had been —what? — my ability to take charge when need be, how could that have become my weakness? Was I taking charge just to take charge? Walking loudly carrying a little stick?

That's it — *walking loudly with a small stick.* Sugar knew. Like the water spider, I have become less than the impression I give. And he saw that, the son of a bitch. Did it happen all the way back in Philadelphia when we played the Russians?

How long, then, before everyone knows?

I ran a little faster, still lagging behind my heart.

I knew I was coming alongside the middle of the swamp because I could smell it. The stench clung heavily along the path and there was the light click of frogs diving for safety. Here the fog was so thick it was as if I floated through the clouds, me alone with the sound of my breathing and the crunch of the Nikes, the smell and the bracing wash of fog on face, chest, forearms, thighs, a touch as light and startling as chilled cobweb.

Ahead of me, just where the road would rise to the cedar knoll heading up to a rock face overlooking the swamp, a sun pocket lay in waiting. But I did not see it until I entered. It was like passing into a small room of dazzling light and heat. Four long strides and I was through — a light switched on at night, then instantly off — and the higher fog was already swallowing me when I spun in mid-stride.

Batcha had been standing there!

My ankle caught and I stumbled, skidding on the grass embankment along the side, falling heavily to my knees in the gravel and stopping on all fours, my palms pounding the loose stone through.

I felt my heart catch. The pounding began slowly, heavily, and rose quickly to slide down like a hand over piano keys, the notes darkening. I lifted my hands and hit them together, blood and stone falling, pain rising.

"Batcha?"

I called, but no answer. I stood up, the gravel announcing itself now in my knees and I buckled back down on one and checked the other: more blood, small stones clinging like buckshot. I rose and stretched the knee, feeling it lock, and stepped uneasily back into the spreading pocket of sunlight.

"Batcha?"

But nothing. I looked at all sides of the strip of bright morning. There was the path, wet and glistening, the silver poplar trunks, dew in the cedar, some dry blueberry bushes, the blue sky in a narrow gap above, the fog banks on all sides — but not Batcha.

Yet I *had* seen her. She wore her heavy black wool shawl, held over her head as if it were raining and pinched tight to her neck. She had stared at me as I came through the fog, her head bowed but tilted so her eye could greet me with gathered hatred. There was no way she hadn't heard me coming. She had been waiting.

I called, louder. "*Batcha!*"

Nothing.

I stepped back into the fog bank and followed the path several yards, but there was no sign of her. The fog felt ice-cold after standing out in the sun, welcome on my palms and knees but causing my legs to stiffen. I turned and ran back the way I had come, passing again the sun pocket and thinking, for a moment, I might overtake her on the path. But there was nothing. I limped past the cedar and on toward the small platform Poppa used to use to pile pulp and flushed a partridge, assuring me no one else had passed this way recently. Where had she *gone?*

I moved slowly back along the return path to the house, and by the time I reached Jaja's old potato patch the fog had lifted entirely and the day was steaming off the roof tiles. I sat down on a soaked, rotting car seat back of the shed, checking my knees and hands. The bleeding had stopped. I knocked the remainder of the small stones free and tried to press the flesh back into its previous form, but it was no use. Small rinses of blood rose in each crater and settled just under the top layer of skin. By tomorrow I would be in a knee brace of bruise and scab.

Inside, Poppa was leaning over the double boiler, stirring the porridge. He looked up as I came in, smiled, then saw I was limping.

"What the heck happened?"

"I fell."

"Fell? You okay?"

"Do I look okay?"

"Nothing broken?"

I shook my head. "Just scrapes."

"There's Mercurochrome in the cabinet. Make sure you put some on. All over."

I took down the small bottle, removed the cap and dabbed at the hurts with the glass stem, highlighting the damage in orange.

"You want a bandage?" Poppa asked.

"Nah. I'll let the air work at them."

"Suit yourself. Here," he said, moving toward me with two bowls of porridge. "You'd better eat something."

He set the bowls down and opened up the bag of sugar. I sat in my place, moving my legs under the table with some difficulty. Poppa got the milk and then, on second thought, began dishing up a third bowl.

"Batcha!" he called. But there was no answer.

"*Batcha!*" he shouted. "I got your breakfast out!"

Still no answer. I was about to speak when I heard some movement in her room, the springs knocking as she eased herself from the bed.

She came to the door and pulled it open, hobbling into the kitchen. She moved so slowly, so weakly, that it would have taken her a month to get that far back in the bush.

"Good morning!" Poppa called out cheerfully. "She's a beautiful warm day out."

Batcha said nothing, staring straight at me, her lips turned to disgust. When she got close enough, she nodded, but whether in greeting or confirmation, I could not say.

Management was furious. Two guys reported to camp overweight. Another had a blood disorder they figured was mono. But all of this was predictable, all of this was part of training camps everywhere. But not Batterinski. Batterinski arrived in camp looking like a two- year-old who had yet to master running. Great scabs had formed over my knees, making me move like a short man on stilts. Infection had set in on my palms and I couldn't even put on my gloves, let alone hold a stick.

But the biggest change in the Kings' camp went right by management. Torchy Bender found God. When I woke up on the first Monday back the dildo was gone from his bedroom door handle; inside, the trapeze was down, the posters stripped, the drawers emptied. The small cigarette case of cocaine vanished from behind the bar, as well as the grass from the kitchen cupboards. All because of Tracy.

She had been waiting in the lower exit from the Forum business offices one afternoon after practice. Torchy figured she was just another nubile looking for the legend and went up matter-of-factly and told her he'd been waiting for years for her to walk into his life. It was line #325 from the Torchy Bender hustle repertoire.

Tracy took it as a sign.

She went back with him to the house on Friday and on Monday moved in permanently.

She made the house over in her own image. Cut flowers on the dining room table. The furniture reeking of lemon oil. Windows clear as baptismal water. She stood at the sink, arms buried in white bubbles, humming things that had last been in Julie Andrews' throat. I was fascinated by the curl of her blonde hair, by the smallness of her nose and by the enraptured tilt of a mouth that seemed to be leaning toward a communion chalice. Tracy looked like the angel opposite the confessional at St. Martin's. All she needed was a skull to stand on.

She turned. "Hi."

"Hi."

"My goodness you boys have let this place run down."

She sounded like Mrs. Cleaver. "Yah," I said. "I know."

I could tell she wanted me to say what the place needed was a woman's touch, but I couldn't.

"Dry?" she asked, nodding to a towel.

"There's a dishwasher, you know."

"This gets them cleaner," she said, as if we were involved in serious, scientific conversation. "We'll cut through the grime first, then see what's best."

She meant the same for Torchy. The garbagemen began to treat the Palos Verdes pick-up like a grab bag. The sexual devices were followed by four huge boxes of the kind of magazines that come wrapped like cheese slices, the magazines by a quarter-ton of neck jewelry, the jewelry by fishnet shirts, jockey briefs, a couple of dozen of Torchy's prized T-shirts — I'D LIKE TO TIE YOU UP IN KNOTS, WOMEN WORKING BELOW, CAPTAIN HINDGRINDER'S FISHY STICK — and even his collection of cowboy hats and boots. Within three weeks Torchy looked like a door-to-door Mormon.

I wasn't sure what was worse, the old Torchy or the new. The old Torchy used to say the only way you can get the true measure of a woman is when she was on her knees. The new Torchy was himself on his knees, with Tracy, the house filled in the late evening with their mumbled prayers. Down went the posters of Marilyn Chambers. Up went the pictures of Christ, the inspired scripture, the church calendars. By the end of a month the house looked like a millionaire's version of a Pomeranian shack.

Coincidentally, Los Angeles also started to win. We went six-four- one on a road trip, the tie against Montreal in the Forum, and back home went three straight. We were on a tear. Torchy moved from fifth in *team* scoring to twenty-fifth in the *league*, and instead of crediting Dionne, who set him up on sixty percent of his goals, or me, who kept the Plagers and Williams and O'Reillys off his case, Torchy told the L.A. reporters it was all thanks to God.

BORN-AGAIN SCORER PLAYS FOR GOD.

I had expected it, and was hardly surprised when Tracy came into the television room one night and asked if she and Torchy could talk to me. She had on a track suit with a cross over the breast. I had on *Charlie's Angels*, with a thin T-shirt over the breasts.

"Bats?" she said, voice expectant as a collection plate.

"Yes?"

She paused, half-distracted by the television. "Do you think maybe Torchy and I could talk to you?"

"Shoot."

She eyed the set: Jill was running; as always, the motion harder on my breath than hers.

"In the dining room?"

She meant the chapel. I no longer even ate there, preferring the nook in the kitchen to having every bite, chew and swallow examined by a jury of Jesus Christ, Simon and Peter, Moses with the Commandments and Jacob trying to figure out his ladder.

"Once the program's over?" I suggested.

She glanced at the television suspiciously, sure the devil had bought the time. "Okay," she agreed reluctantly. "We'll be waiting."

I felt a fool walking in on them. I'd rather have stormed Torchy's bedroom in the old days and found him hanging naked from his ankles in the trapeze and completely coated in Dream Whip while two underaged groupies tore at him with spoons than walk into the shrine of our dining room, with its delicate lights and inspirational music rippling from the stereo.

I stopped at the head of the table and they looked up from their prayers, smiling.

"Sit down old friend," Torchy said.

I sat and they sat. No offer of a beer or drink, not even of one of Tracy's tasteless herbal teas, mandarin orange spice or some other light stain on water that was guaranteed to improve your outlook on life for a mere thirty-two cents a bag.

"Bats," Torchy began, "I'm worried about you."

I wanted to say I was worried about him, but didn't. I waited, knowing what was coming. The only difference here was that Torchy, unlike Father Schula, didn't have a heavy blood-red drape to keep between his envy and my fear. Fear at first; later, outrage.

"Torchy tells me you used to be a good Christian," Tracy said, voice as soft as a choir gown.

I smiled. "He wasn't there."

Bless me, Father, for I have sinned and I confess to Almighty God and to you, Father.

How long since your last confession?

It has been one week, Father.
And what have you done?
And what have you done?
And what have you done?
AND WHAT HAVE YOU DONNNNNNE? . . .

Torchy smiled his friendly-uncle smile. "Bats used to be a server, didn't you, Bats?"

I smiled back, not answering. I thought of Danny, his tongue thick with sacrificial wine, pocket thick with offerings. If there was truly a gate to heaven, Danny would be met by a police roadblock.

How could they be taking this seriously? Only someone as absurd as an Athlete for Christ would be able to see a connection between role and reward. Serve and ye shall one day serve God. Check hard and ye will keep the devil bottled up in his own end.

"Torchy says you were raised Catholic."

I nodded at Tracy but I was looking at Torchy. He had trimmed his hair back to pre-expansion standards. The red flame was turning to ashes now with gray; the loose, freckled face now tightened like a beaver pelt in the sun.

"Do you no longer go to mass?" she asked.

"No."

"May I ask why?"

She spoke with a smile, but with Father Schula peeking out from behind it.

I stared directly at her. "No."

Tracy looked down, hurt. Torchy's face crinkled like cellophane as the blood roared up and returned him, just for the moment, to the old carrot-head of Sudbury.

"Hey, Bats. No need to get so touchy. Tracy's concerned, that's all."

Touchy? Who's getting touchy?

Tracy looked up, leaned forward as if going for the unleavened bread.

"We just want to know where you're coming from, that's all."

I nodded, but I wanted to puke. Here I was in a California confessional, friends exorcising my demons.

Confiteor Deo, omni potenti. No. I was not going to give in to these two, either.

Tracy must have felt the power, because she was willing to try again to reach the atheist. "Was it the Roman Catholic faith itself?"

"I don't follow."

"Did you get turned off by the church?"

"I just stopped going. Like school, eh?"

"But something must have turned you away, surely?"

She was not going to give up. But I could not tell her. I could not go over Ig's death with someone like her. Not even with Torchy. Not even with the old Torchy. I couldn't even go over it with myself. There weren't thoughts to ride with the feelings.

I quoted from Revelations. "But because thou art lukewarm, and neither cold, nor hot, I will begin to spue thee out of my mouth."

Torchy looked up, the smile dropping. "What's *that?*"

I was amused. "How can you come on so holy all the time and not know anything about the Bible?"

Tracy smiled. "There's more to being a Christian than reading the Bible, Bats."

"And more to it than luck too."

She was perplexed. "What's that supposed to mean?"

I laughed, too loud. "Look at your convert, for Christ's sake." I pointed unnecessarily to Torchy, who seemed hurt. "God is nothing more than a rabbit's foot to him. If he plays well with God he'll hang onto God. If he goes into a slump he'll try some new tape or a new stick or a new pair of skates — more likely a new God."

Tracy's eyes were watering. "That's *not* true!"

"It *is* true and he knows it." Again, I indicated Torchy unnecessarily. "You come onto me like I'm some kind of heretic or something, but look at yourselves. It's a joke. Do you know what they're saying about you?"

I stared at Tracy, waiting. I wanted to stop, but couldn't. This was like a hockey fight, time not quite slowed until I'd landed a punch, hard.

"No," she said, voice thin as prayer book paper. "What?"

I made it up. "That Torchy got religion just so he could get you."

"Cool it, Bats," Torchy warned. It was his voice before being bornagain, the old Torchy speaking.

Tracy turned to Torchy, then back to me. "That's *not* true!"

"*Bats.* . ." Torchy's voice was hard, threatening, like dropping gloves.

I dropped mine and swung hard.

"Look — I don't give a shit what you do. Just don't sit in judg-ment of other people, that's all. And don't try and force your bullshit religion on me, either. You just watch, old friend. You run into trouble and you'll drop this phoney shit in a second."

I was wrong. Torchy showed true Christian charity that night and didn't put a chair leg through my head. But Tracy stopped speaking to me and barely said another word all winter and on into the spring. Without discussing it, we divided up the house. They got the chapel and the whole quarter around Torchy's bedroom. We took shifts in the kitchen. I got the pool mornings, they had it afternoons; the hot tub we split the other way around. They probably saw it as heaven and hell.

The Kings flattened out as quickly as they'd risen. We dropped from second to third to fourth and began worrying about the cellar. Torchy's scoring fell off but — much to my surprise — not his prayer meetings nor his obsession with Tracy.

That didn't end until the following season, on a red light at Santa Barbara. Torchy and Tracy had spent the weekend hiking between the Santa Ines mission and Santa Barbara, leaving just enough time to spare to make it back for a night game against Minnesota. Torchy must have been hurrying. He cut the caution light a little too fine and swung out onto 101 straight into a black Cadillac barreling down from San Francisco.

We didn't hear about it until after the game. Some of the guys were bitching about Torchy not showing and the boss was talk-ing about a fine when the phone rang. One of the rookies over-heard Torchy's name being mentioned and assumed it was a trade or, more than likely, considering the way he'd been playing of late, a quick trip to the minors for the fading veteran. But it was neither.

Torchy was in a coma at the Santa Barbara hospital. His leg was broken. He had undetermined internal injuries. Someone else had been in the car and was dead.

Torchy came to the next day and three days later was listed in "fair" condition, able to receive visitors. Some of the guys wanted to go as a team, but I said I had to see him alone and they understood. Most knew how long our friendship went back, none knew how far our differences stretched.

He was sitting up when I entered. I had a card signed by everyone on the team, a separate card from management, a box of strange goodies from Hirohito, the gardener. But Torchy wasn't interested. He was wrapped where the glass had gone into his temple and the skin near his eye was the color of the Sudbury sun going down behind the smelter. His leg was wired up and weighted. A tube went in through the forearm, dripping.

He stared as if not sure who it was. I smiled but he did not smile back. I laid the cards and gifts on the night table but he never even followed with his eyes.

"Hi," I said.

He nodded. I stared at him and could see the water rising in his eyes and spilling. He made no move to wipe them. He tried to speak but his jaw hurt him and he held it to finish.

"Satisfied?"

It was Torchy's old voice. I stared, not comprehending. He looked through tears, but the eyes themselves were frozen solid, sharp as icicles. And then the eyes closed and I was gone. Shut out.

I went out running, up Hawthorne and across the Palos Verdes hills toward the ocean. The wind was out of the southwest, at my back, as I picked my way along the shore between the Point Vincente Lighthouse and Rocky Point, where the best view of the sea was. When I made it, I figured to have come better than twelve miles in less than ninety minutes. My UCLA shirt was stuck to me, my thighs raw along the inside where the shorts rubbed, the outside tendon of my left knee stiffened to the point where it burned to step forward on any downgrade. When I reached the point I climbed to the highest overhang and sat, arms wrapped around knees, Nikes and socks off, breathing deep. Below, the sea broke on the outrocks, the crush so violent it soothed, the sea spitting up at me, as I deserved.

Torchy was finished hockey even before he had predicted he would be out. And, just as he had said, I lasted a bit longer because no one ever expected fists to travel quite as fast as legs. But the day came —yes, as he had said it would —when I might have been better advised to use my legs rather than hands, and scram.

I'd known it was coming since the start of the 1978–79 season, when a goddamn college punk decked me during an exhibition game in Minnesota. It made a big splash in all the papers, and I think only because this big goof was an American and the Yanks saw it all as some kind of American invasion or something. Victory over a foreign power, that sort of thing. Whatever it was, no one bothered to mention it was a sucker punch, which it was, and no one seemed to take much note when in the first regular game against the North Stars I cut the creep for ten stitches late in the third. What they did note was that we blew our lead and they came back to score twice and win with us at a man disadvantage. The man, me. Batterinski fading.

Since then it had been, in a single word, *embarrassing*. A month down at New Haven in the minors, two months back with the Kings. Six months with the Kings, four in the minors. It made no difference to my pay, but it hurt in other ways. I made noises in the press about wanting a trade — I figured sure one of the old World Hockey teams coming into the NHL, Hartford say, could use me regularly — but the Kings leaked to the press that I'd been put on league waivers several times without so much as a sniff from another team. It was my big contract, of course. When Vincent Wheeler negotiated an extension through to June of 1982 he hamstrung both me and the Kings. I was being paid well, but I was miserable. And if I was more like Torchy I would have prayed to God to arrange a conference call to get me out of this mess. I wanted to go. They wanted me to go. And we just needed the right person to ask. Hartford, Winnipeg, Quebec, I didn't care. I just wanted the one last chance to prove I could still do it, and then go out the champ. Surely anyone could understand that . . .

God must have been listening in on the game, because the call finally came. March 11, 1981. They caught me at home. It was the general manager, George Maguire, and I was instantly grateful that I wouldn't be hearing about it this time through the press, as had happened in Philadelphia. I was neither curt nor hurt over the phone, but completely decent. This would be a gentleman's agreement, of mutual benefit to both parties.

Hartford, here I come!

"Dr. Buss wants to see you, Bats."

The owner himself. It *had* to be good.

I drove straight up the San Diego Parkway, hoping a direct route might mean a straight deal. Why Buss? No one had been able to figure him out since he bought the team from Cooke. He was a strange, sad-looking man with a Marlboro mustache, thinning hair and a voice that couldn't possibly belong to a land developer who might soon be a billionaire. The team was fascinated with Buss and what he might mean for us. He'd already come up with $600,000 a year to keep Dionne happy. Maybe he was prepared to buy my contract out at face value. I might clear $200,000. Maybe more.

I raced in past the secretaries. Buss was sitting in his black leather chair, feet up, eyes closed, and I thought for a moment I might be interrupting him — Torchy had said Buss was so smart he and a friend used to play Monopoly without a board, just the dice — but his eyes opened slowly and fixed on me with their slow sadness.

"Felix. Come in, please. We've been waiting."

I entered and noticed there were two other men already inside. And Maguire too. I had seen nothing of them. Had they waited patiently while I drove and Buss slept? The two men did not look hockey. Both were sitting extremely straight, with sober gray suits and slick, patent leather briefcases on their laps. They did not look at all like scouts.

All stood when I entered.

"Felix," Maguire began as he came from the side, face hanging like a hound. "This is Mr. Cousins and Mr. — eh —"

"Dunton," the smaller man offered. Bald, with thick glasses, he looked like a banker. The other man, despite the similar suit and briefcase, was taller, leaner and with short-cropped brown hair looked like a detective. It was he who stepped forward to speak, taking my hand like a priest at a funeral.

"We're with the IRS, Mr. Batterinski."

My heart skipped and swallowed a small cough. Income tax?

"Please," Buss said. "Everyone sit down."

We sat. The smaller man, Dunton, opened his briefcase and hauled out a thick document.

"We understand you to be a client of Mr. Vincent Brammer Wheeler of New York City and New Jersey. Is that correct?"

"I am."

He handed me the document. "This, Mr. Batterinski, is a subpoena. I'm sorry to have to inform you of this, but Mr. Wheeler has been charged by the United States District Attorney's office of New York City with 103 counts of fraud."

"Vincent?"

"Yes sir."

Buss rattled the top off a jelly bean jar and popped a handful, talking through the chew. "He stole your money, Felix."

I stared at him and then at the other two men. "Is that true?"

Cousins spoke, his tone like the cop at the catch end of a radar trap. "It is alleged Wheeler misappropriated funds that were held by his company in trust. The 103 charges involve monies belonging to you and sixteen other professional athletes."

My eyes spun about the room. Maguire was staring into his hands. Buss was picking jelly beans from his gums. Dunton was scribbling in a notebook and Cousins was staring at me, smiling, the glad bearer of bad news.

"How much?" I asked.

"Nothing has been proved in a court of law, Mr. Batterinski."

"How much do you think?"

"His records have been confiscated. But I'm afraid we don't know yet."

"But you must have some idea?"

He must have detected the desperation in my voice. The cop uniform slid off momentarily. "Off the record?" he asked.

I nodded. This sounded like our locker room.

"If the charges are correct he's bilked you out of maybe $300,000."

"Three *hundred* thousand?"

He nodded and Dunton shook his head and *tsked*, but whether in disapproval of what Cousins was saying or of what Wheeler had done I couldn't say, or care less.

Dunton suddenly spoke up. "You weren't the worst hit, if it's any satisfaction."

No, it wasn't. Our dry-wall idea had gone bust; now I felt my apartment building caving in on top of me, and my investments closing in like muck around a rubber boot.

I turned back to Cousins. "Why would he do it?"

"The state is going to contend to pay off gambling debts."

What did it matter how he'd done it? All the time I thought he was up in Torchy's room beating himself to death he was actually screwing me. It didn't matter how or why. Just that it happened. I was not only thirty-six years old, over the hill, washed up and finished. I was broke.

"You're welcome to come to camp, you know."

I looked up at the general manager, grateful for the thought. But I knew, too, it was useless. I hadn't played more than half the games from the all-star break on, sitting in a dozen different press boxes while leeches asked me about my pulled groin and I lied to them that it was getting better. It wasn't getting any worse, either. It barely existed. Apart from existing to give me a little dignity, that is.

"Is there any use?"

Maguire closed his eyes. "We had a good draft. You know that."

"I know."

We sat silent, the truth so obvious we could not even see how to lie around it. Finally I stood up and walked to the framed team picture, staring at myself as I asked, "What do you want me to do?"

"Buss will honor your contract if you go permanently to the minors."

"Thank you, and I mean that. But no. You understand."

Maguire nodded. "The best we can do is buy out your contract."

They were generous, but in the end it was all meaningless. Wheeler had finally pleaded guilty, with me and six other NHLers and two NBAers and a single ball player ready to skin him alive if he walked out a free man, and he'd gotten eight years. But what good did that do us? We all had lawyers' fees, and even if the players' associations picked up a big portion of it, it was still going to cost me big. That plus the fact that Wheeler had somehow spent money of mine I hadn't even received from the Kings yet meant I was down to $20,000 clear, with luck. And not even in Pomerania do you retire on that. My pension wouldn't come through for eight more years.

Maguire, bless his heart, called me in again.

"There's one more thing. The NHL Players' Association is trying to help out all the guys caught in this. I've someone wants to talk to you as soon as you can call him, okay?"

"What for?"

"There's a coaching job up."

Me? A coach? So soon?

"That might be all right. Where?"

Maguire smiled, his hanging face working up pulleys and blocks and tackle until it stood out sideways on both cheeks. He looked underwater, sinking down.

"Helsinki."

"Where the hell's that?"

"There are those who go through life gently touching those they meet, and those whose every touch hurts. Examine Batterinski: the uncle who died when hit by a half-ton when Felix was racing to a party; the best friend, Danny, who told me he gave up trying to prove who was the better player of the two because it obviously meant so much more to Batterinski, and who returned to whatever future the impenetrable bush of Pomerania would yield; Torchy Bender, the one-time NHL all-star now baring his soul on morning religious programming; Erkki Sundstrom, unfairly fired from his job as manager of Tapiola Hauki, his stomach a Swiss cheese of ulcers —all of this thanks to Felix Batterinski.

Intriguingly, none are women. Batterinski, known to enjoy the 'bonuses' of road life, never managed a lasting relationship with a woman in his life. There was, apparently, a friend in Finland, but he refused to tell me her name or to even talk about her. I discovered much later she was Kristiina Jalonen, an architect, who refused to be interviewed for this story. We spoke but briefly and by telephone, and the single emotion that spilled out before she cut off the call was neither pain nor anger, but a strange and weary sadness. She would not, however, talk about it.

How intense this relationship between a hockey player and an architect could have been is something we cannot know, but it is fair to say that Felix Batterinski was a throwback socially as well as athletically. According to those who knew him best, Batterinski viewed women as either fallen or precious saints. Danny Shannon told of Batterinski's first experience, when he was a raw teenager in Vernon, and how even the local prostitute laughed at him. Who knows how many blows he would later land on the ice thinking it was her he was striking out against?

He came from a closeted world where women had a specific function, and he was never able to realize that when he moved into the modern world it was *he* who could not function properly. Just as hockey was surely passing his kind by, human relationships had left him behind right from the start.

So when I said that Kristiina Jalonen seemed struck with 'sadness,' the temptation was strong to resort to another, perhaps more condemning word: 'pity.' But we shall never know.

What was it about Batterinski that made him such a critical

force in so many lives, albeit usually a negative one? It could be nothing more than that he was accident-prone — although his hockey career was remarkably clear of serious injury — but certainly his touch seemed to spread like iodine on a potato, forever blackening. . . ."

Excerpted by permission from "Batterinski's Burden," by Matt Keening, *Canada Magazine*, June 1982.

WE ARE A TWO-HOUR DRIVE DIRECTLY NORTH OF HEL-
sinki in a small city called Lahti for the deciding
game of the first-round play-offs and I don't give a
sweet fuck who wins. Tapiola has already managed the impossible.
Thanks to the second-best record in the league since Christmas,
we're the talk of the country. None of the analysts can figure it
out. And I'm not saying.

My own season has also been a delight, the incident in Sweden
excepted. In thirty-six games I scored eleven goals, had twenty-
three assists and served a mere fifty-two minutes in penalties, a
career low. To put it in proper context, though, I still led the league.

Kovanaama. Bully. It seems to have become my third nickname.
Not as fine as Frankenstein, but a whole lot better than Canucklehead. Since the Swedish thing, hardly a day has gone by without
my name getting into the news. So I was not only selling seats for
Erkki, I was selling newspapers. But I also had a problem, and it,
too, involved the press. Despite my attempts to block him, that
son-of-a-bitch Keening had come over from Toronto. First I knew
of it was a telegram giving his arrival time, where he'd be staying
and that *Canada Magazine* wished us luck in the play-offs. Sneaky.

He caught me at the worst possible time. We'd just trounced
Helsinki Jokerit 8–3 at the Ishallen to make the play-off cut, and
I'd been the star of the game with a goal and three assists. I was
sitting naked in front of my locker, sucking on a Koff beer and
smiling for the cameras while a camp of Finnish journalists asked
simple questions in simple English. *Are you happy? Can you beat
Lahti? How does this compare to the Stanley Cup?* (Yes, yes and a
diplomatic fudge.)

"Super game, Felix."

I looked up, startled by the accent. He was so clearly a Canadian sportswriter that he could have formed the mold: thick glasses
over nervous eyes, balding, a too-eager-to-please smile, cheap
clothes in need of press and coordination, the kind of body that
should say nothing but goes on forever about jogging and tennis
and all those other bullshit words they invent to replace ability.
The body of a true athlete speaks for itself. When a true athlete
says "tennis," he means the same thing as if he'd used the word

"beer" — something social rather than beneficial.

"Matt Keening," he said, shoving out a hand. A nail-biter. I took the hand slowly. Sweat. "Did you get the telegram?"

"Yah."

"Good. I tried to call a dozen times, but you were always out."

"You should have left a message."

"I did. Didn't you get them?"

"No."

"Shit, that's too bad. I swear I left them."

I leaned back to haul out my shoes and socks, escaping to my own lingering equipment smells. "You should have checked with me first."

Instantly defensive, eagerly apologetic — how typically the Canadian sportswriter. "It was my fucking editor," he said. I caught the swear word as it was intended — a gift, to show he was of the earth, an athlete, perhaps, who through injury (brain damage?) became a sportswriter — and I let it bounce away, ignored; I would clean up my own speech in retaliation, letting him worry that perhaps he'd offended me. "He booked the plane and I had to go, eh? I'd never do it this way myself, you know. But it was out of my hands."

Why are they always this way? If they truly live a life where all things — deadlines, pictures used, whatever faceless editor decided to cut out the important or put in the insignificant — are always beyond their control, why bother with such a life? They would have nothing if not for us. Yet they hold others responsible for everything; themselves for nothing.

"I hope you don't mind."

I was tempted to say nothing, but I was game star, feeling generous. "Well, you're here. It's your money you're wasting."

"It won't be a waste, Felix."

"I can't give you much time," I say. We are standing in the lobby of the Mukkulan Kesähotelli and he is begging for the interview.

"Problems?"

"I just get there early, that's all."

He accepts because he has no choice. "Where'll we go?"

"You know as much about this place as I do," I say wearily. "Anywhere you want."

"Guy at the desk said there was an okay place called the Pizzeria Rosa or something. Can you believe it? Pizza, in Finland?"

"I'd rather just walk," I say. Not because I would rather walk, really, but because I can't resist being mean.

"A walk!" he says. "Super idea."

We set off toward the three ski jumps that bow toward the arena where our season will be decided in ten hours' time. I am glad to be walking, when I think about it, but would prefer to be alone. And I know precisely what I would do too. Straight down toward the thick, red-bricked town hall Timo pointed out on the bus ride in, straight to where the statue stands in a small square swept with black, crystalized snow from the roads. From the bus it was difficult to make out, but it seemed to be a statue of a gladiator, left arm raised in odd salute, right arm wrapped around one of those helmets you imagine Victor Mature was born wearing. But all that I could care less about. What I really like is that the statue is bare-assed naked. There is no Paavlo Nurmi to pat here in Lahti, and I forgot to go for some good luck before we left Helsinki.

We are not two friends out for a stroll. We are a stubborn ram and a sheep dog, and the dog, for all his scheming, tail-wagging and circling, knows the ram has no fear and will do as he pleases. Keening talks about the cold, the town, Finland, the flight, his hotel, how much he liked Erkki and then, warned by my snort, how he saw through the amiable facade of Erkki and knew him for the asshole he truly is. The sportswriter trying to ingratiate himself. That, not the typewriter, is the most important tool of his trade.

We turn into a coffee shop for warmth, and the note pad makes its first appearance. It is time to begin.

"Just coffee for me," I say to his suggestion of drinks. "But you go ahead." And he does, ordering a Koff. I can see he is clearly disappointed not to have alcohol doing part of the interview for him.

We talk for a long time, me working through three coffees, which are going to have me short-circuiting by game time, Keening matching me beer for coffee, his hand circling like a vulture as he looks for corpses to pick at. But I am tossing him bones. We discuss the make-up of Tapiola Hauki, the company's involvement, the NHL Players' Association's part in getting me here, the trial of Vincent Wheeler, the years in Los Angeles, Torchy . . .

"I guess you heard all about him," Keening says with a smile.

"Torchy? No, what?"

"You haven't?" Keening acts like he thinks I'm putting him on.

"No. Is he all right?"

Again, the laugh. "I suppose. You know he's got his own television show, eh?"

"Torchy?"

"Yah, Torchy Bender."

"What kind of television show."

"It's called *The Torch* — It's one of those religious talk shows for shut-ins and little old ladies. Only his guests are all athletes."

"No!"

"Yes. I've seen it. I bet he's put on fifty pounds too. And he's got this beard that makes him look like a damned Mennonite."

The beard I understand — the scars. The show I guess I can too. The scars. He's willing to talk on about Torchy but I am not. Keening would never understand. He sees I am uncomfortable.

He asks me about my Stanley Cup ring and I am grateful for the change. I take it off and he tries it on; it looks like a truck tire on a Volkswagen. I grab it back and put it on quickly, laughing. He writes something down, probably pride. We leave Torchy and move through the WHA, the junior years. We cover more than I thought possible and I sit stirring my coffee watching faces in the small whirlpools: Gus, Sugar, Sanderson, Shack, Lafleur, Dionne, and always Orr, Orr, Orr, forever in mid-air with his hands raised in victory, his knee first to hit the ice.

"Tell me," he says, as we head back out into the wind. "How does a hockey player prepare for something like the end of his career?"

"You can't," I say. "And anybody who says he does is lying. It's like a car accident. If you could prepare for that you'd avoid it, wouldn't you? But you never even see it coming until it hits you."

I think of Torchy. I think of Ig.

"Not at all?"

"Not at all."

"Does it seem to happen quickly?"

"One day you think you've arrived, the next day you're gone."

I am falling into my own mouth again. And do not like it.

"So this is a bit of a lifesaver for you, then?"

"I guess. Kind of."

"You need the money, eh?"

"Yah."

"But what if it doesn't work out?"

I stop, turn on him, tilting my head into the wind.

"I just had the best season of my career."

"But let's say sometime down the road it stops being fun or worthwhile. What if this doesn't work out, either?"

I tell him with my eyes as much as my tongue. "It will."

"I'm sure it will. But is there anything you could do if you quit hockey altogether? Do you have a trade?"

Worms? Bait? Outhouse painting for the highways?

I decide to laugh it off. "Well, there's always used cars to be sold in Renfrew."

"Renfrew? What's it like up there?"

"It's God's country."

"Heavily Catholic?"

"*Very* heavy."

Keening laughs, a touch forced. "Did you have a sense of God there watching while you played?"

I should stop, but don't. "Well, you were always told He was. But it was pretty hard to believe He had time to take out for a hockey game."

"But they said He was?"

"They said whatever it took to keep you in line."

"But I understood you to have been a server."

"Who told you that?"

"Torchy. Why, are you embarrassed by it?"

Torchy — had they discussed Tracy, the accident? What else?

"No, of course I'm not. All the guys were."

"So you were a true believer?"

"I guess."

"Do you think He approved?"

"Who?"

"God."

"God? Approved of me? Are you nuts?"

We have not moved. We are still stopped in the middle of the street, with Finns moving curiously around us. I move deliberately but regret it. Keening will think I am running from the point — whatever the point is.

"Well, if you thought He was watching you, you must have

thought He was thinking about you. So you must have wondered what He thought of what He saw."

"Huh? I wanted Him to like me. Like any kid."

"But did you feel at all . . . guilty about playing the way you did?"

I see now where the bastard's going. "You mean violence."

Keening backs off, pretending he, too, has just seen the connection. I almost admire him. He's got more than one move. But he cannot get around Batterinski.

"Well," he says. "Not exactly violence. Aggression. Your style, you know. Did you ever feel you were perhaps playing too aggressively?"

"Not much."

"What about that time in North Bay?"

The Billings fight. Torchy probably told him all about that too.

"I don't know. Maybe."

He laughs, catching me off guard. "It served its purpose, anyway."

I laugh, too. "Yes, it certainly served its purpose."

"Have you got enough?" I ask on the way back to the hotel. Keening seems hurt, but I suspect he has heard it before, just as I have heard his answer.

"Well, I'd kind of hoped I'd be able to hang around you as much as possible. You know, to pick up the textures."

"Yah, sure. But just give me some time alone, first. I want to get prepared for the game, you know."

He does not know at all, but he says: "Sure."

"I'll see you later then. Okay?"

Completely agreeable, he steps off the curb into the dark slush toward the direction of the hotel. I watch him up and around the first corner and then turn, retracing our steps until I reach the street that leads to the town hall.

There are pigeons all over the park. Someone has spread dried bread all along the shoveled paths and I presume the dumb birds have mistaken me for whatever fool is bothering to feed them, for they run at me like I am a three-day-old crust myself. I am afraid I am going to step on them. I shake a leg and they scatter, flying up like a small twister and circling onto an area in front of a bench, landing in what appears to have been strip-mined with toothpicks.

I stand staring up at the tall statue and I think of home and everything in between. I know my nostalgia is caused by the interview. But this time there are no words to trace the time and the faces whip up like the rising pigeons and do not settle. The gladiator has a flat nose like Ig's, almost as if the sculptor had dropped his work face first before the clay had hardened. But the eyes, the eyes are deep-drilled hollow holes and I see Batcha accusing from within. I see Batcha dying and I wonder — will Ig be there? I doubt it. If *I* cannot understand what happens to someone when they die, then how could someone like poor Ig ever hope to? He'd be scared. He'd arrive in heaven more frightened of it and God than he was of the half-ton plowing across the gravel at him.

I jump up quickly, reaching onto the statue's helmet for grip and gain a leghold on the pedestal. I reach quickly and give one quick slap to the gladiator's bare, frozen ass.

No one has seen and it is done. We will win.

I feel full of energy, but when I skate out I find I am concentrating, and that is not me. Batterinski does not need to think when he plays hockey.

I am thinking too much of Kristiina and how she should be here. She was sorry enough for tears, I know and saw that. She promised on her soul to come to the next game if we go on. I heard that. But I am still not convinced. Her damned architectural bunch are on a three-day blitz to meet some deadline only a complete asshole like Jorma could care about. A sanctuary for battered children or some damned fool thing. Shit, if they put it up in Pomerania they'd have to add five floors and a morgue. I am thinking too much of Jorma, as well, still not convinced there is nothing there. And what I need to be thinking about is absolutely zero — my mind as clear as the next play.

I feel strange, slow, cumbersome. Methodical rather than magical. I know that this is apparent only to me. I play the position perfectly, but am useless to the team. I fail to anticipate a reversal in flow, and when the puck suddenly stops dead at our blueline, it is not me suddenly filling the empty space between it and their net with a break, but a circling winger from Lahti scooping the puck as I slide to block, the puck turning over me in slow somersaults until their center baseballs it out of the air and it goes in off Timo's hip. The lights go on, the arena erupts and all look accusingly at Timo, failing to see the fault is mine, alone.

"*Hakkaa päälle!*" Timo shouts as we exit for the third period, down 3–1. Pekka shouts half-heartedly because he sees me look at him. So far not one has even earned the minimum 50 Finn-marks for a good hit.

Can Keening possibly be here in Finland to record the life of Batterinski and see but one terrible game? I am now glad Kristiina isn't here, but she has seen me play well so many times before. As for this Keening dink, I have no sense of him having ever seen me play before. Except on television, of course, but television is as badly suited to hockey as radio is perfectly suited to baseball. If he has seen me only on television, then he has watched a game I had nothing to do with. He has had his focus delivered to him. He has watched the puck and the puck alone, and that is about as close to what a hockey game is all about as is watching a paper boat float down a stream. It shows you where it's going, how fast, and what it is passing, but nothing of the undercurrents, the bottom structure or, for that matter, the life beneath. A player like Batterinski shows up very little on a televised game. But the true fans in the arena know he came to play.

It would not be right to leave Keening with this impression.

About halfway through the final period, with us down 3–1, Niemenranta, one of Lahti's better goal scorers, comes up across center, slips the puck one way around Pekka and darts through the other, running on the tiptoes of his skates and looking for a play. I catch him flush before he regains his footing and he grunts and rolls up my back and over in a complete circle, landing square again on his skates, the skates catching and sending him head-first into the boards, where he lies twisting. The arena is silent but for a single whistle. The referee has wisely called the play dead to tend to the player.

I skate around Orr-like, staring first at the ice, then up at the clock, as if I am working out an equation. Three goals go easily into twelve minutes and twenty-seven seconds. But I know in my heart it does not go at all, that we cannot win. Still, I am at least content with my own play, at last.

"*Sakko,*" the referee says. Then very slowly: "You have penalty."

Penalty? I am not sure I hear him right but he points toward the penalty box and nods sternly.

"*What for?*"

He crosses his fists to indicate interference.

"*What?*"

I cannot believe it. In twenty years I have not delivered a cleaner, harder bodycheck. It is the perfect check to go out on, the perfect moment to be remembered for: Batterinski doing what Batterinski does best. And now they are denying it happened.

I look for help. The players are still around the Lahti player, but two of them have him rising now. He favors one leg, but whether because it is broken or just because the skate blade snapped on the fall I can't tell. Nor do I care.

"Pekka!" I shout.

He turns, John Wayne eyes raising in question.

"Pekka! Find out what the hell's going on here."

Pekka skates to the referee, who takes his approach as a personal affront, backing up with his arms folded over his chest and simply shaking his head in response to Pekka's questions. Pekka shouts at him and he shouts back, rolls back his sleeve and begins a countdown on his watch.

"He says you'll have a match penalty if you don't leave."

"I'm not leaving until he explains what the fuck for," I say. "*No way* that was interference."

Pekka shouts back to him. The referee slaps his watch and signals a match penalty to me and backs to the scorer's bench. I cannot *believe* it! I skate after him but he turns, shakes his head and closes his eyes, shutting down on me.

"You don't have a *fucking clue*, do you?" I shout.

The eyes open and he stares at me, mouth trembling but arms folded firm.

"That was a perfectly fair check and you know it."

"Bats! Forget it!" Pekka shouts.

"No. I won't forget it! This asshole knows sweet fuck-all about hockey and I'm going to tell him so."

"Go off," Timo says, and places a glove on my shoulder.

"*Fuck off!*" I scream at Timo, batting his hand down.

The linesmen are in to help now. I have lost. I take one final burst toward the referee and he backs so startled that he loses his footing and falls. The arena screams like a binding beltsaw. I suppose *this* is my fault too.

I lean into him as I pass, speaking loud enough to carry through the whistling but slowly enough that he may understand.

"You dumbfuck Finn."

What is the use of even staying to watch this fiasco? I kick through the penalty box, snap my stick in half on the boards, and walk straight through toward the dressing room, where a fat little man in a ski jacket hurries ahead to unlock our door. I step in and kick the door shut, muffling the whistles that will not stop for the rest of the game.

Why do they call it all anger? There is fury against an opponent, which is something I enjoy, and there is frustration, which I despise. Yet they call it all anger. If what I had done out there was intentional I would sag in my locker and enjoy letting the fury wash through. And by game's end I would be as peaceful as a nun. But this, this keeps on growing. I kick and stomp and hammer my hands along the walls, but nothing works. I pick up Timo's new shipment of sticks from Koho and break each one methodically, but it does not help. I take out one of the practice goaltender masks and spring on it with my skates until it cracks like a rifle, but not even that helps. I kick through the bathroom door, smash a skate through the toilet seat, elbow the paper dispenser off the wall, cuff out the soap, lean on the sink until it collapses with the plaster from the wall and shimmies like a jack-in-the-box.

But nothing helps. Frustration has no cure. I have done my job perfectly, as well as ever before in my career, and one single son-of-a-bitch has said it is all wrong. He has called me a liar. He has seen something that did not happen. He has penalized the reputation, not the man. He has wronged me, and if he were in here I would set the record right by standing on his jugular until the hollow ground worked through. And when his last air bubbled up and out the cut throat I would look down at him, blow his own whistle and give him an extra ten minutes, just so he could feel it all over again, the miserable bastard.

It is the morning after and Erkki is sitting behind his desk looking remarkably relaxed. There are no nails in his mouth, no twitches, nothing. I cannot believe it.

"Look at this," he says, and hands me a piece of paper with meaningless numbers and Finnish typing. "We made a profit in our first year of operation. I doubt that any team in Finland has ever done that. Most of them are heavy losers."

"You haven't built your rink yet, Erkki. Don't forget that."

"Aha, but that is just the point, Felix. Now we will get our rink.

I've just come from the board of directors and they are most pleased with our season."

"Bullshit."

"I'm serious."

"They're not upset we lost out?"

"They're businessmen, Felix. They look at the year's overall performance. And you know better than anyone how far we've come. Nobody said we'd be anything but last when the season started, did they?"

"Sounds like you're starting to take some credit for it all, Erkki."

"Well . . . why not? We're a team."

"You didn't want to pay to have winners, remember?"

"But I did pay. And I'll tell you another thing too. I paid for last night."

"What about last night?"

"The toilet. The sink. Two doors. A mask."

"I tripped."

Erkki laughs. Strange, this. "Yes, I'm sure. It's not important."

I sit down, completely perplexed. This can't be Erkki the Jerk. He sounds almost reasonable.

"What's going on here?" I ask.

Erkki smiles at me, his pie face rippling into meringue smiles, eyebrows, eyes, cheeks, mouth all leering at me with delight. "I think it is about time you and I became proper friends, Felix. After all, we're in this together. When one prospers, the other prospers."

"Are they going to keep my contract?"

"Of course they are. I told you they were very happy with our performance."

Our?

"But there's a hitch, right?"

"I'm sorry. A . . . ?"

"Something you have to discuss with me, right?"

"What makes you think that?" Erkki asks, the first temptation to pop a nail in his mouth showing through the smiles.

"You called me in. You wouldn't do that just so we could announce our friendship."

"Well, there is a small matter."

"Which is."

"The board of directors has been fortunate enough to arrange for an exhibition game in Leningrad. The board of directors is very high on this idea. They think it would help promote better relations between our two countries. And they have asked me to ask you if you could keep the team together for two more weeks. All expenses will be covered and all salaries extended, of course."

A *Batterinski* go to Russia? Not on your life. Jaja would twist in his grave so hard he'd bring down Black Donald Mountain.

"I'm not a fucking Communist."

"Nor are *we* Communist, Felix. But we have to live beside the Soviet Union just as you have to live beside the United States. We may not like it, but there is nothing we can do about it. This would be good for relations."

"What's in it for them?"

"Who?"

"Your goddamned board."

"As I said, good relations."

"Come on, Erkki. Don't bullshit me."

"Well, it is a large market, of course. And we do a great deal of trade in kind. Not money, but trade. You know."

"Fish lures for what?"

"Wood. Other things we can trade better. Oil. Iron ore."

"And we're to soften up the Russians, is that it?"

"No. That is not it. You are simply to go and show what a fine team you are."

"Which is why you're sucking up to me, right?"

Again, the perplexed look. "I'm sorry?"

"You know precisely how rotten this team is without me."

"Well, it would be preferable if you did play."

"But still, you're worried?"

Erkki closes his eyes and leans back, sighing. "We can't possibly have another incident like Sweden, Felix. It would have terrible results for us, and not just in trade."

"But you can't afford to leave me at home."

"We don't want to leave you at home. Particularly you."

I smile. Of course —what could please the Commies more than to stick it to another Canadian? "Then you must be petrified."

"Not at all. I have a deal with you, okay?"

"What deal?"

"I will pay for your girl, Kristiina, I think it is, and she can come with us."

Of course. A bribe to chain the animal. "If I promise to be good."

"Yes."
"Let her bring her friend Pia."
"Only one. Yes."

Keening has been hounding me for time before his flight and so I take him to the Viisi Pennia. It is a stroke of genius. In the three hours he sits with his tape recorder and a continual supply of Koff beer, courtesy of the Batterinski tab, I tell him everything he needs to know. We go over "Canucklehead" until he finally has it straight. I tell him all about Sugar. I straighten him out on the McMurtry Report by asking him the obvious question: What can some academic from Ontario possibly know about big-league hockey? Say their universities are in trouble — do they come to Batterinski or Schultz or Moose for an answer? I guess not.

Eventually, Keening leaves, carrying me in the tape recorder. If nothing gets erased by the metal detector, in a few months from now I will have my say. I will be described sitting happily in the Viisi Pennia while every Finn hockey player who comes in pays homage to the great Batterinski. Almost as if it was planned. Which it was. A photographer will shoot me in Leningrad — Keening has some arrangement with *Sanomat* — and soon enough I will have the truth out about Batterinski.

I don't know whether to put it at the start of the scrapbook or the end.

Kristiina's reaction is not as I had imagined. She is in the bathroom, throwing up. On the phone she said that she had the flu that is going around and asked me not to come over, but I had to tell her. Leningrad, I said. *Sanko*, she said. Pail. And reached for the plastic bucket beside the chesterfield.

She seemed transparent, her skin bluish, her hair greasy and plastered to her head like she'd just removed a hockey helmet.

She puts a cool washcloth over her face. I don't know what to do. I try to take over the dabbing but she recoils from my reach.

"Please," she says from behind the cloth. "You must not touch."

"Okay, okay," I say, sounding like the one hurt.

She breathes heavily, the intake louder than exhaling, and every so often a moan sounds like it is coming from somewhere else in the room.

"Geez, you're really sick," I say.

She moans.

"Did you try and eat?"

She moans louder.

"What about a doctor? Did you call?"

A moan, or no, I'm not sure.

This is the reverse of the ferry ride to Stockholm, but I do not have Kristiina's natural gift for comforting. When I offer something it only seems to make matters worse. Speaking doesn't soothe, it frustrates. I touch and she shivers. All I can do is follow orders. She wants a blanket and I run for a blanket. She wants the blanket off and I peel it like wet wallpaper from her sweating body. She wants a drink, the pail, another drink, the pail again, help to the washroom, a tissue, a drink, a hand to hold.

And now she wants me to go.

"No way. You need me."

She shakes her head, breathing heavily from her nostrils, as if exhausted. "No," she says, her voice very weak. "I just want to sleep. Please, you do not have to stay."

"Sleep," I say. "I'll be here."

She looks up and forces a smile, but it does not catch. "Please go, Felix. I will be better alone."

How can I argue? I place my hand on her shoulder. She pulls my hand down and kisses the back of my wrist. She is very hot and clammy and I curse myself for hoping I don't catch whatever she has. I want to grab her and hug her, but I am afraid of hurting her.

"I love you," I say.

Kristiina does not answer. She presses tight to my forearm, then moans. But whether in pain or pleasure I cannot say.

The two weeks pass quickly. I let Timo all but take over the coaching chores leading up to Leningrad. He, after all, has played the Soviets some twenty times and understands all that madness about double circling and five-man units and pic-ing. My experience with the Communists is so limited that I've basically got it all down to one play: send Eddie Van Impe out to beat the piss out of the first Red over our blueline. But I doubt the board would go for it.

Timo is as excited as a child about the trip. I had come to think of him as just my big dependable defensive partner and had forgotten that Timo is first and foremost an art historian with the government archives, with a particular interest in Russian art. Back home your teammates played hockey for a living, period; I had forgotten that in Finland hockey is little more than a hobby. It's like finding out Tiger Williams teaches linguistics off ice.

Kristiina says she can't go. The flu barely cleared and it is back again, worse than ever. She has lost weight. Her doctor says her red blood cell count is way down. He's booked her into the Kirurgimen Sairaala for a complete physical. And if Kristiina is not going, Pia has decided not to either, leaving Erkki chainsawing his nails over the possible effect on our deal.

"It's nothing serious?" I ask at her apartment the evening before our flight.

She smiles and shakes her head. She looks so much better lately I cannot believe there could possibly be anything worth going to a hospital over. She's probably got mono, like Torchy in his second year in Philadelphia.

"This is common practice," she says. "I want to anyway. I keep putting it off."

"You look fine now."

"Surfaces can be deceiving," she says, forcing a smile. "I still do not feel very well, you see. The doctor, he thinks it is some kind of small infection that takes over when my blood goes down. It is nothing to be concerned about. I will be out when you get back and we can go up to the cabin if you should like."

"Alone?"

"But of course."

I lean over to kiss her and she accepts me, mouth opening and ripe with the scent of toothpaste. It has been two weeks since we last made love and I can feel myself jump with eagerness. I shift on the couch and place a hand over her breast, slipping in through her gown. But she folds the gown on my hand, as if it might erase the intention. I move back and look at her, eyes begging.

"When you get back, okay?" she says. "I am afraid I don't feel up to it."

I try to make light of the matter. "Well I sure do!"

She does not laugh. She does not even smile. She holds my head down onto her shoulder like I have hurt myself and need comfort.

I stay there, holding my breath, staring over her shoulder in search of something to focus on. But there is only the empty room and the sense of her too close to be seen.

On the afternoon of the departure I am waiting in the Inter-Continental lobby for the bus to the airport, which is late. And when I am pacing I notice a large envelope stuffed in slot 622, my room. I ask for it and am hardly surprised it is from Poppa. The bus horn blows and there is nothing to do but shove it in the zipper pouch with all the other letters and Jaja's story and hope to read it on the flight over.

The loading goes well. We are up and away in a sky as clear as the 7-Up Pekka is pouring into a glass already half full of his beloved *koskenkorva* drink. I order a nice cold Lapinkulta beer, watch while we shoot out along the coast for signs of ice breakup, see none, and then turn to Poppa's letter with a second beer.

March 23, 1982

My dear son Felix,

By the time you receive this letter you should be very nearly through your season, according to your most recent letter which we received on the eighth of this month. It just doesn't seem possible to me that time has flown by so quickly. But in a way, it can't go fast enough here, for at least a while. We've just been through three weeks of solid ten to twenty below zero.

There was a big story in the Ottawa *Citizen* about your old buddy Torchy Bender. What's wrong with that boy? It makes you wonder about that California. Everything's got to be a trend, eh? I saw him the other day on the television and he was making a fool out of himself. May as well have been begging on the street for his money. You think about it, son, you never hear of a good Catholic going that way.

Back home, your old friends are doing a bit better. Danny got promoted full yard foreman down at O'Malley's and his head's near as big as his stomach now. Building a big new place up Schama's sideroad back of the Mountain too. One of them Viceroy homes, comes just like a toy all boxed up and you just stick it together with spit. (*It's gorgeous, really, and I hear it cost them nearly $18,000 — can you feature that? Hi Felix, Marie.*) They got another kid, too, him and Lucy, but I've lost count how many all told. (*Three — Marie.*)

288 The Last Season

The worst news I have to pass on is about our beloved
Batcha. She's very, very ill, Felix. The doctors say it won't
be long now. Her blood's just running out. Doctor gave her
a transfusion last week and she fought like the dickens.
He's also left us some painkillers, but she won't have nothing to do with them. I'll let you know the moment anything
happens, don't you worry.

I almost forgot. (*I didn't — Marie.*) Our Marie has a job
coming up over in Renfrew. (*It's in the Manpower Centre,
Felix, they must have gotten so sick of me coming in bellyach-
ing all the time that they hired me just to shut me up. Ha! Ha!
— Marie.*) I'm sure going to miss her. You can't believe, son,
what a help she's been in all this. We're close to finishing
up, at least the stuff I mark off. I doubt anyone would ever
get through it all, and, quite frankly, some of it's not worth
bothering with.

I'm going to tell you about something, Felix, that I want
you to know in case I'm not around once you get to Jaja's
works. Marie and I found a sealed envelope in the last big
box, down near the bottom, and it has a handwritten note
from Jaja on it that simply asks us not to open it until his
immediate family is gone. I'm not sure what he means by
that. Him and Batcha, I think, but Marie says I'm immediate family too. It might be the deed they got when they
took up here, I don't know. Whatever, I'm going to honor
it at least as long as poor Batcha's still with us. Then you
and me can make the decision together. One thing I know,
it's not money. There never was any around to put in.

You'll notice I've included a few more clippings you might
be interested in. You can thank Marie for them because
she picks up things she thinks I might be interested in when
she's in Renfrew. (*It's nothing, really — Marie.*) *Time* magazine
made Lech Walesa "Man of the Year," did you see that?
Every Pole throughout the world can be proud of that, I
say. We can lay claim to the two most inspirational leaders
in the world, his Holiness Pope John Paul II and Walesa.
The radio here has said Jaruzelski will not even permit
Walesa to attend his baby daughter's christening. He has
not even seen his baby, you know. You know what Jaruzelski's real fear is? The Roman Catholic Church, that's
what. He's afraid to let Walesa be seen near a church in
case he asked the bishop for sanctuary. With Walesa under

the blessing of God, the Communists would be destroyed and they know it. So pray for Walesa and for Poland.

You read Jaja's accounts carefully, Felix. You will see that there is nothing new on this earth if you are a Pole. Jaruzelski has been around before, in different disguises. When your great-grandfather died so valiantly, Jaruzelski was known as the Marquis Alexander Wielopolski, a Russian flunky who was set up as dictator. He was a Pole by name and birth only. In soul, if they have one, which I doubt, he was a cursed Russian. Just like Jaruzelski.

Enough of that. There is more intelligent stuff in Jaja's papers, selections of which we are enclosing. I have only two more points to mention, one good, one I pray is not as bad as it at first sounds. The good is your Kristiina. She sounds lovely and intelligent. You know well my thoughts on a grandson to carry on the name of Batterinski, so I won't go over them.

The other point concerns a photograph that appeared in several of the Canadian newspapers. Certain highly respected people in Pomerania have brought it to my attention, (*Not me, I swear. If you're wondering who, you might try a certain "highly respected" person at St. Martin's. —Marie.*) The picture shows a hockey player spitting in the face of a man from Sweden. I cannot clearly see the face, but the newspaper says it is my son. I have faith in you, son, and have told people it is all a mistake. I am sure you will prove me right.

We are all praying for you. You pray for Batcha. She needs you.

Your loving father,

Poppa.

I will pray for Batcha, all right. "Oh Most Merciful Father, make it quick. I wish no pain on anyone. Amen."

I can feel the jet sag, the whining slow. We are descending on Leningrad. There is only time to quickly scan Jaja's notes. I will have to get back to them later.

How appropriate that the Poles, my people, who came to Canada would end up being sent into the worst kind of

wilderness to build what was called a "settlement road."
We were sent up the Bonnechere River and then further
up the Opeongo into the hills. All the men knew what
their job was, to build roads good enough that the Scots
and Irish could come along behind and cut down the
white pine for shipment back to Europe. We, the Poles
who had waited over a hundred years for Europe to come
in and give us back our home, we were thousands of
miles from our beloved homeland, sleeping in swamps,
fighting flies and trying to lay down roads on topsoil that
turned into pure granite two inches down, all so we could
help to build a Europe that would never come to our aid.

But we were not bitter. What we saw, only the Poles
would like. To the east, west, north and south there was
only more bush and more hills and more swamps and
more mosquitoes. No Germans. No Prussians. No
Russians. No false promises from other Europeans. Poles
stand alone, and here we would be allowed to stand just
that way, forever. We chose the highest hill for the
church, so that no matter where we were in the bush we
could see the steeples and pray and be thankful. . . .

Thankful. Thankful for what, Jaja? For a lifelong chance to work
for the Scots and the Irish lumber barons? For the chance to just
maybe get on with the highways and paint shithouses for the
tourists all summer and then be shit on all winter when they lay
you off? For the chance to end up like Danny Shannon, the envy
of the village because he got himself an $18,000 house that fits
together like Tinkertoys?

. . . which I personally consider to be the most emotional
moment of my life. Ignace Jan Paderewski was to play at
Toronto's Massey Hall on Wednesday, April 26, 1905. I
determined I would go somehow and saved for six
months. Everyone knew all about Paderewski and about
how the previous spring he had stood up to the Tsar
himself in the Russian court. "I beg your majesty's
pardon," Paderewski had said, following the Tsar's silly
delight in finding such a great talent in the Russian
Empire. "*I* am a Pole!" The Russians gave him
twenty-four hours to get out of the country and never

return. His concerts at St. Petersburg were cancelled. His name was forgotten.

But not by the Poles. Not in Europe. And not in Canada. To us he was Poland's greatest hero, not just the world's leading interpreter of Chopin. I had to see him.

By the end of March I had saved ten dollars from winter hauling and the previous fall's roadwork. I boarded the Canadian Atlantic when it stopped for water and switched trains twice more, once in Ottawa, once in Kingston, arriving in Toronto on the afternoon of April 26th. I walked up to Shuter Street and found this Massey Hall and was told the concert had been sold out for a month. I turned away, near tears, when the old man at the ticket office simply said: "Don't go far. Wait until the concert begins." He would tell me no more. I figured he meant that I might get to see the great man, anyway.

I stayed all through the day, no lunch, no supper, and felt like a common criminal when the people began to flood in off the main street in their fancy clothes and big hats and chauffeured cars. Not one of them was even a proper Pole.

When the crowd began to clap and cheer I was certain the great pianist himself had come. But the man that descended from the buggy had a huge top hat on, with bare wisps of white hair showing. I knew it could not be Paderewski. Where was the lion's mane of hair? Where was the mustache? I asked a man beside me. "There's the Governor-General," he said. "That be Lord Grey himself, come all the way from Ottawa for this." I told him I, too, had come from a long way, further even than Ottawa, but he just laughed in disbelief.

I was ready to go when the old man who'd been selling the tickets came out and announced that Paderewski himself had arranged that two hundred tickets be held and now released.

I got one of the first for only $1.50, and thirty minutes later found myself in the third balcony staring down past a pillar and from the side, but at least seeing Ignace Jan Paderewski himself walk out. I felt exactly as I had when I looked upon the Black Madonna at Czestochowa. This wasn't a man any more than she was a painting. This was Poland!

I remember every note of music he played. Bach, Liszt,

Beethoven, Schumann, Brahms, then what I had come
for: Frederic Chopin. I still have the program. Nocturne,
op. 62, in B Major; Etudes no. 12, 7, 30; Prelude no. 17;
Valse, op. 42.

I do not remember his encores. I do not remember
coming down the stairs or going out into the night. I do
remember that Paderewski came out and spoke to me
and other immigrants who were gathered there. He told
us not to give up, to pray.

A woman gave him flowers. Roses, they were, and at
that time of year! Once, his gray eyes swept across my
own and I felt I was finally seeing what my father looked
like, but I know now it was just wishful thinking.

It is hard for me even today, April 21, 1951, to believe
what came to pass for this great man. It was Ignace Jan
Paderewski alone who persuaded President Wilson to
fight for Poland after the Great War, and it was
Paderewski who was the new state's first prime minister
in 1919, as was only fitting.

It was Paderewski who, never forgetting for a moment
the monstrous abuse Poland has suffered at the hands of
Russia, refused to allow the Russian troops access to
Polish land during the years immediately after the
Revolution. He refused to permit the easy flow of
Russians. He refused to comply whatsoever with the
Russians. And in my opinion he, more than any other
man, stopped the Communist Revolution from sweeping
down through Europe as all the fashionable Marxists in
Canada were praying.

In 1951, in Pomerania, Ontario, there is one tired old
man who never, ever goes to bed without saying a special
prayer of thanks to Ignace Jan Paderewski through the
Holy Virgin, Our Lady of Czestochowa.

I want my children to know I, Karol Batterinski, saw
Paderewski play and heard him speak. . . .

Jesus H. Christ! Jaja certainly had no trouble squeezing the
Kleenex. I want my children to know I, Felix Batterinski, saw Howe
play and my own ears heard his elbows land. My *children*? Where
are they hiding?

I fold the letter back into the envelope and stuff it back in the
bag, half wishing I'd never started it. What is this shit supposed

to mean to *me*? Does Poppa actually think I spend every waking moment worrying about Poland? Who cares about all that? I truly doubt I will ever even bother to sit down and go through all of Jaja's story — *all* of it, piss, just what I've been sent — and not because I don't have fond memories of him, but because I'd rather think of Jaja hunched over the radio and waiting for Foster Hewitt than making a fool of himself in a fancy theater with a lot of phoney stuffed shirts.

What is the value in a family history anyway? So it begins, so it ends. What if it could be sent in reverse, so that rather than me receiving all these notes, how about great-great-grandmother and great-great-grandfather being sent one of my O-Pee-Chee bub- blegum cards — say the idiotic one from '79 that listed all my nicknames on the back: Frankenstein, Goon, The Bat, *Canuckle- head*, every fucking one of them. Would they hang it on the man- tel and say that knowing this about Felix somehow made all their hardships worthwhile? Bullshit they would.

Poppa and Jaja both go on too much about family history. Heritage, pride, heroes — shit, all I am is a package of hand-me- down chemicals, bubbling along as best I know how.

Christ, what an airport! I thought I had seen them all—squeezed in Edmonton, ignored in L.A., lost in Toronto, cowed in Chicago — but Leningrad makes a trip through any of them seem like a three-on- one break. We're packed tighter than cigarettes into a foyer leading up several steps to large glass doors, and Russia is presumably somewhere beyond. We're given forms to fill out, swearing we have no drugs, weapons, printed material or thoughts that might be considered ill toward the beloved Soviet Union. Finally, after forty minutes, I am in line to pass a booth. Inside, two boy soldiers scowl at my passport, scowl at me, scowl at the passport, at me, at the passport, at me, and then talk together in a strange, angry language and the boy sitting down scribbles a single letter or number on my passport and hands it back to me. I go to the next booth where a team of boy soldiers goes through the same wasted effort, tears off a portion of the visa and stamps the remaining portion. Then, with Timo whistling happily behind me, I pass on into a much larger room where our hockey equip- ment and luggage is piled haphazardly on carts. I find my bags and then yet another line, where adolescent soldiers, a trifle older and a lot unhappier, go through the luggage as if panning for gold.

My man looks more like a Pomeranian potato-farm boy than a Communist. He has the flat, expressionless face of a Slav, pink cheeks and eyes that wear the soldier's weariness badly, as if a laugh might sneak out if he's not careful. He, too, takes my passport and double checks with a zeal that would suggest I have grown a beard between here and the last checkpoint. Satisfied finally that it is indeed Batterinski, he indicates I should dump the bags on the stainless steel table between us.

He takes the equipment bag first. He removes me piece by piece, checking the cloth lining behind the fiberglass of the shinpads, the pad pockets of my pants, even my jock, removing the plastic cup and then rolling the cloth holder around until he seems certain nothing has ever rested there but Batterinski's privates. He indicates that I should open up the second bag. I unzip it and lay it out flat for him and he proceeds to give the same treatment to my pants, shirts, underwear, socks, even my shaving kit. He turns to a side pocket and takes out my training equipment, trying to find out if the Nike heel is all rubber or simply a reservoir for explosives. He checks my sweatsuit, the stopwatch I never use, the sweatbands.

Smiling, he zips it up for me and hands it back. I smile back. Then, as I take it, he notices the flat pocket along the side where I have stuffed all of Poppa's letters.

He reaches out and hauls the bag back, eyeing the zipper as if I have somehow deliberately tricked him.

"It's only letters," I say.

He looks up, not understanding. Timo is behind me and repeats, in Russian. But he is determined to see for himself. I groan, seeing another five minutes wasted while he tries to read between the lines for instructions on how to make a Molotov cocktail in your bathroom.

Poppa's most recent letter seems to fascinate him, yet I already know he does not understand English.

"Mail is a private affair in *my* country," I say very loudly, looking at Timo for a translation. But Timo does not translate. He signals me to keep quiet.

The soldier shouts something that I do not catch. It is not to me, anyway, but to a group of scowling soldiers standing in a huddle near the closest door. They all appear to be generals, all of them puffed up to manufactured heights, all with better-tailored brown jackets, most with heavily embroidered caps with gold embossing, red bands and shiny black peaks. They all turn, scowling deeper, and then hurry over as if glad to finally have something to do.

"What's in the letters?" Timo asks quietly. He has moved up to my shoulder and barely moves his mouth.

"They're just letters from my father, for Christ's sake!"

"I see clippings," he says.

"He cuts things out and sends them to me," I say, growing very weary of this.

"That's a picture of Walesa, though, isn't it?" Timo says, indicating with his nose.

"Yes. Sure. Poppa's a big fan."

"You should not have brought them."

Brought them? He makes it sound so calculated. I never even gave them a second thought, no more than I thought they'd want to take out my jock cup. *What is going on here?*

My man shows the letters and clippings to the generals and they scowl into the pile, picking up random pieces as if grabbing for someone else's French fries. They are delighted, but unable to show it. When they exchange something it is like children trading hockey cards, trying to get the most mileage out of whatever happens to be in their hands. They are far more interested in whatever is written there than I was myself, and yet they are my letters!

I would just go and rip them out of their hands if they weren't an army and this a foreign goddamn country where I haven't a clue what the laws are. I begin to step forward, but my knees seem suddenly without bone. For a moment I am not sure what is wrong. Kristiina's bug? My mouth is dry, my throat pinched so I almost feel as if I will cry if I speak. It is a feeling so strange that for a long moment I cannot place it. I am worried. *No,* I am *scared.*

I do not know their laws!

This is one of those horrors that all your life you're used to waking up from. This is the witch chasing you down into the swamp, the monster beneath the bed. This is my body falling helplessly through space. This is the plane crash. This is Batcha staring in Kristiina's cabin window. *But this time I cannot awake!*

I do not know their laws. I have no control over what is happening!

This must be how Ig must have felt when Lacha's half-ton failed to come out of its fishtail.

The short generals break up their group examination. One takes Poppa's letters and signals toward the corridor; just a simple raised finger and suddenly a severe-looking woman soldier surfaces from the doorway and approaches him. She looks like Pomerania's Sister Agnes Marie out of her habit. She is thick-lipped and snub-nosed, a vast disappointment breeding within. When she reaches the general he leans, speaks, and sparkles, not in language, but gold; more than half his teeth have been replaced with the metal, and when he talks it is something one sees rather than hears —a lighthouse flashing its warning.

The sad soldier woman turns to me. "Mr. Batterinski," she says, "we would like to know why you have this material."

"It's letters, from my father," I say, my voice tight and dry.

"But is typed."

"Yes. So?"

I have spoken too chippily and instantly regret it. Timo steps in, speaking gently, sincerely. "His father had it typed by someone else because he does not write clearly."

She switches from English to Finnish and lectures Timo at length. Then she turns to the general and switches to yet another language. Then back to me, in English.

"We believe it is not a letter. We believe it is a manuscript."

"It is a letter," I say, trying to sound firm. "My father has also enclosed some of my grandfather's memoirs. He's dead. My father is simply having them typed up in English so that I will have them. That's all."

She tells the short general who had been huddling with a wiry little soldier in wire-rimmed glasses. The glasses bounce with a nervous twitch. This general has more of Jaja's memoirs and is slapping them as he speaks. She enters the huddle and they grunt at each other for several minutes, the first general's teeth periodically flashing with delight. I turn to Timo, but he indicates with a finger he has been told to button up. I am on my own here.

"Your grandfather," she says when she returns, "he was from Poland, yes?"

"Yes." But I am not. And he came over a hundred years ago. "Is there something wrong with that?" I ask, no sarcasm.

I feel Timo nudging my leg from behind, the message clear: tread carefully.

"No, of course not," the woman says in a haughty voice. "The Poles and Soviets are friends. We would just like you to wait a few minutes, yes. There is a seat for you here, please."

She indicates a bench to the side, and before I can even think to complain I feel Timo's hand pushing my shoulder in that direction. He follows behind me and when I sit he sits, his big face wrinkling with concern.

"Is everything all right here?" a high, disturbed voice asks. It is Erkki, hanging onto the nail of the small finger, left hand.

Timo speaks. "They are looking at some letters of Felix's."

Erkki sneers like he has known I am a double agent all along. "What *kind* of letters?"

"A letter from my dear old father," I say sarcastically.

"It contains stuff on Poland," Timo says matter-of-factly. "And some clippings."

Erkki reddens, anger and satisfaction rising to do battle. "What an incredibly stupid thing to do, Batterinski."

I say nothing.

He persists. "You really should have known better."

I cannot take it. "Fuck off, Erkki. What do you mean '*known better*'? A letter or two or three from home—is that some kind of international crime or something?"

Erkki shakes his head, his prissy too-trimmed mustache curling in disgust along his upper lip. "What's going to happen?" he asks Timo, as if Timo might himself have once brought letters from Pomerania into the Soviet Union.

"We wait," Timo says.

Erkki nods, as if this satisfies him. "I'll go ahead and be with the team," he says. We nod, not caring.

I wish I smoked. I wish I hadn't come. I wish Kristiina had. I wish Timo had told me to expect this. I fold my arms and they feel stronger now, the strength finally flowing back. Is this the way it is in battle? Soldiers so weakened by fear they can barely raise themselves to fire? I am as appalled by my fear as I am by the circumstance.

It is twenty minutes before the gold-toothed general and the translator return. He still carries Poppa's letters and Jaja's memoirs, but the clippings are missing. And he also has several long documents, as brown and dull as the visa they have taken from me.

"Would you come with us, Mr. Batterinski?" she commands rather than asks.

I turn to Timo for help, the terror washing down and through again. "May I come as well?" Timo, asks forcing a smile.

"No."

I rise, look desperately at Timo, who can only raise his hands helplessly, and then follow them out through yet another heavily guarded exit while the few remaining players of the team, Pekka included, stare after me as if I am slipping from a cliff and they know no one can reach me in time. Beyond the barricade is a long hall and two armed soldiers fall in front of us. They stop at the far end before a large unmarked door and the general flashes his wealth and indicates I should enter.

Inside, a young soldier sits on a stool, eyeing me. No guns are in evidence here, but like a good deer hound, I can sense their presence. The room is starkly lighted by one central, adjustable spotlight, its beam spreading over a second stool a few feet from the soldier. I take this seat, knowing it is mine.

The general smiles, the gold now black, and with great emphasis pulls out one of his own pockets, indicating I am to follow suit. I do, my hand sweatily wrapping around my jackknife on the first dig. The general grunts and falls on the knife when I produce it. He opens the blades and runs a thick thumb over them and taps the handle for hollow chambers. I imagine what is going through his mind: General Ivan Goofov saved the Soviet Union's beloved leader Leonid Brezhnev this morning by selflessly hurling his body on a diabolical new capitalist weapon a Polish mercenary disguised as a Canadian hockey player was trying to smuggle into the country. The Order of Lenin at least.

He goes completely through my wallet, card by card, picture by picture, coin by coin. He then indicates, but not by example, that I am to remove my clothing. I take off everything but my underwear and the general goes through each piece as carefully as the first checker had worked over my equipment. He is scrupulous, fingering my lapels for consistent thickness, my boot-heels for cavities, even my belt for signs of restitching. But still he is not satisfied. He points to my underwear and I instinctively step out of them and hand them to him. But these he does not take. He points with a smile to the young soldier, who leans forward and seems to take them gratefully. He examines the underwear with even more intensity than the others. In his mind, with the general watching, he is rising through the ranks.

The soldier finishes and places them on the stool I had been sitting on. I reach for them, but the general catches my wrist. "*Nyet,*" he says. With a circling finger he indicates I should turn around, and I do. Then I feel his hand on my shoulder, pushing me over. I bend. The soldier pulls the spotlight down and presses it so close to my butt that I can feel its heat and my hairs tickling. I feel hands, the soldier's I know, insulting my cheeks, forcing my legs further apart as he searches. I wiggle out wider on my heels and stare straight ahead. The spotlight, now directly behind me, has cast my stance as a shadow on the far wall, my testicles hanging large as a feed bag.

I know what Torchy would have done in this position, but I do not have his nerve. The light suddenly swings away and the general hands me my clothes so I can dress. But we are not through yet.

In another room, down another hall, there is an interrogation room manned by a surly-looking man in Buddy Holly hornrims. I am told to sit and do.

"Mr. Batterinski," this new general says in perfect English, "what is the intention you have for this material?"

"It's just letters," I say. "From my father. I suppose I'll keep them and take them back to Canada with me."

"But why, then, bring such material into the Soviet Union?"

"I didn't even remember they were in the bag. I honestly never thought about them, I swear."

"Are you not aware, then, that you have here much material that would be considered harmful to the Soviet Union?"

"A letter?"

The new general peers down at his files, turns a page in Jaja's memoirs and taps a section before turning it. It is Jaja's account of his father's death. I pretend to be reading it very seriously.

"This happened over a hundred years ago," I say.

"On the contrary," he says. "It did *not* happen, ever."

"But it's just a letter. One man's opinion."

"It is not the truth, Mr. Batterinski. But that is a small point. We find throughout the letters much seditious material, much to be concerned about."

"My father simply included them for my interest." I say in a suck's voice. I am beginning to see the only way out of this, to turn Batterinski into something Batterinski would despise. But I'm not going to get through unless I do.

"I had nothing to do with them."

"Then you're saying you don't need it."

All I want is out. "No. I have no need of it."

From beneath, he pulls out a formal-looking document and scans through it. "This," he says, "is merely a formality. You are saying you have no use for such material and had no intention of distributing it in the Soviet Union. We will put the letters where they will be safe."

"Then I'm okay to go ahead?"

"Certainly. You simply have to sign these forms, that is all."

He turns them to me and sets a thick pen down on the papers. With a pencil he indicates where I am to sign.

I balk. "What is this?"

"Simply a formality. A receipt."

"I like to know what I'm signing, though."

"You wish it read to you?"

"Yes. Please."

He glances up quickly at the first general, then grandly picks up the document and begins reading — in *Russian*!

Is this a joke? I look up at the gold-toothed general, but he is listening intently and nodding his head as if in agreement. I look at the woman translator, but her expression is as vacant and businesslike as Sister Agnes Marie on Ash Wednesday.

"Wait!" I say.

He looks up, surprised. "Too fast for you?"

"I don't understand Russian."

"But the document is written out in Russian. I am reading it to you, as you asked."

"What does it say in English?"

"The same thing."

"You won't translate it?"

"You will require no copy of it. This is for our files."

"Give me the pen."

Erkki is livid. He sits in his usual spot, directly behind the driver of the gray and red Intourist bus, then stands to tap a reddened finger on his wristwatch as I board to the cheers of the rest of the team. "Two and a half hours!" he says, shaking. "We've missed our dinner."

I ignore him and acknowledge, instead, the cheers. It is almost like being back in Philadelphia, but the difference is that I have myself felt for the first time the terror of intimidation. Erkki returns a half-chewed hangnail to his mouth and I push down toward an empty seat at the back, shaking hands and accepting backslaps as I go. They think I did it deliberately, to rub the Russians' face in it. I am glad there was no one to see me weaseling free, treating Jaja's years of work like it was nothing more than a day-old newspaper, signing something that may be a full confession for all I know. But what choice did I have? I sit down and close my eyes, discreetly counting the pulse in my wrist. It feels like a bare electrical wire.

Our hotel is in the northwest end of the city, and it is necessary to travel the entire length of Leningrad's main street to get to it. There is little traffic. The guide, a short, grumpy woman with the air of a Grade one teacher about her, barks continuously into a microphone: hothouses for tomatoes in the winter, don't take any photographs of factories, this a war memorial, that a war memorial and, yes, Leningrad suffered so. Tough titty! She ought to have gone through what I just went through.

After a while I stop listening and stare out at thick, dismal people standing forever at bus stops, lining up at what I can only presume to be stores — even in Renfrew they would barely pass as feed and seed warehouses — or people simply walking aimlessly, one hand in a pocket, the other around a small string bag with goods wrapped inside the way Poppa used to have his hams done when he went in to town.

Timo has raved on about this place for two weeks, though. It must be like Poppa and his damned *kiska kajanka*, blood sausage with groats, which he makes every Thanksgiving from a hog's head, fresh blood and the large intestine of the porker. No one else will touch it, but to Poppa it's the most divine eating of the year. Timo's Leningrad is obviously also an acquired taste.

Timo and I have adjoining rooms on the eighth floor of this marble maze and we go up together, passing from the elevators down a snaking hall and past the eyes of a miserable old bitch sitting in a corner with a simple table and a large pad of printed material. As we pass, she checks us off.

"What gives?" I say to Timo.

"She's a *dezhurnaya*."

"A what?"

"You'll get used to them. They're everywhere."

I stare at her and slowly she lifts her head, hooded gray eyes — the eyes of Batcha — folding up the way the headlights of the Corvette used to.

"Is she some kind of agent?" I say when we near our rooms.

"Sort of. Everyone is here."

My room is on the side facing the Gulf of Finland. If only my room were high enough and the gulf narrow enough I would jump, I swear. Why did I ever agree to come here?

I toss my bag into the closet and leave immediately, desperate for that drink Timo and I have been planning. Just as I come out the door an awkward-looking man in a crummy brown suit — Lou Myles wouldn't even try it on his hubcaps — sweeps around the snaking corridor and turns sideways as he drifts past, watching me. I watch him continue down the hall to where the next snake will take him out of view, and I am still staring when he turns suddenly and looks back, again startled by my catching him. I kick at Timo's door. He answers foaming at the mouth, toothbrush in hand.

"This place is crawling with spies," I say.

Timo laughs. "From which side?"

"I've just seen one. What do you call them? Their secret police?"

"KGB."

"I thought that was who we were playing."

"No. That is SKA."

"Anyway, I saw one."

Timo thinks it's a great joke. "Oh, how do you know?"

"I know cops. He looked like a cop."

"*All* Russians look like cops. They kill off all the babies that smile."

"Don't put me on, Timo. I'm serious. You still up for that drink?"

"I am, yes," he says, tossing the toothbrush so it lands in the sink. His mouth he wipes with his hand.

We go down the curving halls toward the elevator, again past the frowning old woman, who checks again on her pad. But this time I do not look. I have had enough today already without imagining Batcha. For all I know she could be gone already. Ding, dong. The bitch is dead. I sincerely hope so.

We do not get on the elevator, as I expect. Instead, Timo leads me to the next section beyond and through swing doors to a small cafeteria with a deep line of drunk and soon-to-be-drunk customers coming up like they're in a McDonald's to pick up champagne or vodka or beer or some of the tiny snacks from beneath the counter.

"Hoy!"

It is Pekka's shout. Through the smoke I make him out in a far corner with several other members of the team and we go over into a flurry of forced cracks about me trying to smuggle Western propaganda into the poor innocent Soviet Union.

I say it once and once only: "I don't find it funny." And from behind I sense Timo signaling that they should knock it off. Timo picks up the drinks, two beers for me and a full bottle of vodka, which he deposits in the booze kitty in the center of the table. I pour the drink, thick, brown beer, so clouded that you can't see through it.

"Jesus Christ! This tastes like toad piss!"

They all laugh, a bit too hard because I am coach.

"Just watch yourself," Timo says knowingly, nodding toward the beer.

I laugh. "No one tells an Ontario bushboy how to drink beer."

Soon, in a fog of smoke there are five empty beer bottles before me and I am beginning to sink. I think at first it is the heat, or perhaps the ordeal at the airport was more exhausting than I thought. I look at Timo across from me, good old Timo who wanted to stay with me. Look at him there—grinning, sweating, the glass up, the glass down, up, down—shit! he's fading in and out on me. I wave my hand in front, hoping to clear the smoke.

"Strong beer, is it not, Bats?" he says.

"It's not the beer. Look. I've had only five."

He taps the bottle. "Twenty percent alcohol."

"Gwan!"

"It is. Another?"

I shake my head, stomach rising to accept what's really causing me to feel this way. "What time's the game?" I ask, desperate to steady myself with a new topic.

"Eight tomorrow," someone says.

"You still coming on Timo's tour, Felix?" Timo asks.

"You bet. But first some sleep, eh?"

I wave a small farewell and break free of the bar, its sound receding like the bark of a dog to a passing car. The eighth floor is clear, silent, but I find it tough going, the way the hallway seems to whip toward my room. First my left shoulder rides along the plaster, then my right bumps on the opposite side, and all I have been doing is walking in a perfectly straight line. Beyond the elevators the old woman still sits, her face rising to note me with censuring eyes, an old wrinkled hand moving in the pale light of her desk lamp to certify my existence.

"I'm *home*, Momma!" I shout.

No reaction. I stop directly in front of her desk, bending down toward her.

"Hey, come on, Momma. How's about a little nookie when you knock off for the night, eh? Room 814. Come on down, Momma!"

She stares up slowly, the headlight eyes rising, the face turning in a scowl, the face turning into Batcha.

"*Batcha!* I thought you were supposed to be dying, for fuck's sake! *Aren't* you?"

She says nothing. I blow kisses as I pass down the hall, slamming painfully into the first large twist of the walls. I bounce off, cursing, and look back again, but she has forgotten me and is staring down into her check pad. I know she will have much to write down.

At the first door my KGB agent in his crummy brown suit is walking toward me. He opens the door and holds it, trying to look courteous. He nods a hello.

"*Fuck* yourself, Pinko!" I shout as I push through. I am sick of them all. Why can't they leave me alone, the bastards? What did Jaja say that has them so fired up they've got half their force out on the Batterinski case?

"*My great-grandfather was killed by you cocksuckers!*" I scream at him, walking away backwards. He tries to look like he does not understand, but I know better. They wouldn't put anyone on me who didn't speak English. He knows. He knows all about the Batterinskis, you can bet on that.

Okay, cool yourself, Bats. Slow-down time, okay . . . there, that's working. I know I have had too much beer, but I needed it. I can still think. I'm not stupid. I know precisely what's going on. I turn and he is still staring at me. I stop at room 818, two doors down from my room, and pretend to be a drunk stumbling for his key. I see him watching, still pretending not to understand, but carefully matching the suspect with his cell number. I drop the key. I look back, he shrugs and is gone through the fire doors and around a twist in the hallway. I scoop up the key and hurry down to 814, slipping in quickly, efficiently.

In-fucking-genious!

Cold water on the face seems to clear things a bit. I would use my finger and intentionally throw up, but I am sure the beer will soon pass.

Outside I hear men's voices. Russian. Not Finnish. Not English. But Russian. They seem to be standing there talking. And then they are gone, undoubtedly waved down the hall by the next crew. I am under surveillance. The generals at the airport have contacted the KGB and everyone from the doorman to the old lady whatchamacallit is on to Batterinski. *Assholes.* They'll have no more luck with me than they have with any Batterinski.

Silent as breath I lift the desk chair and then the armchair and pile them against the door. I then put the round coffee table on its side, forcing it so it wedges between the larger chair and the bed, which is itself anchored to the wall. The writing desk I also wedge in between the small closet and the edge of the door. Just let them try. Just let them *try* and get another Batterinski.

Timo and I are standing overlooking the memorial cemetery to the Siege of Leningrad, and though he appears obviously pained by the view, he cannot possibly know what I feel. Head thick as a stump and as sore as if someone's tried to split me with a dull ax. And my damn knee — I haven't been able to straighten it since I jumped up for Timo's morning call and ran straight into the upturned coffee table. But at least it kept the fuckers out.

Timo speaks slowly, low. He tells me of the three-quarters of a million Krauts kicking the shit out of the city for nine hundred days, the full million Russians bombed, shot or, more often, just starved to death. It's comforting for a Pole to know that once in a while at least the dogs turned on each other.

He stands in front of the memorial flame and surprises me with great, fat tears dropping off his cheeks, while I stand thinking only how much the gas smells like eggs we sometimes misplaced in Jaja's coop and could only find with our noses. He shows me what they call the graves. Not even a name. Nothing. Just dates, one for each year: 1941, 1942, 1943, 1944. Four numerical grave markings, each expected to say something special about more than a half-million faceless, nameless corpses.

For this, Timo cries. But I am a Pole and I feel I cannot cry for Russians.

I try to imagine Ig in a grave with two hundred thousand others, him screaming for his Jaja and everyone else shouting at the same time, drowning him out, trampling him as they storm toward whatever false reward they had imagined. Ig lying there with feet kicking him, hair in his mouth, limbs breaking, rotting, stinking, chewed by rats, maggots at his eyes, and him still thinking that Jaja is going to somehow find him and reach down and pull him up. Wash him, maybe, and send down to Hatkoski's for some new hair, maybe a new toque, a few spoonfuls of Nestle's Quik, a bottle of Pure Spring ginger ale to whet the whistle . . .

Ig: 1966.

What does *that* say? Tell me that.

I close my eyes, though I know the image comes from within. I open my eyes and the blur tells me they are wet. I walk off from Timo, so he will not see.

Timo takes me to the Rembrandt room of the Hermitage museum, a big pink palace on a river so filthy a worm wouldn't know whether to dig or swim. To me the pictures seem like faded Xeroxes, each identical one even duller than what has gone before. But Timo babbles on. He looks at paintings as if they were television screens, active, with breasts bouncing, guns shooting, people falling. For his sake, only for his sake, I make a single effort.

In the picture I'm looking at there is a boy in rags and he kneels with one torn sandal hanging off his foot. He is leaning into the comfort of an old man with several shadowed figures, four I can make out, looking on from behind. They have looks of pity on their faces. I check the placard. *The Return of the Prodigal Son*, c. 1665. I try all different approaches to the painting to try and please Timo. I examine every small detail, but so much of it is as fogged, murky and dense as the river outside the window. I stare carefully at the boy but cannot really see him at all. His face is turned slightly to the right and there are no clear features to make out, only the hint of discomfort. I look again at the old man, his forehead high, nose long, eyes shrouded and kind, beard beginning black but growing to white, full and tangled. I stare and stare and stare again; and then, twenty-five years released in a blink, I see who the old man is.

Jaja.

The sports palace looks like a poor man's L.A. Forum, and Erkki, hardly the poor man's Jerry Buss, is waiting for us just inside the glass doors, pacing.

But no, Erkki is not angry or even nail-biting. When he sees Timo and me, he comes over, nodding kindly to big Timo, and takes my arm, leading me away.

"I have a telegram for you," he says, his voice soft and practiced.

He hands it over. "URGENT REQUEST FROM FATHER TO CONTACT FELIX BATTERINSKI ON FAMILY MATTER STOP GRANDMOTHER DEAD STOP FATHER MOST ANXIOUS STOP"

"I'm sorry," Erkki says. He puts his hand on my arm as if we are brothers.

"It's no surprise," I say. "I expected this."

"She'd been ill?" Erkki asks, still dripping with understanding.

"Cancer."

"Oh, I see."

I fold the telegram and place it in my pocket, not thinking of Batcha but of Poppa, now completely alone. Like me.

Erkki continues to hang onto my arm, squeezing. "I called our office, Felix. Your father is most concerned. I've arranged for you to fly back early, if you wish."

I stop and stare at him. *What for?* Pekka couldn't get out of practice the day an uncle died and now they want to let me go home for an old grandmother I hated? What gives?

"And miss the game?" I say.

"It would be all right."

"Do you *want* me to go? Is that it?"

Erkki blinks, acting surprised. "Your family needs you."

"What for? What could I possibly do now?"

"Your father says it is urgent."

"You'd like me to go, wouldn't you, Erkki? Then you wouldn't have to worry about your silly 'deal' — isn't that it? Without Kristiina here you're afraid of what I might do."

Erkki squeezes my arm harder, delighted for once to take on the calm role after so many months of hysterics. "Look, Felix," he says. "I can well understand your being upset. I'll leave you to think about it, okay? But do you see that man standing over there?"

I follow his finger to a Soviet in a terrible blue suit, who nods toward me. More KGB?

"He is a taxi driver, and he's instructed to take you to the airport if you wish. You're booked on the eight o'clock flight."

I look at Erkki, bewildered. "It's your decision," he says. "I assure you, if you go home the board will understand perfectly. The president himself says you should go."

He turns and walks away before I can question him further. I pull the telegram back out from my jacket. Why urgent? Poppa knows there is nothing anyone can do at this stage. Wouldn't he just tell me in the next letter? He knows what I thought about Batcha . . .

. . . And I want to play. I want to hit every Leningrad KGB or whatever they're called as hard and as slow and as sweet as I ever hit the kids in Renfrew or that turkey Billings or Orr or Unger or any of the thousand other bodies, ankles, faces or fists that have given way to Batterinski. The team needs me. . . .

They do not need me. Erkki does not even want me. *I stand alone.*

Why is Poppa so anxious? I crush the telegram and look back at the taxi driver. He smiles and nods on cue.

There is more at work here than coincidence. I have been away only slightly more than a day and someone has been at work on me. I came down off the Aeroflot flight, through customs and the exit door, and the flashes began popping before I got halfway down the escalator. I knew them instantly: Jarvi, Repo, Torkkeli, most of the others, all the old begging faces from the dressing rooms, the hands behind the microphones, the scribblers. And I also knew instantly that they were not after a comment on Batcha's death.

Torkkeli didn't even wait for my full descent. "Mr. Batterinski!" he shouted, his television crew scrambling behind him. "We've had a report that Tapiola Hauki has played since Christmas un-

der a bonus system that pays for rough play — do you have anything to say on the matter?"

I smile into the camera and say, "Where do you hear that?"
But my mind is not on the words. Who has done this?

"An unnamed source," Torkkeli says. "Is there any truth to
the accusation."

"None whatsoever."

Suddenly the air is alive with my name. I wish I had showers
or a training room to hide in and figure this out. It has to be that
loser I turfed off the team when we played in Sweden . . . What
was his name?

"Are you familiar with a Matti Kummola, Mr. Batterinski?" one
of the scribblers shouts.

Of course — it was Matti. "Yes," I say. "He played one period of
exhibition hockey for Tapiola."

"Is it true, sir, that he was taken off the team by you because
he would not take penalties?"

"Not at all. Matti wouldn't take the game seriously, that's all.
We believed the game should be taken seriously."

"He says you deliberately encouraged violence."

"Me?" I say, forcing a laugh. "I want my team to be physical.
Hockey is a physical game. Body contact. It's a game of strength
and skill. Sure we played hard, but we also won, didn't we?"

"Kummola says it is his understanding there was a system of
monetary payments for players who fought."

"No. We paid bonuses for good hockey, same as any team."

"Are you saying Kummola is lying?"

"I'm saying Kummola was not good enough to play for Tapiola
— we are a good, honest, competitive hockey team and we play a
tough brand of hockey. What's the point you're trying to make?"

"The point would be that someone was rewarding violence,"
says a surly-looking young man with a hand-held microcassette.

"Hard-hitting hockey is its own reward," I say, proud of my
comeback.

"Did *anyone* pay?" one of them shouts.

"Please," I say. "Only Erkki Sundstrom can answer questions
relating to finance."

I push through them, ignoring further questions and shouts,
pushing a path, elbowing off micophones, out through the automatic doors to the taxi area, the sharp night air welcome on my

face. I realize I am covered in sweat as the night pours up my sleeves and down my open throat, circling, teasing, alerting, telling me the problem has not been left scrambling around the luggage carousel.

On this side of the room I am stark naked, wilting; on the far side of the room I am again pushing through the airport crowd, my last comment fingering the Jerk. Torkkeli is on air now, backdropped by the Ishallen and the orange and purple Tapiola Hauki team banner. He has the look of television sports announcers everywhere, always speaking directly to their Grade six teachers who never thought they'd amount to anything.

"Quick! What's he saying?" I call out.

The saloon doors to the kitchen swing open and Kristiina's shadow moves into the room, the glow of the television rippling like moonlight over her nakedness. She carries two vodkas, my sixth, her third. Unfortunately, since I arrived only the drinks have been stiff. My fault completely. I am not myself.

Kristiina listens intently, handing me the drink without looking. Matti's picture, then Erkki's, slip onto the screen.

"Well?" I say, sweat bubbling again.

"Shhh — wait."

Torkkeli signs off and fades from the screen, back to the anchorwoman. Kristiina turns off the set and sits down, her leg rubbing along mine with no visible effect.

"The Finnish Ice Hockey Federation has announced a full inquiry into the charges," she says.

"Jesus Christ! What else?"

"They have tried to contact Erkki in Leningrad for comment, but did not get through — as usual. Matti Kummola says he will say in any court that the allegations are true."

"What did he say about me?"

"That you were evasive. That given your reputation as a *kovanaama* it seems quite possible to him."

"He doesn't even know me."

"He says you would be a perfect candidate for such a scheme."

"And that's it?"

"Pretty much. Tapiola spokesmen have denied it and said the company would not be associated with any such tactics."

"That'll be Erkki's line too."

Kristiina takes a drink, then turns, worried. "Is it true?"

"In a way."

Kristiina seems disappointed. I try to explain: "Well, it's not the big thing they're trying to make of it, that's for sure."

"But did the players get paid for taking penalties?"

"They got paid for aggressive play. If a penalty came out of it, that had nothing to do with the system. I just wanted the players to show a little balls, that's all."

Kristiina laughs. "A little what?"

"Balls, you know."

"No. I don't."

I illustrate. "These!"

She laughs, louder. "A bonus just for *having* them?"

"For *showing* them!"

"It is no wonder they are holding an inquiry," she says, teasing.

I go to her and we meet, fitting together like clamps, swaying back and forth in the silence. Both my arms are about her neck, the soft silk of her hair light as gossamer on my forearms. I pull her tight; she smells and feels again like the Kristiina I love.

"Feel all right?" I say.

"Just fine," she says, weary of the convincing. The doctors have given her a clean bill of health, she says. Just some low-grade virus that wouldn't leave her system. She's fine now; there never was anything to worry about.

But now she is worried for me. "How about you, okay?"

"I'm not sweating it."

"No. I mean about the news from home."

"You know my feelings on her," I say. "I just want to talk to my father, that's all."

"My big darling," she says. "Felix is not having a very good time of it."

"I'll be just fine as long as I have you," I say, kissing her shoulder, teasing with my tongue. I feel warm inside, the vodka burning, and Kristiina feels warmer still, her breasts flat against my chest, her long lovely hand rubbing up and down the inside of my legs, her nails turned to barely touch what the team was supposed to show, the nails walking lightly out along what was impossible only minutes before.

I fall into her mouth, pushing, being swallowed, our tongues arguing for space. My hands fall along both sides of her, in and then out, the curves leading on. I turn inside, rubbing, circling, rubbing, opening. I move into Kristiina and away from the world. I am the squirrel reaching the stone fence, the partridge turning into the spruce. I am Batterinski, running from his own creation.

At three the radio buzzes and skips into all-night programming. I awake and realize I am still hiding in Kristiina, her arms and legs around me, my own legs tucked up like a baby's. I resent moving, but I know now I will be able to reach Poppa. Finally. He will have to be at home now.

The line crackles, spits and hums with distance, but I am walking down Batterinski Road once the first ring sounds —one long, two short; one long, two short; one long, two short —and I can sense Poppa moving in from the kitchen, his long thin finger twisting and reaming an ear so he will hear better. For Poppa the telephone remains an invention, not a necessity, and he still treats it as if he is being marked on performance.

"Ahhh — Yallo."

"Poppa! It's me!"

"That you, Felix?" he shouts. *Dat. Yes, dis is me.*

"I got your telegram, Poppa."

"I tried to phone."

"I was in Leningrad."

"*Russia?*"

"Yes."

"*What* were you doing in Russia?"

"We had a game. They telegraphed from the team office here."

"That was good of them." *Dat. Dem.*

"You sounded worried."

"Didn't they tell you your Batcha was dead, Felix?"

"Yes. When?"

"Early yesterday. Funeral's tomorrow. She's in Renfrew."

"In Renfrew? Why there?"

"Can't have her here. Place's burned pretty bad."

"*Burned!* What do you mean burned?"

"The house. They told you that, didn't they?"

"No! Nothing. What happened?"

"Your Batcha died in the fire, son."

Batcha? In a fire? What is going on here? I sit down, legs buckling.

"Not cancer?"

"No. The shed caught fire and I wasn't here. I saw the smoke and came running, but I couldn't do much. We almost lost the house. Shed's all gutted. I dragged Batcha free, but it was too late. Couldn't save her."

"What was she doing there?"

"She tried to put it out herself. But she was too old, eh? I'm too old too. I got burnt pretty bad myself."

"You?"

"My right arm. Don't worry. I'll be all right."

"How badly burned are you? Tell me, Poppa."

"I'm okay."

"How bad?"

"I can't use the arm. My eye got it a bit too."

"I'm coming home, Poppa."

"You don't have to, son. Jan's helping. We can handle it all."

"The hell you can. I'm coming home."

"The funeral's tomorrow."

I can tell how desperately he wants me to come. He wouldn't ask. He wouldn't even hint if he didn't need me. "I'm not sure I can make it. I'll try. I pick up six hours, remember."

"You're sure you want to do this?"

"I'm sure."

"If you're sure, then, your Poppa would be grateful."

"I want to do it, Poppa."

"Can I ask you a favor?"

A favor? What has he already asked?

"Anything."

"Will you bring back the letters I sent you?"

"The letters?"

"Not the letters from me. Jaja's memoirs, okay? Forget the other stuff, but would you bring back the stuff Marie typed for you?"

I can't! I don't have them! They're in Leningrad.

"Yah, sure."

"God bless you, my son."

"I'll call when I get in," I say.

"I will pray for a safe flight," he says.

"Goodbye, Poppa."

"Thank you, Felix."

"Goodbye."

I leave Kristiina sleeping and with a small note tucked between her legs, where I am certain good memories of Batterinski will remain forever. She will find it in the morning and read it over coffee:

> My dearest, sweetest Kristiina,
>
> My father needs me, as I suspected. My grandmother died not of the cancer but in a fire that also burned my father, though not badly. I must go and help and I know you will understand better than anyone. I have a predawn flight and decided not to wake you. But I kissed you on the lips, and also here, while you slept. I love you dearly, my darling. And since I cannot find the courage to ask in person, do you think you could ever imagine yourself married to a big galoot like me? Nothing would please me more, you know it.
>
> I love you forever,
>
> *Felix*

The phone rings while I pack back at the Inter-Continental and I grab the first two calls thinking it is Kristiina, who might have discovered the note. But it is the press both times. I put the receiver back without even admitting it is me. The ringing continues off and on, but I refuse to answer. What the hell does it matter? To them, a dead line is as good as an interview anyway: *"Batterinski was not available for comment, but returned home to Canada on a morning flight, claiming pressing family business."*

The flight is calm, the skies open well out into the North Sea. For the longest time I simply stare down, watching the shoreline recede beneath me. I feel Finland drawing itself back into my past, the first statistics I have accumulated that have nothing to do with the rep, but everything to do with the future. A single number, one, Kristiina. And with dawn creasing and her rising to find my offer tucked so gently between her thighs, it may well be that Batterinski no longer has to stand alone. Hockey may well be over. Life may finally be beginning.

How can one who has not passed through the experience hope then to pass on what it was like? When have we ever had a player who could articulate the pain of the end? What was it Felix Batterinski felt as he flew from disaster in Helsinki toward further horrors at home? He had to know it was over. There would be no more cheering.

Driving up through the Ottawa Valley toward Pomerania for the funeral, Batterinski would have passed through the small town of Renfrew, where he had often played hockey as a youngster. Long before he was born, however, it was home for one of the Ottawa Valley's greatest hockey legends, Fearless Frank Finnigan, whom it's almost certain a man with Batterinski's education would never have heard of. But Finnigan, like Batterinski, was a hero in the small lumbering towns of the valley. And when it was over, as for Batterinski, there was nothing. Finnigan's daughter, Joan, would one day try to put it in a poem she called 'Grey Is the Forelock Now of the Irishman.'

'. . . I remember my father, too,
    in the headlines,
on the gum cards, in the
    rotogravure,
and how, in the pasture, there
    was nothing
to charge but shadows and,
    in the dark beyond night,
bright enormous butterflies
    crossing the moon
of his disenchanted vision; I
    heard him cry out to them
in another room but they
    stayed in his eyes
until we were all well-marked
    by the days
of his going down into ruin.

'Wrinkled now is the brow of
    my all-star father
standing in the doorway
of the house of his grandsons
who yet must learn,
in smaller forums and with less
    limelight,
how heroes are really made.'

Going to find Felix Batterinski that day in Pomerania, I remember thinking there were neither children nor grandchildren who would one day try to come to terms with him. There was only me.

Excerpted by permission from "Batterinski's Burden," by Matt Keening, *Canada Magazine*, June 1982.

POMERANIA IS IN THAW. AS I DRIVE DOWN BLACK DONALD Hill, down past the hardware store and Hatkoski's barber shop, down toward what used to be the White Rose station and the turn, the kids playing up the Schama sideroad decide to burst their dam. They came running downhill alongside it, the water racing below the ice lip, them sliding above on the final crust. It bursts through the lowest slush ridge and out over Highway 60, and I have to slow to let them cross, five youngsters in mud-soaked mittens, toques pushed high on their heads, five future river-runners for the mills. If only they still used river-runners.

It looks like a war movie. I have to leave the rented car at Jazda's and hike the rest of the way in, sticking to the high side and hanging onto wet alders to keep from sinking through the thick crystal of the plow banks. Twice I break through badly, once losing a boot which I must root for with a branch. On the first corner past Jazda's I see where Poppa has tried to run it in the half-ton but sunk through to the axles. His steps, wide-spaced and deliberate, are still punctured in the cold muck leading away from the door. I step in his tracks the rest of the way home.

There is no mistaking the fire. I see exactly what happened as soon as I get to the laneway. The shed is badly burned but still standing on the house side, though Poppa's green siding has been charred. Yet more than seeing things, I can smell. A smell sadder than burning leaves, the ugly smell of a mistake. Oil and paint, certainly. Cloth, perhaps. Shingles. Plastic. But none of these describe how rancid the smell is in total.

Batcha? Could it be her?

Poppa is inside, trying to measure out coffee, and when he turns to the sound of the opening door it is as if I have come upon a stranger pretending to be Poppa. It is not just his arm that is wrong, but his whole side. Above the ear the hair has been burnt away, the ear and exposed flesh glowing red and glistening with Vaseline. Over one eye there is no eyebrow, just a swollen, whitish ridge. He drops the spoon, staring at it momentarily as if someone else has thrown it, then carefully holds the arm in tight and comes toward me. We say nothing. He hugs with his good arm and I touch as if he has been constructed of newspaper and flour glue.

"You're hurt, Poppa," I say, my voice thin and stretched.

"I'm okay," he says. "It just hurts to touch. The air is good on it."

"How did it happen?"

Poppa seems reluctant to say. He backs away, back toward the kitchen and the pot of hot water. "I'm making coffee," he says. "You?"

"Yah, me."

But he cannot handle two cups. I move in and take over and he makes no protest. He sits in his usual chair, taking care not to let the arm brush the table or the backs of the other chairs. When his weight shifts he winces, and he sounds short of breath.

"You'd better tell me," I say.

"I had to drag her out," he says, voice swollen as his face. He speaks slowly, but not from reluctance. He wants to tell. "Her clothes were on fire and I tried to roll on her. It was pouring rain . . . and there was still plenty of snow. But it was no good. She never came around. I thank God for that fire extinguisher you put in. I saved the house, anyway."

"I saw the truck on the way in. Were you going for help?"

"She was already dead. I just wanted her buried from here. I thought maybe I could open the road."

"How did they get her out?"

"Jazda's snowmobile. He's been good to me. Jan's been good. You been good coming like this."

Dis. And so I am home. The calendars still flutter on the wall from the slight furnace draft, Poppa sits with his coffee staring into the backs of the cereal boxes, and I sit in my old chair at the far end, overloading my cup with sugar, stirring slowly, thinking. It's as if I just walked in from setting some new shiners in the minnow pool. But eighteen hours ago I was in Helsinki, twelve hours before that in the Soviet Union. I have crossed nearly half of the world to be here. I have been body-searched, outraged, nearly arrested, deceived, attacked, laid and have asked a woman to marry me. But yet I have nothing to say to my own father about any of it.

"You've had some calls," Poppa says matter-of-factly. It *could* be me just in from the minnows. It could be Danny on the phone with word the smelts are running.

"Oh? From where?"

"From over there." He indicates the pump with his thumb. He means Finland. "Person-to-person. I could hardly understand them."   "How many?"

"Three. Twice in the middle of the night."

"Sorry."

Poppa looks up, worried. "No trouble, I hope."

I shake my head. "They were probably just trying to let me know the score."

"You didn't play in Russia?"

"No. I left before."

Poppa seems more upset with this than with the fire. "I hope they gave those bastards what for."

"They would have tried, Poppa. I'm going to look in the shed, okay?"

I get up. Poppa doesn't move; he doesn't even turn in his seat because of the pain; instead, he speaks straight ahead, as if I am still there. "There's not much to see," he says.

But he is wrong. The shed has become a black shell of the Batterinski years here. Poppa has been moving about in it, his gumboots by the doorway caked gray with soot and his trail through the debris marked by periodic sweeps where he has kicked at things. The rain has hardened the ashes and I can see precisely where he went, but not whether the kicks were in anger or in search of things. The house wall is hardly touched, the old harnesses, lamps, snowshoes, found wire, coats, cables and rusted tools still hanging on their spikes. But the far wall is gone entirely, the charred frame only hinting at what was once there. Poppa's .22 lies in the soot, the stock now as narrow and black as the barrel. There are ragged coats, tarpaulins, charred canthooks, rakes, a fishnet, meaningless without its string, dozens of burned and wrinkled magazines, their pages buckled and twisted as if trying to escape, newspaper scraps, wooden boxes, cardboard trunks, burst tins, paint cans, bottles, sealer jars and, everywhere, small scraps of paper — a corner, a half page, almost an entire page — but with whatever was once on it erased by the fire or faded to nothing by the rain.

Behind me the door kicks open again and Poppa steps onto the ledge in his gray socks, a sweater loosely draped over his injured arm and held away from the skin by his good hand.

"A hell of a mess, eh?" he says sadly.

"How did it start?"

"I don't know. Spontaneous combustion, I suppose. Place was full of rags and old paint tins."

"You're damn lucky the house didn't catch."

"Yah," he says half-heartedly.

"Mostly junk here anyway," I say.

Poppa says nothing. I kick a burnt crate and when I look back at him his eyes are glassy. The wind? The burn?

"Are you okay, Poppa?"

"We lost Jaja's memoirs, Felix."

His mouth trembles and he looks down and away, not wanting me to see.

"What do you mean you 'lost' them?"

Poppa shouts, impatient. "They *burnt*! The fire got them. They're gone!"

I don't understand. "What were they doing out here?"

"We stacked them here as we finished. We were almost finished."

"You lost *everything?*"

"There's one box in the basement still."

I breathe easier. "Thank God."

"Don't bother," he says. "It's just the financial records. All the history was out here."

I am afraid to look at him. His voice tells me he cannot keep back the tears.

"I thought Marie was getting copies in Renfrew."

"She was, but just of what was sent to you. It was here, too. We never thought — we should never have been so stupid."

I go over and nudge one of the box skeletons with my toe. Inside there is mostly ash, but a few papers remain, pasted along the side with ash and ice. They have their form, almost, but none of their content.

"I'm just so glad we at least have your copies," Poppa says to my back.

My back answers him, head nodding, lying, afraid to turn.

Bless the telephone. Before Poppa can move on to ask to see the letters ("Tell me, Poppa, have you ever heard of Pulkovo Airport?") a one long, two short gives me the chance to duck past him and in the back door. "Must be Jan now," he says as I pass.

But it is not. It is person-to-person, from Finland.

"Yes, you're talking to him," I say.

Vaguely I hear something in Finnish, then a switching and a voice, suddenly loud.

"Felix Batterinski?"

"Yes."

I catch the first name — Voitto — but not the second, and the newspaper, *Sanomat*. He says we have spoken many times before and I am sure we have, but that is for him to remember, not me.

"Erkki Sundstrom has admitted the penalty pay-offs were paid," the voice says. "But he says that you originated the idea."

"He does, does he?"

"Yes, he does. May I ask you for a comment?"

Poppa has come through the door and stares at me as he carefully sets down the sweater. I pretend I'm having a hard time hearing and wave him away. Good old Poppa: he walks through the kitchen and out into the front room, closing the door behind him until it binds on the lay of the floor. I hear him on the stairs.

"Who called them 'penalty pay-offs,' Voitto?"

"They are referred to as that here. It is a bit of a national scandal, you see. You were the subject of a wild debate in our parliament today."

"For what?"

"Many Finns are very upset about your bringing North American tactics to Finland."

"Are they interested in making your hockey better?"

Voitto laughs. "May I quote you on that?"

"Sure. Finnish hockey players have all the skills but one. They can skate, pass, shoot — but they show no heart. All I did was try to give them heart."

"Some would say that isn't something you can buy."

"We made the play-offs, didn't we? A team everybody laughed at the first of the year — everybody including yourself, if I remember correctly." I do not remember at all, but I do know that what one sportswriter thinks, they all think.

"Yes," Voitto says, hoping to entrap me with his ready laugh. "I did. But the question is whether making the play-offs is justification enough for paying for penalties."

"Aha — but I have never said we paid for penalties, have I?"

"Sundstrom admits it is so."

"Then it is just one other thing that poor bastard doesn't understand. I wanted a simple bonus system for hard play, that's all. Show a little heart and we'll reward you. But it is a lie to say we *paid* players to take penalties."

"Sundstrom has produced a score sheet, though. So much money for this, so much for that."

That bastard jerk Erkki.

"Well, we had to have some way to measure aggressiveness."

"I see. But you still deny the charges."

There's no way Jerkki is getting away with this. "I go by whatever Erkki says. We were in it together, completely, and as manager he's far better able to comment on it than I am. The coach just follows orders. And you can quote me on that too."

"I will. And thank you very much."

"Just a second. Do you know the score from the other night?"

"The Leningrad game?"

"Yes. Do you have it?"

"Yes. Just a second. It's here, somewhere." I can hear him calling in Finnish over the muffled phone. He comes back on but I do not think I hear him right.

"Again?"

"12–1."

I hang up, smiling. I do not need to ask who scored the 12.

I hear Poppa on the stairs, then cracking back the door. He seems unsure of himself. His hand shakes as he loosens his grip on the chiseled hole that never received a knob. I am suddenly struck with how old he is — seventy-five. He now stoops worse than Jaja ever did. His mouth precedes his speech, like an out-of-synch movie.

"What was it, son?"

"Nothing, Poppa. Just some business with the team. They're going to be drafting next week. They need some idea on who to go after, eh?"

Poppa smiles, satisfied. "Build with youth, son. Just like the Islanders."

"Yah," I say. I cannot believe Poppa knows what he is saying. I am now older as a hockey player than he is as a human. As of this telephone call, Batterinski is dead.

The coffin is closed. Considering how Poppa looks after just trying to beat the fire from the bitch, I assume she is little more than caked ash herself. I cannot look at the box without feeling her hatred for me. Poppa dragged me over to see the wreath sitting on the head of the casket; I found it difficult to swallow — not from sorrow, but from my own anger. The wreath had a red ribbon banner with "FAMILY" etched in green, but I could not feel it had come from anyone but him. Batcha never was my flesh and blood, never will be.

Poppa has said it was no way to die, but what way is there? Would she have preferred the cancer? Or Ig's way, staring down the road at a half-ton and a windshield full of his nephew's laughing, drunken friends? Or Jaja — the last thing he heard the squawk of chickens, their wings offering wind for his fall? Or Matka, knowing that my cry should have been hers? How can he say that, *no way to die?* Batcha is dead and I, quite frankly, don't give a sweet damn about her. I have come for Poppa's sake, not the bitch's.

There are so many others in this room now, and I know them all and also not at all. Uncle Jan, Cousin Jazda, Schama, Shannon, Murray, Toposki, Batterinski, Father Schula, Dombrowski, Hatkoski — and as I stare at them or shake their hands I sense that they are much the same as before, though worn. Like the newspapers Poppa stacked in the shed: discolored, wrinkled, but filled with the same words. Uncle Jan and I talk of how it was and what a shame it was about Batcha, and eventually he gets around to the one thing that he really wants to talk about: is Gretzky better than Orr? There is no comparison, I say, and leave him to make his own.

What is it that happens to uncles? I remember my childhood and how Jan always meant excitement, new gimmicks, candy, pop, a chance to take over the steering wheel, look under the hood, spit from the window. Jan always made me feel special as a kid. But now when I look at him I think only of death. The last few times I have seen him have been at funerals. The Batterinski family has become nothing other than ceremonial, something dragged out in bad times and displayed as proof that at one time, somewhere, for some reason, they were all in this horror together. No wonder they flee and only gather again at the next death. Can this possibly be what Jaja meant when he talked about heritage?

Jan is changed. Thinner, bald now as Ig was, and not even the laugh remains. He pulled up to the Catholic funeral home in a broken- down Ford stationwagon that rattled and spit through twenty seconds of pre-ignition when he turned it off. And just as the car contradicts my memory, so too does Jan's marriage. He has become quiet and brooding. His wife, Sophia, whom I remembered as silent and frightened, is now loud and bossy and known to Poppa as "The Whiner." Their little girl has grown up, run away from home at sixteen with a cadet from the Petawawa army base and hasn't been heard nor seen in the two years since. Thank God, I say, that Jaja is no longer here to record us.

"Felix."

The voice is soft, tentative. I turn, expecting the priest.

"Danny!"

He nods and smiles shyly. I am so glad to see him that I want him to scream "UGGA-BUGGGAAAAA!" so loud ancient Aunt Jozefa will scald herself with tea.

Lucy has also come. She has a new dress on and it hides her weight well. No, she has lost some, enough that I wish again I were coming up behind her with the top down and the FM turned up loud, her seventeen-year-old bottom exhausted from churning down Batterinski Road. When she smiles I see she has new teeth. A sign of her poor past, of Danny's improved present. The yard foreman's wife gets to hand out the turkeys at Christmas, and by God she had better look like the boss's wife when she does it.

I take Danny's hand in mine and it feels like two Dannys. He has stretched himself into a new Renfrew suit that some Toronto retailer has sent to the minors. The lapels are wrong, the wide gray stripes a nudge against Danny's fat, the knees cracked and folded where it has been insulted by a hanger. Lou Myles would be outraged, but Danny thinks he's the cock of the walk. He looks old. The hair is thin as balsam now. If Kristiina saw us standing together right now, she would assume I was talking to a friend of my father's. Which I suppose Danny is now. More than mine, anyway.

"Thanks for coming," I say, after some useless talk.

But Danny shows no signs of moving on. Lucy does, toward the coffee and *placeks* at the far end of the room.

"So," Danny says, breathing deep, the formalities done with. When he smiles my Danny passes through Poppa's Danny and I smile back, glad to see him finally. "How's she been going for you?"

I pretend it is a thought that has seldom crossed my mind. "Good, I guess."

"Finland okay?"

"Been great. We got beat out in the play-offs."

Danny pulls out a cigarette, taps it carefully on the edge of the box. "Too bad," he says.

"Ah," I say. "It doesn't matter."

What kind of talk is this? Where are Danny and I, fishing off the creek bridge, dreaming about the NHL, planning how we'd get into Lucy Dombrowski's pants, saying everything and anything that popped into our minds. There was no patrolling what you said then. I think something new, but cannot say it. *Danny, you should see Kristiina. You'd love her. Personally, I'm just as glad Batcha's dead. Isn't my old man looking old? Do you ever look at yourself, Danny, and say "Holy old baldheaded, where did I go to?" Do you, eh?*

"Poppa says you're doing good at the mill," I say as Danny lights up.

He gives his answer in skywriting, the exaggerated nodding and absent-minded look at the ceiling sending the smoke arrogantly up.

"I'm doing okay," he says.

"Good," I say.

Danny smiles the old smile. He thins before my eyes, hair growing and curling once again around his head. "You've made a bit of the news, eh, lad?"

"You've seen?"

"Sure. Everybody got the picture of you spitting. I *loved* it."

"Poppa's not so pleased," I say, nodding toward the old man in a far corner.

"Fuck, everybody thinks it's a hoot. That's me old buddy, eh?"

I smile, feeling my own years shed. Soon we are standing there bouncing on the balls of our feet, laughing quietly at nothing in particular, just the warmth of our own longstanding.

"You've had some troubles, lad," Danny says.

"Yah, that son-of-a-bitch of an agent" — did I just say *dat?* — "I'd kill him if I ever saw him, you know."

"And I'd be right there to help you."

Soon I can see the conversation will not be able to help itself. When Danny finally asks, as I know he must, I sense he feels as awkward as I.

"You figure you're through playing?"

I surprise myself with the answer. "Probably."

But Danny surprises me even more with what he says. "We're not kids anymore, are we?"

We? Kids? I stare at Danny but he does not see me, his pig eyes sealed with delight. *Why would he say that?* I have not mentioned how fat he has gotten. I have not asked him where his hair went. I have not said that Lucy, compared to Kristiina, looks like a black bear in that stupid dress. He cuts me with banter and I build him up by saying nothing.

I let it go. I know why Danny must say these things. He knows that I know there is nothing inside that fat. He knows that I know the truth about his hockey dreams and he is damned if I will live mine out without him pissing in the bed.

Eventually Danny drifts to where the old men are lying about their pathetic lives. Fish are recaught, timber refelled, weights relifted, but no matter how many times they redo it they cannot get it right because it will always be them telling the lie, not the man they imagined holding the rod, the ax, the canthook.

Father Schula conducts the funeral, the same stringy voice that used to tell me to keep my head up now asking me to keep it down for something I can't quite buy. I hold Poppa's good elbow and he weeps into a hanky, pretending it is a cough. I do not once think of Batcha, but only of myself and Danny standing while he blows smoke and tells me my whole life — a life that makes his look like a mayfly's in comparison — has been nothing other than an exercise in growing up.

We're not kids anymore, are we?

Who does he think he is? *Where's your heart, Danny? Take a look at your own rep: fat boy, baldy, loser* . . . I'm too kind, too kind. If Batterinski had the same instincts in real life that he has in hockey, it would be Danny in that box they're carting out to the cars now. Thank God I am also human, too human.

Father Schula cannot help but smile as we squirt through the muck up toward St. Martin's cemetery. He would just as soon forget the formalities and show us all how the parish's proud new purchase has eliminated the need for a vault for all but the deepest winter months. From first thaw on he has a second-hand John Deere to do in an hour the work old Tomasz Kukurski used to take three days with a spade and pine shoring to complete, and Kukurski could only dig from May through October. The John Deere is still warm, melting ice periodically dripping down onto the manifold and steaming quietly into the air. Beyond John Deere, Batcha's grave has been dug, a high mound of oily, black muck standing vigil by the near fence.

We bury Batcha for good by returning to the church for the coffee, tea, *mazureks* and *placeks* and uncrusted breads the women's auxiliary are putting out in the basement. But first Poppa and Jan take me back into the church proper, where they genuflect and pray to the Black Madonna while I stare at my hands and wonder if they will ever again sing with the rush of blood. Danny's sly crack is still bothering me.

I light one of the candles on the gospel side of the altar and slip two quarters into the small slot underneath a Scotch-taped sign asking for two dollars. Poppa sees me lighting the candle and nods in solemn approval. He does not know it is not for Batcha. It is for me.

On the way out, I walk slowly around the church, past the oak confessional with the drapes of dried blood, past the plaster angels standing on the skull, the screaming residents of hell below, down all the way to the rear of the room where there is nothing but the baptismal font and the smiling, confident faces of the four dead soldiers.

I still do not feel as old as any of them, even the nineteen-year-olds. Perhaps, though, I now feel like them at the moment they realized the Lancaster was headed into the black pull of the gulf. Did they, too, sense that this was all a crazy mistake going on here and somehow they'd become trapped in it? Did they scream that it wasn't time yet? Did they expect to pull out of the dive? Did they, too, believe the best was supposed to lie ahead?

The cheat was on for them, just as it's now on for me.

When the telephone rings in the morning I do not know where I am. I recognize the rings before I recognize my own room, and before I can place myself I am downstairs in my underwear, the air strange about me and the linoleum ice-cold on my bare feet. It might be Kristiina.

I shout, expecting Finland. "Hello!"

The voice is close, surprised by my velocity. "Felix? Is that you?"

I tone down. "Yah."

"Matt Keening here, Felix. From *Canada Magazine.*"

"Oh yah, how are you? That story out yet?"

"That story isn't finished yet, I'm afraid. What's this crap coming out of Finland all about?"

"What crap?" I ask, but I know.

"You haven't seen the *Globe?*" Fool, he asks as if there's a box at the subway stop in front of the house. The only time people in Pomerania ever see the *Globe* is if they order china dishes from the catalog.

"We don't get it here."

"You're on the front page. Erkki Sundstrom has accused you of illegal pay-offs. It's a wire service story —Reuters —not much detail, but it says Tapiola had an illegal penalty pay-off system worked out with the players. True?"

"Not quite, no."

"The Finnish Ice Hockey Federation has voted to suspend Tapiola's operations. They might be expelled from the league."

"For that?"

"They're really worked up about it, Felix. You're a *cause célèbre* over there. I tried to call you and finally got Pekka and he said you were back home here. Sorry to hear about your grandmother."

"Yah."

"Pekka, by the way, thinks the pay-off thing's all a big joke."

"He would."

"He asked me to tell you that Kristiina's gone back into the hospital but you're not to worry. He says he'll call you himself. But he said it's nothing serious, that she'll be out soon."

I can feel the sweat forming on my forehead, the phone slipping in my hands, my heart changing gears. "Tell me *exactly* what he said about her."

"Just that. He said it was routine and you had no worries, but he wanted you to know, okay?"

"I'll call him."

"Look, I'll call back for you, okay? Save you the money."

"No." *Who does this guy think he is?*

"Okay, but look —I've got to talk to you more, okay? We can't have this story come out without clearing up these accusations, can we?"

"Can't we just forget the story?"

"Can't. The color's already locked in. We got nothing from the Leningrad shoot, of course, but research dug up some first-rate stuff from Helsinki. And of course there's the NHL stuff."

"You can't hold back on the story?" I ask.

"Uh-uh. Look, the timing is to your advantage. Fight fire with fire, I say. I can't move the editor on this, so we got two choices. One, we can either go with what we got, with an italicized news update at the end — but with nothing from you. Or we can do it right, rework it all to deal with this whole kefuffle in mind, with your own say in the matter."

He has me and knows it. Suddenly I need him more than he needs me. If I'd only said no in the first place I could just hang up now and forget it. But that is the press: give them enough rope and they'll hang you.

"Okay," I say with a long push of air. "Shoot."

"Over the phone?" He seems surprised.

"You're on deadline, aren't you?"

"The editor's stretched it another week. He wants me to drive up and see you personally."

"Why? You know what I look like."

Keening sputters. "But it would be so much better, Felix. I could capture some of that homey atmosphere, show you as a real genuine person, with feelings. You know. Make your say a hell of a lot more sympathetic. I promise you that, friend."

"No."

"No? You mean you don't want me to come up?"

"Not now. Please understand — these are not good times."

"It would be so much better if I could — "

"You can call me back the day after tomorrow. Okay? I'll be here."

"Well, okay, but — "

"I got to go now. Talk to you then."

I hang up without farewell. When I turn to run upstairs for Pekka's number I am blocked by Poppa, standing in his long underwear by the doorway, blocking me. There is fear in his eyes.

"Who was that, son?"

"Just a reporter from Toronto. The weekend magazine is doing a feature on me and just wanted some more details."

"A feature?" But Poppa's delight turns instantly to concern. "What *kind* of feature?"

"You know, my view of European hockey, that sort of thing."

"You fix that lie about you spitting, eh?"

"I fixed it, Poppa. Don't worry."

He scratches, thinking. "I couldn't sleep."

"Go back to bed, then," I say, more crossly than intended. I am instantly sorry.

"We could easily have another fire here, eh?"

"Don't worry about it," I say. "You won't."

"But we could. And I'm thinking about what we got left of Jaja's memoirs we should do something about. There's a machine at the newspaper office in Renfrew. I'd like to get copies of your letters and maybe leave them with Jan, what do you think?"

Think! What do I *say?*

"Sure, Poppa. But let me do it for you, okay?"

Poppa's face settles. I tap him on his good shoulder and bound by him up the stairs and into the room where I will dress, dig out Pekka's number and try to figure out how long I can continue lying to Poppa.

Poppa is outside hacking trenches with his one good arm to drain off the hollow in front of the bait shed. I can hear the steady chop of the ax in the late ice; I can imagine Poppa's face turned up against the spray; I can see him flinch with every blow, but satisfied with my great lie about Jaja's letters. How ironic that I am in here demanding the truth, shouting thousands of miles at poor Pekka, who keeps insisting there is nothing for me to be worried over.

But I am. "*How* do you know that?"

Pekka laughs. "Because, old man, Pia just got back from seeing her."

"Is Pia there now?"

"No. She is out shopping. But she would tell you the same thing, I assure you of that."

"You're sure she's all right, then?"

"Positive, old man. Pia says they may let her out tomorrow. Is that not proof enough?"

"Where is she?"

"The Kirurginen Sairaala."

"How do you spell that?"

"Don't bother. It's the surgical hospital."

"*Surgical!*"

"I have told you—women's troubles. But it is nothing, obviously. Here, let me get you the number, please . . . Pia has it written down here somewhere . . . yes, here—one seven . . . three seven one."

I scribble quickly. "What does that mean, 'women's troubles'?"

I hear shouts in the background, the line hissing through the distance as Pekka muffles the sound. He comes back on.

"Pia just came in. She'll talk to you."

The receiver is put down, picked up clumsily. Pia sounds either out of breath or nervous. "Hi Felix, how are you?"

"Fine. What's with Kristiina?"

"Pekka told you. She was not able to end that sickness. There was some minor surgery and she is just fine now. I have seen her. She was asking about you." A giggle. "Of course, everybody's asking about you now."

I respond with sarcasm. "So I hear. Look, what precisely was wrong with her?"

But Pekka has pulled the receiver away, shouting. "Hey, Bats, you're big news over here, old man. Did you know that?"

"I heard."

Pekka's old laugh ripples through. "You got Erkki in some hot air — water — you know, 'trouble,' old man. They fired him this afternoon. It was just on the news. You remember Voitto down at the *Sanomat?* He really did a large story on you both. Erkki came out looking like a liar and you like a German SS officer. I think the team's going to be disbanded."

"You'll be out of a job."

"It's just a game — who cares?"

I care, you stupid fucking Finn! It is *not* just a game! "Yah, true enough."

"You cannot imagine the coverage here. Front page. Television. Half seem to want to toss you and Erkki in prison, half are saying you're telling the truth and, of course, Finns don't want to hear it."

"It *is* true."

"It must be true. I was just talking to Timo and he's had offers from both Tampere and IFK if Tapiola folds. I had a call yesterday from Lahti. Everybody wants to find out just what Batterinski did to pull us up so high. What'll happen to you, old man?"

If I only knew. "I don't know. I got next year's contract, so I presume they'll honor that. Right now there's lots to do here."

"Everything's okay there?"

"Yah, fine. I just got things to do."

But when I hang up I realize I have only things to *un*do. Poppa still works on the trenches, every wet thunk telling me his energy comes from knowing I have salvaged all his work on Jaja's memoirs. Somewhere Danny is talking about me and laughing. *We're not kids anymore, are we?* And Kristiina—what's with her? What does she feel about my note?

But the hospital will not accept my call. Someone eventually comes on whose English I can understand and she tells me that only family can call. I say I am Kristiina's fiancé and all she will do is promise me that she will check with the patient. And she will not check now, but later, after the rounds. I can call back, if I wish, in a few hours.

Poppa comes in from his ditch construction, scraping the muck off on the side of the door frame. He leaves the boots on the steps and walks out of them, gripping the first chair so his socks don't slip on the floor. He looks at me and smiles.

"What do you say then, shall we take them in?"

"Huh?" I am still in Finland. "Take what in?"

"Jaja's papers. The copying, remember?"

The papers! Who cares about the goddamned papers?

"Poppa, I'll do them, okay? I said I would." I am almost shouting. He recoils, every part of him snapping but his eyes. They rest on mine, measuring.

"I could go in with you," he says.

"I'll go in myself. I want to think, okay?"

The eyes blink. "Is everything all right, Felix?"

I should have more patience. "Yes, everything is just fine, Poppa. Now get off my back, okay?"

The eyes apologize. "I'm sorry, son. It's been a bad week."

"Tell me about it!" I shout, grabbing my coat and slamming the door on him as I leave.

Outside, his trenches run like crooked spokes out from the center of the forming pool. Six exits, only one of them open, and in that runs laughter, the runoff snickering as it passes down the Batterinski lane, across the road and onto the brown ice of the swamp, where it freezes in layers, solid, waiting for the sun.

The kids are engineering again on the Schama sideroad. I honk when I pull onto the main highway and when they wave back I find I am pulling over and they are standing around looking frightened, as if I might be from the highways office down in Renfrew.

"Hi, kids!" I shout in Clarkie's hospital-visiting voice.

"Hi!" they shout back, relieved.

There are five of them, four boys and a girl, and they are shy, yet friendly. Untroubled Pomeranians with nothing to prove because there is no one to notice, just yourself in another house or on another farm. Their faces are all wide, flat and solid, except for one boy whose curly black hair has stuck to his head with perspiration. But even he has their eyes, eyes that reflect nothing and capture little. These kids are just another part of the landscape, even in their own minds. When they wake up tomorrow the hill will be there blocking the sun; there will be church on Sunday, potatoes for the plate, O'Malley's mill when they are old enough to work, the liquor store, the public house, fists to fit their faces, faces for their fists, trips to the used car lots in Renfrew, near fatal and fatal accidents on the way home . . . and eventually the graveyard at St. Martin's.

Why can it not be as simple for me? These kids haven't the slightest worry about reps. They arrived already defined: Pomeranians. And I could have stayed one if —

"Aren't you Felix Batterinski?" the curly-haired one says.

"That's right," I say, putting my hands into my jacket pocket and smiling. The hockey player's sheepish pre-autograph pose.

"I'm Tommy Shannon," the boy says.

I look at him. Yes, but grown. He has Danny's hair. That's where it went.

"Danny's young lad?" I say, already knowing.

"That's right," he says. The same words I used, but here no hands-in-the-pocket humility. I find my own hands fidgeting. *What has Danny told him about me?* He plays with a button and pulls back his shirt. "I still got it," he says, reeling out my old shark's tooth, the gold chain slightly green. I smile, warming to him.

"Your daddy's my best old pal, you know?" I say. The other kids look at Tommy, impressed.

But Tommy isn't particularly. "You and my dad used to play together in junior, eh?" he says, smiling.

Junior? The closest Danny Shannon ever got to junior were the letters I wrote him from Sudbury.

I have the power to hit back at Danny now. I can get him for the crack, get Tommy even. All the kids are looking at me, awed.

"That's right, Tommy," I lie. I cannot hurt Danny, no matter what he has done. I pull my hands from my pockets and run one through his hair. "You play?"

"He's our best!" a boy in a torn grease-red ski jacket says.

"Who're you?"

"Danny Dombrowski — he's my cousin."

Danny? Danny. Danny is the hero here. They even name their children after him. *Where is Felix?*

"What's your team?" I ask.

"St. Martin's."

"You're not still playing in that old rink," I say, indicating with my thumb the shack in the distance.

"No where else to play," Tommy says.

"Who's your coach?"

"Father Schula," the new Danny says proudly.

"Father Schula! For God's sake!"

"We're in first place," Danny says. "Except we got no more ice. We're playing Renfrew Saturday for the district, eh?"

"Renfrew. They're good, I guess," I say.

"We already beat them good," the new Danny says. "Tommy got four goals."

I look at Tommy Shannon and he is staring down, hammering a toe into the muck with pride. I cannot believe this. Father Schula's St. Martin's boys are still playing Renfrew. And winning! And because of a Shannon!

Danny is here twice. A son. A nephew. *WHERE IS FELIX?* How can they play Renfrew without Batterinski?

"You got anybody tough on your team?" I ask, kicking my own muck.

"No," Tommy says.

I smile, staring down so they won't see.

"There's no body contact," the new Danny says.

No body contact! Outlawed for all groups below bantam. Every two years it goes up a level. At that rate in eight more years it would reach the NHL. *No body contact.* Strike Schultz and Williams and Batterinski from the record books forever. We need more pages for Gretzky . . .

I drive around but there is no place to go. The pub is open but I am afraid of talk. The woods are too wet for walking, the back roads too mucked for a six-cylinder, rear-wheel-drive rented shitbox. There is really only the highway, both directions leading out of town, both leading back in. With not even a ten-mile drop in the speed limit in honor of Pomerania, the highway does not even acknowledge that the place exists.

I drive slowly up over the hill toward the church with my window open, the cold promise of spring in the air. I can smell the earth where it rises in a driveway, and everywhere there is water, rippling fast and clean down the center of the road, trickling brown and slushy along the sides. Let them talk of robins arriving to herald spring; they do not speak for Pomerania; here, spring is the first sound of rubber on asphalt. But when I try for it, the rented car does not have the horses.

At the hardware store there is a large green truck with its gate down and the driver is jockeying out a mattress. He is jacketless, wearing only a black T-shirt, and when I double-take on the absurdity of dressing this way I realize I am looking twice at Bucky Cryderman, my old teammate from Vernon.

"Hey, Bucky!" I yell out the window.

He stops, still not recognizing, then: "Holy shit! Not Batterinski?"

"It is!" I get out and we shake hands warmly, both sizing up. If we went by volume, it would take me twice as long, for Bucky is even fatter than Danny, but he is also the same Bucky: same hairstyle, not a touch of gray or the sixties, seventies, eighties, same boyish tough face that wouldn't faze a rabbit. What changes does he see in me?

"I seen you on the television the other night," Bucky says, black teeth finally showing his age.

"Me?" I say, laughing but clinching inside.

"You in Sweden."

"Finland."

"Wherever. You sure got them D.P.s pissed off at you, lad."

"So it seems."

Bucky laughs, the laugh of the night with Maureen. "Fuck 'em, eh, Bats?"

"That's what I say. How you been, anyway, Buck?"

"Good! Pretty good!" Bucky practically shouts, perhaps in defense. He pulls a package of cigarettes from under one sleeve and pinches one free — I imagine he still calls them weeds.

"You got a family?"

He lights up, hand shaking. "Five kids. Only one boy, though."

"Five!"

"Maybe six now," he says, laughing. "I left at sunup."

"Who'd you marry?" I ask.

"You wouldn't know her," he says. But in the way he glances toward the safety of his cab, I think perhaps I do: Maureen the Queen.

I change the subject for him. "You see much of Sugar lately?"

Bucky looks back from the cab to me, and I know instantly that Sugar Bowles is dead.

I have not prayed in so long that I hardly remember how. I am sitting — no, kneeling — in the Batterinski pew, but it is not the pew that I grew up in. Poppa has been moved further back to a smaller pew. The Batterinskis are fading and they no longer need the space. Soon Poppa will need only a folding chair at the rear doors, one of those Danny and I used to put out for the Christmas midnight mass. Soon Poppa will no longer be sitting in his beloved St. Martin's. For his last visit, they will let him lie down.

It is so quiet in here that I can hear the ice melting and sliding off the southeast corner. I sit listening like a doe with a spring fawn, worrying about every creak in the floor and draft in the curtains. I do not wish my tears to be seen by anyone.

But I cannot stop crying. I have tried to imagine this God listening, but it does not quite work. What can I do? Pray for Sugar? He's dead and hardly needs a late reference from the likes of me. Pray for Jaja, Ig, Matka? Does God continually have their souls monitored to see if enough prayers are being said in their favor? And what of someone like me? If I die and leave no one to pray for me, am I then doomed? And if not, then what is the use of ever praying for anyone?

Yet I can pray for Kristiina, the living. But I can't concentrate. My thoughts feel like they are in Kristiina's blender, each turning into the next, one cutting another.

In the end I am just a Pole. Alone. All I can truly pray for is Felix Batterinski, the poor dumb bastard. But pray for what? It is beyond my comprehension how so much could possibly have gone wrong. Right from Leningrad on. No, not there, from Sweden on. In Helsinki. Hell, with Wheeler in L.A. In Philadelphia, I suppose. No, in Sudbury, the summer Ig got it. When Batcha turned on me the day Jaja died. Maybe when Matka died, right from the first.

What was it that Batcha called me?

I cannot remember the word. Just the translation. *Monster.*

I cannot believe I even have such ludicrous thoughts in my head. If this is part of prayer, then prayer is for fools.

I get up and leave, determined not to bow or genuflect or even act impressed. I got into this on my own. I will get out on my own. Alone. Just like always.

On the far side of Black Donald Lake is a picnic site, the tables stacked under the high white pines, the orange garbage containers turned upside down for winter, the washrooms locked. There is also a pay phone, filthy with caked snow and spray from the winter's snowplowing. I pull off as far as I dare onto the shoulder and leap the ditch, sinking to my knees in hard-packed snow. There is the ghost of a winter trail to the booth, probably a motorist who slid off the road months ago calling for a tow truck, and I use the hardened parts of the trail for footing. I half expect the phone to be ripped from the box, but the old Danny is now too old and respectable, the new Danny and Tommy too young, and the phone sits intact and working, waiting for a quarter.

I place the call, charging it to Poppa's number.

The Kirurginen Sairaala switchboard is receptive this time. I can sense my name on a sheet and almost instantly I can hear the phone ringing in Kristiina's room. And then her voice, weak, tired, but my darling Kristiina.

"Hi babes! Canada calling."

"Felix!" Her voice perks up. Good. "Where are you?"

"In the middle of the bush."

"Are you here?"

"I told you. I'm in a phone booth in the middle of nowhere."

"How did you find me here?" She sounds mildly irritated, typical of those who never wish to be seen to be sick.

"Pia. Pekka. They told me."

"Told you what?"

"Told me where to reach you. Why do you say that?"

"No reason. I'm sorry. I am just tired. Please."

"How did it go?"

"Fine. Perfect. I'll be out in two days."

I am not sure I want to ask, but: "What was it all about?"

I can feel her pause. I wait, afraid to even breathe. "It was that infection," she says. "It was what was making me sick. It was not important."

"But why an operation? Why are you in a surgical hospital? Why couldn't they treat you with penicillin, or antibiotics?"

Again, the pause. "It was, I think they say 'women's problems' . . . you know."

When I shout I see my breath is forming in the booth. It is colder in than out. "No, Kristiina, I *don't* know!"

She laughs, but it is not quite her laugh. It is what she thinks her laugh sounds like. "Then you should not worry about it. It was nothing, really. I miss you, you know."

"I miss you too. But I still want to know what was wrong."

"Nothing. Believe me, please."

I say it before I even consider it. The thought forms in my mind and takes shape on my tongue, my mind recoiling from the suggestion.

"You had an abortion, didn't you?"

There is no answer. But there is, too.

"Didn't you?" I say.

"What did Pia tell you?" she says weakly.

"Pia told me nothing."

"What makes you think it was that?" Her voice is filled with air, floating on hope.

"I'm not stupid," I say angrily, my own voice heavy with hurt. "Am I right? It was an abortion, wasn't it?"

Her voice is as small as the distance is large: "Yes."

I feel as if the gloves have dropped. Time slows. Batterinski moves in, attacking, in charge. "Don't you think it is something we should have discussed together?"

"There was nothing to discuss," she says, voice growing with defiance. "It was my decision. The doctors said the pregnancy was not going well. I was very sick, you may recall."

"My mother lay in bed for two months before I was born."

"Your mother died, you told me. Is that what you wanted of me?"

"Not at all. I just think I had a right to know, that's all."

"I'm sorry, but what right?"

"I was the father, dammit!"

"Yes, if there had been a child. There isn't going to be a child now."

I can feel time quickening. I must go back on the attack. "You never even gave me a chance," I say. "We would have gotten married."

She laughs, this one not an imitation but the real thing. "Is that the way you fix these things where you come from?"

"It would have been the thing to do. Didn't you get my note?"

"Yes. And it was sweet. Thank you." .

"'*Thank* you'? What the hell is that supposed to mean?"

"Just what I said. Come on, Bats. What's with you?"

I am angry again, time slowing. "What's with *you?* Would you or wouldn't you?"

"Would I or wouldn't I what?"

"Marry me."

"Oh please — we must not talk about that now."

"No. I want to talk about that, okay? Would you? Will you?"

"Not now, please. Not now, particularly. Marriage is the last thing I want right now. I just want to go home and rest."

"What about later, then. I love you, you know. Even after this."

"'After *this*'? Look my Canadian darling, you must not make this look like I've done something wrong to you. What I do with my own life is my business."

"*My* business when you're pregnant."

Her voice suddenly grows cross. "Not your business then, either. And especially not your business when I'm not pregnant. Understand?"

"What about later?"

"Later for what?"

"For us getting married, Kristiina. What in heaven's name is wrong with you?"

"There's nothing wrong with me. It is with you. And if you must have an answer, the answer is no."

"No?"

"No."

"Why?"

"Because I'm not ready, for one thing. Because even if I ever am ready I doubt we would be right for each other. You will understand."

I can say nothing. I stare at the receiver. Ice has formed on the mouthpiece but it should be on the ear.

She fills the gap. "You asked."

I sputter. "Okay, but what about us together. What was all that about?"

"Fun. Fun for me. Fun for you, too, I hope."

"Just fun?"

"Sure. Fun. What else matters? Look, I still love you in my own way, isn't that enough?"

I am suddenly back walking on the ice of Helsinki harbor with her. She has let go of my hand deliberately. *You're different*, she says. Now she says *fun*. Batterinski is her toy —isn't he? —nothing but a goddamn fucking toy you take off the shelf when you're bored and kick under a chair when you've better things to do. *Enough*, she says.

"No! It is not enough!"

I am screaming. I hammer the receiver down so hard it buckles the cradle. I can't even phone her back to finish. I yank the receiver as hard as I can, ripping the phone and cable free from the box and sending my shoulder stiffly back against the still folded door. I turn and I kick and the door gives slightly, but the snow has packed hard around the track and it cannot shut tight. I kick again and again and the door bursts, the thick glass shattering but holding together in patches. It falls, folding, the sound like a well-greased rifle bolt accepting its charge. Which, in a way, is precisely what Batterinski is doing.

Holding the receiver by the end of the cable, I whip it like a club against the three sides of the booth, stomping around the outside, falling in the drifted snow to my knees. The booth turns to cobwebs, the cobwebs falling in on each other.

I take the telephone and twirl it like a lariat over my head, then send it full force against the door of the washroom so it leaves a deep gash and black skid. They will have to paint that again. Just like Jaja painted the goddamned things every year for bugger-all. That blow is for him.

I kick at the glass and turn to the sound of a logging truck gear-

ing down for the slope. I don't even care. I stand proudly beside
my shattered phone booth and stare straight at him, defiantly,
but the bastard does not even take his eyes off the upcoming
curve. Like everyone else, he seems convinced Batterinski no
longer exists.

I know from Poppa's eyes that he is deeply troubled. When I first
drove back out I hoped I'd be able to cheer him up with news
that the road was opening up. Anything to avoid Kristiina or all
this shit going on in Finland. But I knew by the time I reached the
lane that all was not quite right. No outside light for me. Just a
sad glow from the kitchen where he sat with a coal oil lamp burning in a recently rewired house. Not too subtle a slap, and I did
not miss it.
    He rises slowly from his contemplation of the wick.
    "You should have called. I had supper ready."
    "Sorry."
    Sorry be damned. This is 1982, not 1962, but suddenly I can
taste toothpaste in my mouth. It is as if I've just come in from
drinking in the gravel pit with the rest of the gang and I've
squeezed the tube directly into my mouth. But Poppa always knew
then. He knows now.
    "You had calls," he says.
    "Yeah? Who?"
    "Everyone, it seems. The CBC. The *Toronto Star.* The *Globe and
Mail.* Finland."
    "Who from Finland?"
    "They left their number."
    He picks up a piece of folded paper. I see he has been looking
through my scrapbook. The paper I take from him and unfold.
Voitto. The nerve of him, to call back.
    "What is going on, son?" Poppa asks sadly.
    "It's a misunderstanding, Poppa. Same as the thing in Sweden.
I tried to teach them how to be winners and now they're trying
to treat me like I'm some sort of criminal or something."
    "Are you?"
    "Poppa! Come on now! We gave out bonus money for aggres-
sive play, it's as simple as that. Never for penalties. I turned a
bunch of losers into winners, Poppa, and now they're saying they'd
rather be losers."
    "Did you lose your job?"

"I guess. I've lost jobs before, Poppa."

"But you won't be going back to Finland . . ."

"I guess not. It's beginning to look that way."

Poppa closes his eyes, closes in on what has really been troubling him. "Then how will we get Jaja's memoirs?"

He can't possibly know about Leningrad! He just wonders where they are.

"I'm sorry, Poppa. I just completely forgot. I had so much on my mind today."

"You didn't forget, Felix. You don't have them, do you?"

"Of course I have them."

"I went through your luggage, son."

"They're in the trunk then."

"Are they?" His eyes light up, apologizing and embracing me at the same time. I cannot do this to him.

"No. They aren't there."

Poppa's face collapses. "But why, son? What did you do with them?"

"I lost them, okay? In Russia. They took them away from me. It wasn't my fault."

"*Who* took them away?"

"The police. The KGB. I don't know. They took them from me at the airport. I didn't even know I had them. And even if I had I still wouldn't have thought about it. But they took them."

"Why?"

"The Polish stuff. And all those clippings you kept sending me. They read it all and then they wouldn't let me have them back."

Poppa's eyes are glistening in the bad light.

"Poppa, please! It was an accident. Just like this was. Don't you see?"

But Poppa just shakes his head. The tears are dropping now. "This was not an accident, son."

I do not follow. "What do you mean?"

"Batcha set the fire on purpose. I was upstairs sleeping."

"But you said —"

"I said so she could be buried from the church. She deserved that, at least. I couldn't save her, Felix, because she and every goddarned piece of paper out there was drenched in coal oil. She did it all deliberately. She even managed to drag those boxes out from under her bed."

"But why?"

"She'd hardly spoken to me all winter. Once Marie and I set to work on Jaja's memoirs she wouldn't have anything to do with us. I put it down to her sickness — but why she did it is beyond me."

"She wanted to *destroy* his history?"

"What else? She was going to die anyway. She was hardly in any pain."

"But you didn't tell anybody?"

"No."

"Why?"

"I couldn't. I knew nothing I did would ever bring them back. That's why I was counting on you, but even that —"

Poppa wipes his one good hand over his eyes. He is blaming me. Even Poppa is blaming me. It is all my fault, everything. Right from Day One.

Marie Jazda is shaking as she reaches for the sugar dispenser. She has tried every excuse to get out of this meeting. Too much work. Dentist. A meeting with the Manpower higher-up. But I have driven all the way over to Renfrew to find out something far more important than anything she could possibly be doing. And I have told her that. And in the end she has agreed to join me at Prince's for lunch. Chips and gravy, Coke, Boston cream pie with coffee. No wonder Marie remains unmarried: her fingers look more suited to canthooks than rings.

But I know her heart is also large. Marie is my cousin, but I lost track of her somehow between childhood and Poppa's letters. We have kissed as cousins, wrestled, run away from home, spied on animals doing it, beaten up on her brothers, lied to our parents together. But now we are strangers, forced into the same red- freckled Formica booth by ill luck, her hurrying to eat and get out before the dark stranger opposite dares try and make conversation.

But I want to know why she was not at Batcha's funeral.

"I had to work, Felix."

She didn't sign the guest book at the funeral home, and that was right here in Renfrew.

"I had the flu that week, sick as a dog."

She didn't call.

"Still haven't got my phone in."

Poppa hasn't mentioned her.

"Yes, I suppose he hasn't."

There is something in the way she looks up from her coffee, small brown eyes opening wide, then ducking, that tells me there is more here than I am catching.

"Did something go wrong between you two?" I ask.

"He didn't think much of me getting a job," she says. *Tink*, after all that schooling. The small voice and stare into the coffee tells me this is a lie.

"He told me you were finished."

She grasps, pouring more sugar. "Well, the things he'd marked off, yes. You should know. You got them."

Tings.

"I lost them."

The eyes widen over the coffee. It is the stare I have seen in a hundred arenas. Only the cup is different here. "For good?"

"For ever."

The eyes close. She probably knows even better than I what they meant to poor Poppa.

"Did you know Batcha set the fire on purpose?" I ask.

Marie glances suspiciously around as if we might be taped. "Yes."

"How?"

"I knew the second I heard. The boxes weren't even kept in the shed. We piled what we finished in the kitchen corner."

"Then she had to haul them out?"

"I imagine."

"Were they heavy?"

"Were they *heavy?* Are you kidding?"

"Then how did she manage?"

For the first time Marie smiles. "With your Batcha you don't ask questions."

"Does anyone else know what you know?"

"I don't know. There was some talk. It certainly seemed strange to everyone. A bed-ridden old lady. And I heard some say there was coal oil all over her and the shed."

"But no one said anything to the police."

"Why would they? What good would it do?"

"I suppose."

"Father Schula would throw a fit, you know him. Them that say she killed herself say they'd have done the same if they was dying from the cancer."

She takes a long sip of coffee, relaxing for the first time. Perhaps she thinks this is all I came to hear.

"But you know it wasn't because of that."

Marie keeps the cup high to her mouth, muzzling herself. She waits, then puts it down. "Yes, I know."

"Do you know why she did it?"

"I don't know that, no."

But I am not convinced. "You *must* know, Marie. For Christ's sake! I'm your own cousin."

"Can I get another coffee?"

I wave over the waitress. "Tell me what you know."

She waits for the coffee and for the waitress to move off, then checks around for further surveillance and leans forward to whisper. Anyone watching would assume we were plotting an affair, and they would have to wonder what it is she has, or I lack.

"Your father and I had quite a falling out, you know."

"I was beginning to suspect."

"I doubt he'll ever speak to me again."

"What happened?"

"You remember that sealed package? The stuff your grandfather set aside? Your Poppa told you about it in your last letter, I think."

"Yes, I remember."

"Well, your father took that stuff pretty seriously, eh? No way he was even going to peek."

I see now. "But you did, is that it?"

Marie blushes, the color returning her to the eight-year-old I remember playing with.

"He used to go out and do whatever the hell he felt like while I sat there and was expected to type all day. I didn't mind at first, but it got to be a real bore after a while. All he had to do was read, eh? I had to translate it all and then type it up, and take care of *her*, too, for that matter."

"Batcha?"

"She could be a real test when she was ill, Felix."

"She was always a bitch. You don't need to tell me."

"He was out checking his damned rabbit snares and I figured he'd be gone at least until lunch. I got a bit ahead and then took a look at the package. I steamed it open. I didn't mean no harm. I wouldn't even tell anyone, but I figured it would be a heck of a lot more interesting than another twenty pages of that boring Bismarck crap, eh?"

"I don't blame you," I say, encouraging.

"All I did was read it, some of it. And *she* caught me."

"Batcha?"

"I didn't even hear her. She came in from her bedroom, from my back. And she must have been standing there looking over my shoulder. I don't know how I didn't hear her. You know how she walked in those boots. And that floor! And no cane, either. It was like she floated, eh? She half scared me to death. She reached over and grabbed them right out of my hands and started hitting on me."

"Batcha?"

"Can you believe it? She was yelling at me in *her* Polish, which I can barely understand. She called me *mora*. It means bloodsucker. She didn't hurt me, but she scared me so bad I threw up before your Poppa got back."

"What happened?"

"She had the stuff in her bedroom. She called him in. I was so sick, Felix, it was awful. Then he came out and told me to take my stuff out to the truck. He'd drive me home. He never spoke to me again."

"But why? What was in the package?"

"I didn't have a chance to read it, Felix."

Why is she being evasive? "But you read some of it."

"It didn't make much sense. It was in a strange Polish. Your father was much better with the old Cassubian than I was. But even he might not have known some of these words. It was really strange."

"But you must know what it was about, Marie. Surely."

She can only shake her head.

"Does that mean no, or you won't tell me?"

She swallows. "You don't want to know. I shouldn't have been into it. Your father was right."

"Tell me."

"No."

"Marie! I have a *right* to know!" I realize I am almost shouting. The waitress is looking at us, and other diners. But Marie also notices and perhaps this is good luck. She cringes, would like to be elsewhere. I know instantly I can use this to my advantage.

I maintain a loud voice. "You'll have to tell me, Marie! and *now!*"

She is the color of the Formica now. Marie shrinks into her seat and stares at me with a fear that suggests I am Batcha returned from the dead, about to flail at her yet again for her ignorance.

"It was mostly about you, Felix."

Me? Why would Jaja seal what he wrote about me? Why would he write *anything* down? And why those words? All Marie could recall were words, certain words . . . *mucka,* something on the head of the baby. On *my* head! And *vjeszczi . . . vjeszczi . . . vjeszczi* . . . Of course — the word the bitch used when she ripped my neck. Monster. *Me?*

Not just about me, but about her too. And maybe he kept it quiet—kept *what* quiet?—only so long as the bitch was still around. Maybe he thought whatever it was would go with her. But she hadn't gone. He had. And that's right — it was only after he was gone that she dared set herself up as a *càrovnica.* But she must have *always* been a witch. And somehow he wouldn't let her.

But he had to have been worried about her. Otherwise why write it down?

Of course, of course. He didn't write it down to *keep* it from me. He wrote it down *for* me. So I would have it in case I needed it. Good old Jaja. That was why I saw him in the painting. He was calling me home to get it. But why would I need it?

And what *is* it?

Who can tell me?

Not Marie. Not Poppa. Not Batcha. Maybe that's why she killed herself. So I'd never know. So she'd win either way, dead or alive.

Someone has got to know!

Old Frank, the Black Donald Lake *jiza,* is still alive but drunk, probably drunk for years for all I know. The garbage he has just slopped straight out the door, twin gray breasts of ashes and eggshells and tin cans and tea bags and busted bottles on both sides of the landing, most of the boards broken or rotted through and the door window broken and replaced by an old torn camp blanket. I knocked, but no answer. I knocked again, rousing him barely.

"Uhhhnnn?" he grunts from inside.

"Is Frank home?" I call. I don't know what else to say.

I hear bottles falling and spinning across the floor from his footsteps. He peers out through the blanket, red, rheumy eyes blinking with light and the white paste that has formed around their seams. When he winces his upper lip rises and his beard drops, opening a brilliantly red, empty hole in his face. The sunlight makes him sneeze, and he turns and explodes five straight times onto the floor.

"Are you Frank?"

He blows his nose and pulls the door. "Who're you?"

"Felix Batterinski."

He blinks and wipes away some of the paste, but it makes his vision blur. He turns and works on his eyes with his shirt, blinking several times until I come back into focus.

"Karol's boy?" he sniffs, thinking not of Jaja but of Batcha, his competition.

"Walter's. Karol was my grandfather."

He nods. "I was sorry to hear about the old lady," he says, sincerity lacking. The door opens and the stench pours out. A sewer, small, rotten, festering. I feel like throwing up. In the corner closest to the door there is an overturned white enamel pail with newspapers piled on it and ax blows through the floorboards for a rough hole. His toilet. The sewer smell. There is a bed, sagging with a yellow water-stained mattress and several more old gray camp blankets on it. A broken wooden icebox for a table. Some police magazines, some cups, spoons, tobacco tins, papers, candles, cans, papers, garbage, garbage, garbage.

But in the far corner, cleaned and exact, a small crucifix hanging from the wall, a prayer bench and a bewilderingly clean white napkin under an expensive candle holder. The candle is out, but burned halfway. The holder and napkin hold no sign whatsoever of the tallow droppings.

"Come."

I go all the way in, swallowing heavily, trying to minimize my breath. Old Frank goes to what must have once been a kitchen — a broken green Coleman camp stove piled high with filthy pots and pans — and he pulls two chairs, one with a broken back, one with no back, out from the newspapers. He brushes them off and sets them out by the chapel.

"Sit."

I sit, glad the air is more bearable away from the hole. He sits and stares again at me, then smiles.

"A Batterinski has need of old Frank, eh?"

"I want to ask some questions," I say, not at all sure how to talk to this hermit.

Again the smile; his swollen gums glisten, the red within like scarlet lipstick.

"You would ask for free at home."

For a moment I do not understand. I look up into the glistening grin and see the red eyes dance with small jokes. Slowly, I re-work the phrase and understand perfectly. I pull out two ten-dollar bills, thinking to give him one now and the other if he earns it, but he snatches both from my hands instantly. He shoves them inside his shirt, then the mouth reopens.

"*Chłopa pjisca mjerza.*"

"I'm sorry. My Polish is really pretty weak, I'm afraid."

The lips have sounds; they scrape out and wheeze into what, in fading, I realize is a laugh. He reaches over and touches my hands. I recoil but hold them still, the sensation not unlike when Danny once blindfolded me and placed my hands in peeled grapes, telling me they were children's eyes. Old Frank's temperature does not seem human: the hands are like ice, long knobby fingers with mats of black hair over the joints.

"'A man is measured with the fists'—that's what it means. It is an old saying, very old."

I look at my hands. What has he seen there? He knows who I am, a Batterinski, but can he possibly know what I also am, as well? Is it written there for him to see?

"I play hockey," I say.

He nods enthusiastically.

"The word *vjeszczi*—what does that mean to you?"

His hands instantly leave mine, the left going to his waist where he tucks the thumb behind the band, sign against *wurok*, evil eye. Can the word be that powerful?

He licks at his lips. "The work of *smantek*," he says.

That word I know well enough. *Devil.*

"Why?" I ask.

Old Frank spits out a green slime and admires it for a moment before running a boot over it to smooth it into the rest of the grime on the floor.

"A true *vjeszczi* is a vampire. So is *wupji*."

"They mean the same?" I ask.

He shook his head. "Both monsters, but they are *not* the same at all! A *wupji* is far more dangerous. You can do nothing until a *wupji* is dead to make sure." He shrugged. "If a *wupji* does not lose its color, you can always fix him in the box." He chuckles at the thought.

"I don't understand."

"Many ways. Put a half nickel in his mouth. Put a brick under the chin. Turn him upside down so he claws out the wrong direction. Throw a net over him so he has to untie all the knots. There are many things you can do if you're sure it is a *wupji*."

"Do? But why?"

He looks at me as if I am crazy. "*Why?* So he won't come back for you, that's why."

"But there's no such thing," I say.

Frank shrugs. "Suit yourself. I have known them. I have seen them. I have dealt with them many times. Just as I know your grandmother would have. Is that why you have come to me, to tell me there is no reason for any of this?"

"I want to know about *vjeszczi*."

The smile, glistening.

"Much easier. The *wupji* is born with two teeth. You must immediately check the baby's mouth. A *wupji* you can do nothing about until he is dead, and by then there may not be anyone around who remembers how he was born. A *vjeszczi* is a much simpler matter. The baby is born with the caul. *Mucka.*" — Yes, another of Marie's words —"You simply scrape the little cap off the head and save it. When the child is seven years old the caul is ground up and fed to the child in his food. He never even needs to know. Once he eats it he is no longer *vjeszczi*, see?" The smile.

"How would he know if he had or hadn't?"

"He wouldn't."

"Why when he's seven? Is that important?"

A shrug. "Seven is the lucky number for the Poles. Maybe only for extra luck. You should wear that number when you play your hockey, Batterinski." The smile, dripping.

"It's mine."

Again the hands on my hands, strangely warmer. "Then you will always have luck with your hockey."

I ask him just before bed, over his final coffee. "Poppa, was I born with a caul?"

"A *what?*" The spoon rattles against the cup, splashing.

"A caul. You know, a *mucka*, a cap of extra skin. On my head."

"How would I know?" He continues stirring, calmed now and methodical, deliberately paying little attention to me.

"You were here. I was here. You would have known."

"So what if you were? What difference would it make?"

"Was I?"

He lifts the spoon and taps it dry on the oilcloth before looking up. "What is the point, Felix?"

"I want to know."

"You're talking stupid, son."

"Just tell me, yes or no. I have a right to know for myself."

"Well, then you were."

He is asleep now and I can hear him moaning. I should go up and fluff his pillows, turn him a bit, perhaps bring some Vaseline, but I cannot bear to see him now. His coffee still sits here, cool now, untouched since our conversation ended with him standing up and heading straight for bed.

Not even a grunt for goodnight.

I am thinking crazy thoughts. Poppa has turned into Jaja. I am turning into Poppa, a dragonfly shedding the shell of the waterbug to find his wings have already been pinched off. I feel the way Poppa looks to me — defeated. Now it is me sitting here alone, just as Poppa would, me drinking his *sliwowica* prune vodka. The only light is the coal oil lamp on the kitchen table. The spoon has stuck fast to the oilcloth where he tapped the coffee off. I am even sitting in his chair.

Look, he has had my scrapbook out again, leafing through the Flyer years like I am forever skating around, Schultz and me, the Stanley Cup over our heads while the Philly fans erupt in appreciation. The book is less thumbed after the Flyers. Poppa looks just so far and then quits.

He turns to something else like this damned paperback on Lech Walesa and the Solidarity movement. Walesa and his big walrus mustache staring out like he's the Black Madonna himself, for Christ's sake. Poppa is obsessed with Walesa, praying for him, praying *to* him, for all I know. All he wants to talk about is Poland

and Walesa and the goddamned Russians. It is as if he sees the Russians holding Walesa captive on the evidence they found in Jaja's memoirs.

Only a Pole could hold himself so responsible.

He reads up to the Flyers and the Cup, and then turns to Walesa, leaving little doubt in my mind just who Poppa believes is the champion of the world today.

Fine, Poppa, fine. You lie up there and you moan like a baby. And if you cry loud enough maybe Walesa will hear you and come running with comfort.

Me, I'm going out.

The moon is like a nail clipping, but enough. I can pick my way up behind St. Martin's with ease. I know the ground; I know the trail from a dozen funerals; I know where she is and what she is doing. I hear the bitch laughing.

No one sees me. I leave the car in the hardware lot and walk up the school kids' trail back of the store, cut across the Schama sideroad and up through the cedars to the church. I scare up a hare coming through.

Batcha would say that was bad luck. But this time for her, not for me. I am sick of her controlling my life. Sick and tired and fucking well finished with it.

The ground is frozen stiff, our tramping three days ago into the graveyard has turned to scabs of snow. It is impossible to step without slipping or stubbing, so I go up high on the bush side and circle around on Batcha. This way the bitch won't see me coming.

She really is a *čàrovńica*. A true witch. Not just a *jiza* with folk medicines and superstitions, but a true witch with real powers. Evil powers. I know that now. The poplar crosses, the pins, the evil eye, the mole claws to scratch cow udders, the buried hearts — it all makes perfect sense to me now. It began with Matka's death. My fault. And Jaja wouldn't let her take over when they saw what I was. That's why she hated me. Why he wrote it all down . . . It should have been me pouring the wax in *her* keyhole. Bitch.

And I can see now that she never let up. Kristiina, for sure. Batcha was there too. The night in the cottage with Pekka and Pia in the next room. Of course. It would have been that night Kristiina became pregnant. And Batcha killed the baby, sure as shit. Why didn't I ask Kristiina if it had been a boy or a girl? Would they tell her? Would they know? Was his little heart still pumping when they dropped him in the garbage? He was a boy. I know that now. He was Jaja's dream of the Batterinski name continuing. That's what that painting told me in Leningrad, sure. He was my gift back to the family and Batcha couldn't bear it that I would take over from her, that *I* would control what became of us all. Bitch.

She was behind Wheeler too. She fucked Philadelphia. She fucked L.A. She fucked Helsinki. She fucked me in Leningrad. It was always her, always at the window, laughing. Just like I heard her the other day. Wasn't the water at all. And she's still laughing.

Bitch!

Laugh, you fucking bitch! Laugh all you want!

I knew there would be no key needed. A thumb starter, hand clutch, four-gear snap shift on the floor, scoop-operated by swiveling the joystick. Not much different from what they had in Sudbury. I still remember.

I press the starter and the battery turns the starter engine, but it will not catch. Of course, the choke. I have to wait for the moon before I can find it. I slide it out to full and push again. The starter engine whirrs, then catches, and the main engine coughs into action. I push in the choke to quieten it, but kill the engine. Again, and again they catch. I let it idle loudly, then slowly press in the choke. Check to see that the scoop is up, then shift into first, release the clutch, step on the gas and the John Deere moves into action, howling across the crust.

But I could care less. This has to be done.

I have the decency to skirt the other graves. I come in on Batcha from behind, grateful there is not yet a marker. I dare not try the headlights, but it doesn't matter. In the thin moon I can make out the mound and the flowers, frozen in full bloom. I back the John Deere in, swivel the scoop and shift seats to work it.

This is far more difficult. There are three joysticks, and with the scoop switched over I find one operates the up-and-down motion, one the scoop itself, and one the thrust. But I cannot coordinate them! I bump against the grave and the frozen earth knocks the John Deere straight back. I have not put down the pods. I turn back to the seat, search out a lever and press it. Hydraulics hiss into action and I feel the machine rising. I move the lever and the machine settles as if in water.

Back to the scoop. I pull it in tight, then press straight down. The blade hits badly. I try again and this time the scoop bites in. I push and it moves stiffly into the earth and bounces off. I try again, and this time it bites deep. But I lose it on the lift. I try again, and this time, finally, I come up with earth. It rises high over Batcha's grave and I feel like cheering.

But why am I doing this? What the fuck am I doing here? What good will this do?

I don't want the bitch up. I want her gone forever. I don't even know now what I was going to do with her.

I shake my head. Poppa's vodka. I am not quite right. I feel cobwebs wrapped about my body. I squirm.

Of course! *She* is doing this to me. She *wants* me to dig her up! She's not yet through with fucking me around.

"YOU CAN'T FOOL MEEEE!"

I pull up the scoop and dump the earth. It falls badly, spreading over Jaja's snowclean grave.

"YOU GODDAMNED BITCH!"

I pull the scoop to its rest position, change chairs, work the hydraulics so the pods vanish, shift gear and turn the John Deere completely. I put it into bull low, crank up the gas, and grade straight up onto the grave mound.

The John Deere hangs there a moment, weaving, then the earth gives, sinks and the big machine settles.

I am sure I hear the box crushing below.

Fools! How can they expect to catch the person who made the trails? I saw the cops' lights flashing long before they made the turn at St. Martin's. I saw Father Schula scurrying out to point. By the time they headed up toward the graveyard I was long gone, tucked into the cedars like a partridge.

Batterinski has a few moves left yet.

Poppa is still asleep, but the moaning has stopped. And I know why too. I know now what took me to the John Deere: not me, but her, but I fixed her proper. The bitch. His moaning had to stop. And now it is time to fix my own.

I just have to find that goddamned caul.

I must remember all that Old Frank told me.

Chłopa pjisca mjerza. A man is measured with the fists. I have been measured. I came out all right. *Wupji.* No, that is the teeth. You can do nothing about the *wupji* until he is dead. And I am most certainly not dead. The bitch is dead. I cannot control my hand. It moves on its own, thumb hooking in under the belt, the sign against *wurok.* So I am still afraid of her. But just for a little longer.

But where is it? Where is the caul? I know she kept it. *That* was what gave her power over me. *That* was what she used to fuck me around with. But where is it?

In her room! Poppa won't hear me. I can hear him snore now, deep in sleep, the sound like the starter engine on the John Deere. I will look and find it and eat the cursed thing and then everything will be fixed right. The bitch will be entirely dead.

Poppa has fixed up Batcha's room just as I last remember it. The bed is made. Her rabbit-fur slippers are even on the throw mat. There is no overhead light —she wouldn't let the electrician in, would she? She knew I would try one day. The only light is her Christ table lamp. I turn it on but the light below is cut off by the shadow cast by the dresser. I have to grab Christ around his wounded chest and lift him, knocking off the red shade as I do. The cord, fortunately, has enough slack that I can aim the light around like a mechanic's lamp. But there is no longer anything stored under her bed. Nothing. Holding Christ in an armpit, I go through her drawers but there is nothing here but the smell of cedar boughs and the pitch black of Batcha's inside: stockings, underwear, slips, shawls, sweaters, all black and formless as herself. In the top drawer there is a heavy old Bible with a carved wooden cover and underneath it a small chest. I take the Bible and place it on her bed and turn with hope to the chest, but it is only a tangle of hair nets, some manicure scissors and a small pouch filled with nail clippings.

The closet is more difficult to search. I have to lift the door and slide the lamp cord under it to gain enough length, and the door snaps at the lowest hinge, cracking through the house. I freeze and listen. Poppa snorts, coughs, catches and is off again snoring. I move and realize I am soaking with sweat. My shirt grabs across the shoulders, my pants catch at the knee. My heart pulses in my neck and I can feel it against the starch of the shirt collar. It is too close in here. The closet is filled with dark garments, dresses, coats, vests. On the floor there is only a yellow chamber pot, matched and stacked black shoes, a single pair of unused winter boots. On the shelf only hats, toques, muffs, gloves. A hat box in one corner contains dozens of poplar crosses, pins, paper, two old and blackened Polish books.

But nothing else. I poke Christ into all the corners, but there is nothing left. Yet I know better. Marie said she dragged some of the memoirs out into the shed. She might also have taken the boxes from under her bed.

Perhaps I went up in ashes. Perhaps her main reason for lighting the fire was to burn the caul. To make it so I could never fix things. The *bitch*. I wish I had the sound of her box-crushing on tape, the way Torchy used to tape his sex sessions. I'd listen and I'd applaud. And then listen again.

I come back into the kitchen but cannot find the flashlight. There is only the old hurricane hanging on the spike. When I shake it there is the slosh of coal oil, so I take it down and set it on the table, checking first on Poppa's snore — still regular — and then the time: 5:35. The glass is filthy with dust and I have trouble lifting it and wiping it clean, frightened of breaking the mantle. I pump it, open the release valve, lift the glass again and strike one of Poppa's long wooden matches and insert it. The lantern bursts, shards of flame shoot through the vents and wrap themselves in a deep blue and yellow around the entire glass. I am afraid I have pumped too hard, or else the flame is working down the delivery tube, but suddenly the larger flame tapes high and vanishes into a thick black smoke. I adjust the mantle and the pin glow grows to a tight wrap around the entire cloth. It clears the glass and fills the room with its light, a better glow even than Christ gave off.

As quietly as possible I pop the back door and step out and down, into the shell of the back shed.

There is a flutter under the eaves, then movement, swooping. A bat! *Smentek!* It twists through a missing wallboard and disappears into the night. Good! I place the hurricane down where it will be best protected, but the night wind still finds it, toying with the flame so my shadow sways through the remaining walls like black fire.

There is a burned trunk I do not remember off to the far side.

It might be blue, but there is more black from the fire than whatever color it once was. It is behind the crates I know held Jaja's memoirs. Poppa might have pushed it there so he could concentrate on Jaja's stuff. There is so much extinguisher powder around that it sifts like fine talcum and has actually formed drifts around the base. But there might be a chance.

Poppa has piled things on the trunk, all of them useless. One of Jazda's workhorse collars for the pulp hauling, two tractor wheel rims, some twisted, rusted and now charred cable. I clear them quietly, glad there is enough ash and snow and paper char on the floor to soften any blow. The top of the trunk is badly burned, almost as if this was where she had poured her coal oil. I pull and the cardboard tears. I lift up the lamp and tilt it so I can see inside.

Poplar crosses! There must be thousands of them. How they failed to catch is beyond me, they feel so dry and old to the touch, but the flame never made it quite through the surface. There is only some drifted ash inside; otherwise, it has been untouched.

There are more books inside, all Polish, all incomprehensible. And several tins, some containing beads, some buttons, some empty.

But nothing else. I yank the box so it comes completely free, and as it turns I notice on the side most badly burned there is a hole, but whether caused by the fire or by Poppa's rats I cannot be sure. Several bottles have broken and spilled against the framework of the shed; they might well have slipped from the box as poor Poppa kicked it aside to get closer to the doomed memoirs.

I get down on the floor and sift among them with my bare hands, touching very lightly for fear of broken glass. The jars are badly charred and my hands become inked with their coating. Some are broken. Some contain nails. More buttons. One has coins . . . And one is neither clear nor burnt. It is blue ceramic, about eight inches tall, flanged in the middle, untouched.

I reach and grab the jar, lifting it like a chalice. It has a ceramic top with a cork base built on, all held in place by an attached clamp. The clamp is fastened tight and rusted in place. Probably for years.

But it seems empty. I weigh it and it seems no heavier than what can be seen. I shake it and nothing. I shake it again, my ear riding with it, and I think I can hear something ever so vaguely. Something light as powder. Light as dried skin!

Clutching the jar I grab up the lantern and make it back into the kitchen, where I close the valve on the flame and set the jar down carefully on the oilcloth, smudging everything. There is a washcloth hanging on the old pump. I take it off, wet it under the tap and clean up the soot, wiping the table clean, moving the scrapbook and the Walesa book and placing the ceramic jar dead center, where I can take a good look at it.

But I do not want to see it. I want to see inside. I *have* to see inside. I can barely negotiate my own fingers. They grab badly at the clamp and the jar nearly slips from my grasp. I grab again, holding it with both hands and push up on the clamp with my thumbs, but it does not give.

Poppa always has penetrating oil around and I find it on the sill. I try to pour it on, but my hands are shaking too badly. I have to put the jar down, smear the oil on my fingers, then work the oil in along the clamp, using the washcloth again to clean up. And then I have to let it work in. I take my pulse because I do not know what else to do. One hundred and forty beats per minute. A five-mile run. I take the scrapbook up but find I have no stomach for it: each picture is like one of Danny's lies, serving a momentary purpose but then gone. I cannot look back on what I should still be looking forward to. And damn! I've gotten oil on it anyway. I get the cloth again but the oil has caught in the newsprint of the scrapbook pages, spreading out, spreading back, the smudge being passed from one page to the next.

Goddamn it all to hell!

I try the clamp again and it budges. A deep breath, a second effort, and this time it gives completely. The cork lifts free of the ceramic neck and a stale, putrid smell wafts lightly and is gone. I stare immediately down the throat but it is pitch black inside the bottle, and no matter how I angle it to the overhead light I cannot see because of my own shadow.

From the cupboard I take down a cereal bowl. I place it in front of my own chair and then pump the ceramic jar like a ketchup bottle, tapping the neck and then the bottom with the edge of a straightened finger. For a moment I panic, convinced there is nothing inside. But then a gray, matted powder trickles out. Nothing else.

What would I look like? If I am thirty-seven years old this powder should also be thirty-seven years old. I don't even have a clue what a fresh caul would look like, let alone one that's thirty-seven years old.

Thirty-seven . . . the number seven . . . I am still seven . . . it is not too late.

I am afraid to touch. I grab one of Poppa's wooden matches and dab at the powder and some of it sticks to the match. I pick it up and stare at it, the match head an inch or so from my eye. It is nearly transparent, layered, more dust than skin, but like something that has been deliberately powdered. Like I was.

It has to be me!

One long, two short. *The fucking phone!* At *this* time? I jump for it, worried about Kristiina, worried about Poppa.

"Hello!"

The voice at the other end seems surprised at the speed. He chokes for words. Not Kristiina! Shit, shit, shit, *shit!*

". . . Would this be Walter Batterinski?"

I find I am hissing, an angry goose. "I'm his son. What do you want at *this* hour?"

"I'm sorry, sir. This is Constable Dupuis with the Renfrew detachment of the OPP. We've had a case of vandalism overnight, sir. At the cemetery."

"Yes? What?"

"A grave on your site, sir. It was somewhat damaged, I'm afraid."

"By who?"

"We don't know, sir. We were wondering if perhaps you had any ideas or whether this was just a case of random vandalism."

"Well I'm sure I have no idea who would do something like that. You're sure it was in the Batterinski plot."

"Yes sir. A recent grave. Mrs. Karol Batterinski."

"My grandmother."

"I'm sorry, sir. I — "

I hang up the receiver, smiling. Then lift it off again quietly so they cannot call again. I have work to do.

What do I do with this stuff? Say I follow through with what Old Frank said and eat it. Will that prove the bitch was right? She *had* to be right — I'm surrounded by proof. But what can doing it now do for the thirty years since I was seven?

It can't bring back Jaja. Or Ig. Or Philadelphia. Or even Helsinki.

But maybe Kristiina. Perhaps it can still save Kristiina for me. Perhaps it can still save me. What the hell — what have I got to lose? So what if it can't fix the past. It just might save tomorrow. Look, there's the dawn, pink and full of promise.

But how will I eat this? It's already in a cereal bowl, so perhaps that's a sign. I look in the cupboards and come up with a huge plastic bag of rolled oats. I put on the double boiler, heat the water and dump in some salt and two cups of oats. I turn it slowly, no longer even thinking, entranced by this new calm. It is like a fight I am winning. I no longer feel fear. Nothing. I know from the cop call that I really was at her grave. It was not a dream. I know also that I have picked the right jar. *I have found myself.*

Porridge is perfect. The oats burp big circles of steam and the mix thickens. I turn off the stove and hold the pan under the tap, letting cold water run along the sides to cool it, then I drop four tablespoons of it into the bowl with the powdered caul, turning it over and over until the gray powder is no longer visible through the light brown and white of the porridge. I won't even see it.

Nor taste it. The secret here is brown sugar. I take Poppa's big jar off the high shelf and spoon in three giant scoops, tossing and turning it through the mix until it glistens with sweet mica. Then some cold milk and I am ready.

I sit down in my own chair and breathe the steam of the porridge deep. I am even hungry. The vodka has worn off entirely and I am clearheaded. I pick up the first spoonful, tilting for extra milk to flow in, and raise it first to my nose. I cannot help but smile at the very idea. I hold my past in my hand, myself thirty-seven years ago. I have found Batcha's curse. I am devouring my past to nourish my future. Just like Jaja.

I take the first bite, swallowing quickly. It tastes like porridge, not Felix Batterinski. Batcha should have done this thirty years ago. For God's sake, I wouldn't even have noticed!

Think of the trouble it would have saved everyone.

I take another bite, this time chewing, enjoying.

Delicious!

"'It's Felix,' the old man said the morning I came up to him as he stood crying at the well pump. Nothing else. Nothing else was necessary.

He did not know me. He did not even know I was coming. Yet he sent me into the house almost as if he knew that I had to see how the story would end. Perhaps he felt that someone else could better make sense of it all.

I went inside and Felix Batterinski was slumped face down on the floor, his tongue twisted, blood clotted across his forehead. The kitchen table was knocked over. There was porridge all over the floor. Rolled oats. And a smashed cereal bowl.

I did not know then that it was more than simple porridge. Nor did the coroner down at Renfrew know until the report came in that so stunned the world of hockey. Felix Karol Batterinski, holder of the NHL's single-game penalty record, had committed suicide by deliber-ately mixing rat poison with sweetened porridge and eating it. A calculated, desperate act by a troubled man.

But why had no one —myself included—seen what was happening to this simple man? Sure, the Ontario Provincial Police had called about vandals at the local cemetery. By terrible coincidence the violation had been on the fresh gravesite of

Felix's beloved grandmother. And when his father found the family Bible sitting on her bed he knew that his son had been up that night reading it, remembering her. But that sad coincidence cannot explain it all, surely.

Are the still-unknown vandals any more guilty of setting Felix Batterinski off than, say, the management of Tapiola Hauki, who conspired with him in a bizarre and highly controversial scheme to bring North American blood (and guts) to Finnish hockey? And is anyone more to blame than the National Hockey League itself, which used Batterinski's fists until they were worn out and then turned him away without an explanation? Or the agent, the infamous Vincent Wheeler, who bilked Batterinski out of his graceful retirement plans?

For that matter, can there be any more guilt than that which falls on the fan? Who was it but the average fan who made of Batterinski a false god? And who turned from their worship when the god was cast down? Where were the cheers on Felix Batterinski's last lonely night on earth?

We can only pity poor Walter Batterinski, who says it is all his fault for having the rat poison where his son could find it. But of course it has nothing to do with him. Felix may have found the container in the burned shed, but we all know that, in truth, he brought the poison home with him, all by himself.

Perhaps it was not suicide at all. Perhaps it was murder. One basically good man turned evil and eventually destroyed by a callow system. And perhaps we are all to blame.

All Walter Batterinski is left with today is the scrapbook of his son's tragic life. He made me go through it with him when I stayed for the funeral and Felix's subsequent burial in the St. Martin's plot next to his grandmother. He smiled and pointed highlights out to me right up to the second Stanley Cup the Philadelphia Flyers won in 1975, then he abandoned me to finish on my own. Beyond Philadelphia the pages were seldom thumbed. There was nothing on Finland, most certainly not the spitting incident in Sweden (see photo top right, page 22). Someone had spilled oil and neglected to clean it up, almost as if hoping the oil would somehow make the letters run together in a more pleasant configuration.

The last six pages were empty. Walter Batterinski mentioned this to me when I handed him back the scrapbook. I believe he wanted me to fill them in, to complete the story of Felix Batterinski.

'We know that hockey is where we live,' Fred Shero had once written on the dressing room chalkboard when Batterinski was still in Philadelphia, 'where we can best meet and overcome pain and wrong and death. Life is just a place where we spend time between games.'

Felix Batterinski, a simple, uncomplicated man from simple roots, would have bought that idea completely. When there was no longer a time between games for him, there was no longer life. And so it ended. A simple, sad story of hockey meaning everything, and in the end nothing."

Excerpted by permission from "Batterinski's Burden," by Matt Keening, *Canada Magazine*, June 6, 1982. (Winner of the 1982 Canada Foundation of Investigative Journalism Gold Medal).

National pastime, rite of passage, family tradition — hockey is integral to the lives of fathers and sons, and much of what happens between them starts to unfold the very first time a young man leads his children onto the ice.

THE HOME TEAM

ROY MacGREGOR

When we watch the major league players, there are those thrilling moments of play when we feel for the players the kind of adulation felt by children for their heroes. We wonder how they got to where they are, where they got their start, and what set them apart from the other kids who crowded onto the ice every Saturday morning.

The Home Team features in-depth interviews with many of hockey's best-known names — Bobby Orr, Wayne Gretzky, Mark Messier, Bryan Trottier, Pat LaFontaine, the Drydens, and the Howes — as well as those lesser known — Gino and Joe Odjick, from an Algonquin Reserve in the North, the Yashin family from Russia, Quebec's Alexandre Daigle — to explore the special father and son relationships that, when it comes to hockey, are truly the ties that bind. Featuring stories of tragedy and triumph from both the famous and the family next door, this poignant collection of father-and-son memoirs is a celebratory tribute to the grand game which — in Canada, in some special way — touches us all.

Look for
The Home Team
in bookstores everywhere